Racism

An American Cauldron

SECOND EDITION

Christopher Bates Doob
Southern Connecticut State University

 HarperCollins*CollegePublishers*

Once again, to Carby

Acquisitions Editor/Executive Editor: Alan McClare
Project Coordination: York Production Services
Cover Design: Scott Russo
Manufacturing Manager: Hilda Koparanian
Electronic Page Makeup: R.R. Donnelley and Sons Company, Inc.
Printer and Binder: R.R. Donnelley and Sons Company, Inc.
Cover Printer: Color-Imetry Corp.

Racism: An American Cauldron, Second Edition.

Library of Congress Cataloging-in-Publication Data
Doob, Christopher Bates.
  Racism: an American cauldron / Christopher Bates Doob.—2nd ed.
    p. cm.
  Includes bibliographical references and index.
  ISBN 0-673-99485-6
  1. United States—Race relations. 2.Racism—United States.
I. Title.
E184.A1D66 1995   95-31714
305.8'00973—dc20   CIP

95 96 97 98   9 8 7 6 5 4 3 2 1

Brief Contents

Detailed Contents

Preface

In the brief span since the first edition of this book was published, great tumult has occurred on our planet. Sometimes exhilarating and often frightening, these changes, both at home and abroad, have often centered on race and ethnicity and have involved different groups' drives for freedom, equality, and opportunity as well as efforts to thwart these drives.

The tumultuous nature of American racism is apparent in the book's title. The cauldron imagery is also consistent with the conflict perspective provided by the internal-colonialist theory introduced in the opening chapter and used throughout the text.

The central issue here is racism as suffered by large racial minorities in this society—African Americans, Mexican Americans, Puerto Ricans, Native Americans, Japanese Americans, and Chinese Americans—as well as by the majority group it also ensnares. The book avoids lengthy and often discursive material about individual racial minority groups in order to hold readers' attention. In particular, I have provided studies and illustrations that demonstrate why institutional racism persists and how it affects people's lives. The use of internal colonialism helps keep students focused, guiding their analysis of material. I chose this theory because its application can make students keenly aware of the nature of racism and, in particular, of its economic and political sources.

The opening chapter presents basic concepts and analyzes the significance of racism in American society. Chapter 2 examines theories of racism; Chapter 3 introduces the largest American racial minorities. Chapters 4 through 8 explore minorities' exposure to racism in politics, the criminal-justice system, violent situations, work, housing, education, the family, and the mass media. Chapter 9 analyzes racism in South Africa and Brazil; the final chapter discusses possible solutions to racism.

I have focused on producing a readable book. Vignettes introduce each chapter and inserted sections offer narratives of specific incidents or experiences to keep the presentation interesting and informative. However, the book also provides a substantial body of factual information, including historical sources, recent studies, and up-to-date statistical information.

Certain changes are apparent in this edition. It contains over 225 recent sources, thus offering a substantial body of new substantive material for a fairly short text. In addition, there are prominent new sections—including an analysis of the transformation of a Ku Klux Klan member, a discussion about Indian-owned casinos, a discourse about women of color, and an extensive updating on race-related issues in South Africa.

A number of individuals have played critical roles in this book's development. The following colleagues in sociology have given invaluable analysis on the second edition. The reviewers were: Alvaro Nieves, Wheaton College; Donna J. Hess, South Dakota State University; and William A. Schwab, University of Arkansas.

As acquisitions editor at HarperCollins, Alan McClare has continued to provide a firm but gentle guiding hand.

Once again Teresa Carballel's wise, humane commentary helped keep the project progressing smoothly and efficiently.

Recognizing how interesting and valuable readers' input can be, I encourage any instructor or student with a comment or question about this book to write me at the address below. I promise to answer all letters.

Chris Doob
Sociology Department
Southern Connecticut State University
501 Crescent Street
New Haven, CT 06515

Chapter
1

Significance of Race and Racism

A light breeze stirred the assemblage of cypress, cedars, eucalyptus, and Monterey pines that stood in green relief against the sharp blue sky. In the ample space between trees were many sets of sturdy wooden ladders, slides, stairs, and platforms, with the general impression produced that trees and children's things were organically blended.

But attractive as it was, the physical environment was much less striking than the children who ranged between infancy and about 12, spoke various languages, and represented a diversity of racial types. Smiles, laughter, and pleasure dominated the scene as children and parents enjoyed the idyllic setting. Was it the family version of the Garden of Eden, or, perhaps more appropriate for this generation of children, a moment from "Sesame Street?" Actually it was a real place—the children's playground in San Francisco's Golden Gate Park.

At the edge of the playground was a pavilion where refreshments could be bought. Suddenly about a dozen eight- or nine-year-old African American boys approached the pavilion. They started to line up, then broke out of line, and one reached into a relish container on a shelf next to the refreshment window, grabbed a handful of relish, and threw it pointblank at a companion's head. The victim retaliated, and several other boys joined in. A shout from inside the window, and the boys quickly moved away from the refreshment area. A middle-aged white woman turned to her grandson and said deliberately, "Those are bad boys, Freddy, very bad boys. I want you to stay away from the likes of them." She looked at the relish container and ruefully shook her head.

Meanwhile a white man walked over to where the boys were now sitting. "That's no way to act," he said. "Food's to be eaten, not thrown." He started to walk away, then turned back to the boys and asked, "Have you kids got money for lunch?" The boys stared blankly at the man, and as his eyes traveled down the row, each, in turn, shook his head. The man looked at the list of items sold, shrugged his shoulders to suggest that buying lunch for the entire group was too expensive, and then bought each boy a ticket for the nearby carousel.

This situation seems to epitomize the overall racial picture in this country. There are moving illustrations of racial cooperation and harmony; support exists from political and economic leaders as well as the majority of Americans for improving interracial relations. On the other hand, lurking in the shadows, often unobserved, especially by white Americans, is the ever-present reality of poverty and racism. Most Americans don't consider themselves racists and do not believe that they encourage it, but under pressure, like the grandmother, they often reject members of different races if they feel turmoil and violence about to descend. Many Americans manage to either keep racial issues out of their lives or to interact interracially under easy conditions, such as in the children's playground at Golden Gate Park.

Before we leave that scene, one more point about it should be emphasized. Qualities about that situation were peculiar to the modern era. A century, even a half-century ago, such a rich racial assortment of children would not have occurred. In parts of the country, segregation laws would have prohibited children of different races sharing the same facilities; in other areas, perhaps in San Francisco, informal standards maintained by both whites and racial minorities would have discouraged such a sharing.

This book focuses on racism among large American racial minorities—African Americans, Mexican Americans, Puerto Ricans, Chinese Americans, Japanese Americans, and Native Americans.* By 1990 nearly one in four Americans had African, Hispanic, Asian, or Native American ancestry, a sharp increase from 1980 when the proportion was about one in five (Barringer, 1991). By 2010 about 38 percent of children under 18—nearly two in five—will belong to racial minorities (Schwartz and Exter, 1993:101).

---

*Currently several racial groups are referred to by more than a single term. My response to this ambiguity is to interchange the terms "blacks" and "African Americans," "Chicanos" and "Mexican Americans," and "Indians" and "Native Americans."

In this book we need concepts to analyze our modern world of racial diversity. One of these concepts is "norms." A **norm** is a standard of desirable behavior. Norms are rules that people are expected to follow in relations with each other. Norms not only provide guidelines for appropriate behavior in a given situation but also supply people with expectations of how others will respond.

Throughout this book we see that norms determine people's outlooks and behavior in interracial situations. Parents belonging to different racial groups are more likely to bring their children to a racially integrated playground than they would to a playground where local residents would oppose their presence. The vast majority of the time nearly all of us follow the prevailing normative structure: We are creatures of current social custom.

ANALYSIS OF RACISM

Studying a sociological topic like racism requires an approach similar to building or bridge construction; in both cases tools are necessary. As befits an intellectual exercise, the tools used here are not material but analytic, sociological concepts that define certain key issues that will frequently arise throughout this work. In the pages ahead, we examine two sets of concepts—majority group, minority group, prejudice, and discrimination and then race, racism, and related concepts.

Majority Group, Minority Group, Prejudice, and Discrimination

A **majority group** is a category of people within a society who possess distinct physical or cultural characteristics and maintain superior power and resources. In contrast, a **minority group** is any category of people with recognizable racial or ethnic traits that place it in a position of restricted power and inferior status so that its members suffer limited opportunities and rewards. Minority-group members are inevitably aware of their common oppression, and this awareness helps create a sense of belonging to the group. It is important to understand that majority or minority status has no intrinsic relationship to group size. For instance, sometimes a minority group has been many times larger than the dominant group in the society. Such a situation existed when the European countries established colonies in Africa, Asia, and the Americas. In other cases—African Americans in the United States, for instance—the minority group is smaller in numbers than the dominant group. Minority status is the result of a subordinate position in society, not of the size of its membership.

Prejudice is a highly negative judgment toward a minority group, focusing on one or more characteristics that are supposedly uniformly shared by all group members. If a person rigidly believes that all members of a racial or ethnic group are innately lazy, stupid, stubborn, or violent, then that person is prejudiced toward the group in question. Racial, ethnic, and religious prejudice are the most prominently discussed types; in general, prejudice is not easily reversible. The fact that prejudice is not easily reversible distinguishes it from a "misconception," where someone supports an incorrect conclusion about a group but is willing, when confronted with facts, to change his or her opinion. While prejudice involves a negative judgment toward a minority group, discrimination focuses on the limitations imposed on a group. **Discrimination** is the behavior by which one group prevents or restricts a minority group's access to scarce resources.

The basic position throughout this book is that while discrimination and prejudice influence each other, discrimination has had a greater impact in the social world. Historically the majority group has discriminated against racial minorities for their own political, economic, and social advantage. Prejudice has been a rationalization for this exploitation. In fact, researchers have found that discrimination can occur without prejudice (Campbell and Pettigrew, 1959), and prejudice is neither necessary nor sufficient to produce discrimination (Kutner, Wilkins, and Yarrow, 1952; Warner and DeFleur, 1969). Since discrimination involves behavior and prejudice does not, the priority given discrimination is consistent with the attention to be paid to norms in this book. Norms regulate behavior, including behavior which relates to the topic of discrimination.

Racism involves both discrimination and prejudice as the following analysis indicates.

Race, Racism, and Related Concepts

In the previous section, we saw that a given group's access to power has played a significant role in race relations. That pattern is also apparent in the present discussion.

We begin with the distinction between social and biological definitions of race. *Social races* are categories of people that the majority group designates as sharing membership that endures throughout the lifespan and conveys certain rights and obligations. At first glance this might seem like a straightforward description, but it involves practical difficulties. While sometimes members of a given social race might appear racially similar, in other cases they do not. So under the latter condition how is membership in a social race established? Generally there has been one way—descent: Regardless of racial appearance, individuals belong to a social race if they are at least partially descended from individuals who are confirmed members. But what if the particular society, such as Brazil, does not use descent as a basis for establishing membership in a social group, or what if an individual comes from mixed parentage? Then social-group membership is difficult or impossible to establish convincingly (Harris, 1968).

Biological definitions of race have been equally confusing. While many criteria, including skin color, hair and eye color, hair texture, nasal index (the relationship between the nose's length and width), lip form, head shape, and genetic distribution, have been used to distinguish racial types, none of the criteria taken singly have been able to establish distinct racial groups. For instance, skin color, widely considered the most obvious criterion for distinguishing races, is not an obvious indicator when analyzed thoroughly: There are wide variations within what are designated the major racial divisions of human beings, and considerable overlap among these racial divisions also exists (Molnar, 1975; Montagu, 1974).

Over the past several centuries, however, the danger of imprecision did not discourage efforts to develop racial classifications. In 1735 Carl von Linne produced an analysis of human varieties in which American Indians (Native Americans) were summarized as reddish in color, with thick black hair and a personality that was considered "persevering, content, free;" Europeans were described as "light, active, ingenious" and "covered with tailored clothes"; Asians were labelled "severe, miserly, haughty"; and Africans as "crafty, lazy, negligent, anointed with oil" and "governed by whim" (Count, 1950:359).

This scheme was influential, and yet a rival outlook also developed during that era. The eighteenth century was a period in which leading scholars believed that the influence of education and the natural environment could exert a powerful impact on human beings. A prominent European belief held that the great apes were actually human beings whose progress had been blocked by an unfavorable environment. In the United States, Samuel Stanhope Smith argued that dark skin color was a physical phenomenon like freckles and that with sufficient exposure to the sun, whites could become blacks. Smith contended that the reverse process occurred in the celebrated case of Henry Moss, a Virginia slave who appeared to have lost skin pigmentation after moving from the South to the North.

By the early nineteenth century, however, leading thinkers rejected the conclusion that short-term environmental factors affected people's racial type. Because of a growing understanding of geology, scholars began to realize that the human species had evolved over a much vaster length of time than previously recognized, and thus while scientists still accepted the idea that savages could become English gentry, whites or Caucasoids were considered thousands of years more advanced than the other races (Harris, 1968). By the middle and late nineteenth century, prominent leaders supported social Darwinism, which, as we see in Chapter 3, claimed that a white elite's uncompromising pursuit of their self-interest would promote the most universally beneficial social evolution.

Whether social or biological criteria are used, the designation of people's racial membership is an imprecise process. Most frequently **race** refers to a classification of people into categories falsely claimed to be derived from a distinct set of biological traits. Racial classification proves useful to the majority group, which is able to use its power both to subbordinate minority groups and to establish claims of their inferiority. Some recent historical investigations continue to examine the process by which racial classification occurs. In particular, experts are analyzing the steps by which whites' sense of racial superiority developed and thrived during colonization (Wade, 1993).

Racism is the belief contending that actual or alleged differences between different racial groups assert the superiority of one racial group. A racist outlook opposes a belief in racial equality, which contends that if the members of different racial groups are given equal opportunity to develop their talents, then a similar distribution of talent will appear in each group (Hacker, 1992:24–25).

Two types of racism exist: There is individual racism and institutionalized racism. **Individual racism** is an action performed by one person or a group that produces racial abuse—for example, verbal or physical mistreatment. Frequently this type of racism is intentional, but it need not be. One might argue, for instance, that individual racism occurs when a white customer seeking information approaches a group of five store employees and addresses the only white member, assuming that this individual is better informed than the others.

Currently individual racism remains fairly common. In lengthy interviews with 37 middle-class blacks, 24 respondents reported incidents in the previous two years concerning individual racism in workplaces, schools, restaurants, and retail stores, and 15 research subjects revealed incidents of street discrimination (Feagin, 1991).

While individual racism is surely less common than in the past, the fact that it is unusual implies that the impact of particular incidents can be shocking. Consider this response to a questionnaire item in which a student asked her respondents whether or not they had ever been the victims of racism. A 20-year-old black woman replied:

> I was at the corner of a street getting ready to cross when about five white males ran the red light, drove as close to the curb as possible, and screamed in my face, "Run the nigger over!" I jumped back to avoid getting hit and looked in bewilderment searching for this "nigger." That was my first racist experience, and the first time I had ever been called a "nigger." I became overwhelmed with hate, anger, and fear. (Cloud, 1994)

Unlike individual racism, institutional racism is not an immediate action but the legacy of past racist behavioral pattern. Specifically **institutional racism** involves discriminatory racial practices built into such prominent structures as the political, economic, and education systems. The idea of institutional racism is distinctly sociological, emphasizing that social structures establish norms guiding people's behavior. By accepting the norms maintained in racist structures, individuals invariably perpetuate discriminatory conditions. Institutional racism is the prime factor maintaining racism.

It seems useful to examine institutional racism in detail since many people find this important concept difficult to grasp, not realizing that within many structures of American society—for instance, schools, work organizations, the criminal-justice system, government agencies—the impact of institutional racism has dramatically limited many citizens' chances for success.

Inner-city schools with students that tend to belong to racial minorities often suffer institutional racism. Local and national spending for these schools tends to be modest. Court orders requiring legislators to equalize tax allotments in neighboring school districts are likely to encounter footdragging from the representatives of wealthier districts reluctant to lose their funding advantage. In April 1994 28 states were involved in court battles over school finance.

The most celebrated case started in March 1968. At that time Demetrio P. Rodriguez, a Mexican American man whose five children attended a poorly funded school in San Antonio, Texas, filed a suit citing the funding disparities between rich and poor districts. Over a 13-year period, the Texas legislature developed five new funding plans. Four were challenged and later scrapped, either criticized by poor districts because they did not appropriate enough money or opposed by wealthy districts because they had to give up too much of their funding; the fifth plan seems no more promising than its predecessors. In spite of the long fight,

Rodriguez and many other proponents of funding equalization have remained active. Rodriguez explained, "I keep fighting because I want my grandchildren to have what I and my children never had" (Celis, 1994:31).

Like Rodriguez many people realize that the limited educational opportunity produced by institutional racism impacts deeply on children's lives. Different groups associated with poorly funded schools—administrators, teachers, parents, and the students themselves—go through educational motions but recognize that inner-city students are casualties of society, with bleak futures. A writer summarizing the feelings of a mother sending her children to an inner-city school whose students were 98 percent African American observed that the woman felt that such schools "were hardly schools at all, . . . more like warehouses where the kids were stored for a few years, sorted, labeled, and packed for shipment to the menial, low-paying jobs at which they would be doomed to labor the rest of their lives" (Lukas, 1985:104). Institutional racism, in short, involves a discriminatory legacy of structures and practices carried over from eras when racist actions were widely and openly supported.

Institutional racism can spread from one institutional structure to another—for instance from the educational to the economic area. Minority-group members attending the kind of ineffective schools just described are less likely than whites, who generally attend better schools, to have educational credentials making them eligible for many jobs. Thus minority-group children can grow up victimized by limited access to schools, jobs, and other important facilities. Institutional racism is impersonal, lacking the dramatic, newsworthy quality of individual racism, but it nonetheless is potent and destructive.

While institutional racism is more concerned with discrimination than with prejudice, other important concepts are focused on the meaning and significance of prejudice. A **stereotype** is an exaggerated, oversimplified image, maintained by prejudiced people, of the characteristics of the group members against whom they are prejudiced. In an early study of stereotypes, blacks were considered superstitious, lazy, happy-go-lucky, ignorant, and musical while Jews were designated shrewd, industrious, grasping, mercenary, intelligent, and ambitious (Katz and Braly, 1933). In a recent investigation, sociologist Mitchell Duneier concluded that blacks males have often been stereotyped as wasteful, pretentious, lazy, uncommunicative, impatient, flashy, irresponsible, and exploitative of women. His research on working-class black men who met regularly in a Chicago restaurant demonstrated that the men, who tended to scrupulously subscribe to a demanding moral code, did not remotely approximate this stereotype (Duneier, 1994).

Individuals maintaining stereotypes often find that their oversimplified conclusions offer a more orderly, straightforward analysis of a minority group than a nonstereotyped evaluation would provide. Furthermore stereotypes help to either confirm that a downtrodden group should remain in its lowly position or encourage members of the dominant group to push down minority-group individuals who are starting to achieve some economic and political success (Simpson and Yinger, 1985:100–101).

One of the disturbing, potentially tragic qualities of stereotypes is their self-fulfilling nature. A **self-fulfilling prophecy** is an incorrect definition of a situation that comes to pass because people accept the incorrect definition and act on it to make it become true. For instance, if white teachers believe that minority children are superstitious, lazy, happy-go-lucky, and ignorant, then they are unlikely to make a serious effort to help them learn. The students, in turn, will recognize the teachers' disinterest or contempt and will probably exert little effort in school. The teachers see "confirmation" of what they already "know"—that their minority students are inferior. In reality what the teachers confirm is the process performed by the self-fulfilling prophecy. This concept vividly illustrates how prejudice serves as a rationalization for discriminatory behavior.

One more issue to consider is whether minority-group members' stereotyping can be considered racist. To begin, minority-group members sometimes develop stereotypes that assert their own superiority. For instance, Leonard Jeffries, a political scientist at the City University of New York, described whites as "ice people," who are materialistic, greedy, and driven to domination while blacks are characterized as "sun people," who are kind, caring, and communally oriented (Hacker, 1992:28–29). These descriptions qualify as stereotypes, but it is debatable that they are racist. Many analysts of race and racism believe that behavior only qualifies as racist if it has the capacity to hurt the members of another racial group, and minority-group members' stereotypes generally lack the power to inflict such damage.

SIGNIFICANCE OF RACISM IN THE UNITED STATES

Although such prominent social theorists as Émile Durkheim, Karl Marx, and Max Weber differed on many issues, they agreed that ethnicity and race were relatively unimportant concepts. Analyzing the development of industrialization, they felt that both the social bonds and conflicts created by people's ethnic or racial status were characteristics of preindustrial times and would disappear in the industrial world, where discriminatory tendencies associated with those narrow, prejudice-laden ties would give way to more rational relationships that would transcend ethnicity and race and help accomplish the practical goals of modern life (Bell-Fialkoff, 1994; Blauner, 1972:3–4).

The tendency to dismiss or deemphasize the importance of race and racism is not limited to the past. In *The Declining Significance of Race,* William Julius Wilson (1978) concluded that while modern American capitalism has maintained an underclass of poor people, many of whom are black, the process producing that result has been largely color blind (Wilson, 1978; Wilson, 1987).

According to Wilson, there have been three stages of American race relations between blacks and whites. The first stage was blatantly racist, with African Americans exploited as slave workers on plantations and farms. The second stage occurred with the emancipation of slaves; during the next half-century, industrial expansion was accompanied by both class conflict and racial oppression. The third stage currently exists and involves the transition from racial inequalities to class inequalities.

Wilson concluded that for modern African Americans barriers no longer concern legalized racial inequality. The passage of equal-employment and affirmative-action legislation has made it possible for blacks with appropriate educational and training credentials to get good jobs and move comfortably into the middle class. In contrast, African Americans, other racial minorities, and, in fact, whites who do not have the credentials making them eligible to move into the industrial and government sectors find job possibilities increasingly limited. Wilson contended that affirmative-action programs, set up with the best of intentions, have increased opportunities for privileged African Americans but have not improved chances for poor blacks, thus producing growing economic class divisions among blacks (Wilson, 1978:19).

Wilson's conclusion that a variety of current economic factors diminish opportunities for poor people, regardless of color, is widely supported. However, two limitations to his central conclusion about the declining significance of race seem apparent, one involving the continuing objective significance of racism and the other its current subjective importance.

First, evidence indicates the extensive persistence of racism in both individual and institutional form. In the chapters on politics and the criminal-justice system, work and housing, education, the family, and mass media, there are studies showing that while racism might often be more subtle than in the past, it remains alive and healthy. Particularly significant is the continuation of institutional racism. Racist policies established in the past produce increasingly destructive impacts for minority-group members even though government officials and business leaders are no longer openly promoting those policies. For instance, once ghettoes inhabited by racial minorities are established, they continue to grow in size, providing highly restrictive educational and occupational opportunities for the steadily expanding residential body (Rusk, 1993:47).

Second, there is the subjective dimension of racism. Political scientist Andrew Hacker suggested the significance of this issue while discussing blacks' representation in the mass media. He wrote, "When black Americans go to movies, turn on television, or simply scan the comic strips, it seems as if their nation hardly knows or cares they exist" (Hacker, 1992:22). A recent study found that blacks are more inclined than whites to see black-white relations as problematic. Compared to whites, blacks perceive both more widespread black hostility toward whites and also more white hostility toward blacks (Sigelman and Welch, 1993). Another investigation compared blacks and whites of similar socioeconomic status in their reports of psychological well-being and quality of life over a 14-year time span from 1972 to 1985, with differences between whites and blacks on these reported feelings remaining stable for the time period. The overall result was that blacks had lower life satisfaction, less general happiness, less trust in people, less marital happiness, and lower self-rated physical health than whites. The researchers concluded that being black means "a less positive life experience than being white" (Thomas and Hughes, 1986:839). A recent study compared mean-income figures for black and white males ranging in age from their 20s to their 60s and covering the years from 1940 to 1990. With the exception of males aged 20 to 29 during the 1970s, white-male income was always more than black-male income. The greatest disparities occurred in the 30 to 50 age range. The researchers emphasized that this largest gap was significant because "blacks in the 30 to 50 age group are in their 'prime' in terms of raising children, establishing careers, and building wealth" (Thomas, Herring, and Horton, 1994:624). In the 1980s blacks' earnings in that "prime" 20-year age span was slightly less than 87 percents of whites'.

Consider a personal testimony. In *Makes Me Wanna Holler,* journalist Nathan McCall (1994) indicated that growing up black in American society, he felt devalued. Like Andrew Hacker, McCall referred to blacks' representation in the mass media. Sitting spellbound in front of the television, he would drink in the beauty of white's "ivory skin, which seemed purer, cleaner than my own." At the age of seven or eight, McCall saw a Clairol haircoloring commercial where there was a close-up on a pretty white woman "who sensually tossed her blond mane backward and forward all over her face. Near the end of the commercial, a throaty voice chimed in and asked, 'Is it true blonds have more fun?'" The image stuck with McCall. A group of whites riding in a convertible with their long hair blowing in the breeze reminded him of the blond's flowing hair. Yes, he decided, whites have more fun (McCall, 1994:11–12).

As a journalist at the *Atlanta Journal-Constitution,* McCall continued to confront the issue of race. He met blacks who denied that race remained a significant factor—that it was time for African Americans to stop using racism as an excuse for their own shortcomings. Such people, McCall indicated, promoted a detached attitude toward racial issues. He wrote: "The suggestion was that, somehow, if you had allowed racism to make you mad, then you were defeated. I felt the opposite. I felt that any black person who had *no* anger was defeated" (McCall, 1994:292).

A final comment on Wilson's thesis. The position asserting the declining significance of race raises a useful point: That modern conditions limiting minorities' opportunities extend beyond the issue of race. While acknowledging that point, I believe there exists ample evidence indicating that in the modern world, racism remains a powerful, destructive reality.

In a provocative article, Troy Duster (1987) suggested that when two distinctive social groups, such as whites and African Americans, are in contact, and the members of one group plan to study the other, the most fundamental issue involves what questions are posed and answered. For instance, whites, who have supplied the majority of race-relations researchers, have often begun an investigation of blacks focusing on a question similar to this one: Which group is more likely to have members living in poverty? The answer, Duster indicated, is that African Americans are about three times more likely than whites to be living in poverty. From this information researchers are likely to pursue studies of welfare and its apparently debilitating effect on black communities as well as the absence of a strong work ethic. Recommendations emerging from such research will emphasize the necessity of workfare programs that force "the lazy parasites" to support themselves and to stop living off productive tax payers.

On the other hand, Duster indicated, researchers studying black citizens might begin with this question: Between blacks and whites in America, which group is more likely to earn their income by working? The answer is that while blacks obtain 80 percent of their total income from wages and salaries, whites receive only 75 percent of their total income from that source. While blacks receive about $1.2 billion from private property or investment sources, whites obtain $87 billion. From this perspective it seems that whites, not blacks, are more inclined to live off "the fat of the land." Investigators primed with the answer to this second question are then likely to initiate an investigation that is distinctly different from the first one. They might be particularly interested in discovering why the once highly regarded American work ethic seems less apparent among whites than among blacks.

Thus questions asked are fundamental, structuring the substance of research, its results, and the recommendations investigators make. Coming back to the present work, we need to find a question broad and incisive enough to guide our inquiry. Duster suggested the following question: "How and why has race been the persistent category of advantage throughout every generation of the nation's history?" (Duster, 1987:12).

Starting with Duster's question, analysts recognize that American society has consistently practiced racism, with racial minorities invariably losing out in the process. One possible reservation about Duster's question involves the word *the* in the phrase "the persistent category of advantage." Many sociologists would argue that social class has been equally "persistent," and it seems impossible to determine whether race or social class wins the persistence contest.

Duster's question suggests the importance of historical analysis. To understand why racism has been so persistent in American society, investigators must dig into history. Not only academic specialists but activists recognize the importance of this point. A recent examination of 40 speeches made by Jesse Jackson indicated that he has often emphasized the importance of history in helping to grasp the current impact of racism (Callahan, 1993). In this book the importance of historical discussion is apparent not only in Chapter 3, which is devoted to history, but also in major sections focused on historical analysis in various other chapters.

Duster's question also suggests a conflict-theory approach. **Conflict theory** contends that the struggle for power and wealth in society should be the central concern for sociology. Over the past half-century, this perspective has been widely applied to racism. For instance, John Dollard (1937) and W. Lloyd Warner and Leo Srole (1945) indicated that when slavery was abolished, white Southerners established a caste system maintaining segregation in all private and public facilities and ensuring blacks' economic, political, and social disadvantage.

More recently such conflict theorists as Mario Barrera (1979) and Robert Blauner (1972) have described **internal colonialism,** where the control imposed on indigenous racial minorities passes from whites in the home country to whites living within a newly independent nation. This approach appears in the next section and throughout the book.

Why use this theory? Internal colonialism addresses what Bill Lawson (1992) has called "the moral discourse" of minorities' discrimination. While whites often acknowledge the historical inequities imposed on minorities, the discussion and analysis of those issues emanates from theirs—the oppressors' cultural tradition. Thus they fail to appreciate the concrete realities of racism for current minority groups. The tenets of internal colonialism are different: They address, or at least attempt to address such realities and thus seek to show how racism impacts on its victims' daily lives.

INTERNAL COLONIALISM

The ideas of "control" and "exploitation" are central to internal-colonialist theory. Like colonial subjects, members of American racial minorities are subjected to a battery of extreme political, economic, and social discriminations. They receive limited representation in the political process, and they are restricted on where they can live and work. They work long and hard for low wages, and they receive inferior food, housing, education, and medical care.

Four conditions of internal colonialism, all of which have been present in American society, are (1) control over a minority group's governance, (2) restriction of its freedom of movement, (3) the colonial-labor principle, and (4) belief in the inferiority of racial minorities' culture and social organization (Blauner, 1972:53–70). Each point is briefly discussed and at least one modern illustration is included in the analysis.

Control Over a Minority Group's Governance

Historically whites imposed governmental control on racial minorities, making the decisions that determine major outcomes in their lives. A recent study found that on the Fort Yuma Reservation in California, where Quechan tribespeople are permitted to elect their leaders, government officials still impose a great deal of control—for instance, not providing federal funding for business development unless their favored governing style is maintained. Quechan leaders indicated that while their approach supports more argument and leadership turnover than officials wanted, the Quechan style represents a modern application of their traditional approach—improving people and practices by a process of continuous criticism. Government officials were unimpressed and threatened to cut funding (Bee, 1990).

Restriction of a Racial Minority's Freedom of Movement

Whites stringently limited Indians' and blacks' freedom of movement. Indians had their native land invaded, and for over 400 years, they were systematically deprived of their land and freedom and eventually forced to settle on reservations. Blacks, on the other hand, were transported against their will from Africa to the United States, where they were enslaved until the end of the Civil War and then, while technically freed, have continued to encounter limitations on their physical freedom. In modern times such limitations still persist. A half-dozen studies conducted in England and the United States indicated that police were more likely to stop, search, and interrogate blacks than whites (Norris, Fielding, Kemp, and Fielding, 1992).

The Colonial-Labor Principle

The colonial-labor principle indicates that racial minorities must serve white controllers' interests and needs. While capitalist theory emphasizes a free market and free labor, these privileges have primarily been restricted to whites. Historically racial minorities have been required to serve at the pleasure of those who owned or employed them. They have been expected to "know their place," appreciating the necessity to be resigned to a less-than-full participation in society—denied the rights and privileges reserved for whites. This limitation even applies to occupational areas where minorities have been very active. In April 1994 Nolan Richardson, the coach of the Arkansas men's championship basketball team, remarked that whites retain narrow perceptions of blacks' role in sport, including the coach's role. Whites, Richardson said, recognize that black coaches can be good recruiters and effective motivators. He added, "But we're never great coaches" (Rhoden, 1994:4). Whether the reference is coaching or some other occupation, whites have generally believed that the top thinkers, the master strategists, are invariably like them—white.

Historically in the United States, illegal Mexican immigrants have been at the mercy of the colonial-labor principle—starting in farming, mining, and railroad work, then becoming involved in assembly-line activity, and now finding themselves in farm labor, custodial work, and domestic tasks. As illegal aliens they have been under employers' control—forced to accept illegally low wages and vulnerable to layoffs during economic downturns (Hraba, 1994).

Belief in the Inferiority of a Minority Group's Culture and Social Organization

Finally a basic tenet in the internal-colonialist scheme has been the prejudiced position that racial minorities' culture and social organization are inferior to whites' and that, therefore, these groups should readily discard their traditional culture and embrace that of the dominant culture. Thus traditional cultures have been undermined or destroyed, and racial minorities wishing to obtain at least some of the privileges of the dominant culture have had to focus on mastering its knowledge and skills. From the seventeenth century to the present, Europeans and later white Americans have issued relentless claims about cultural superiority, often making distorted observations about the content of other racial groups' cultural patterns. While historically such claims have tended to go unchallenged, this is no longer the case. In December 1993 Senator Ernest Hollings of South Carolina commented on African diplomats coming to Switzerland for international trade agreement talks, saying that "rather than eating each other, they'd just come up to get a good square meal in Geneva" (New York Times, 1993:B16). When the remark drew angry criticism, a Hollings' aide defended his boss by saying that Hollings had just made a harmless joke. In an era when cultural putdowns are no longer publicly acceptable, that response produced little sympathy.

Minority-group members often find it particularly galling that even in the midst of their own communities, the celebration of the dominant culture persists.

A Chinese American writer noted that in the 12 blocks of San Francisco's Chinatown, there are 42 Christian churches. He added:

> On the walls of Chinatown there's a plaque honoring the song "Grant Avenue"; a plaque marking the birthplace of the first white child in San Francisco; a monument to the first white school. *Nothing* for the Chinese. There is one exception: a monument to Sun Yat Sen. He was a Christian. (Terkel, 1992:312)

Table 1.1 demonstrates the relationship among some issues we have just analyzed.

Throughout this chapter we have been examining concepts and a theory. Now for the first time, we analyze a concrete situation demonstrating the occurrence of racism in people's lives. These sections, which occur in every chapter, represent good opportunities to see how norms governing racism develop at the **micro level,** that is, in situations involving the structure and activities of small groups.

A Ku Klux Klan Member's Rejection of Racism

An additional concept supplies the starting point of this discussion. **Social distance** is the feeling of separation between individuals and groups. In the 1920s psychologist Emory Bogardus developed a scale to measure social distance. The scale asks people to indicate their willingness to interact with various racial and ethnic groups in certain social situations, which represent seven degrees of social distance. The seven items involve an increasing social distance as one moves down the list. The first item is kinship by marriage, followed by regular friendship, and the last item involves exclusion from the country.

As a result of racist practice, blacks and whites often perceive a great social distance between each other. However, while suspicion and uneasiness are widespread, the gulf between members of the two groups would seldom be as great as between a Ku Klux Klan member and a black activist.

C. P. Ellis is a white man who has spent his entire life in Durham, North Carolina. When he was in the eighth grade, his father died, and he had to quit school and start supporting the family. It was a constant struggle, with over half of his wages going just to pay rent. As time passed, Ellis became more and more bitter, feeling that there was something seriously wrong with the country and that he

Table 1.1   DISCRIMINATION, PREJUDICE, AND RELATED ISSUES

Discrimination	Prejudice

Racism: a form of discrimination
  a. Individual racism
  b. Institutional racism
Internal colonialism: a theory
  analyzing the oppression of
  American racism, with more
  emphasis on discrimination
  than on prejudice
	Stereotype: image maintained by prejudiced people
	
	Can support self-fulfilling prophecy

needed to find someone to blame. He explained, "The natural person for me to hate would be black people, because my father before me was a member of the Klan . . . It was the only organization that would take care of the white people. So I began to admire the Klan" (Terkel, 1992:272).

Initiation into the Ku Klux Klan was a momentous event. Suddenly for the first time, this man who had struggled all his life felt he had achieved something meaningful. Ellis was led into a large meeting room that contained at least 400 people. The lights were dim, and in front of him was an illuminated cross. He knelt before the cross, vowing to uphold the purity of the white race, fight communism, and protect white womanhood. At the end of the oath, the Klan members applauded loudly. Ellis was thrilled.

He became a prominent organizer for the Klan, recruiting young, poor white men who like him had felt deprived of full membership in society and felt thrilled at the opportunity to have a chance to belong to an organization in which they were valued. Ellis rose to the position of Exalted Cyclops of the Klan's Durham chapter. He visited city leaders in their homes and sometimes received calls from them to attend city-council meetings to represent white interests against the growing number of activist blacks.

Ellis explained:

> We'd load up our cars and we'd fill up half the council chambers, and the blacks the other half. During these times, I carried weapons, outside my belt. We would wind up just hollerin' and fussin' at each other. As a result of our fightin' one another, the city council still had their way. They didn't want to give up control to the blacks *nor* the Klan. They were usin' us. (Terkel, 1992:273)

At first, however, Ellis didn't realize this. He simply focused on the black protesters, whose picketings and demonstrations infuriated him. In particular, he had "a purple passion" about one protest leader—a woman named Ann Atwater, who led a series of demonstrations. Several times the two of them had furious shouting matches.

Then one day Ellis was walking downtown, and he saw a city-council member whom he knew well, approaching from the other direction. Ellis expected to shake hands with the man and have a friendly chat since he had often spoken to the man on the phone and visited him at home. However, the city-council member crossed the street and ignored him. For Ellis the incident was a painful revelation. He spent many sleepless nights struggling with the humiliating conclusion that the political leaders were using him and other Klan members. He brought the issue up at a Klan meeting, saying he did not like being used. The others were unimpressed and simply declared that they should just "keep fightin' them niggers" (Terkel, 1992:274).

The situation wore on Ellis. While he still did not like or trust African Americans, he would see a poor black man with ragged shoes and clothes walking down the street and dimly would begin to feel a kinship with him. Eventually Ellis wanted to leave the Klan, but he felt unable to take the step.

A turning point occurred when a meeting was convened to figure out how to spend a federal-government grant of $78,000 provided to help solve racial problems in the local schools. A variety of groups were asked to participate, including Klansmen and black activists—too many blacks for Ellis to feel comfortable, he told a friend. But the friend persuaded him to go. It was hardly reassuring to walk in the door and immediately see Ann Atwater.

The meeting, Ellis noted, was run "by a great big black guy, but he was very nice." The moderator explained that all participants should feel free to say whatever they wanted. Several blacks indicated that white racism was the source of racial problems in the schools. Ellis listened for a while, but when he could stand listening no longer, he asked for the floor. The reason for these problems, he declared, was "black racism. If we didn't have niggers in the schools, we wouldn't have the problems we got today" (Terkel, 1992:274). What happened next amazed Ellis. Howard Clement, a black man, stood up and indicated that Ellis was the most honest person at the meeting and that it was a good thing he had shown up. As the meeting broke up, a number of blacks tried to shake hands with Ellis, but he refused and walked away.

Nonetheless the following evening, Ellis was back for another meeting. He had gotton his feelings off his chest and felt more relaxed. Still he was surprised and distinctly uneasy when a black man proposed that he and Ann Atwater be the cochairs of a committee that would work out the guidelines for how the government money would be spent. Ellis wondered what to do. It seemed impossible to work with Ann Atwater, and yet from the beginning, he felt pride in being asked to cochair the committee: Here for the second time in his life was a meaningful opportunity for him, a low-income white person, to do something that would produce personal recognition.

One night he telephoned Atwater, saying that while the two of them had had their differences, there was a chance for them to do something important. Would she be willing to put aside their past disputes? Atwater said that she was willing if he was. So they agreed to meet for dinner, along with Bill Rigg, the black man who had been moderating the meetings. Atwater explained that at the cafeteria "C. P. kept pacing up and down the floor." With other whites in the room he "didn't want to be seen sitting at the same table with two blacks" (Terkel, 1992:280).

It was hardly an easy experience for Ellis. He was struggling to confront his racist past, to work on a project that involved drastically shorterning the social distance with black people, whom he had always feared and hated. At night his old friends would sometimes telephone, asking why in the hell was he spending time with black people. Was he selling out the white race? Some support came from Duke University, where he had been doing maintenance work. In recognition of the importance of the biracial effort to relieve racial tension in the schools, the president of Duke gave C. P. Ellis ten days off with full pay.

Atwater and Ellis struck ahead. Seeking support for their program, they went knocking on doors, but this odd couple was too much for most people, whether black or white, to accept. One day taking a few minutes break from their arduous effort, the two of them started what at first seemed an idle conversation. Atwater indicated that life had become real tough. Not only was she poor, supporting her family as a domestic, but this committee work was starting to have an impact on her children. Recently her daughter had come home crying because the teacher had made fun of what her mother was doing. Ellis was startled. The same thing had happened to his son, who had come home crying when the teacher had joked about his father. As Ellis explained what happened, he paused, swallowed hard, and stifled a sob.

> I begin to see, here we are, two people from the far ends of the fence, havin' identical problems, except her bein' black and me bein' white. From that moment on, I tell ya, that gal and I worked good together. (Terkel, 1992:275–276)

Recalling that special moment, Ellis broke into tears.

Twelve years later many changes had occurred. On the job Ellis was elected business manager of the local labor union, which had a two-thirds black membership. Ellis's conception of social distance had changed dramatically. Now he felt comfortable with most black people and estranged from his former Klan friends. His current friends were people who shared his progressive goals emphasizing the importance of working toward a better life for all poor people. Ellis noted, however, that "their station in life is higher than mine. I don't feel comfortable in their homes. Sometimes I find myself standing in the corner in a social gathering and that ought not to be" (Terkel, 1992:279). The reader comes away with the feeling that C. P. Ellis feels good about himself and what he is doing but that he also feels somewhat uprooted, separated from the intense support and camaraderie the Klan had provided.

The last point is instructive and sobering, emphasizing a basic sociological reality: People are strongly influenced by the social world in which they live. If a Klansman stops hating blacks and pursuing the organization's racist activities, he loses his fellow members' friendship and support. At that juncture the friendship such a group provides will disappear, and it can be difficult to replace. Thus an important conclusion that emerges from Ellis's experience is that while individuals' struggles against racism can be uplifting, even inspiring, such personal victories can promote other difficulties in people's lives.

In the next chapter, we pursue the task of understanding racism by examining theories addressing the topic.

REFERENCES

Barrera, Mario. 1979. *Race and Class in the Southwest.* Notre Dame, IN: University of Notre Dame Press.

Barringer, Felicity. 1991. "Census Shows Profound Change in Racial Makeup of the Nation." *New York Times* (March 11):A1+.

Bee, Robert L. 1990. "The Predicament of the Native American Leader: A Second Look." *Human Organization* 49 (spring):56–63.

Bell-Fialkoff, Andrew. 1994. "Ethnic Conflict," pp. 198–204 in John A. Kromkowski (ed.), *Race and Ethnic Relations 94/95.* Guilford, CT: Dushkin Publishing Group. Fourth edition.

Blauner, Robert. 1972. *Racial Oppression in America.* New York: Harper & Row.

Callahan, Linda F. 1993. "History: A Critical Scene within Jesse Jackson's Rhetorical Vision." *Journal of Black Studies* 24 (September):3–15.

Campbell, Ernest Q., and Thomas Pettigrew. 1959. *Christians in Racial Crisis.* Washington, DC: Public Affairs Press.

Celis, William, III. 1994. "A Long-Running Saga over Texas Schools." *New York Times* (April 10):Sec. 4a, 30–31.

Cloud, Alaina. 1994. "African-Americans' Responses to Racism." Student project, Southern Connecticut State University.

Count, Earl. W. (ed.). 1950. *This Is Race: An Anthology Selected from the International Literature on the Races of Man.* New York: Schuman.

Dollard, John. 1937. *Caste and Class in a Southern Town.* New Haven, CT: Yale University Press.

Duneier, Mitchell. 1994. *Slim's Table: Race, Respectability, and Masculinity.* Chicago: University of Chicago Press.

Duster, Troy. 1987. "Purpose and Bias." *Society* 24 (January/February):8–12.

Feagin, Joe R. 1991. "The Continuing Significance of Race: Antiblack Discrimination in Public Places." *American Sociological Review* 56 (February):101–116.

Hacker, Andrew. 1992. *Two Nations: Black and White, Separate, Hostile, Unequal.* New York: Charles Scribner's Sons.

Harris, Marvin. 1968. "Race." *International Encyclopedia of the Social Sciences* 13:263–269.

Hraba, Joseph. 1994. *American Ethnicity.* Itasca, IL: F. E. Peacock Publishers. Second edition.

Katz, David, and Kenneth Braly. 1933. "Racial Stereotypes of One Hundred College Students." *Journal of Abnormal and Social Psychology* 28 (October):280–290.

Kutner, Bernard, Carol Wilkins, and P. R. Yarrow. 1952. "Verbal Attitudes and Overt Behavior Involving Racial Prejudice." *Journal of Abnormal and Social Psychology* 47 (July):649–652.

Lawson, Bill. 1992. "Nobody Knows Our Plight: Moral Discourse, Slavery, and Social Progress." *Social Theory and Practice* 18 (spring):1–20.

Lukas, J. Anthony. 1985. *Common Ground.* New York: Alfred A. Knopf.

McCall, Nathan. 1994. *Makes Me Wanna Holler: A Young Black Man in America.* New York: Random House.

Molnar, Stephen. 1975. *Races, Types, and Ethnic Groups.* Englewood Cliffs, NJ: Prentice-Hall.

Montagu, Ashley. 1974. *Man's Most Dangerous Myth: The Fallacy of Race.* New York: Oxford University Press. Fifth edition.

New York Times. 1993. "A Senator's Cannibal 'Joke' Angers Blacks." (December 16):B16.

Norris, Clive, Nigel Fielding, Charles Kemp, and Jane Fielding. 1992. "Black and Blue: An Analysis of the Influence of Race on Being Stopped by the Police." *British Journal of Sociology* 43 (June):207–224.

Rhoden, William C. 1994. "Arkansas's Richardson Delivering a Message." *New York Times* (April 3):Sec. 8, 4.

Rusk, David. 1993. *Cities without Suburbs.* Washington, DC: Woodrow Wilson Center Press.

Schwartz, Joe, and Thomas Exter. 1993. "All Our Children," pp. 101–103 in John A. Kromkowski (ed.), *Race and Ethnic Relations 93/94.* Guilford, CT: Dushkin Publishing Company. Third edition.

Sigelman, Lee, and Susan Welch. 1993. "The Contact Hypothesis Revisited: Black-White Interaction and Positive Attitudes." *Social Forces* 71 (March):781–795.

Simpson, George E., and J. Milton Yinger. 1985. *Racial and Cultural Minorities.* New York: Plenum Press. Fifth edition.

Terkel, Studs. 1992. *Race: How Blacks & Whites Think & Feel about the American Obsession.* New York: New Press.

Thomas, Melvin E., Cedric Herring, and Hayward Derrick Horton. 1994. "Discrimination over the Life Course: A Synthetic Cohort Analysis of Earnings Differences between Black and White Males, 1940–1990." *Social Problems* 41 (November):608–628.

Thomas, Melvin E., and Michael Hughes. 1986. "The Continuing Significance of Race: A Study of Race, Class, and Quality of Life in America, 1972–1985." *American Sociological Review* 51 (December):830–841.

Wade, Peter. 1993. "'Race,' Nature, and Culture." *Man* 28 (March):17–34.

Warner, W. Lloyd, and Leo Srole. 1945. *The Social Systems of American Ethnic Groups.* New Haven: Yale University Press.

Warner, Lyle G., and Melvin L. DeFleur. 1969. "Attitudes as an Interactional Concept." *American Sociological Review* 34 (April):153–169.

Wilson, William Julius. 1978. *The Declining Significance of Race: Blacks and Changing American Institutions.* Chicago: University of Chicago Press.

Wilson, William Julius. 1987. *The Truly Disadvantaged: The Inner City, the Underclass, and Public Policy.* Chicago: University of Chicago Press.

Chapter
2

Racism Theories: Perspectives on Intergroup Oppression

*A*t the age of 13, I was living with my family in Durban, on the east coast of the Union of South Africa. One morning we were at the docks, watching the unloading of a fishing boat.

I left the spot where I'd been standing and walked over to speak to one of my brothers. Suddenly a voice behind me said, "So you're moving because it sickens you to stand next to a dirty Indian." Surprised I turned around to see a young Indian man, probably in his middle 20s, frowning at me intently.

I started walking away but then stopped and moved back toward him. "I didn't even see you there," I said.

Instantly the frown was gone. "You're an American!" he shouted. "I've never met an American! Tell me," he continued, signaling to come closer, "have you ever been to Chicago?" I shook my head. "No matter. Perhaps just living in the states, you'll know enough. I've got an absolute obsession about Chicago, especially Chicago of the Prohibition era. Tell me. Do shoot-outs between crime families still take place on the streets there?"

We talked for 10 or 15 minutes, and then it was time for us to leave. The rest of the day and for many days to come I thought about the encounter. I was old enough to have a general sense of the virulent racism that dominated South Africa. But this encounter had been personal, graphically demonstrating the potent impact of racially linked symbols: A white skin could instantly create anger and frustration for a minority-group member, and yet when it became apparent that the white skin covered an American, the sense of oppression could be immediately washed away. Following that incident I was left with the shadowy outlines of questions which I have pondered ever since: Why does racism develop? Who benefits from it and how? Just what damage does racism produce for the members of both the minority and dominant groups? And, above all, how can racism be eliminated?

In the intervening years, I've found that while sociological theories analyzing racism have not provided complete answers to these questions, they do address them. To combat and ultimately eliminate racism, we must first understand it. Theories are a major source of understanding. Theories, in short, are not simply abstract, formal statements: They can be practical steps toward comprehension and change.

Many theories analyze either the macro-level or the micro-level issues. **Macro-level** topics involve the large-scale structures and activities that exist within societies and even between one society and another. As we noted in Chapter 1, **micro-level** subjects concern the structure and activities of small groups. Table 2.1 lists the theories included in this chapter.

MACRO-LEVEL THEORIES OF RACISM

As we noted in the opening chapter, conflict theory contends that the struggle for power and wealth in society should be the central concern for sociology. Many people are restricted or controlled by limits powerful members of society impose, and such restrictions create or at least encourage conflict. According to the proponents of this theory, conflict inevitably produces change.

Table 2.1   THEORIES INCLUDED IN CHAPTER 2

Macro-Level Theories

A. *Structural-Functional Theories of Race Relations*
   1. Park's assimilation theory
   2. Gordon's seven-level assimilation theory
   3. Glazer and Moynihan's pluralism theory
B. *Conflict Theories of Racism*
   1. Davis, Gardner, and Davis's caste theory
   2. Dollard's caste theory
   3. Cox's theory of racism
   4. Wilhelm's theory of racism
   5. Internal-colonialist theory

Micro-Level Theories

1. Allport's social-psychological theory of prejudice
2. Frustration-aggression theory

Structural-functional theory is less concerned with conflict and change. **Structural-functional theory** suggests that groups in interaction tend to influence and adjust to each other in a fairly stable, conflict-free pattern. According to this theory, these groups are mutually supportive and interdependent, and each group contributes to the overall stability of the society. Since World War II, most advocates of structural-functional theory, notably Robert Merton (1968), have acknowledged conflict and change play roles in social relations, but those factors are less prominent than in conflict theory. In this section we see that there remains a distinct difference between structural-functional theory and conflict theory when applied to the conflict-laden issue of race. One might argue that the structural-functional theories center on race relations and that the conflict theories focus on racism.

In this discussion we examine prominent examples of both theoretical types.

Structural-Functional Theories of Race Relations

In the opening decades of the twentieth century, one of the most eminent American sociologists was Robert Ezra Park. Park recognized the existence of racism, but based in part on his positive experience serving as secretary to the moderate black leader Booker T. Washington, he remained optimistic that it would eventually be eliminated (Bulmer, 1993:354). Park wrote: "The race relations cycle, which takes the form . . . of contacts, competition, accommodation and eventual assimilation, is apparently progressive and irreversible" (Park, 1950:150). We consider Park's four steps.

Park indicated that contacts between different racial groups occur when explorers from one group discover new areas that can serve as sites for economic gain. Then, according to Park, competition develops. But it is not uncontrolled competition; rather members of the different racial groups must act within established customs and laws. They adapt to the new environment, finding work that, while not necessarily what they would choose to do, contributes to the emerging economy. Eventually a new division of labor forms, incorporating the different racial groups.

With the division of labor in place, accommodation begins. Park asserted that within any established economic system, even one which is as oppressive as slavery, intimate and personal relations among members of different racial groups develop, undermining the more sinister elements within the system. According to Park, one sign of such accommodation during American slavery was that in spite of legislation and custom strongly supporting the system, the number of slaves given freedom by their masters steadily increased (Park, 1950:150).

Assimilation—the elimination of separate racial interests and the development of a common identity involving all racial groups within a society—is the final step. Park suggested that invariably some racial groups would assimilate more rapidly than others, and writing in the 1930s, he conceded that African Americans had still not fully assimilated—that "though the white man and the Negro have lived and worked together in the United States for three hundred years and more, the two races are still in a certain sense strangers to one another" (Park, 1950:76).

Park was vague in analyzing the precise nature of African Americans' incomplete assimilation, indicating that while they were not fully assimilated "in just what sense this is true is difficult to say" (Park, 1950:77).

Milton M. Gordon (1964) sought to be more precise than Park, developing a seven-level framework for analyzing different types of assimilation. To illustrate his scheme, he suggested the existence of two hypothetical ethnic groups—the Sylvanians and the Mundovians. Originally they had separate homelands, but at one point Mundovians started moving to Sylvania. By the second generation, the Mundovians were completely assimilated. What precisely did this mean?

First, it meant cultural assimilation, by which Mundovians adopted all the patterns of the host culture—the language, education system, religion, beliefs, values, and norms—and put aside their own previous cultural standards.

Second, the second-generation Mundovians achieved structural assimilation, making friends by joining cliques, clubs, and other Sylvanian organizations and thereby receiving full acceptance in their residential communities.

Third, the new arrivals obtained marital assimilation, intermarrying in large numbers with native Sylvanians.

Fourth, second-generation Mundovians had developed identificational assimilation, meaning that their sense of themselves as a people was linked to the host culture; in short, they now considered themselves Sylvanians, not Mundovians.

Fifth, the second-generation Mundovians enjoyed a prejudice-free assimilation; the Sylvanians did not feel and thus did not convey a sense of inherent superiority.

Sixth, the Mundovians also benefitted from a discrimination-free assimilation; in no manner were they treated as second-class citizens by the Sylvanians.

Seventh, the final step is civic assimilation, in which the group seeking assimilation—in this case the Mundovians—did not make any significant demands on the host culture requiring a change in its established ways of thinking and acting.

Gordon seemed to be less confident than Park about complete assimilation in the United States. When he examined Americans' friendship patterns and club memberships, it was readily apparent that most preferred to associate with their fellow racial- and ethnic-group members. On the other hand, Gordon noted that by choice some people reached out beyond their own groups and sought the friendship and stimulation of those with diverse racial and ethnic backgrounds. Furthermore contacts among Americans of varied heritages occurred because of the racial and ethnic mixing produced in the industrial work world and in higher education systems. Gordon wrote:

> Ethnic communality will not disappear in the foreseeable future and its legitimacy and rationale should be recognized and respected. By the same token, the bonds that bind human beings together across the lines of ethnicity and the pathways on which people of diverse ethnic origin meet and mingle should be cherished and strengthened. (Gordon, 1964:265)

In later years Gordon acknowledged conflict theory's perspective, admitting that groups with greater wealth and power are able to use those scarce resources to exploit groups that are less well situated. His use of conflict theory, however, was brief and unsystematic, failing to analyze in detail the sources and effects of the unequal distribution of wealth and power (Gordon, 1978).

Pluralism is another structural-functional theory concerned with race and ethnicity. **Pluralism** is a theory emphasizing that a dispersion of power exists in government or other structures within American society. Unlike assimilation theory pluralism does not contend that all cultural differences will ultimately fade away. In fact, a proponent of the theory has argued that in modern times racial and ethnic identities have become stronger than in the past (Scott, 1990).

Nathan Glazer and Daniel Patrick Moynihan (1963), supporters of pluralism, produced a well-known book with a decidedly nonassimilationist title. *Beyond the Melting Pot* was a clear statement that the nineteeth-century idea emphasizing that all ethnic and racial groups would simply disappear in the great "American melting pot" has been proved inaccurate. Analyzing the major ethnic and racial groups in New York City, Glazer and Moynihan concluded that common history, community ties, organizational linkages, and often religion and language have united members of a given racial or ethnic group, making it likely that the group will serve as an interest group and provide the most efficient means for members to achieve full participatory rights in the political and economic systems.

When a racial or ethnic group lacked those rights, members of the group needed to be mobilized to function as an interest group. For example, Glazer and Moynihan contended that in order for blacks to achieve equitable participation in modern society, new, effective African American leaders capable of demanding full rights for their people had to emerge. Writing in 1963, Glazer and Moynihan suggested that while there had been some promising signs of the emergence of such a leadership over the past quarter-century, black leaders had recently proved ineffective. This failure, the authors argued, was significant, because only African Americans could lead their own people in certain problem areas. They wrote:

> It is probable that no investment of public and private agencies on delinquency and crime-prevention programs will equal the return from an investment by Negro-led and Negro-financed agencies. It is probable that no offensive on the public school system to improve the educational results among Negroes will equal what may be gained from an equivalent investment by Negro-led and Negro-financed groups. . . . (Glazer and Moynihan, 1963:84)

Solutions to such pervasive problems will prove formidable and expensive. To expect the emerging African American leadership, in fact the leadership of any single ethnic or racial group, to play a major role in their solution is unfair and unrealistic, particularly in the financial area.

A decade later Glazer and Moynihan reasserted the earlier thesis, emphasizing two points: first, that by the middle 1970s, there were more interracial struggles for prestige, respect, political power, and access to economic opportunity than in the past; second, that the use of ethnic groups as interest groups had become a more persistent trend in recent years (Glazer and Moynihan, 1975:5–7).

Once more, in 1990, Glazer and Moynihan reevaulated their thesis during a panel discussion that occurred at the time of the trials for two white men accused of participating in the killing of a black man in the Bensonhurst section of Queens,

New York (discussed in Chapter 4). They suggested that the racial unrest and hatred the killing had produced underlined the relevance of their thesis and invalidated an assimilationist perspective—that, as a reporter cryptically phrased it, "the melting pot metaphor was a crock" (Roberts, 1990:B1). Mr. Moynihan, now Senator Moynihan, took the opportunity to criticize Marxist thought, suggesting that the beyond-the-melting-pot thesis, which emphasizes the prominent role of race and ethnicity, has refuted Marx's claim that industrial forces would annihilate the significance of race and ethnicity and create a unified working force whose only interests were those shared by an oppressed, exploited class. Giving his colleague major credit, Moynihan said, "What Karl Marx proposed in the British Museum, Nat Glazer disproved in the New York Public Library" (Roberts, 1990:B1).

As we noted in the first chapter, it is true that Marx was one of several prominent social scientists—Durkheim and Weber were others—who discounted the significance of race and ethnicity as major forces in the industrial world. In that regard Moynihan was correct: Undeniably ethnicity and race play important roles in affecting political, economic, and social events in modern society.

On the other hand, the Moynihan and Glazer thesis, which emphasizes that racial and ethnic groups serve as effective interest groups for their members, has often not proved accurate. For instance, Glazer, who wrote the original chapter on African Americans in *Beyond the Melting Pot,* conceded that his claim that blacks would manage to be as economically and politically mobile as white groups proved naive (Roberts, 1990:B1).

Whether assimilationist or pluralist, structural-functional theories fail to address harsh realities of wealth and power inequalities. They simply assume that different racial and ethnic groups have essentially equal access to these scarce commodities and that therefore they will have similar opportunities to receive the prized benefits of society. If, as in the case of African Americans in the early 1960s, many group members have not been successful economically and politically, then, according to Glazer and Moynihan, responsibility rests with the group's leaders, who largely on their own must learn to resolve their group's enormous difficulties. Since such structural-functional theorists never directly analyze issues of unequal distribution of wealth and power, it is hardly surprising that they do not realistically assess the massive mobilization of funds and personnel needed to resolve such problems.

In contrast, conflict theories focus on issues of wealth and power and racial minorities' historically unequal access to these prized commodities.

Conflict Theories of Racism

One of the prominent conflict theories of racism is the caste analysis. A **caste system** is a socially legitimated arrangement of groups in which the ranking of the different groups is clearly designated, members' expected behavior is specified, and the movement of individuals from one group to another is prohibited. In the 1930s and 1940s, social scientists first applied the concept to American race relations, and in recent years researchers have continued to analyze the idea of caste (Forbes, 1990; May, 1992; Oommen, 1994).

In *Deep South*, Allison Davis, Burleigh B. Gardner, and Mary R. Gardner (1941) studied a small southern city with nearly 10,000 inhabitants, about half of whom were black, along with the caste system maintained in that city. One feature of the caste system was the established set of beliefs subordinating blacks. Whites generally felt that African Americans were inherently inferior—that they were a lower form of organism which was mentally deficient and emotionally undeveloped. Whites believed that in some general sense, blacks were "unclean," and thus it was unfitting for whites to eat from dishes or wear clothes that African Americans had used. The researchers also found that local whites felt that the caste system was the "will of God." A physician explained:

> The way I look at it is this way: God didn't put the different races here to mix and mingle so you wouldn't know them apart. He put them here as separate races and He meant for them to stay that way. . . . I don't think God meant for a superior race like the whites to blend with an inferior race and become mediocre. I think God put all the different races here for a purpose, and He didn't mean for them to mix. I think I am right in saying that, and my attitude is Christian-like. (Davis, Gardner, and Gardner, 1941:17)

In addition, whites contended that blacks were "childlike" and would never grow up, living entirely in the present with no regrets for the past nor fears about the future. Since southern whites believed that blacks were childlike and thus irresponsible, whites were convinced black servants would steal from them. It was in their nature, and thus blacks could not be held responsible. Since whites were the ones capable of such preventative actions as locking liquor cabinets or keeping a check on stockings, handkerchiefs, and food, they bore the responsibility for preventing such infractions (Davis, Gardner, and Gardner, 1941:20).

Davis, Gardner, and Gardner indicated that certain social practices, which they called "rituals of subordination," maintained the caste system. These rituals included spatial separation, with southern blacks and whites always knowing that public facilities were segregated; and deferential behavior, which meant that blacks were always expected to respond respectfully to whites, using titles of respect and letting whites be served ahead of them in stores and offices.

Essential for maintaining the caste system was endogamy, the prohibition of interracial marriage. Had African Americans and whites been permitted to intermarry, it would have been much more likely that individuals could pass from the black to the white caste. Such a prospect represented a frontal assault on the caste system.

Blacks, the system dictated, needed to be kept in their place. When this occurred, whites received a variety of benefits. In a study conducted in another southern town during the 1930s, John Dollard (1937) suggested that local middle-class whites received three principal gains from their dominant position in the caste system. First, there was an economic benefit. Middle-class whites were able to avoid menial, often physically demanding jobs. Generally they did not mow their own lawns, cook their own food, nor clean their own houses. In what was largely an agricultural area, most of the farming, including the backbreaking work of cotton picking, was blacks' responsibility. Furthermore while blacks' work was more taxing physically than whites', it also paid considerably less. Thus many whites could use advantages they obtained from blacks' low-paid employment to maintain a luxurious lifestyle.

Second, Dollard discussed whites' sexual gain, meaning that because of their superior position in the caste structure, white men had unchallenged sexual access to both African American and white women. Dollard suggested that southern white men's traditional outlook toward white women enhanced the significance of this issue. Southern white men were expected to idealize the white women, celebrating their beauty and chastity and restraining erotic feelings and behavior. While sexual activity with their wives was necessary to produce children, southern white men felt guilt-ridden about it. For uninhibited, passionate sex, freed from "cares, threats, and duties" (Dollard, 1937:144), they often turned to black women, many of them prostitutes.

Third, southern whites received a prestige gain. Simply because people were white, they were able to demand forms of deference from blacks that would enhance their self-esteem. For whites, Dollard suggested, the prestige gain created an illusion of greatness similar to alcohol's intoxicating effect. The difference was that this benefit was not an illusion but "a steadily repeated fact." Dollard wrote:

> From the standpoint of the white man the crucial thing may be that his aggressive demands are passively received; this gives the gratification of mastering the other person. Still more important perhaps is to receive the deference in advance of demanding it, a submissive affection which is freely and automatically yielded. (Dollard, 1937:174)

The prestige gain, in short, provided whites gratification on the spot, and it also served to emphasize the legitimacy of the caste system, in which blacks were classified distinctly inferior to whites and controlled by them.

During the same era, Oliver Cromwell Cox (1959), an African American, Marxist sociologist, analyzed the relations between African Americans and whites. As a supporter of Marxist thought, Cox accepted Marx's claim that under capitalism modern societies would be divided into two basic classes—the ruling class, whose members owned the factories and farms that were sources of wealth, and the working class, whose members depended on wages. Capitalism, Marx emphasized, was exploitative, paying workers barely enough to survive and forcing most of them to do assembly-line work that was repetitive and boring. Eventually, Marx indicated, workers would recognize that as a class they shared common grievances against the ruling class and the capitalist economic system. Organizing themselves into an army, workers would overthrow the ruling class and establish a new economic system—socialism—in which all citizens would own the means of producing wealth (Marx and Engels, 1959).

Writing in the 1940s, Cox extended the Marxist analysis to include blacks' oppression. He suggested that as members of the working class, blacks in capitalist society faced all the limitations and problems imposed on white wage earners. In addition, they were racially exploited, designated inferior to whites and denied many of the modest rights available to members of the white working class. In Richard H. Thompson's phrase, blacks faced "double exploitation" (Thompson, 1989:151).

Cox concluded that the core of the American racial problem was that blacks wanted to assimilate, obtaining equitable opportunities in modern society and reducing greater exposure to disease, unemployment, poverty, and illiteracy. The white ruling class, however, opposed blacks' assimilation. Its members felt that it was to their advantage to keep blacks and other racial minorities economically, politically, and socially disprivileged.

While whites used various techniques to keep blacks in an oppressed state, Cox believed that lynching was the "fundamental reliance" of the white ruling class. Although the practice occurred more frequently in the South than in the North, Cox contended that support for the practice—what he called "the lynching attitude"—existed among whites throughout the country.

Cox defined **lynching** as one group's use of mob action to kill a member of an oppressed group, thereby warning members of that oppressed group either to accept an even more lowly status or to forsake any developing plans to rise above their subordinated position (Cox, 1959:549).

Because of the purpose lynching served for whites, the actual victim was unimportant: What was necessary was that some black person's violent death conveyed a warning. Cox believed that sending a warning to local blacks was a central element in the cycle producing lynchings. The process involved the following steps. First, a growing belief developed among local whites that in some respect, such as gaining wealth or acting self-assertively, local African Americans were getting out of hand. Second, discussing the issue among themselves, whites reached the conclusion that blacks in the area represented a distinct, immediate threat. Third, there was a rumored or actual occurrence of some outrage committed by a black person against a white individual. If tensions among whites were extreme, some of them simply created an incident. For instance, they falsely accused a black man of making sexual advances toward a white woman or of stealing from his employer. Fourth, once the incident took place, the white mob mobilized, and a black victim was burned, hanged, or shot in public, preferably before the court house to emphasize the legitimacy of the savage act; then the victim's remains were dragged through the black section of town. In the fury of mob violence, other African Americans were often killed or beaten, and considerable property belonging to blacks was destroyed. Fifth, within two or three days, the mob had achieved its emotional release, and a movement for judicial investigation occurred. Sometimes on the Sunday following the violence, courageous local ministers preached that lynching was barbarous and un-Christian. Eventually a grand jury returned the finding that the deceased individual met death by burning, hanging, or shooting at the hands of unknown parties. Sixth, a new racial adjustment developed, with blacks becoming very cautious in dealing with whites and accepting even more oppressive relations and conditions than previously. If, at this time, some black people dared to defend their rights against whites, most local blacks were much more likely to be critical than supportive. For most black citizens, the major task at hand was to get on with life and to convey to whites a sense of normalcy— that they, the blacks, bore whites no malice. Cox wrote, "The lynching had accomplished its purpose, . . . and the cycle . . . [was] again on its way" (Cox, 1959:551).

Cox suggested that the extraordinary violence whites inflicted on blacks might have been necessary to overcome "possible inhibitions of conscience" occurring because of black and white workers' common plight as exploited wage earners within industrial capitalism. Cox asserted that one of the significant effects created by racism was that it prevented black and white workers from appreciating that under capitalism they shared common grievances that could have served as the basis for an organized interracial effort to overthrow the ruling class and the capitalist system. Were Cox alive today, he might conclude that modern outbreaks of violence against racial minorities have produced a similar divisive effect.

Cox believed that in order to encourage structural changes that would eliminate violence against them and permit them to seek a full share of the rights and privileges of modern society, African Americans needed effective leadership. Cox indicated that in spite of many blacks lamenting the fact that no great leader had emerged among them, the absence of such leadership was inevitable. Why? The key, Cox claimed, was blacks' position in society: "The destiny of Negroes is cultural and biological integration and fusion with the larger American society" (Cox, 1959:572). Like other Americans, blacks were pursuing their individual destinies, seeking assimilation into the economic, political, and social structures of modern American life. A leader who either promised to carry the entire race to glory or who negatively represented whites and white-dominated society would work against individual blacks' efforts to obtain success and satisfaction.

According to Cox, Marxist analysts of race relations needed to appreciate that blacks were only a small part of American workers' struggle for political and economic power. Cox believed that for blacks and whites alike, the most effective leadership would undoubtedly come from white leaders who sought to improve downtrodden poor people's lives, regardless of color. Without any undue concern for "the Negro problem," President Franklin D. Roosevelt did more to elevate blacks' status than any other leader of the first half of the twentieth century (Cox, 1959:582).

A recent study of Cox noted that in his later years, he became more willing to make concessions about American society, moderating his earlier position about the necessity to overthrow capitalism and declaring that racial equality would most readily be produced by reforming current political and economic systems (Snedeker, 1988).

However, Cox and other early conflict theorists dealing with race and racism had limited impact in their lifetimes. From the 1930s until the late 1960s, structural-functional theory remained dominant, with its emphasis on cohesion, conformity, and cooperation. As we have noted, its applications to race relations—the assimilation and pluralism theories—were widely accepted. Then in the middle and late 1960s, widespread protests, which included a deep concern for racial and economic injustice, promoted a sharply increased interest in conflict theory in general and conflict theories of race and racism in particular (Monk, 1994:xvii–xviii).

Sidney Wilhelm (1983) is a modern proponent of a conflict theory of racism. He has developed an idea similar to one already mentioned twice in this book: Like Marx before them, modern Marxist thinkers have failed to recognize that racism exists independently of economic forces. Marx believed that as capitalism advanced, narrow allegiances that produced racism would disappear. Modern Marxist theorists have tended to conclude that socialism would provide that benefit. According to Wilhelm, these theorists concluded that "the destruction of capitalism will immediately eliminate any economic necessity for the continuation of racism" (Wilhelm, 1983:129). But Wilhelm suggested that racism is also the product of noneconomic factors. Currently racism cuts across all social classes, with blacks and other racial minorities who are spared oppressive economic conditions nonetheless vulnerable to racism. Certainly ample evidence in this book supports that claim.

Wilhelm's second principal conclusion is that many African Americans represent a special category of disadvantaged people—those who are permanently unemployed. Historically blacks have had uniquely restricted educational and occupational opportunities, and as a result many of them have been much less prepared than other groups to prosper in the computerized, automated postindustrial world. Wilhelm indicated that African Americans "are not so much oppressed as unwanted; not so much unwanted as unnecessary; not so much abused as ignored" (Wilhelm, 1983:233). Both past and present Marxist theory, Wilhelm claimed, have failed to appreciate how historical conditions have placed poor modern African Americans in a position of unique economic exploitation.

Some commentary on conflict theories of race relations seems appropriate. To begin, it should be emphasized that some of the observations about racism offered here are dated; for instance, the southern caste system with associated lynching and other horrors has been largely dismantled. Nonetheless we might consider the possibility that some oppressive social patterns described in this section are still applicable; for instance, while lynching no longer occurs, a similar process of terror and intimidation occurs in modern situations in which whites initiate violence against African Americans and other racial minorities.

Modern conflict theorists, perhaps the Marxist theorists in particular, need to address the respective impacts of race and social class on racial minority-group members' lives. For example, evaluating Wilhelm's conclusion about modern blacks' high level of unemployment, Richard H. Thompson indicated that one can dispute his claim that Marxist theory fails to provide conceptual analysis of blacks' high level of unemployment in modern capitalism. Thompson contended that traditional Marxist theory contained the concept of surplus labor that addressed such an issue (Thompson, 1989:166–167). On the other hand, Thompson and many other conflict theorists would agree that Wilhelm is correct in asserting that more than traditional, class-oriented Marxist concepts must be used to analyze the causes of modern American racism. A major challenge for the advancement of conflict theories of race is to sort out the respective impacts of race and social class on racial minorities' lives and on modern society itself.

Analyzing racism, some conflict theorists would include a third factor—gender. They have argued that poor women of color are most effectively understood if their three minority statuses are considered simultaneously. Several scholars are developing a unified theory of class, race, and gender, which considers diverse combinations of these three factors (Collins, 1989; Sacks, 1989).

Many conflict-theoretical analyses of American racism, such as Oliver Cox's work, are compatible with internal-colonialist theory, emphasizing that whites have systematically controlled and exploited racial minorities and focusing on minorities' governance, restriction of movement, work, and supposed cultural inferiority.

In this section devoted to conflict theory, it seems appropriate to evaluate internal colonialism, which was introduced in the previous chapter and is used throughout the book. If you wish to review the theory's content, turn to pp. 11–14.

It appears that three criticisms most frequently directed against internal colonialism are doubts about the accuracy of the analogy between colonialism and internal colonialism, neglect in addressing class divisions among dominant whites (Feagin and Feagin, 1993:39–40), and underestimations of minorities' ability to determine their own destiny.

First, we consider the criticism of the analogy between colonialism and internal colonialism. Supporters of this point emphasize that unlike colonial subjects American minorities are not confined to a restricted territory nor are they subjected to control imposed by an intermediate elite similar to the indigenous leaders within a colony that help the colonial power exploit the local people. Advocates of internal colonialism concede that on these two issues, the situation faced by American racial minorities is different from that confronted by the indigenous African, Asian, and American peoples subjected to colonial exploitation. However, the proponents of the theory emphasize that while modern minorities are not confined to a specific territory, they are subjected to significant restrictions of movement; furthermore although American minorities do not need to deal with an intermediate elite, they generally face a highly controlled governance process.

Second, critics claim that internal-colonialist theorists fail to address class differences among whites. After all, they contend, not all minority-group members are subordinate to whites. American minority groups have sizable numbers of people whose educational, occupational, and income levels are above the white averages. This conclusion is true. Like any social theory, internal colonialism does not address the totality of social reality. In fact, the theory's emphasis is not on class differences among whites but on the power whites as a group can impose on a given minority group: That because of the greater political and economic resources possessed by the dominant white group, racist insults and injuries can be directed against many minority-group members readily, even unexpectedly. Supporters of internal colonialism recognize that American minorities have improving opportunities and achievements. However, the proponents emphasize, these accomplishments do not invariably protect minorities from racist oppression.

Third, critics of internal colonialism have indicated that the theory underestimates racial minorities' ability to control their own destiny. While analysts must consider harsh realities of racism, they should not overstate their case, failing to assess minority individuals' capacity to confront or surmount those harsh realities and obtain various successes. Some theorists have been aware of this point. For instance, one writer contended that any theory of race and racism produced within American society will fail to fully grasp the structural limitations historically imposed on minorities and provide ineffectual or illusory means to escape racial oppression. It is essential, she concluded, to evaluate racial issues from a perspective rooted outside of traditional American culture—in her case from an Afrocentric perspective (Van Dyk, 1993).

It seems that the modern observer of racism must steer a narrow course: on the one hand, thoroughly examine the devastating impact of racism—and internal colonialism proves useful here—and, on the other hand, acknowledge minority-group members' successful efforts to control their own lives, perhaps with strategies developed from their group's unique cultural points of view.

Let me conclude the commentary on conflict theories of racism with a personal observation. Frequently sociologists find that both structural-functional and conflict theories offer useful analysis of major sociological topics. For instance, in my own introductory sociology text (Doob, 1994), the two theories complemented each other effectively in examining the functions of religion, the impact of education in modern society, and the concentration of political authority. But while structural-functional theory's perspective emphasizing stability and harmony and downplaying conflict and wealth and power inequities can provide some insight, I find such emphases especially hard to accept when the cruel, crippling realities of modern racism are readily apparent. Or, to phrase it differently, the only way I could comfortably write this book was if a conflict perspective permeated it.

We now shift from the macro-level to the micro-level and examine social-psychological theories of racism.

MICRO-LEVEL THEORIES OF RACISM

Theories in this section examine the small-group context encouraging prejudice and discrimination. In *The Nature of Prejudice,* Gordon Allport (1954:307–310) suggested that prejudice is a three-stage learning process to which children in American culture are exposed. The following situation illustrates the first stage: Janet, a six-year-old girl, comes running home and asks, "Mother, what is the name of the children I am supposed to hate?" In Allport's apt phrase, Janet "is stumbling at the threshold of some abstraction" (Allport, 1954:307). She identifies with her mother, seeks her approval, and wishes to fuse her obedience to her mother with appropriate feelings toward her own social contacts. The child, Allport contended, engages in *pregeneralized* learning, having accepted the information that a certain African American boy is dirty or a particular Native American woman is not to be trusted, but generalizations involving prejudice toward entire racial or ethnic groups still elude her. Language is the key to the development of racist thought. Listening to her mother, father, other adults, and older children express their prejudices toward different groups, Janet will gradually be able to grasp which racial and ethnic groups are the culturally approved objects of prejudice.

In Janet's case the second stage in learning prejudice begins with her mother's response to the question about the children Janet is expected to hate. The mother might reply, "I told you not to play with black children. They are dirty; they have diseases; and they will hurt you. Now don't let me catch you playing with them." Such a directive can initiate the period of *total rejection:* Prompted by parental order, the child vigorously rejects all members of a certain racial or ethnic groups—in this case African Americans. For Janet and other six-year-olds, total rejection of a particular group might prove unsystematic since, according to research, until children are eight, they do not have a clear, stable sense of people's race and ethnicity (Aboud, 1984). By ten or eleven, when white children subjected to a prejudiced upbringing answered a series of questions comparing blacks' and whites' qualities, the whites were scored higher on every question. Allport concluded that these children "had learned to reject the Negro category *totally*" (Allport, 1954:309).

The third stage involves *differentiation.* Now the child has become more sophisticated, learning to make gracious exceptions when it seems appropriate: "Some of my best friends are Puerto Rican." Or: "How could I be prejudiced against Asians? The woman who took care of me when I was a kid was Chinese, and I loved her dearly." By about age 15, young people have become sophisticated enough to turn the racism faucet on and off at will. As part of the package, they have learned what Allport called "the peculiar double-talk appropriate to prejudice in a democracy"—speak in favor of individual rights and equality and simultaneously support prejudice and discrimination (Allport, 1954:310).

Recent research has examined the impact differentiation produces. Preschool and young school-age children of all major racial groups generally demonstrate more positive attitudes toward whites and greater identification with them. For adolescents the pattern is not as distinct. More independent than young children, they appear much more capable of combatting the impact of racial stereotypes imposed either on their own racial group or on other groups (Aboud, 1988; Spencer and Markstrom-Adams, 1990).

Another social-psychological perspective is the frustration-aggression theory. Consider the following situation. A four-year-old is scolded by an angry father. The child, in turn, is angry and frustrated and glances up at dad, momentarily wondering whether she might risk kicking him in the shins. But dad, his towering height convinces her, is much too formidable, and so taking a less satisfying but somewhat satisfying action, she slugs her innocent two-year-old brother. The **frustration-aggression theory** emphasizes that people blocked from achieving a goal are sometimes unable or unwilling to focus their frustration on the true source, and so they direct the aggression produced by frustration toward an accessible individual or group. The displacement of hostility from the true source of frustration to this substitute—a so-called "scapegoat"—permits a release of tension called "catharsis."

Three conditions make it likely that a racial or ethnic group will become a scapegoat. First, the group must be easy to identify, whether by skin color, a tattoo, or some insignia such as the Star of David Nazis forced Jews to wear. Second, the group selected must be weak enough so that it is unlikely to retaliate. Third, to qualify as a scapegoat, a group must be physically accessible (Simpson and Yinger, 1972:66–69).

For racist individuals, scapegoating is often an emotionally charged process, quickly meeting their needs at a given time and place. In his study of poor southern whites in the 1930s, Leonard W. Doob indicated that at least half a dozen white men informed him that when farmers for whom they were working forced them to leave the cabins in which they were living and replaced them with blacks, their immediate impulse was to kill the blacks. Before pursuing the impulse, however, each concluded that "killing the nigger wouldn't get me anywhere, since there are plenty of other nigger families for the place" (Doob, 1937:471). The quotation is notable because it suggests that even though the frustrated poor whites eventually toned down their initial aggressive reaction toward blacks, they were still in the grips of the frustration-aggression perspective, which protected them from facing the painful truth that the real source of their frustration was the powerful, inaccessible farmers.

While the frustration-aggression theory is a useful analytic tool, it could be refined. Sometimes frustration does not produce aggression, and thus it would be useful to determine when a frustrating situation produces an aggressive act and when it does not. Furthermore even when aggression is the outcome, it is not necessarily focused upon a scapegoat. In particular, the theory does not specify the conditions under which aggression is directed against a scapegoat or against the true object of frustration. In addition, the theory specifies little about the process of scapegoating—in situations where several potential scapegoats are available, it is not clear what social factors encourage oppressors to tyrannize one particular group and not another (Marger, 1994:94; Schaefer, 1993:44).

Discussion now shifts from the analysis of theory to a case study. In the following section, we consider how internal colonialism as well as other theoretical perspectives and concepts prove useful in the analysis of racist events.

Ishi, the Last Surviving Yahi

Early in the morning of the August 29, 1911, in a small northern California town, the sharp barking of dogs made workers at a slaughterhouse aware of a man crouching against a nearby fence. He was emaciated, dying of starvation, and his hair was closely shaved—a sign that he was in mourning. In the months that followed, it became apparent why Ishi was in mourning. He was the last surviving member of the Yahi tribe, whose other members had been mercilessly hunted down. Ishi's story is a stark account of what can happen to a highly oppressed group whose members are brutalized victims of internal colonialism.

With the discovery of gold in northern California in 1848, whites began coming to the area by the thousands. Some were law-abiding citizens and others were not, but the new settlers shared a sense of racial and cultural superiority: Native Americans were inferior beings who should be exploited as servants, slaves, or sex objects. Any white man who actually married a Native American was viewed with contempt. Thus early white settlers drew caste distinctions. Indians, even so-called "good" Indians who lived on or near white homesteads, were always classified as lower-caste members.

Inevitably stereotypes accompanying this classification process proved deadly for northern California Indians. White immigrants had come across the plains where they had encountered Indians who were mounted on horses and were often armed with rifles. These were formidable opponents, and the whites adopted the convenient rationalization that the Yahi and other northern California Indians would be equally dangerous. Significant differences—that these Indians were on foot and without guns—apparently escaped the recent settlers. Many whites made little or no effort to distinguish different Native Americans' abilities and motivations, and some killed Indians with little or no discretion. No saying more clearly demonstrates Indians' stigmatized status than the well-known, nineteenth-century phrase, "The only good Indian is a dead Indian."

With such an outlook, no Indians were safe. The Yahi and other northern California tribesmen sometimes responded to the frequent threat of being tracked and killed by turning against whites and robbing or killing them. Following such acts trigger-happy whites were likely to murder any Indians, including "good" Indians. Because of their inability to fight back and their accessibility, these Indians served as scapegoats for the whites.

Until the 1880s, however, the Yahi had few encounters with whites. Certainly the members of this tribe were aware of the invaders and viewed them as an oppressive force. However, their nomadic life, which kept them gathering fruits, nuts, and berries and hunting game, confined them to hilly country, far from the new settlements. Eventually whites' livestock began roaming the hills, destroying many plants that were a major source of Indians' food. At the same time, settlers began to pollute the streams, which provided salmon and other fish. For the Yahi survival had always been precarious, but now it became even more so. Using all the skills developed living close to nature, they fought back. They raided the whites' homesteads and stole livestock and other food. When whites began killing them, they too killed in return. Theodora Kroeber indicated that the Yahi image "of the white man became fixed during those days when it was a careless boast that 'You can't tell one Indian from another.'" The Yahi "found themselves, too, indifferent to making distinctions between one white person and another" (Kroeber, 1969:49–50). This situation illustrates how stereotypes can create a self-fulfilling prophecy. When whites and Indians began to stereotype each other as indiscriminate murderers, they became convinced it was necessary to kill or be killed. As a result, members of each group became even more committed to indiscriminate murder.

Ishi was probably born in 1862. By that time the surviving Yahi had grasped one of the central ideas of internal colonialism—that their freedom of movement was highly restricted and that they could only survive if they used all their skills to avoid whites. But avoidance sometimes was impossible. When Ishi was about three, a raiding party attacked the Yahi camp. Most of the Yahi were killed, but he and his mother escaped. As Ishi grew up, he learned to hunt and fish and to live on the run, hiding from whites. Always threatened by starvation, the diminishing band sometimes raided white farms and stole food. Such a difficult life took its toll. By 1870 only about 16 Yahi tribespeople survived, and by 1906 just four remained. At that point a surveying party discovered the hidden Yahi camp close to a stream. Three members fled, and the fourth, Ishi's crippled mother, was discovered by the whites. They took the Indians' food and weapons but left the old woman unharmed. Shortly afterwards Ishi returned and carried his mother to a secluded spot, where she soon died. Ishi never again saw the other two tribal members. He was convinced that they must have died, or otherwise he would have encountered them. For the last three years in the wild, Ishi was entirely alone—the sole survivor of a tribe that had been systematically reduced to a single person by whites' genocidal efforts.

This is hardly an inspiring account with which to conclude the chapter. Unfortunately as we examine the history of American racism in the next chapter and then move on to consider current racism in later chapters, we see considerably more evidence of racial oppression. The role of theory for analyzing racism will also be apparent.

REFERENCES

Aboud, Frances E. 1984. "Social and Cognitive Bases of Ethnic Identity Constancy." *Journal of Genetic Psychology* 145 (December):217–230.

Aboud, Frances E. 1988. *Children and Prejudice*. New York: Basil Blackwell.

Allport, Gordon W. 1954. *The Nature of Prejudice*. Cambridge, MA: Addison-Wesley.

Blauner, Robert. 1972. *Racial Oppression in America*. New York: Harper & Row.

Bulmer, Martin. 1993. "The Apotheosis of Liberalism? An *American Dilemma* after Fifty Years in the Context of the Lives of Gunnar and Alva Myrdal." *Ethnic and Racial Studies* 16 (April):345–357.

Collins, Patricia Hill. 1989. "The Social Construction of Black Feminist Thought." *Signs* 14 (summer):745–773.

Cox, Oliver Cromwell. 1959. *Caste, Class & Race: A Study in Social Dynamics*. New York: Monthly Review Press.

Davis, Allison, Burleigh B. Gardner, and Mary R. Gardner. 1941. *Deep South: A Social Anthropological Study of Caste and Class*. Chicago: University of Chicago Press.

Dollard, John. 1937. *Caste and Class in a Southern Town*. New Haven: Yale University Press.

Doob, Christopher Bates. 1994. *Sociology: An Introduction*. Fort Worth: Harcourt Press. Fourth edition.

Doob, Leonard W. 1937. "Poor Whites: A Frustrated Class," pp. 445–484 in John Dollard, *Caste and Class in a Southern Town*. New Haven: Yale University Press.

Feagin, Joe R., and Clairece Booher Feagin. 1993. *Racial & Ethnic Relations*. Englewood Cliffs, NJ: Prentice-Hall. Fourth edition.

Forbes, J. D. 1990. "The Manipulation of Race, Caste, and Identity: Classify Afroamericans, Native Americans and Red-black People." *Journal of Ethnic Studies* 18 (winter):1–51.

Glazer, Nathan, and Daniel Patrick Moynihan. 1963. *Beyond the Melting Pot*. Cambridge, MA: M.I.T. Press and Harvard University Press.

Glazer, Nathan, and Daniel Patrick Moynihan. 1975. "Introduction," pp. 1–26 in Nathan Glazer and Daniel Patrick Moynihan (eds.), *Ethnicity: Theory and Experience*. Cambridge, MA: Harvard University Press.

Gordon, Milton M. 1964. *Assimilation in American Life: The Role of Race, Religion, and National Origins*. New York: Oxford University Press.

Gordon, Milton M. 1978. *Human Nature, Class, and Ethnicity*. New York: Oxford University Press.

Kroeber, Theodora. 1969. *Ishi in Two Worlds: A Biography of the Last Wild Indian in North America*. Berkeley and Los Angeles: University of California Press.

Marger, Martin N. 1994. *Race and Ethnic Relations: American and Global Perspectives*. Belmont, CA: Wadsworth. Third edition.

Marx, Karl, and Friedrich Engels. 1959. "Manifesto of the Communist Party," pp. 1–41 in Lewis S. Feuer (ed.), *Marx & Engels: Basic Writings on Politics & Philosophy*. Garden City, NY: Anchor Books. Originally published in 1848.

May, Ann Mari. 1992. "Caste, Class, and Social Change: An Institutionalist Perspective." *Journal of Economic Issues* 26 (June):553–560.

Mead, George Herbert. 1934. *Mind, Self and Society*. Chicago: University of Chicago Press.

Merton, Robert K. 1968. *Social Theory and Social Structure*. New York: Free Press. Third edition.

Monk, Richard C. 1994. "Introduction: Issues in Race and Ethnicity," pp. xiv–xxi in Richard C. Monk (ed.), *Taking Sides: Clashing Views on Controversial Issues in Race and Ethnicity*. Guilford, CT: Dushkin Publishing Group.

Oommen, T. K. 1994. "Race, Ethicity and Class." *International Social Science Journal* 46 (February):83–93.

Park, Robert Ezra. 1950. *Race and Culture*. Glencoe, IL: Free Press.

Roberts, Sam. 1990. "Moving Beyond the Melting Pot 25 Years Later." *New York Times* (May 17):B1.

Sacks, Karen Brodkin. 1989. "Toward a Unified Theory of Class, Race, and Gender." *American Ethnologist* 16 (August):534–550.

Schaefer, Richard T. 1993. *Racial & Ethnic Groups*. New York: HarperCollins. Fifth edition.

Scott, George M., Jr. 1990. "A Resynthesis of the Primordial and Circumstantial Approaches to Ethnic Group Solidarity: Towards an Explanatory Model." *Ethnic and Racial Studies* 13 (April):147–171.

Simpson, George Eaton, and J. Milton Yinger. 1972. *Racial and Cultural Minorities: An Analysis of Prejudice and Disrimination*. New York: Harper & Row. Fourth edition.

Snedeker, George. 1988. "Capitalism, Racism, and the Struggle for Democracy: The Political Sociology of Oliver Cox." *Socialism and Democracy* 7 (fall/winter):75–95.

Spencer, Margaret Beale, and Carol Markstrom-Adams. 1990. "Identity Processes among Racial and Ethnic Minority Children in America." *Child Development* 61 (April):290–310.

Thompson, Richard H. 1989. *Theories of Ethnicity: A Critical Appraisal*. Westport, CT: Greenwood Press.

Van Dyk, Sandra. 1993. "The Evaluation of Race Theory: A Perspective." *Journal of Black Studies* 24 (September):77–87.

Wilhelm, Sidney M. 1983. *Black in a White Society*. Cambridge, MA: Schenkman.

Chapter
3

Passage to Racism

*T*he best-known estimates of the number of slaves brought to the New World range between 9 and 15 million, with perhaps half dying during the infamous "middle passage" from Africa to the Americas. Is it surprising that so many died? Consider the prevailing conditions.

After being branded and chained, the captured Africans were rowed out to slave ships, where they were packed into areas sometimes no more than 18 inches high. One captain said, "They had not so much room as a man in his coffin, either in length or breadth." Here they lived from six to ten weeks, in conditions horrible enough to drive people mad and often worsened when epidemics of dysentary, smallpox, or the flux, an illness which spared whites, swept the ships.

Suffocation in the unbearably close quarters was frequent, and in the frenzy to obtain more air, some men strangled those next to them. So many dead slaves were thrown overboard that reports indicated sharks would pick up a ship off the coast of Africa and follow it for its entire journey (Bennett, 1982:49).

How could one group of people treat another so savagely? To analyze the historical development of racism, we can use a final theoretical framework. It is Donald L. Noel's (1968) theory of ethnic stratification, which concerns how ethnicity and race become central factors for determining people's access to valued political, economic, and social rewards of their society. This theory represents an additional conflict-theoretical perspective. While the theory can apply to diverse ethnicities, including different white ethnic groups, our focus in on race.

According to Noel, three conditions permit racial stratification to develop. First, there must be **ethnocentrism,** which is the automatic tendency to evaluate other cultures by outsiders' cultural standards. Ethnocentric individuals believe that their way is the correct or most appropriate way, and if other cultures have different standards or ways, they invariably are inferior. The more one culture differs from another, the more likely people's ethnocentric tendencies appear. Nineteenth-century white Americans were ethnocentric toward African slaves, because slaves differed from them in many ways—language, clothing and appearance, social norms, religion, and other cultural standards.

Second, competition for scarce resources is a necessary factor. Competition can be between or among different racial groups or simply within the dominant group. Two conditions affecting the extent to which competition produces racial exploitation are (1) whether or not custom or law puts limits on how much the minority can be oppressed and (2) whether the dominant group's opportunities are static or expanding. Both conditions favored extensive exploitation of slaves. Owners' treatment of slaves was almost completely unrestricted, and during the first half of the nineteenth century, use of slaves in the South greatly increased agricultural production and profit.

Third, as we have noted with internal colonialism, for racism to occur, one racial group must possess superior power. Without it there will be intergroup relations ranging from peaceful coexistence to conflict, but one group cannot consistently impose its will on the other. Frequently when one group possesses superior power, it is likely to try to produce structures and practices that permit it to keep control indefinitely. When blacks were brought to America, they were at the mercy of their masters, who went to great lengths to create a slavery system that would last forever.

In analyzing the process by which whites subordinated racial minorities, Noel's scheme proves useful. Internal colonialism seems a more appropriate perspective once the minority group's subordinate status has been established.

THE PREINDUSTRIAL ERA OF RACE RELATIONS

Whether Dutch, English, Portuguese, or Spanish, Europeans who encountered racial minorities used their superior power to deprive them of two precious resources—their material wealth or their labor. Physical conditions determined the most efficient means of exploitation. When inhabitants were fairly sparsely settled, as in the Americas, they were either driven back—the North American technique—or exterminated—the approach in the West Indies and the South American lowlands. When the population was densely settled, a more practical or efficient policy was to enslave the local people—the approach used widely in Africa and in Indonesia (Cox, 1976:9–10).

With the opportunity to exploit the minority members of technologically simple cultures, Europeans used ethnocentric stereotypes as rationalizations. By the middle of the sixteenth century, the Spanish declared that they enslaved Indians to work in tropical mines "because, among other things, of their 'barbarous natures,' 'their sins,' their need of religious instruction, and because their labor was naturally due to a people of such 'elevated natures' as the Spaniards" (Cox, 1976:26).

During the preindustrial era, European explorers and settlers to what is now the United States dealt primarily with two minority groups—Native Americans and African Americans, originally slaves from Africa.

The Art of Making Breakable Treaties

The Tainos Indians who received Columbus on the island of San Salvador made a very favorable impression on the explorer. Writing to the King and Queen of Spain, he enthusiastically noted how peaceful they appeared, observing, "They love their neighbors as themselves, and their discourse is ever sweet and gentle, and accompanied with a smile; and though it is true they are naked, yet their manners are decorous and praiseworthy" (Brown, 1972:1).

To Columbus, like the European hoards that followed, these positive qualities were clear signs of weakness. The Indians were sweet, pliable, but definitely savage children, who, Columbus believed, should be "made to work, sow and do all that is necessary and to *adopt our ways*" (Brown, 1972:2). Columbus initiated a policy where white explorers, colonists, and settlers pursued a system of racist exploitation that incorporated the three factors in Noel's scheme: They used their greater power to seize what they considered the Indians' most precious commodity—land. This land permitted whites to steadily expand their economic activity, and neither law nor custom imposed much regulation on land takeover and other dealings with Indians. In addition, ethnocentrism helped rationalize the takeover: The Indians benefitted greatly, the ethnocentric argument went, because they were now recipients of whites' supposedly superior cultural offerings.

For the millions of European settlers arriving in what was to become the United States, land acquisition was the basic necessity. To facilitate this process, Europeans and later Americans began establishing treaties with Native Americans and then invariably breaking them. The first treaty between Indians and Europeans occurred in Massachusetts. When English settlers landed in Plymouth in 1620, they received aid from several Indians, who gave them corn and taught them where and how to fish. Without this help the Pilgrims undoubtedly would have perished. Five years later the colonists asked one of these Indians, a Pemaquid chief named Samoset, if they could have an additional 12,000 acres of Pemaquid land for accommodating the steady stream of English settlers. Like other Native Americans, Samoset believed that people could no more own land than they could the sky, but he was willing to humor the colonists, with whom relations had been good, by putting his mark on a piece of paper.

In the following half-century, most arriving colonists did not bother with treaties, simply appropriating land to meet their needs. Metacom, the chief of the Wampanoags and the son of one of the four men who aided the original Plymouth settlers, realized that Indians would be pushed relentlessly westward unless they resisted, and so even though the colonists flattered him by crowning him King Philip of Pokanoket, he dedicated himself to establishing military alliances with the Narragansetts and other local tribes. In 1675 under Metacom's leadership, the Indians attacked 52 English communities, completely destroying 12 of them and suffering substantial losses themselves. After being captured, Metacom was drawn and quartered, and as a warning against further rebellion, his skull was displayed on a pole in Plymouth for the next quarter-century. Meanwhile European settlement expanded, and many tribes continued to resist (Brown, 1972:3–4).

During the seventeenth century, some Indian tribes allied themselves with the French, who were more inclined to hunt and trap than settle the land. When the British defeated the French after a ten-year war, they had to confront an array of hostile tribes. In 1763 these uprisings encouraged a Royal Proclamation in which the King of England declared that exploration and settlement of all lands west of the western slope of the Appalachian Mountains would cease until completion of negotiations with all tribes involved. The settlers, however, kept appropriating land.

More than 20 years later, in 1787, the U.S. Congress was also conciliatory, offering the following solemn pledge:

> The utmost good faith shall always be observed toward the Indians; their land and property shall never be taken from them without their consent; and in their property, rights, and liberty, they shall never be invaded or disturbed, unless in justified and lawful wars authorized by Congress; but laws founded in justice and humanity shall from time to time be made, for preventing wrongs being done to them, and for preserving peace and friendship with them. (Deloria, 1972: title page)

In the early 1800s, Supreme Court decisions established the principle that Native American societies were self-governing nations with a right to their land and that the American government must abide by the treaties that it made with them. But the steady influx of settlers to the frontier undermined that position. Congress passed what became known as "Pre-emption Acts," which validated settlers' claim to lands that treaties had assigned to Indians. In 1824 the Bureau of Indian Affairs was established to coordinate relations between Indian tribes and the federal government. Its major task became Native Americans' relocation. The "utmost good faith" expressed in the lofty statement of 1787 was discarded under what Noel's theory considered the pressures of an expanding, competitive society.

In 1829 Andrew Jackson became president. Known as "Old Hickory" by whites and "Sharp Knife" by Indians, Jackson exhibited a tough, adversarial approach to Indians, whom he had fought throughout the southern states and considered incapable of living peaceably with whites. Jackson claimed that the best solution for all concerned was to move all Indians west of the Mississippi, where, he promised them,

> your white brothers will not trouble you; they will have no claim to the land, and you can live upon it, you and all your children, as long as the grass grows or the water runs, in peace and plenty. It will be yours forever. (Bailyn et al., 1976:441)

To any Native Americans who were students of diplomatic relations with whites, this message must have seemed ominously familiar and provided little sense of consolation or security. Though phrased in peaceful terms, its author was an enthusiastic advocate of whites' use of superior military power against the Indians. Certainly it was realistic to be pessimistic, because within a few years settlers were streaming into territories west of the Mississippi, and so what had once been considered "the permanent Indian frontier" was steadily shifted westward.

Reading this material, you might begin to wonder whether racism is the central issue. After all, you might say, the primary motive for removing the Indians was economic—the settlers' need for land. A critical point is that if settlers and officials had not classified Indians as inferior, they could not have so easily exploited them economically. Racist and ethnocentric assessments were apparent from colonial times. The first settlers' written records indicated that they considered Indians "depraved, savage brutes, as impious rascals who lived in filth and ate nasty food" (Jacobs, 1985:110). A major element in the eighteenth- and nineteenth-century stereotype of Indians was that they were all nomadic hunting people wandering free-as-the-wind over thousands of acres of virgin wilderness. While this image simply ignored the obvious fact that many of the eastern tribes lived in stable towns and villages, such prominent individuals as President John Adams and General William T. Sherman found it a fine rationalization for depriving Indians of their land (Jacobs, 1985:111).

The most famous racist rationalization was the concept of "manifest destiny,"which described Indians' culture as inferior to whites' and then suggested that this supposed inferiority should serve as the basis for their exploitation. According to the concept of manifest destiny, God ordained that Americans should liberate the continental territory and direct native people's movement toward participation in modern political and technological life. The idea proved convenient when gold was discovered in California in 1848, and many thousands of fortune seekers once again violated treaties and annihilated the idea of "the permanent Indian frontier" as they pushed nearly to the Pacific.

So it was clear that no treaties would stop the whites' advance. During the second half of the nineteenth century, the Sioux, Cheyenne, Arapaho, Kiowa, and Apache under such leaders as Sitting Bull, Crazy Horse, Cochise, and Geronimo fought soldiers and settlers in a vain effort to retain their land and way of life. Eventually they were killed or passified and placed on reservations. Ethnocentrism was apparent in systematic efforts to destroy Native American cultures. Officials compelled many Indian children to attend boarding schools, where they had to abandon their native languages and customs. In 1892 the Commissioner of Indian Affairs issued a directive requiring all male Indians to keep their hair short; he also banned wearing paint and holding tribal dances and feasts and discouraged wearing blankets (Nichols, 1986:133–134). Native American cultures were inferior, the whites argued, and so such measures were believed beneficial for everyone, including the Indians.

The preceding discussion has outlined some of the major historical developments in early contacts between whites and Indians. Shifting from macro-level to micro-level analysis, we examine racism in the life of an Indian chief and his people.

Little Crow Goes to War

In 1862 Little Crow was a 60-year-old warrior, whose people, the Santee, steadily lost their homelands as 150,000 settlers extended the "permanent Indian frontier." Furthermore local traders and Indian agents were constantly cheating the Santee out of most of the annuities they received as compensation for their land loss.

Little Crow had adopted some aspects of white culture, exchanging breechcloths and blankets for trousers and brass-buttoned jackets, joining the Episcopol Church, building a house, and starting to farm. At the same time, he had severe problems with white officials. As a chief within the political system imposed by the American government, he had signed two treaties that had not only led to the Santee losing their land but also to their being tricked out of most of the financial compensation owed them.

In July 1862 several thousand Santees gathered at two Indian agencies seeking money, which the government owed them and which they needed to buy food. Realizing that their people were hungry and approaching starvation, Little Crow and several other chiefs rode to one of the agencies and asked the agent to issue food which was in the warehouse. Eventually he complied, and the Indians left quietly.

In the second agency, however, the agent refused to pass out food until the money arrived. Angered, Little Crow said that they had waited a long time for money owed to them and that it was the only way they could pay for food. He continued, "We have to get it. We have no food, but here are these stores, filled with food. We ask that you, the agent, make some arrangement by which we can get food from the stores, or else we may take our own way to keep ourselves from starving."

Instead of answering Little Crow, the agent turned to another white man, a trader, and asked him what he should do. "So far as I am concerned, if they are hungry let them eat grass or their own dung," the trader replied (Brown, 1972:40). For a moment the Indians were silent, and then in unison they stood up and left.

Little Crow went home, and the following Sunday he was in church, where he listened to a sermon, shook hands with other worshippers, and then returned home. It was an unhappy time for Little Crow. Earlier that summer his people relieved him of some of his duties, showing that they had lost confidence in him because of the two treaties he had signed. Had Little Crow been able to convince the agent to give them food, his prestige probably would have been restored. The trader's insult eliminated the possibility. Before the arrival of the white man, Little Crow would have been able to win back his honor by leading his people to battle, but the treaties prohibited him from going to war.

Little Crow's predicament was a distinct illustration of internal colonialism: He and his people were controlled and exploited by whites, who systematically deprived them of their land and made them dependent on whites for their survival. In spite of his oppressed status, Little Crow tried to get along with whites, adopting some of their cultural standards.

But it was a situation that Noel's scheme would analyze as encouraging increasingly rigid racial stratification—because whites' drive for more land was very strong and because their custom and law placed few if any restrictions on their treatment of Indians. Many encounters could set off incidents in which whites' greater power, coupled with a sense of caste superiority (illustrated here by the trader's comment), permitted them to tyrannize the Indians. The incident just described is a case in point, and it put Little Crow and his people in a life-threatening situation where their limited power provided little or no opportunity to produce a favorable outcome.

In this context the sequence of events is hardly surprising. Late that Sunday night, Little Crow awoke to hear many voices outside of his house and a group of Santee entering his bedroom. Several young men in their tribe had raided a farm and killed three white men and two white women. No Santee would now be safe from whites, the men claimed, and reluctantly Little Crow agreed to lead them to war. About ten months later he was killed, and soon afterwards 38 Santee were hanged in the largest mass execution in U.S. history (Brown, 1972:42–65).

During preindustrial times whites were equally systematic in oppressing blacks.

Behind the Cotton Curtain

As we noted earlier in the chapter, the American slavery system is a clear illustration of Noel's theory of racial stratification. Whites used their power to establish a system of nearly complete control which thrived in an expanding economy and involved almost no controls on owners' conduct toward slaves. Whites' ethnocentric attitudes towards blacks also contributed.

For the first 40 years of American settlement, there was little slavery. Instead of slaves, early colonists were more likely to have indentured servants, whose passage to the New World and room and board were financed in exchange for a specified number of years of unpaid employment.

But eventually settlers became convinced that for several reasons slavery was more efficient. First, since slaves were owned, they could be forced to accept whatever living conditions would be most advantageous to their owners. Second, even though settlers could recruit a fair supply of servants, there simply were not enough of them to work on the steadily growing number of tobacco, rice, and indigo plantations in the South. These first two points are consistent with the Noel theory's emphasis on the significance of competition: Lack of regulation and the need for a vast supply of laborers in an expanding economy encouraged the development of slavery. Third, indentured servants' contracts were often a source of dispute, with servants either suing their masters or simply running away. In contrast, slaves could be purchased outright and thus contracts with them were unnecessary. Finally maintaining slaves was distinctly cheaper than hiring indentured servants (Franklin and Moss, 1988:32).

Slavery existed through the seventeenth and eighteenth centuries and was always most widely practiced in the South, which, unlike the New England and Middle Atlantic states, had large agricultural crops that could effectively use a large slave population; by the early nineteenth century, the northern states had outlawed slavery. Until the end of the War of 1812, in fact, the growth of slavery was relatively slow, even in the South. Then with the virtual elimination of war in the Western world, trade with Europe flourished, and a great demand for cotton developed. Massive cotton production depended on large numbers of unskilled laborers, and with the growing demand, slavery expanded. In 1790 there were fewer than 700,000 slaves; by 1830 the number had reached 2 million; at the last census before the Civil War, the slave population had nearly doubled to 3,953,760 (Franklin and Moss, 1988:112–113).

According to one historian, the American slavery system developed into "a social system as coercive as any yet known." Most slaves served on farms and plantations, and about two-thirds of them worked on cotton plantations. These plantations varied considerably in size. In 1860 about 88 percent of slaveowners possessed fewer than 20 slaves, and evidence suggests that the most profitable economic unit contained between 30 and 60 slaves. While not maximially efficient, large plantations were enormously productive, especially in the states where King Cotton prevailed—Mississippi, Alabama, Louisiana, and Georgia (Bennett, 1982:86–87).

Slavery was an economic system which permitted owners to use fellow human beings brutally to maximize profits, and the cotton plantation, which was a totalitarian system established with this goal in mind, controlled slaves' lives from birth to death. Generally there was a nursery where a slave often designated an "aunty" cared for young black children while their mothers worked in the fields. At about the age of six or seven, slave children started working, and when they reached ten or twelve, they received a full set of adult tasks.

One ever-present danger slaves faced was the possibility that the owner would find it economically productive to sell or hire out a family member, and thus many children were torn from their parents and often never saw them again. Frederick Douglass, who later became a prominent opponent of slavery, recalled seeing his mother only four or five times. She lived 12 miles away and had to receive permission to walk the distance on foot after a full day's work in the fields; she faced a whipping if not back before sunrise. Douglass wrote:

> I do not recollect of ever seeing my mother by the light of day. She was with me in the night. She would lie down with me, and get me to sleep, but long before I waked she was gone. Very little communication ever took place between us. Death soon ended what little we could have while she lived, and with it her hardships and suffering. (Douglass, 1968:22)

Like Douglass's mother most slaves on large plantations were field hands. The cultivation of crops was a demanding undertaking, and planters felt that the system proved most successful when slaves were scrupulously supervised by the owner or a hired overseer. Planting, cultivation, and harvesting of cotton, tobacco, rice, and sugar cane required minimal skill but considerable time and effort. For slaves the most demanding time of the year came during the harvest season. Worried about inclement weather destroying crops, planters sometimes forced slaves to work 18 to 20 hours a day (Franklin and Moss, 1988:116–117).

Most owners managed plantations themselves, but overseers were necessary if a plantation possessed more than 20 slaves or the owner was frequently absent. Overseers, also known as drivers, tended to be poor whites who often despised and resented the slavery system, feeling it responsible for their own poverty and that slaves, in particular, bore major guilt. Setting high production quotas for their overseers, planters placed few limits on their authority as long as slaves, admittedly valuable property, were not permanently damaged. Sometimes, however, drivers exceeded even these liberal limits as Frederick Douglass noted in the case of his master's cruel overseer:

> The overseer's name was Plummer. Mr. Plummer was a miserable drunkard, a profane swearer, and a savage monster. He always went armed with a cowskin and a heavy cudgel [club]. I have known him to cut and slash the women's heads so horribly, that even master would be enraged at his cruelty, and would threaten to whip him if he did not mind himself. (Douglass, 1968:24)

Slaves experienced different degrees of misery. It was generally preferable to be on a small plantation than a large one, because then one would work directly with the master, and they tended to be less ferocious than overseers. Masters also differed markedly, ranging from cruel and sadistic to, if one might use the words loosely, kindly and caring. Yet one should remember that simply by owning fellow human beings, even the most benevolent masters were committed to the slavery system, and when faced with a situation where they had to choose between their economic welfare and their slaves' well-being, they seldom opted for the latter (Bennett, 1982:94).

Besides work, other daily issues in slaves' lives were food, clothes, and housing. Slaves' food was often a problem for planters, who were preoccupied with producing their staple crops and frequently had to purchase food both for themselves and their slaves. Food for slaves was carefully rationed—a week's supply was about a peck of corn meal, three to four pounds of bacon or salt pork, and sometimes supplements of sweet potatoes, peas, rice, syrup, and fruit. Some slaves maintained their own gardens but risked possible punishment if they spent too much time at this activity. On most plantations slaves were fed fairly well because owners recognized that decent food was necessary for efficient work. They reached no such conclusion about clothes, and most slaves wore crude, homespun garments known as "Negro clothes" and poorly made, skimpy shoes called "Negro brogans." Housing too was poor, with slaves generally living in small, crudely made huts that had no windows, little furniture, and usually no beds. Worse than the absence of comforts, however, was the crowding. A Mississippi planter kept 150 slaves in 24 tiny huts that were only 16 by 14 feet each. An ex-slave noted, "Everything happened in that one room—birth, sickness, death—everything" (Bennett, 1982:89–90; Franklin and Moss, 1988:120–121).

Like whites dealing with Indians, slaveowners used racist rationalizations to justify the oppression in which they engaged. Slaveowners claimed that blacks were inferior and destined to occupy subordinate positions and that southern whites, far from being corrupted by the practice, had developed a uniquely refined culture which would have been unable to evolve without slaves performing the menial tasks (Franklin and Moss, 1988:174–175).

To legitimate slavery, southern whites cited the biblical accounts of Cain and Ham. These stories helped slaveowners rationalize that blacks were evil, cursed by God, and fully deserved to be condemned to slavery (Allahar, 1993:46).

Southerners further legitimated slavery by enacting what became known as Slave Codes, a body of laws covering every aspect of slaves' lives. While the Slave Codes differed from state to state, the general point of view was that slaves were property, not people—that the laws were supposed to protect ownership of that property and to ensure that slaves were maintained under repressive conditions that would promote a maximum level of production. Thus most of the laws focused on exclusion, indicating activities slaves were not permitted to do—for instance, leave their plantations without authorization, possess firearms, hire themselves out without owners' permission, buy or sell goods, or visit the homes of whites or free blacks. Most of the petty offenses were punished with whippings while the more serious ones produced branding, imprisonment, or death. Arson and conspiracy to rebel were capital crimes in all slaveowning states (Franklin and Moss, 1988:114–115). The Slave Codes made it clear that the only legal regulation that occurred during slavery solidified racial segregation: Owners' rights were carefully protected while blacks' rights were scrupulously denied.

In spite of slaveowners' intimidating control, resistance occurred. Diaries, logs, and historical accounts indicate that some blacks opposed enslavement in a variety of ways, including armed insurrection, physical attacks on masters or over-seers, escape, starvation, and suicide (Forbes, 1992). Furthermore a recent study has suggested that a larger group of whites opposed slavery than historians gener-ally acknowledge. According to Herbert Aptheker, these courageous people were more likely to be women than men, and more frequently were poor than affluent. In his book Aptheker provided evidence of persistent white opposition to slavery and racism in the writings of preachers, teachers, antislavery workers, and ordinary people as well as whites' support for slave flights from servitude and active involve-ment in slave uprisings (Aptheker, 1992; Solomon, 1993).

In the early-industrial stage, new economic and political conditions produced some changes in racial minority-group members' lives.

THE EARLY-INDUSTRIAL STAGE

According to Oliver Cox (1976:14–15), industrial leaders have always been willing to accept racist outlooks and practices. Their dominant motivation has been to expand their economic enterprises, and racism has generally not hampered that expansion.

Soon after the Civil War, Herbert Spencer thrilled most prominent Americans with the doctrine of social Darwinism, which loosely built upon Charles Darwin's research done with plants and animals. Spencer declared that as a fundamental sci-entific principle, the most intelligent and capable people would invariably rise to dominant economic and political positions and that society would evolve most rapidly and efficiently if citizens recognized that this "survival of the fittest" was the natural and proper order of things. Those who failed to rise to the top—some whites and all racial minority-group members—were simply proving their inherent inferiority. The timing of social Darwinism was perfect for wealthy and powerful whites, appearing just when American industry was rapidly expanding and justifying its leaders' success and prominence. We wouldn't be at the top if we didn't deserve it, they triumphantly declared, and John D. Rockefeller enthusiastically lectured about social Darwinism to children in Sunday school and industrialist Andrew Carnegie felt privileged to consider Herbert Spencer a close friend (Hofstadter, 1955).

Spencer and the other social Darwinists, of course, had never heard of the self-fulfilling prophecy and if they had, undoubtedly would have dismissed it as the muddled thinking of sentimental, unscientific minds. There is little doubt, however, that what social Darwinism did was to offer a giant boost to those already well located and, conversely, a shove toward the bottom for those who were not.

It was not just the leaders who subscribed to this doctrine. Members of various social classes read and applauded Spencer's work (Hofstadter, 1955:34), and it seems likely that the racist position inherent in social Darwinism must have readily blended with racist views already firmly fixed in American culture. Whether recently arrived or already settled, it was not a good time to belong to a racial minority in America.

We now consider experiences for Indians, African Americans, Chinese, Japanese, Mexican Americans, and Puerto Ricans during the early-industrial era.

Native Americans' Reservation Life

Througout this period Native Americans continued to experience the racist treatment inflicted on them since Columbus's time: In their passion for what they considered the Indians' one precious resource—land—white Americans used their superior power to subdue the native inhabitants and to relocate them on reservations, where they fell under the control of the Bureau of Indian Affairs. At the same time, whites' ethnocentric outlook drove them to provide their victims a new and "better" culture and way of life.

In 1887 the passage of the Dawes Act mandated the end of common land holdings on reservations; instead, each single Indian adult or family was supposed to receive a 160-acre plot. One immediate effect of the Dawes Act was that millions of acres of so-called surplus reservation land not included in the allotments was taken from the Indians and sold to white farmers, miners, and corporations.

For many Indians the 160-acre allotment provided inferior land which was inadequate for crops or grazing animals. In other instances, however, land quality was good, and Native Americans were able to lease it to farmers and ranchers for substantial income. While many Indians were pleased with this arrangement, white reformers obsessed with the work ethic were disturbed, feeling that such a system made Native Americans unproductive and lazy. These people reasoned that if the Indians could sell at least some of their land, then they could buy machinery and homes that would allow them to become effective, hard-working farmers in the best American tradition.

The reformers convinced congressional members of the righteousness of such an approach, and between 1902 and 1910, Congress passed legislation permitting the sale of all Indian-owned land. Within a decade over half the Indians who had received allotments under the Dawes Act had sold their land at far below market value and were both landless and penniless. Landless Indians were in a much more economically deprived state than landless whites, because they were unprepared educationally and culturally to face the white work world, whose members tended to respond violently to Native Americans venturing outside of reservations (Berthrong, 1986:204–209).

During this era, missionaries, officials of the Bureau of Indian Affairs, reservation teachers, and personnel at federally funded boarding schools tried to impress the importance of dropping traditional ways and learning white people's culture. Indian boys and young men were supposed to receive training as farmers or laborers while Indian girls and young women were prepared for housekeeping and domestic tasks.

In the late nineteenth century, boarding schools, which supposedly trained young Native Americans for jobs in the industrial world, reached their highest level of enrollment, with 25 schools containing over 6,000 students. The schools had major deficiencies, however. The young people were lonely living in a culturally alien atmosphere, and they were repelled by the inevitable emphasis on military organization: By the middle 1890s, both girls and boys were placed in drill companies on the first day of school, were required to wear uniforms, and were led by student officers following army drill regulations. Ethnocentric in outlook, most school officials praised the military structure, contending that it

> served to develop a work ethic; it broke the students' sense of "Indian time" and ordered their life. The merits of military organization, drill, and routine . . . were explained by one official who stated that "it teaches patriotism, obedience, courage, courtesy, promptness, and constancy." (Trennert, 1986:225)

Imbued with a sense of cultural superiority, teachers often humiliated their students. In an autobiographical account, one Native American indicated that in class a teacher asked him to read a paragraph, and he did so without error. The teacher, however, criticized the reading and demanded that he read it again, and again, and again. After the eleventh reading "everything before me went black and I sat down thoroughly cowed and humiliated for the first time in my life and in front of the whole class" (Luther Standing Bear, 1978:146).

By the early 1920s, the Indian boarding schools ceased. Gradually educational officials recognized that while government personnel might have established the schools with the intention of preparing Indians for work in the white world, actual training occurred in an atmosphere conveying a sense that they were racially and culturally inferior beings. Furthermore jobs for which they were trained were rarely available, and Indians' condemnation of the boarding schools was growing (Trennert, 1986:229–230).

During the late nineteenth and early twentieth centuries, blacks faced new forms of oppression.

African Americans' Survival in the "Survival-of-the-Fittest" Era

While the end of slavery meant that blacks were technically free, an oppressive system of racial stratification continued. Whites were still much more powerful than blacks, using them to financial advantage in the expanding, early-industrial economy.

After the Civil War, most ex-slaves found little reason to celebrate their recent freedom. The land had been devastated, with many blacks and some whites suffering from disease and starvation. Furthermore southern whites, determined to retain as much power as possible over the newly freed blacks, passed the infamous Black Codes, which provided blacks scarcely more rights and opportunities than under slavery. In addition, President Andrew Johnson was sympathetic to white southerners, declaring that African Americans were not ready for the privileges of citizenship and vetoing congressional legislation in their behalf. A fight between Congress and the president broke out, and in spite of Johnson's strenuous campaign for his program, the people sided with Congress, providing an overwhelming mandate to Thaddeus Stevens and other congressional supporters of blacks' rights.

For blacks it appeared to be a great moment. Historian Lerone Bennett, Jr., concluded, "Never before had the sun shone so bright" (Bennett, 1982:214). The Reconstruction Act of 1867 passed, and all southern states had to convene racially mixed constitutional conventions, which outlawed slavery, eliminated race as a criterion for determining a person's right to possess and inherit property, and extended the vote to all black males. Suddenly whites' overwhelming political power was threatened. In the next few years, blacks served as lieutenant governors in Mississippi, South Carolina, Louisiana, as secretary of state in Florida, on the state supreme court in South Carolina, were a majority in the South Carolina House of Representatives, and held a host of less influential but important posts in southern state and municipal governments (Franklin and Moss, 1988:206–220).

Change was social as well as political. In South Carolina, probably the most racially liberal southern state, dramatic developments were occurring. One account noted:

> The social life was gay, glittering and interracial. A dashing militia captain gave a ball, and blacks and whites—some of them native South Carolinians—glided across the polished floor. At official balls, receptions and dinners, blacks and whites sat down together and got up in peace. (Bennett, 1982:216)

But it was no more than a quick burst of sunshine. American public opinion was turning against people of non-Anglo-Saxon background in what was soon the heyday of social Darwinism. The Supreme Court adopted the tone of the times, emasculating the Fourteenth Amendment, which insured that African Americans were citizens with full rights and privileges, by ruling that the amendment prohibited states but not individuals from discriminating. Many whites expressed their racism less elegantly. A group of South Carolina whites, whose state we already noted had the most liberal racial policies, appeared before Congress in 1868, protesting African Americans' participation in politics and vowing to carry on the fight until once more blacks were subordinated. Expressing their racism proudly, they declared:

That is a duty we owe to the land that is ours, to the graves that it contains, and to the race of which you and we alike are members—the proud Caucasian race, whose sovereignty on earth God has ordained. (Bailyn et al., 1977:766)

For blacks Reconstruction had seemed to be an era of great hope and promise, but by the middle 1870s, it was clear that no significant economic, political, or social reforms would emerge from it—no guaranteed 40 acres of land and a mule (as one congressional supporter had promised), no guaranteed citizens' rights, no guaranteed boost in social position, but only a full share of racism and terror.

The terror struck with full force at the turn of the century, primarily in the South. Two general factors seemed to lie behind the beatings, shootings, and lynchings—the desire to drive blacks out of political activity initiated during Reconstruction and into terrorized submission; and a general sense of social crisis generated by economic depression, with blacks serving as scapegoats for fearful, frustrated whites. A recent study of lynchings occurring in Georgia between 1890 and 1900 found that counties demonstrating intense economic competition between blacks and whites had a greater number of lynchings than counties where that competition was less intense. Between 1882 and 1901, 1,914 African Americans were lynched. While still alive, victims were sometimes roasted slowly over fires or had limbs or sexual organs amputated. Castration occurred in hundreds of lynchings, with the impulse to castrate black males popularized in white literature and folklore. After death, pieces of the victim routinely were distributed to onlookers who wanted souvenirs of the notable event (Marable, 1994:71; Shapiro, 1988:30–31; Soule, 1992).

During that era whites often believed that most lynch victims had raped white women. Records, however, do not support this conclusion. In the first 14 years of the twentieth century, just 315 lynch victims were accused of rape or attempted rape while over 500 were accused of homicide and others of robbery, insulting whites, and a variety of nebulous "offenses" (Franklin and Moss, 1988:282).

How did the people of that era feel about lynching? Unfortunately systematic survey research did not start for several decades. In 1905 one writer, however, did have the initiative to record the following data: In the trial of white men accused of burning two black men to death, 76 of 110 prospective jurors (69 percent) indicated that even if evidence clearly demonstrated that the defendants had taken part in the murders, they would not have favored their conviction (Baker, 1973a). Such sentiment was consistent with the Slave Codes and other norms for whites' unregulated treatment of blacks established during slavery.

Even more threatening to blacks than lynchings were race riots, which were not directed at individuals but ranged across large areas and could involve any African Americans unlucky enough to be in the vicinity. In the early 1900s, while the number of lynchings slowly decreased, the frequency of riots rose in both southern and northern cities. As black immigration to the North increased, hostilities grew proportionately, and in 1908 the riot that occurred in Springfield, Illinois, during which two black men were killed within a half-mile of the only home Abraham Lincoln ever owned, was as ferocious as any that occurred in the South (Franklin and Moss, 1988:282–286).

Violence against African Americans was simply the most vicious example of the racism they encountered. In 1908 a writer asked blacks in both the North and

South to summarize their chief complaints. In the South the first problem cited was almost always the separate and inferior railroad cars or facilities in railroad stations, followed by references to injustice in the courts, the low quality of schooling, and the prospect of physical violence. In contrast, in the North, overwhelmingly the most frequent complaint involved discrimination in the work place, even though job opportunities were much more extensive than in the South. To the southern black man, the North proved to be a shock. He was seeking work where he would be "judged at his worth as a man, not as a Negro: this he came North to find, and he . . . [met] difficulties of which he had not dreamed in the South" (Baker, 1973b:279).

Black leaders responded in different ways to the violence and discrimination their people suffered. On September 18, 1895, Booker T. Washington, a very moderate leader, made a famous speech, which became known as the "Atlanta Compromise." Appearing before a segregated, all-white crowd, Washington drew loud applause when he described blacks as "the most patient, faithful, law-abiding people the world had seen" and promised the increasingly enthusiastic audience that in all social areas, blacks would accept racial separation. A decade later W. E. B. DuBois and a group of black militants repudiated this position, claiming for themselves "every single right that belongs to a freeborn American, political, civil, and social; and until we get these rights we will never cease to protest and assail the ears of America" (Bennett, 1993:133–134). To help accomplish such goals, these black leaders founded the National Association for the Advancement of Colored People. It was the first major organization formed to promote blacks' interests—certainly a formidable task at a time when most African Americans were poor and powerless.

Until World War I, most blacks were in the South, but then several conditions encouraged them to leave. Because of a series of disasterous floods, the devastating impact of the Mexican boll weevil, and low cotton prices, many southern planters shifted from cotton to food crops and livestock, which required fewer workers. With declining demand for workers, wages plummeted. A noneconomic factor—the threat of lynching—also spurred a number of southern blacks to head north. A study covering the years 1910–1930 found that African Americans' migration was heaviest in southern counties where more lynchings had occurred. While some factors pushed blacks to leave the South, others pulled them to the North. The outbreak of World War I contributed to a northern labor shortage in two ways. A sharply increased demand for northern industrial production of war supplies coincided with a cutoff in the supply of European laborers. This combination of conditions encouraged black laborers to respond favorably to recruiters who came south seeking workers.

Southern whites were alarmed by African Americans' flight and took measures to limit it. In Jacksonville, Florida, a local ordinance declared that all labor recruiters needed to pay a license fee of $1,000. In many southern towns and cities, whites threatened departing blacks, and the local newspapers urged that they remain. But blacks recognized that this was their chance to participate, if modestly, in the bounty of the industrial age. Northern employers appreciated the influx of African Americans at a time when otherwise they would have remained understaffed. Furthermore patriotic Americans realized that without blacks the labor shortage would have significantly hampered the country's war effort. In the decade 1910–1920, the black population in the northern and midwestern states increased by about 525,000 people; during the 1920s about 877,000 African Americans left the South (Franklin and Moss, 1988:251–252, 305–306; Massey and Denton, 1993:29; Tolnay and Beck, 1992).

In the 1890s the typical African American resident of a northern city lived in an area that was 90 percent white. When large numbers of southern black workers started to arrive, whites' views toward African Americans quickly hardened. Northern newspapers participated enthusiastically, using such racist terms as "nigger" and "darkey." Between 1900 and 1920, race riots broke out in a number of northern and midwestern cities. The worst riots occurred during the so-called "red summer" of 1919; throughout the country 26 riots broke out as returning white soldiers feared competition for jobs from African Americans. Blacks living outside recognized "black" neighborhoods had their homes ransacked or burned. To survive, African Americans had to move to recognized black areas. By about 1940 the segregated urban pattern leading to modern black ghettoes had been established (Massey and Denton, 1993:29–31; Schaefer, 1993:196).

We move now from the macro-level analysis to the micro-level, considering one young African American's struggle during the early twentieth century.

Perils of Being Black in the Early Twentieth-Century South

When famed writer Richard Wright was growing up in the South, the Civil War had been over for about a half-century. For those 50 years, African Americans had been technically free, but, in the well-known phrase, they were expected "to know their place"—to accept that they would be deprived of full rights and privileges in society.

As the introduction to a book of short stories entitled *Uncle Tom's Children,* Wright wrote an autobiographical essay that showed how perilous the lives of young black people could be. One tenet of internal colonialism is the colonial-labor principle, stressing that racial minorities are expected to perform tasks that primarily benefit majority-group members. But what if a young black man ignored this principle and considered work a personal growth experience? Such an approach represents a direct challenge to the current racial order. It illustrates what Erving Goffman called **normification**—behavior that gives the impression that an individual widely considered inferior is trying to deny being different (Goffman, 1974:115).

Wright applied for a job at an optical company in Jackson, Mississippi. The interview went well, with Wright careful to show the expected deference by pronouncing his "sirs" very distinctly. He was hired, and the new boss indicated that Wright would be able to learn about the business. As a result the new employee had visions of working his way up. The first month went well enough, but while cleaning the shop and polishing lenses, Wright gradually realized that he had no opportunity to learn anything, in spite of the boss's claim.

So one day Wright approached Morrie, a young white colleague about his own age, and asked about his work. Morrie grew red and asked, "Whut yuh tryin' t' do, nigger, git smart?" No, Wright replied, he wasn't trying to get smart. "Well, don't, if yuh know what's good for yuh!" Morrie replied.

Puzzled, Wright concluded that Morrie simply did not want to help him, and so he went to Pease, the other employee, and asked him about his work.

> "Say, are you crazy, you black bastard?" Pease asked me, his gray eyes growing hard.
> I spoke out, reminding him that the boss had said I was to be given a chance to learn something.
> "Nigger, you think you're *white,* don't you?"
> "Naw, sir!"
> "Well, you're acting mighty like it!" (Wright, 1938:xv)

Pease went on to warn Wright to stay away from "white man's work."

From then on both Pease and Morrie treated Wright differently. They ignored him unless he was a bit slow performing some task. Then they called him "a lazy black son-of-a-bitch" and told him to hurry up.

Wright faced other dangerous situations in which normification became an issue. One day entering an elevator along with some white men, Wright had an armload of packages. Because of the packages, he could not remove his hat—as whites always expected of African Americans in their presence. After staring at him coldly, one of the white men removed Wright's hat and stuck it under his arm.

Had Wright thanked the white man, he would have risked a punch in the mouth since such a response would have suggested normification—implying a situation of racial equality in which the white man had done him a favor. The safe course of action would have been to look at the white man out of the corner of his eye and grin. Wright refused to demean himself by taking the easy way out, but he also wanted to avoid a punch in the mouth for making no response. So as soon as the hat was placed under his arm, he used another strategy—acting as though the packages were slipping and seemingly making a highly concentrated effort to prevent it from happening (Wright, 1938:xxx).

In his youth Richard Wright had several painful experiences making it clear that when dealing with whites, black people put their physical safety on the line if they even hinted at normification. In the early twentieth-century South, African Americans were safe only if their words and actions constantly reassured whites that they, the blacks, accepted the caste system and its rituals of subordination (discussed in Chapter 2).

During the preindustrial era, other racial minorities began to reach the United States.

Chinese, Japanese, Mexican, and Puerto Rican Pioneers

In the late nineteenth and early twentieth centuries, the four groups examined in this section started arriving in the United States. The factor in Noel's scheme most saliently affecting their situation is the issue of competition. Workers from these countries were welcomed when it proved beneficial to businesses to obtain cheap labor. On the other hand, frequently white workers found themselves in competition with these immigrants for jobs, and as a result resentment, even violence against them developed, with the law providing minority groups little protection. Noel's two other factors also are relevant: At times whites' ethnocentrism helped make it acceptable to oppress a particular racial minority, and whites' superior power allowed them to establish policies and pass laws limiting newly arrived minorities' opportunities.

Chinese immigrants, who were escaping the ravages of the Taiping Rebellion in southern China, reached the West Coast when gold was discovered in California. At first relations between the races were aimiable because the Chinese were willing to work the areas already abandoned by whites who had moved on to more profitable sites. Eventually, however, the Chinese workers' willingness to put in long, arduous, but productive days proved abrasive to whites; even though the recent arrivals were restricted from the richest areas, they simply were too successful. The remedy was to pass a special foreign mining-license tax imposed once a month almost exclusively on the Chinese. Still they kept coming to California and by 1860 represented nearly 10 percent of its population.

By the early 1860s, the gold supply had started to dwindle, and most Chinese had little to do. White leaders wanted to exploit this eager, hard-working labor source. Would the seemingly puny Chinese be strong enough to lay track for the transcontinental railroad? Widespread debate developed, and eventually Charles Crocker, a contractor for the Central Pacific Railroad, decided to give them a trial. Although scornfully called "Crocker's pets," 1,200 Chinese were hired for construction and between 1864 and 1869 proved to be excellent workers. But then the job was done, and along with about an equal number of non-Chinese, they were out of work. Meanwhile about a million people had moved to California on the transcontinental railroad, and the result was a distinct labor surplus.

In the context of racist, late nineteenth-century America, it was not surprising that the Chinese became scapegoats for white workers' economic plight. At a miners' meeting, the participants concluded that any means necessary should be used to stop the "Asiatic inundation" and that the ruling class and the Chinese shared responsibility for job scarcity. The miners produced a fierce, racist statement flatly declaring that

> the Capitalists, ship-owners and merchants and others who are encouraging or engaged in the importation of these burlesques on humanity would crowd their ships with the long-tailed, horned, and cloven-hoofed inhabitants of the infernal regions. (Daniels and Kitano, 1970:36)

In the 1870s and 1880s, hostility toward the Chinese was more than verbal. Violence started in the mining districts and surged into the cities. Chinese were robbed, beaten, and sometimes killed, but because of the laxity of law enforcement and a statute prohibiting Chinese from testifying against whites, almost no criminal prosecution occurred. Mark Twain wrote,

> I have seen Chinamen abused and maltreated in all the mean, cowardly ways possible to the invention of a degraded nature, but I never saw a Chinamen righted in a court of justice for wrongs thus done him. (Twain, 1868)

One analyst suggested that supporters of the Chinese were "the rich, the good, and the wise"—merchants seeking trade with the Far East, ranchers and farmers looking for cheap laborers, most Protestant clergy, and individuals searching for low-paid, docile servants. The anti-Chinese forces were composed of white working-class people competing against Chinese immigrants for jobs and two groups who needed support from working-class whites to survive occupationally—politicians seeking their votes and journalists requiring their patronage (Daniels, 1988:51–52). Thus the economic factor played a major role in whites' response to early Chinese immigration.

Eventually Congress decided to take a decisive step to quell the violence and to protect jobs for white workers. The Chinese Exclusion Act of 1882 halted the immigration of laborers and helped to alleviate if not eliminate anti-Chinese violence, which continued through the 1880s (Knoll, 1982:24–27).

The Japanese arrived on the West Coast several decades after the Chinese, and they inherited much of the racist feeling. "Now the Jap is a wily an' a crafty individual—more so than the Chink," warned a writer in the *Sacramento Bee* (quoted in Okimoto, 1971:15). To many white Americans, newly arrived Japanese workers willing to labor at the most menial, lowest-paying jobs simply extended the "Yellow Peril," threatening employment, housing, and even American culture itself. As Japanese immigration reached a peak of about 50,000 in the first decade of the twentieth century, Congress passed the United States Immigration Act of 1907, which authorized the president to restrict entrance of foreign workers if he deemed that their arrival would jeopardize opportunities for American workers. The following year President Theodore Roosevelt negotiated a deal with the Japanese government, permitting only the families of Japanese men already owning land or professionals to immigrate. This arrangement precluded the embarrassment of legislation similar to the Chinese Exclusion Act of 1882 and foreshadowed a trend of "symbolic racism," which, as we will see, is now prominent (Ima, 1982:263–264; Knoll, 1982: 53–58).

Unlike Asian Americans, the earliest Mexican Americans (Chicanos) did not immigrate to the United States. They were living in Texas when following the Mexican War, the United States gained permanent possession of the land which currently constitutes the states of Texas, New Mexico, and Arizona. As late as 1910, however, only about 250,000 Mexican Americans, people of mixed Spanish and Native American heritage, were residents of the United States.

At that time a pair of events in Mexico—the release of workers from forced labor on large haciendas (ranches) and the violence produced by revolution—encouraged many Mexicans to flee their homeland. Along the U.S. border, work was available because legislation had compelled many large cattle and sheep ranchers to give way to crop farmers who badly needed laborers. In the 1920s Mexicans also moved to such northern manufacturing cities as Chicago, Detroit, and Milwaukee, where they became factory employees. By the early 1930s, there were nearly 1.5 million Mexican Americans in the United States. During that decade, however, there was a great surplus of workers because of high unemployment accompanying the Great Depression. Out of work, about 400,000 Mexican Americans either returned to Mexico voluntarily or were forced to leave by government officials intent on reducing welfare roles.

With the outbreak of World War II, the employment picture once again changed dramatically. Mobilizing for war, the United States badly needed workers to fill farm-labor jobs left by departing soldiers. In 1942 the *bracero* program, which existed briefly during World War I, was reestablished. It involved a bilateral agreement between Mexico and the United States about the supply of labor. The American government underwrote Mexicans' travel costs and promised both a minimum wage and just treatment for *braceros* (temporary laborers) working on privately owned farms in the United States. Essentially the program provided federal subsidy for agricultural interests, and while originally intended only to meet wartime labor shortages, it continued for a quarter century after the war because it proved useful on both sides of the border. For Mexico the *bracero* program served as a partial solution for high unemployment, and for U.S. farmers it produced a steady supply of cheap labor.

Frequently employers violated the program's conditions, and although the Mexican government protested the violations, few official efforts sought to prevent them; the federal government, in fact, permitted agricultural interests almost complete control of wages, housing conditions, and other factors affecting workers' welfare. Although the *bracero* program officially discontinued in 1964, many American farmers still maintain it informally, illegally hiring Mexican farm workers.

At present about 90 percent of Chicano citizens are living in urban areas, particularly in the Southwest. A substantial number, however, live elsewhere, especially in the Midwest (Feagin and Feagin, 1993:262–264; Heyman, 1990; Keefe and Padilla, 1987; Maldonado, 1982; Stoddard, 1973:2–30).

Puerto Ricans, another major Hispanic group, began reaching the United States in the nineteenth century, but their relations with whites began much earlier. On November 19, 1493, on his second voyage to the New World, Columbus arrived in Puerto Rico. At that time the island inhabitants were members of the Tainos tribe, and when the Spanish conquered the island, most of the Tainos died because of exposure to European diseases. As a result of this annihilation of indigenous people, the Spanish had no source of cheap labor. In 1511 to remedy the situation, they started bringing in African slaves, and the practice of slavery continued for over three and a half centuries until it was abolished in 1873. In 1898 following Spain's defeat in the Spanish-American War, the island became a possession of the United States. American-owned sugar plantations dominated the economy until after World War II when the local government started a program of economic expansion that produced over 1,000 factories by 1970. For American businessmen it has been very profitable to establish factories in Puerto Rico since local workers could be hired for considerably less than mainland laborers (Fitzpatrick, 1987:28–29, 33–34). Commenting on 500 years of white exploitation, Jesus Colon wrote:

> The first thing we must realize is that . . . strangers have been knocking at the door of the Puerto Rican nation for centuries always in search of something, to get something or to take away something from Puerto Ricans. This has been done many times with the forceful and openly criminal way of the pirate. (Colon, 1961:147)

Before the Spanish-American War, most of the Puerto Rican immigrants were political exiles who used New York as a base for seeking support for the island's independence. Obviously these people were disappointed when the United States took over the island instead of granting independent status.

In the 1950s large numbers of primarily poor Puerto Ricans started coming to the mainland. In 1945 there were about 34,000 departures from Puerto Rico, with people primarily bound to the mainland United States. In 1950 the figure rose to about 170,000, then to 315,000 in 1955, jumped to over 1.5 million in 1971, and remained at or above that number each year through the 1970s and 1980s. A rapidly growing population in an undeveloped economy where unemployment has remained high has spurred the migratory flow. Furthermore as American citizens, Puerto Ricans do not face legal restrictions entering the country, and since the island is close to the mainland, flights from and to the island are fairly cheap.

Race and racism have been complicated issues for Puerto Ricans. While firmly established segregation patterns never existed on the island, Puerto Ricans have been aware of racial differences. Traditionally upper-class individuals prided themselves on what they claimed to be their pure Spanish lineage, and among other social-class groups, there has often been a preoccupation with color. But while a concern with people's skin color and other racial characteristics has existed, Puerto Ricans claim that social-class location, not race, determines how one person will treat another. In Puerto Rico, they say, an upper-class white Puerto Rican will treat lower-class Puerto Ricans the same way, regardless of whether they appear to be white or racially mixed. In the United States, in contrast, people's color often determines their treatment, regardless of their social class. For Puerto Ricans with African and Indian heritage, such explicit racial discrimination can be painful to encounter (Fitzpatrick, 1987:18–19, 105–106).

We next move rapidly toward the present, introducing important factors setting the stage for race relations in the late-industrial era, which will be discussed in detail in other chapters.

THE LATE-INDUSTRIAL PERIOD

By the middle of the current century, all racial groups examined in this book had substantial membership in the United States. While significant changes have continued to occur, it appears that the racial-stratification system was essentially in place. Thus at this juncture, it seems reasonable to suspend the use of Noel's theory on the development of racial stratification and employ the internal-colonialist theory. Table 3.1 summarizes the relationship of theory to events in the three historical sections examined in this chapter.

During World War II, an executive order banning discrimination in defense plants and government agencies, along with an acute labor shortage, permitted blacks and other racial minorities to move into semiskilled manufacturing jobs and some white-collar positions. While some individuals belonging to racial minorities lost their positions to returning veterans after the war, the expanding economy provided improved opportunities for many of them.

Table 3.1   HISTORICAL STAGES OF AMERICAN RACISM

I. Preindustrial Stage (analyzed by Noel's theory of the origin of racial stratification)
   A. Ethnocentrism stressing Native Americans' and blacks' cultural inferiority
   B. Competition, with whites experiencing an expanding, unregulated economy:
      Indians' loss of land and traditional subsistence patterns; blacks' slavery
   C. Whites' superior power permitting complete control of Native Americans and blacks
II. Early-Industrial Stage (analyzed by Noel's theory)
   A. Social Darwinism, ethnocentrically declaring racial minorities "less fit" racially and
      culturally
   B. Competition pursued by whites in an expanding, largely unregulated economy
   C. Whites' greater power allowing nearly complete control of policies and practices affecting
      racial minorities
III. Late-Industrial Stage (analyzed by internal colonialism)
   A. Whites controlling the political structure and determining the policies dominating racial
      minorities' lives
   B. Ghettos and segregation forcing racial minorities to live in certain areas and making them
      highly vulnerable to economic downturns; sporadic violence against minorities limiting
      freedom of movement
   C. Consistent with the colonial-labor principle, racial minorities highly overrepresented in
      low-paid, menial jobs
   D. Blaming-the-victim ideology ignoring institutional racism and emphasizing poor members
      of racial minorities possess cultural inferiority

At the time the economy was starting to shift from one focused on goods-pro-ducing industries (manufacturing, construction, mining, and agriculture) to one primarily concerned with service (government, transportation, public utilities, trade, and later, information transmission). In this new economy, members of racial minorities with appropriate educational and training credentials, sometimes assisted by affirmative-action standards, could often locate well-paying jobs (Wilson, 1978:88–93).

But in recent decades racial discrimination has continued to be widespread, and protest against it has been extensive.

Racial Minorities' Protest in Modern Times

On February 1, 1960, four black students from the Negro Agricultural College in Greensboro, North Carolina, entered a variety store, bought several items, and then sat down at a lunch counter and ordered coffee. At the time their action was remarkable, because the lunch counter, like other public facilities in the South at the time, was officially segregated. The students were refused service, but they continued to sit at the counter until the store closed. This was the opening attack of the sit-in movement, which was a peaceful effort to destroy segregation in stores, libraries, hotels, buses, and other southern public facilities.

During the early 1960s, peaceful protests demanding full civil rights for blacks spread throughout the South. In May 1961 the Congress of Racial Equality, a prominent civil-rights organization, sent "freedom riders" into the South to challenge segregation laws in interstate transportation. In several Alabama cities, the interracial teams encountered violence when their buses were attacked. Eventually Attorney General Robert Kennedy sent 600 federal officers to the scene to restore order (Franklin and Moss, 1988:439–444). While blacks' civil rights was not high on the agenda for either Robert Kennedy or for his brother, the president, the Kennedys basically supported freedom riders' efforts. Martin Luther King, Jr., suggested that the Attorney General seek a ruling from the Interstate Commerce Commission establishing the rights of all interstate travelers. At first Robert Kennedy branded the scheme naive, but then he changed his mind, ordering Justice Department lawyers to keep after ICC commissioners until they issued a ruling protecting the rights of interstate travelers. In September Kennedy received the ICC statement. Taylor Branch indicated that Kennedy and his assistants had "telescoped a process that normally took years—even if the commisioners like the proposal, which in this case they did not—into less than four months. Experts considered the lobbying feat a bureaucratic miracle" (Branch, 1988:478).

The unstable partnership between protesters in the South and the federal government also involved school integration and voting rights. Although black and white protesters were sometimes attacked, beaten, and even killed, government forces offered some protection and support. Advances occurred, most notably the Civil Rights Act of 1964 and the Voting Rights Act of 1965, which we discuss in the next chapter.

It took enormous conviction and courage to be a prominent participant in southern civil-rights protests. In 1963 Medgar Evers was the best known civil-rights leader in Mississippi, initiating organized drives for integration in general and equitable employment in particular. More than 30 years later, his wife recalled:

> We both knew the end was near. You don't challenge a system like that without knowing the price to be paid. We lived with threats on a daily basis, and both of us knew in the last three weeks that it wasn't going to be long. (Applebome, 1994:30)

On June 12, 1963, Medgar Evers was assassinated.

Outside of the South, intentionally segregated facilities was not the core problem. In those regions blacks and other racial minorities were victims of institutional racism in politics, work, education, and housing. In 1966 Stokely Carmichael, a prominent civil-rights leader, started speaking about "black power"—that only if blacks provided strong, militant leadership for their own people would they obtain a fair share of the society's political, economic, and social rewards. Black leaders' style changed, and many began to predict that unless blacks started receiving equal rights, massive violence would occur. Riots in Los Angeles, Detroit, Newark, Washington, D.C., Cleveland, and a host of other cities indicated that the black-power leaders were not making idle statements. But while some members of these organizations appeared in public carrying guns, no evidence indicated that they initiated violent activity. They simply emphasized that continuing racial injustice would make rioting and other urban violence inevitable.

During the late 1960s, other racial minorities also became involved in protests. Among Native Americans the best-known protest group was the American Indian

Movement (AIM). Founded in 1968 in Minneapolis, it had over 70 chapters four years later and played a major part in several large protests, including the 71-day, armed occupation of reservation land on the Pine Ridge reservation in Wounded Knee, South Dakota. (Farley, 1988:143; Nagel, 1993:10). In the late 1960s and early 1970s, a group of radical Chicanos, disgusted with the failure of established political organizations to oppose discriminatory policies against Mexican Americans, formed *La Raza Unida,* which ran candidates for statewide and local offices, winning a number of contests and initiating educational and social programs that helped their primarily low-income constituents. In the spring of 1969, some Puerto Rican men in Chicago started the Young Lords, a militant organization, which soon established chapters in other cities. The New York City branch, for instance, occupied the First Spanish Methodist Church for eleven days and started a day-care center, a breakfast program, and a clothing-distribution program. In the 1960s an Asian American movement, led by Japanese American students, began to challenge older leaders and traditional ways. Programs in Asian American studies were established, and in their own new journals, Asian Americans started to encourage their people to develop new ways of producing group pride and collective consciousness (Feagin and Feagin, 1993:191–192, 276–277, 315–316, 351).

The accomplishments of minority-group organizations, however, were offset by the dismemberment of various progressive social programs and policies during the Reagan/Bush presidential years. As a result many middle-class African Americans became deeply disillusioned about what they had started to believe might be an inevitable path toward racial integration and equality. Without faith in black nationalism and the loss of faith in American democratic institutions, they found themselves, in the words of sociologist Robert Washington, "ideologically adrift, groping for a different, more practical conception of black America's place in American society" (Washington, 1993:259). Unfortunately during the past two decades, one prominent reality has exacerbated this trend.

The Double Whammy: Racism and Poverty

Since the 1970s a new complex of destructive economic and social conditions has affected many minority-group members, particularly poor African Americans and black Puerto Ricans. These people, often labelled members of the so-called "underclass," now seem to have little opportunity to escape poverty. One contributing factor has been the loss of jobs for unskilled minorities produced by the decline of manufacturing and the suburbanization of blue-collar employment (Wilson, 1987). In an important article, however, Douglas Massey (1990) argued that the most significant cause has been the recent pattern of racial segregation in housing.

Focusing on African Americans, Massey analyzed the significance of racial segregation in housing. He indicated that in a largely integrated area, particularly if it has diverse income groups, an increase in poverty, such as the one occurring during the economic downturn of the early 1970s, will adversely affect the area but will not alter its basic functioning: The economic strengths of the district will offset increased poverty, which will be dispersed throughout it. In contrast, if African

Americans face segregated housing, they will be forced to live in a restricted number of locales, which, given blacks' history of job discrimination, are likely to be in no-better-than-fair economic condition in the best of times. An economic downturn will not only affect black residents more readily than whites, since blacks' greater poverty makes them more vulnerable to the downturn, but given housing segregation, poor blacks from other locales forced to move by the downturn most likely will be funnelled into the area, contributing significantly to its economic decline. As a result most businesses will fail or be forced to leave; local opportunities for work will decline or virtually disappear; with the loss of local income, clinics and hospitals will leave the area; schooling, which is highly dependent on district funding, will sharply decline in quality; local residents will be less able to maintain their homes, landlords will be less motivated to do so, and with deterioration of residential buildings, the number of deserted buildings will increase; because of the growth of poverty, crime and violence will accelerate. Over the past quarter century, this process has contributed substantially to the rapid increase in the number of poor African Americans.

But for many people, structural conditions producing poverty and racism receive little attention. Focus is on an individual's inability to be successful, to avoid poverty. Social Darwinist or hateful references no longer prevail. The common approach is what some analysts call "symbolic racism"—a combination of traditional American values and antiminority feeling (Sidanius, Devereux, and Pratto, 1992). Individuals engaging in symbolic racism are likely to indicate how African Americans or members of other minorities often lack the work ethic to succeed in conventional educational or occupational structures. Minorities, these people conclude, simply are not sufficiently motivated.

William Ryan (1976) has called such an approach "blaming the victim." The failure to achieve success is described as an individual's personal deficiency and the economic and political conditions severely limiting that person's full participation in society—in short, conditions promoting institutional racism analyzed by internal-colonialist theory—are downplayed or ignored. In modern times politicians, policy makers, and social scientists have often endorsed the blaming-the-victim approach emphasizing racial minorities' cultural inferiority. Widespread support for such a perspective is hardly surprising in a culture which has placed a premium on the importance of individuals' strivings and success in competitive settings.

Certainly minority-group members who are not successful are aware of the victim-blaming labels attached to them. One of the greatest dangers posed by this situation is the potential violence it creates. In a society where individual success is so strongly emphasized, those who see little likelihood of such success readily feel diminished, angry, and frustrated, and, as a result, are often poised to strike out against others—either in their own communities or outside of them. Violence seems to be a growing reality in our society.

Following the Los Angeles riots of 1992, local leaders recognized the need to develop strategies to undercut future violence by opening up economic opportunities for poor minority-group members. A program called Rebuild L.A. was supposed to connect inner-city business organizations with corporations that would help them get started and provide employment for minority residents.

Two years later it was apparent that the program had made limited progress. One problem was that there was constant bickering about racial groups' representation on the board of directors. Although the original director, a white man, recognized this challenge and appointed four coleaders—a black man, an Asian woman, a Hispanic man, and a white man—these leaders often became gridlocked, unable to agree on programmatic goals.

An additional difficulty involved the extent to which corporations have followed through on their earlier pledges. $500 million in corporate pledges came in the form of donated equipment, training programs, and contracts to minority-owned companies but generally not, as often originally promised, in the form of jobs. Furthermore some companies reneged on earlier pledges.

Still because of Rebuild L.A., some poor neighborhoods are better off in terms of financing, stores, and services than they would have been without the program. Mark Ridley-Thomas, a Los Angeles city councilman, suggested that the enormity of the task and the pressure to launch it must be considered:

> I'm not of the view that Rebuild L.A. has been worthless, but they have done far less than anticipated, and that is a function of the challenge being too great and the organization being too new. They had to get to work in a seven- or eight-day period after the riots, and that's hardly the planning one needs to be effective. (Sims, 1994:5)

Meanwhile in November 1994, California residents passed a measure known as Proposition 187, which declared that the state should stop paying for illegal aliens' education and health benefits. While this change in policy could save California taxpayers $3 billion annually, a host of critics point out that the destructive impact on people's lives could be immeasurable, even breaking up families where some members are legal residents and others are not. At this writing the decision about implementing Proposition 187 has been tied up in court (Ayres, 1994).

REFERENCES

Allahar, Anton L. 1993. "When Black First Became Worth Less." *International Journal of Comparative Sociology* 34 (January–April):39–55.

Applebome, Peter. 1994. "A Hot Summer of Bloodshed and Change." *New York Times* (February 6):30.

Aptheker, Herbert. 1992. *Anti-Racism in U.S. History: The First Two Hundred Years*. Westport, CT: Greenwood Press.

Ayres, B. Drummond, Jr. 1994. "New Fears for California's Undocumented Aliens." *New York Times* (November 21):A10.

Bailyn, Bernard, et al. 1977. *The Great Republic*. Lexington, MA: D. C. Heath.

Baker, Ray Stannard. 1973a. "What Is Lynching?" pp. 304–328 in Donald P. DeNevi and Doris A. Holmes (eds.), *Racism at the Turn of the Century: Documentary Perspectives 1870–1910*. San Rafael, CA: Leswing. Article originally published in 1908.

Baker, Ray Stannard. 1973b. "The Negro's Struggle for Survival in the North," pp. 278–289 in Donald P. DeNevi and Doris A. Holmes (eds.), *Racism at the Turn of the Century: Documentary Perspectives 1870–1910.* San Rafael, CA: Leswing. Article originally published in 1908.

Bennett, Lerone, Jr. 1982. *Before the Mayflower: A History of Black America.* Chicago: Johnson Publishing Company. Fifth edition.

Bennett, Lerone, Jr. 1993. "10 Most Dramatic Events in African-American History," pp. 132–135 in John A. Kromkowski (ed.), *Race and Ethnic Relations 93/94.* Guilford, CT: Dushkin Publishing Group. Third edition.

Berthrong, Donald J. 1986. "Legacies of the Dawes Act: Bureaucrats and Land Thieves at the Cheyenne-Arapaho Agencies of Oklahoma," pp. 204–217 in Roger L. Nichols (ed.), *The American Indian: Past and Present.* New York: Alfred A. Knopf. Third edition.

Branch, Taylor. 1988. *Parting the Waters: America in the King Years 1954–63.* New York: Simon and Schuster.

Brown, Dee. 1972. *Bury My Heart at Wounded Knee.* New York: Bantam Books.

Colon, Jesus. 1961. *A Puerto Rican in New York.* New York: Mainstream Publishers.

Cox, Oliver C. 1976. *Race Relations: Elements and Social Dynamics.* Detroit: Wayne State University Press.

Daniels, Edward, and Harry Kitano. 1970. *American Racism.* Englewood Cliffs, NJ: Prentice-Hall.

Daniels, Roger. 1988. *Asian Americans: Chinese and Japanese in the United States since 1850.* Seattle: University of Washington Press.

Deloria, Vine, Jr. 1972. *Of Utmost Good Faith.* New York: Bantam Books.

Douglass, Frederick. 1968. *Narrative of the Life of Frederick Douglass.* New York: Signet Books. Originally published in 1845.

Farley, John E. 1988. *Majority-Minority Relations.* Englewood Cliffs, NJ: Prentice-Hall. Second edition.

Feagin, Joe R., and Clairece Booher Feagin. 1993. *Racial and Ethnic Relations.* Englewood Cliffs, NJ: Prentice-Hall. Fourth edition.

Fitzpatrick, Joseph P. 1987. *Puerto Rican Americans: The Meaning of Migration to the Mainland.* Englewood Cliffs, NJ: Prentice-Hall. Second edition.

Forbes, Ella. 1992. "African Resistance to Enslavement: The Nature and the Evidentiary Record." *Journal of Black Studies* 23 (September):39–59.

Franklin, John Hope, and Alfred A. Moss, Jr. 1988. *From Slavery to Freedom: A History of Negro Americans.* New York: Alfred A. Knopf. Sixth edition.

Goffman, Erving. 1974. *Stigma: Notes on the Management of Spoiled Identity.* New York: Jason Aronson.

Heyman, Josiah McC. 1990. "The Emergence of the Waged Life Course on the United States-Mexico Border." *American Ethnologist* 17 (May):348–359.

Hofstadter, Richard. 1955. *Social Darwinism in American Thought.* Boston: Beacon Press. Revised edition.

Ima, Kenji. 1982. "Japanese Americans: The Making of 'Good' People," pp. 262–302 in Anthony Gary Dworkin and Rosalind J. Dworkin (eds.), *The Minority Report.* New York: Holt, Rinehart and Winston. Second edition.

Jacobs, Wilbur R. 1985. *Dispossessing the American Indian: Indians and Whites on the Colonial Frontier.* Norman: University of Oklahoma Press. Revised edition.

Keefe, Susan E., and Amado M. Padilla. 1987. *Chicano Ethnicity.* Albuquerque: University of New Mexico Press.

Knoll, Tricia. 1982. *Becoming Americans.* Portland, OR: Coast to Coast Books.

Luther Standing Bear. 1978. *Land of the Spotted Eagle.* Lincoln: University of Nebraska Press.

Maldonado, Lionel A. 1982. "Mexican-Americans: The Emergence of a Minority," pp. 168–195 in Anthony Gary Dworkin and Rosalind J. Dworkin (eds.), *The Minority Report.* New York: Holt, Rinehart and Winston. Second edition.

Marable, Manning. 1994. "The Black Male: Searching beyond Stereotypes," pp. 69–77 in Richard G. Majors and Jacob U. Gordon (eds.), *The American Black Male: His Present Status and His Future.* Chicago: Nelson-Hall Publishers.

Massey, Douglas S. 1990. "American Apartheid: Segregation and the Making of the Under-class." *American Journal of Sociology* 96 (September):329–357.

Massey, Douglas S., and Nancy A. Denton. 1993. *American Apartheid: Segregation and the Making of the Underclass.* Cambridge, MA: Harvard University Press.

Nagel, Joane. 1993. "American Indian Mobilization: Tribal, Intertribal, and Supratribal Strategic Political Action," pp. 3–14 in Young I. Song and Eugene C. Kim (eds.), *American Mosaic: Selected Readings on America's Multicultural Heritage.* Englewood Cliffs, NJ: Prentice-Hall.

Nichols, Roger L. 1986. "The Indian in Nineteenth-Century America: A Unique Minority," pp. 127–136 in Roger L. Nichols (ed.), *The American Indian: Past and Present.* New York: Alfred A. Knopf. Third edition.

Noel, Donald L. 1968. "A Theory of the Origin of Ethnic Stratification." *Social Problems* 16 (fall):157–172.

Okimoto, Daniel I. 1971. *American in Disguise.* New York: John Weatherhill.

Ryan, William. 1976. *Blaming the Victim.* New York: Vintage Books. Revised edition.

Schaefer, Richard T. 1993. *Racial & Ethnic Groups.* New York: HarperCollins. Fifth edition.

Shapiro, Herbert. 1988. *White Violence and Black Response: From Reconstruction to Montgomery.* Amherst: University of Massachusetts Press.

Sidanius, Jim, Erik Devereux, and Felicia Pratto. 1992. "A Comparison of Symbolic Racism Theory and Social Dominance Theory as Explanations for Racial Policy Attitudes." *Journal of Social Psychology* 132 (June):377–395.

Sims, Calvin. 1994. "Who Said Los Angeles Could Be Rebuilt in a Day?" *New York Times* (May 22):Sec. 3, 5.

Solomon, Mark. 1993. "Racism and Anti-Racism in U.S. History." *Science & Society* 57 (spring):74–78.

Stoddard, Ellwyn R. 1973. *Mexican Americans.* New York: Random House.

Soule, Sarah A. 1992. "Populism and Black Lynching in Georgia, 1890–1900." *Social Forces* 71 (December):431–449.

Tolnay, Stewart E., and E. M. Beck. 1992. "Racial Violence and Black Migration in the American South, 1910 to 1930." *American Sociological Review* 57 (February):103–116.

Trennert, Robert A. 1986. "Educating Indian Girls at Nonreservation Boarding Schools, 1878–1920," pp. 218–231 in Roger L. Nichols (ed.), *The American Indian: Past and Present.* New York: Alfred A. Knopf. Third edition.

Twain, Mark. 1868. "Persecution of the Chinese in California and Passage of the Burlingame Treaty to Protect Their Rights," pp. 98–99 in Maxwell Geismar (ed.), *Mark Twain and the Three R's.* Indianapolis: Bobbs-Merrill, 1973.

Washington, Robert. 1993. "The Civil Rights Movement after Three Decades." *Politics, Culture and Society* 7 (winter):259–285.

Wilson, William Julius. 1978. *The Declining Significance of Race: Blacks and Changing American Institutions.* Chicago: University of Chicago Press.

Wilson, William Julius, 1987. *The Truly Disadvantaged: The Inner City, the Underclass, and Public Policy.* Chicago: University of Chicago Press.

Wright, Richard. 1938. *Uncle Tom's Children.* New York: Harper & Brothers.

Chapter
4

Under the Thumb: Politics, the Criminal-Justice System, and Violence

*I*n 1954, early in his civil-rights activities, Martin Luther King, Jr., was a leader of the Montgomery bus boycott, in which black citizens were refusing to ride city buses until seating was integrated. At one point African Americans advocating integrated busing and whites opposing it agreed to meet and form a committee that would seek to reach a mutually satisfying resolution.

During one meeting a member of the White Citizens Council, a white supremacist organization, joined the group on the opponents side of the table. Immediately King jumped up and protested the addition of someone else when committee membership had already been established. Furthermore, King added angrily, "We will never solve this problem so long as there are persons on the committee whose public pronouncements are anti-Negro" (Branch, 1988:148).

Henry Parker, a white minister, reacted strongly to King's comment, indicating that the new man had as much right to join the committee as anyone, including King. Then other whites entered the discussion, asserting that King's comment had introduced hostility and mistrust into the negotiations. Some blacks defended King, and the exchanges became angry, with each side accusing the other of initiating bitterness and negative feelings.

Eventually King made a motion for recess, saying that the whites had come to the meeting with "preconceived ideas." This observation infuriated Mrs. Logan A. Hipp, a white woman who had been serving as secretary for the meeting. "You are the one who has come here with preconceived ideas," she told King, trembling with fury. "I resent very deeply the statement that we have come here with preconceived ideas" (Branch, 1988:148).

The meeting broke up, and King felt a "terrible sense of guilt"—that he had not maintained sufficient control, and, as a result, had handled himself badly. The problem was that the whites' reaction had caught him off guard. Most of King's adult years had been spent in integrated situations with whites who accepted moral claims of racial equality, and he had expected whites on the committee to fall into two categories. Either they would have been enlightened and accepted his call for racial equality, or they would have been so blatantly racist that they would have appeared wicked and ridiculous to both African Americans and whites.

It was unexpected to learn that the majority of the whites regarded a declared white supremacist as no more extreme than King and his associates who advocated the "shocking" practice of integrated busing. Taylor Branch wrote, "The whites had spoken as the diplomats of a large country might defend their interests to diplomats from a small one. Their technical approach had deprived King of the moral ground he had occupied all his life" (Branch, 1988:149).

As this episode illustrates, historically whites have controlled American society, and central to that control has been dominance of the political process, where the shadow of internal colonialism remains. While in the past couple of decades racial minorities have made progress in the political realm, they remain relatively powerless, with their governance primarily in whites' hands. Meanwhile in the areas of criminal justice and violence, some whites' sense of perceived threat to their established control still encourages destructive, racist outcomes.

The common factor uniting political activity, the criminal-justice system, and violence is "power." **Power** is the ability of an individual or group to implement wishes or policies, with or without the cooperation of others. **Authority** is power that people generally recognize as rightfully maintained by those who use it. In race relations people's sense of which concept applies to a given situation varies with their outlook. In the opening illustration, whites felt that in dealing with African Americans, they exercised authority. Blacks, in contrast, stressed that whites maintained control by power, not authority: Whites simply had the personnel and weaponry to enforce their dominance. The first major section of this chapter discusses the **political institution,** which is the system of norms and roles that concerns the use and distribution of authority within a given society.

RACIAL MINORITIES IN THE POLITICAL PROCESS

A recent study comparing blacks to three white ethnic groups—Irish, Jews, and Italians—concluded that in the area of politics, blacks were distinctly disadvantaged. The researchers indicated that to a much greater extent than the white groups, the African Americans were forced to battle for basic citizens' rights, such as access to schooling, jobs, and political activity, including the right to vote. Furthermore once blacks were able to enter politics, they faced much stronger resistance from the white political establishment than did the three white groups (Cornacchia and Nelson, 1992). Nonetheless while blacks have been particularly disadvantaged politically, in the past half-century, their opportunities in politics have gradually improved.

With the urbanization of the South after World War II, whites were increasingly exposed to higher education and national mass media—both of which often opposed continuing segregation. Recognizing that political opportunities were starting to develop, African American organizations initiated sit-ins and boycotts to protest the continuation of segregation. Meanwhile during the 1950s and 1960s, an expanded, active black electorate was beginning to make an impact in northern cities. The increased black-voter strength in the North combined with civil-rights protest in the South to give the assertion of African American political rights much greater prominence.

In the late 1950s and early 1960s, black leaders hoped that the media coverage of white southerners' violent reactions to their antisegregation protests would encourage the federal government to overcome its traditional reluctance to interfere with southern local and state governmental practice. This, in fact, did occur. After racial violence in Birmingham, Alabama, President John F. Kennedy proposed the Civil Rights Act, which was passed in 1964 soon after his death, and in 1965 renewed violence against African Americans in Selma, Alabama, and the international uproar produced by this violence helped ensure passage of the 1965 Voting Rights Act.

The Civil Rights Act of 1964 has been the broadest American legislative effort to eliminate racial discrimination. The act covers employment practices of all businesses with more than 25 employees, access to all public accommodations such as hotels, motels, and restaurants, and the use of such federally supported organizations as colleges and hospitals. The Voting Rights Act of 1965 has suspended various qualifying tests for voter registration that many southern states used selectively to discriminate against African Americans, and this act also authorized federal examiners to enter these states and register black voters, greatly increasing their number.

Significantly these two pieces of legislation developed when Americans' support for civil-rights issues was very high. At the time Congress was faced with these two bills, adult Americans indicated that civil rights was the "most important problem facing the country." By 1966 civil rights had lost that priority position, and it has never regained it (Jaynes and Williams, 1989:221–223).

The Voting Rights Act has helped advance political interests of African Americans and other racial minorities. Results have been most striking in the South. In 1952, before the passage of the Voting Rights Act, 13 percent of black adults voted; in 1984 the figure rose to 65 percent (Jaynes and Williams, 1989:234).

Since 1965 African Americans have been elected to every major political office except for the presidency and vice presidency; in November 1989 L. Douglas Wilder was the first African American elected to the other major executive position when he became governor of Virginia. The national total of black elected officials was 7,517 in 1992, 505 percent of the 1,479 elected black politicians in 1970 (U.S. Bureau of the Census, *Statistical Abstract of the United States: 1993*, No. 448). Table 4.1 provides more detailed statistics on this topic.

These figures must remain in perspective. The percentage of black elected officials is very small. As of 1985, 1.2 percent of elected officials were African Americans, with the South's 4 percent the highest of all regions. In a country with about 12 percent of the population black, there is a distinct underrepresentation of elected black officials (Jaynes and Williams, 1989:238).

The figures, in fact, probably overstate blacks' political impact. In a well-known study of policy making in Cook County, Illinois (which includes the city of Chicago), Harold Baron (1968) concluded that the actual power held by elected and appointed African American officials in government, business, labor, education, and other major policy-making bodies was probably about one-third as great as the percentage of posts they held. The difficulty was that these officials primarily worked in black areas or interacted only with blacks and had little or no opportunity to make policy decisions in such critical areas as housing, jobs, and education.

Other racial minorities are also underrepresented politically. Among Native Americans political activity primarily involves reservation elections. Not until 1924 did Indians have the right to vote in elections outside of reservations. By 1967, 15 Native Americans had served in legislatures in six western states. In the 1990s par-

Table 4.1   BLACK ELECTED OFFICIALS BY OFFICE, 1970–1989

	Total	U.S. and State Legislatures[1]	City and County Offices[2]	Law Enforcement[3]	Education[4]
1970	1,479	179	719	213	368
1975	3,522	299	1,885	387	951
1980	4,963	326	2,871	534	1,232
1985	6,312	407	3,689	685	1,531
1990	7,335	440	4,481	769	1,645
1992	7,517	499	4,557	847	1,614

[1]Includes elected state administrators

[2]Composed of county commissioners and councilmen, mayors, vice mayors, aldermen, and regional officers

[3]Involves judges, magistrates, constables, marshals, sheriffs, and justices of the peace

[4]Includes members of state education agencies, college boards, and school boards

Note: While blacks are underrepresented in elected office, there has been a significant increase over time in the number of elected black officials.

Source: U.S. Bureau of the Census, *Statistical Abstract of the United States: 1993*, No. 449.

ticipation increased; in 1992, 35 Indians were elected as representatives in 14 state legislatures, and Larry Echo Hawk won office as attorney general in Idaho. Very few Native Americans have been elected to Congress, with about a half-dozen representatives and two senators having some Indian ancestry (Feagin and Feagin, 1993:189).

While underrepresented politically, a few wealthy Indians have taken steps that could lead to significant influence in politics. In 1993 and 1994, the Mashantucket Pequots, whose Foxwoods Casino has made huge profits, contributed about $315,000 to the National Committee of the Democratic party as well as about $500,000 to Democratic campaigns in at least four states. Initially it was not clear what the Pequots sought in return for their donations. Lobbyists for the tribe simply said that Democrats had been good to American Indians generally and the Pequots in particular, and that on a variety of issues including health care and education the Clinton administration seemed to be on the right track. State Senator James T. Fleming, a Republican and an opponent of casino gambling, could not find fault with the donations. He said, "I would imagine that all they're trying to do is expand their influence. As long as it's legal, I don't see anything wrong with it" (Johnson, 1994:B2). While contributions to individual candidates are limited, the Pequots can give as much as they want to state and national parties, thereby gaining tremendous goodwill from politicians.

Asian Americans have been more successful politically, especially Japanese Americans. In Hawaii they have dominated congressional positions, with both senators and both representatives usually Japanese Americans. In the middle 1970s, a Japanese American senator and representative were elected in California, but in 1990 Asian Americans, who were 10 percent of the state population, were vastly underrepresented. Only 2 members of the state's 47-member congressional delegation were Asian American, and only 1 percent of city council and school board seats were held by Asian Americans. In 1993 Tony Lam became the first Vietnamese American elected to a local-government seat when primarily non-Vietnamese Republicans chose him for a seat on the city council in Westminster, California (Feagin and Feagin, 1993:350; Mydans, 1994).

Asian Americans have encountered a pair of distinct disadvantages for participation in the political process. First, Asian Americans' membership in at least a half-dozen ethnic groups, which further subdivide according to social origins, time of arrival, and religious affiliation, often makes it difficult to find common political interests. Second, many foreign-born Asian Americans grew up in cultural traditions in which public positions on political issues could endanger one's economic standing or physical safety. Changing countries does not necessarily eliminate those old fears, and in many cases American-born children are reared with the idea that politics is a dirty, dangerous business that should be scrupulously avoided (Awanohara, 1993:112–113).

Mexican Americans have had a comparable level of political success. At any given moment, there are about ten Mexican American members of the House of Representatives. In the 1992 California election, Mexican Americans won ten seats in the state legislature. The growth of the Chicano population, along with the elimination of discriminatory statutes, such as a California law requiring English literacy for voters, have encouraged steady expansion of Mexican American voting turnout (Feagin and Feagin, 1993:274–275; Maharidge, 1993). A study conducted in Texas provided two reasons why the Chicano population is increasingly likely to vote. First, Mexican Americans' level of education has been rising, and voting studies indicate that level of education is the factor best predicting people's inclination to vote. Second, with the growth of the Chicano population, both major parties have increased their effort to mobilize support from this group, in particular offering Chicano candidates on statewide ballots (Longoria, Wrinkle, and Polinard, 1990).

In some areas, notably urban sections of California, Mexican Americans face a complicated political future. Illegal Mexican migrants are restricted residentially, moving into low-rent districts that become filled with people who, because legal access to jobs is barred, have little chance to move into mainstream society. While elected officials in such districts are assuredly Mexican American, low voter turnout hardly establishes them as major vote getters in veteran politicians' eyes. Meanwhile the districts they serve usually become increasingly poor and in need of costly services. In the 1970s and 1980s, the prevailing idea was that the Voting Rights Act, which attacked discriminatory actions against racial minorities, would overcome their political disadvantage; for Mexican Americans, however, the reality of illegal immigration has produced new significant political problems (Skerry, 1994). As we noted at the end of Chapter 3, the combined impact of poverty and racism have led to negative conditions not previously anticipated.

Puerto Ricans have been fairly successful at winning state and local offices. In 1992 in New York State, two State senators, four members of the state assembly, and eight members of the New York City Council were Puerto Rican. In addition, there was one Puerto Rican in the lower houses of the state legislature in New Jersey, Massachusetts, and Pennsylvania and three in Connecticut. In the early 1990s, lawsuits initiated by Puerto Rican activists led to two new congressional districts, one in Chicago and the other in New York City. At this time Puerto Ricans have three districts where their numerical domination makes the election of Puerto Rican candidates nearly inevitable (Feagin and Feagin, 1993:313).

In modern times sociologists have recognized that within a given racial minority, variations in background as well as current experience promote different political stances. Among Asian American groups, for instance, Chinese Americans split roughly equally between Democratic and Republican affiliation, Native Americans lean somewhat toward the Democrats, Japanese Americans and Filipino Americans have been largely Democratic, and Korean Americans and Vietnamese Americans have primarily gone Republican (Awanohara, 1993:113).

Conditions Affecting Racial Minorities' Political Success

Minority politicians must be aware that they face limitations seldom imposed on whites. One of the two major political parties—the Republican party—has remained committed to the governance principle contained in internal colonialism, regarding itself almost exclusively as a white ruling party. While a few conservative or very moderate minority-group individuals will receive political appointments or party backing in an election bid, African Americans and most other racial minorities realize that Republicans represent white Americans, defend their interests, and win most elections without minority, particularly black support. Andrew Hacker suggested that by sending this message, the Republican party "feels it can attract even more votes from a much larger pool of white Americans who want a party willing to represent their racial identity" (Hacker, 1992:201).

Many whites simply refuse to support an African American candidate, and the darker the skin, the less likely the support. A random sample of white adult Americans participated in an experiment in which they were told they would assess policy issues in a gubernatorial race occurring in a neighboring state. Each subject received a two-page packet containing information about a candidate's political experience, personal characteristics, and positions on different political issues. These convincing but fabricated portraits presented either a moderate or liberal political position. In addition, the packet contained a portrait of the candidate—either a light-skinned black male, a dark-skinned black male, or a white male, with the photos carefully adjusted to be equal in physical attractiveness. In the packets candidates' political positions and the three types of photos were both randomly distributed, thus permitting the experimenters to determine whether skin color and tone had an independent impact. They did. The findings showed that the three variations made significant differences: Both black candidates lost to the white one, but the dark-skinned black man finished a decisive third (Terkildsen, 1993).

Because of the disadvantages they encounter seeking political office, minority candidates are usually dependent on heavy voting support from their own racial group. A study of mayoral and city-council elections between 1965 and 1986 in New Orleans indicated that in elections where less than 40 percent of registered voters were African American, most candidates were white and those elected overwhelmingly white, with few blacks supporting black candidates. With between 40 and 55 percent of registered voters black, there were candidates of both races, and generally voting broke along racial lines. In elections with over 55 percent of registered voters African American, the majority of candidates were African American, and, in fact, in districts with over 60 percent black registered voters, both candidates were invariably black (Vanderleeuw, 1990).

Sometimes members of racial minorities can be elected even when their group is small. A study of the conditions permitting the election and reelection of Federico Pena, the Mexican American mayor of Denver, suggested two factors that can help accomplish this goal. First, the candidate must obtain almost complete support from his or her own racial group. Even though he did not present himself as a "minority" candidate, Pena was able to perform this task by stressing such issues as "neighborhoods" and "openness"—abstract concerns that had great meaning to Mexican Americans traditionally denied effective political participation but concerns that would not offend whites. Second, the minority candidate must make special efforts to appeal to nonminority voters or, at least, to lessen their opposition. One way Pena accomplished this goal was to emphasize prominent citywide concerns, such as more and better city planning and sounder government management (Hero and Beatty, 1989).

Among black candidates the current evidence suggests that those elected to office in areas with many white voters tend to be mild-mannered people possessing a distinctly middle-class background and style who are perceived to be running more as individuals than as representatives of their racial group. Many, perhaps the majority of whites are frightened when they hear, or think they hear a black candidate referring to "our turn" in politics: To such individuals this candidate seems to be an insurrectional leader who will use an elected office to subject whites to the range of inequities African Americans suffered in the past (Hacker, 1992:206–209). Thus it appears that many whites appreciate the historical realities of internal colonialism in the governance process, fearing that the tables can be turned on them.

Besides seeking political-leadership positions, racial minorities face another important challenge in the political arena: Are they able to accomplish significant political goals? A study of black and Chicano urban leadership in 12 northern California cities produced a notable result: Researchers found that the extent of minority representation in city government was not a decisive indicator of whether or not local government was responsive to minority needs.

Much more significant was what researchers called **political incorporation**—inclusion of racial minority-group members as significant players in political coalitions which contained some whites and successfully challenged established white conservative groups for control over a city's political activity. When African Americans and Mexican Americans achieved substantial political incorporation, significant improvements for their groups were likely to occur. These included:

1. A sharp increase in the city employment of minorities
2. The creation of police review boards, which investigated cases in which racial minority-group members claimed police abuse
3. A significant rise in the numbers of minority representatives appointed to city boards and commissions
4. The establishment of many minority-oriented programs
5. City governments' greater responsiveness to minority interests in the delivery of services and the formation of city policies in such key areas as economic development and education (Browning, Marshall, and Tabb, 1986)

The link between political incorporation and internal colonialism seems clear. The colonial mentality persists among whites, notably the governance principle emphasizing whites' control of racial minorities in political situations. Thus as political leaders, African Americans and other minority-group members are only able to produce significant political change when allied with whites.

For African American mayors, economic impediments to political incorporation can be formidable. Blacks tend to be elected mayors in cities with large African American populations, and these cities tend to be poor. A recent study of seven cities with populations of more than 150,000 citizens indicated that all seven had suffered significant population loss and that unemployment, underemployment, and poverty were widespread problems. With declining economic resources, these mayors' ability to provide affective governance and service delivery or to attract business suffered (Swain, 1993). Because of such limitations, the mayors' support from citizens was likely to dwindle. Once they lose influence with the voters, black mayors' capacity to generate political incorporation sharply declines.

Without political power minority-group individuals are not likely to have the critical information to function effectively in the political process. As a political reporter in Portsmouth, Virginia, Nathan McCall saw that being outside of the power structure, blacks only found out about decisions that would oppose their interests once the deals were made. At that point protests against the closing of a historic school or a real-estate venture that benefitted wealthy white citizens while forcing blacks to leave their homes were no longer effective (McCall, 1994:258).

Minority Politics Outside of Government

One racial minority—Native Americans—has conducted much of its political activity outside of the established governmental structure. Forced to confine most of their political involvement to reservations and supported by governmental emphasis on the revival of tribalism, many modern Indians have started to mobilize politically around issues of tribal identity and reservation roots (Hagan, 1986).

Some Indian tribes have initiated law suits to reclaim tribal lands that were illegally purchased from their ancestors. In 1972 two Indian tribes in Maine claimed thousands of acres of land, and state officials had a good laugh. Two decades later they were no longer laughing. Because of a 1790 federal law stating that no Indian land could be bought or sold without federal approval, the U.S. Supreme Court ruled in 1985 that the law needed to be honored in the many instances where it was either ignored or misunderstood. The land claims in question involve purchases made in the late-eighteenth and early-nineteenth centuries in eight eastern states.

After a U.S. Court of Appeals ruling in 1980, the Maine lawsuit was settled within five months through negotiations among individuals representing the U.S. Department of the Interior's Bureau of Indian of Affairs, the two Indian tribes, and the state. The legal council to the state legislature indicated that there was a prevailing spirit of compromise shown by the three sets of players and that all were quite pleased with the settlement. In other eastern states affected by the 1985 Supreme Court ruling, the Interior Department has been a less willing participant, and this creates a major difficulty. Without that department's support, Congress is not likely to provide its approval as the 1790 law requires (Wager, 1993).

In other instances the treaties were negotiated legally, but the government has not enforced them. Thus members of the tribes that signed the treaties are in a strong legal position to demand that the government maintain these official agreements. In 1984 Ojibway men renewed the practice of spearfishing, which had been a traditional spring practice of the tribe. The fishing is done in the Upper Great Lakes area on land sold to the United States. Treaties signed in 1837 and 1842 permitted the Indians to fish the land, but for over a century, the state of Wisconsin refused to recognize those rights, imposing its fish and game laws and jailing Ojibway people who violated them. In recent years court orders have allowed the activity to continue while the issue is being litigated. Although the tribe's legal efforts have permitted the Ojibway to return to this traditional practice, at least temporarily, there has also been a negative development—extensive, sometimes violent non-Indian resistance to the Ojibway fishing practices (Harjo, 1989).

While pursuing political rights through the courts does not always produce desired results, other benefits can emerge. Since 1920 there have been a string of court cases initiated by the tribes deprived of control of the Black Hills, a huge tract of western land. While this series of lawsuits has been unsuccessful, it has helped maintain a strong sense of unity among members of participating tribes and has won a number of admissions from the Supreme Court, such as their 1975 statement that Indians' treatment in this giant land deal represented "a national disgrace." Such admissions have produced much more national support for these tribes than they could have obtained if they had just made a one-sided presentation of their case (Churchill, 1990).

In April 1994 President Clinton demonstrated awareness of Indian leaders' rising political prominence by inviting leaders of the 547 federally recognized tribes to meet with him at the White House. Three hundred twenty-two tribal leaders accepted the invitation. The president said, "Welcome to the White House. Welcome home," and indicated that tribal leaders should be given the same deference shown to state governments. Some participants responded positively. The president of the National Congress of American Indians said the meeting would "send a message to our people that a new day had begun." In contrast, others had grievances, calling in particular for relief from the recent 13 percent cut for the Indian Health Service (Jehl, 1994:10). An important implication of this meeting is that tribal government, which federal officials have traditionally granted limited authority, has now assumed a prominent political role.

Like Native Americans, Chicanos have also pursued political goals by using organizations outside of the established political process. In 1929 the League of United Latin American Citizens (LULAC) was founded in southern Texas to use moderate political means to oppose discrimination against Mexican Americans. Currently the organization has active councils in 28 states, a national headquarters in Washington, D.C., and a professional staff. White politicians have seldom criticized LULAC's efforts because its heavily middle-class membership has made strenuous efforts to strongly support most American political and economic practices and has never condemned the society as discriminatory. LULAC has approached political activism cautiously, avoiding demonstrations or disruptive practices but using such widely supported techniques as voter-registration drives, petitions, and legal pressure (Marquez, 1989).

In the middle and late 1960s, the Chicano movement developed, with its members viewing themselves as oppressed because of their race and social class. The idea of internal colonialism seemed relevant. One writer noted that Chicanos have been "socially, culturally, and economically subordinated and territorially segregated by white America" (Gutiérrez, 1993:46). As part of the Chicano movement, César Chavez used the union of the United Farm Workers of America to organize agricultural workers throughout the Southwest and militate for higher wages and better working conditions, at least for a few years. In addition, in northern New Mexico and southern Colorado, Reies López Tijerina created the Aliánza Federal de Mercedes, and this organization was able to win land settlements for some Mexican Americans making such claims. Male members within the Chicano movement focused on such issues as the elimination of job discrimination, access to political power, entry into higher education, and community self-determination. While concerned about these issues, female members of the movement tended to emphasize demands for birth control, welfare rights, protection against male violence, and sexual pleasure both inside and outside of marriage (Guttiérez, 1993).

Organizations representing minority groups can readily find themselves in precarious positions. If too militant, whites and perhaps some of their own group are likely to oppose them. On the other hand, if quite restrained, they might lose significant support from members of their own group impatient for major advances. Consider the case of the NAACP.

In 1993 Benjamin F. Chavis, Jr., became the executive director of the National Association for the Advancement of Colored People (NAACP). During his first year in office, he enacted changes that drew opposition from many members of what for decades had been a moderate organization working for improvements in black Americans' lives. For instance, Chavis met with black street-gang leaders and defended "gangster rap" music—an action later repudiated by his own board of directors. In addition, he called for closer ties with the Nation of Islam and its controversial leader Louis Farrakhan. Furthermore Chavis drew the wrath of some environmentalists and lawmakers by advocating the shift of the cost of hazardous-waste cleanup from offending companies to a broad-based business tax. The director's argument was that the waste dumps, which are often located in poor minority neighborhoods, would be cleaned up more quickly with the tax; his opponents said that it was naive to expect Congress to pass another tax on business and that its passage would free polluters from a significant deterrent. While Chavis drew opposition from his board of directors and many moderate NAACP members, he also had strong support. Ronald Walters, chairman of Howard University's political science department, indicated that the board's opposition reflected its long-term policy of avoiding controversy at any cost and demonstrated why "so many young people feel it has become irrelevant" (Holmes, 1994b:6). Predictably the board of directors perceived the situation very differently. To this group Chavez's strong stances on issues was threatening, and in August 1994 he was fired (Holmes, 1994c).

As the following situation illustrates, minority-group politicians often face special challenges.

PACs and African Americans in Congress

By the middle 1990s, political-action committees (PACs) had a bad name among American voters, invoking images of wealthy businessmen giving huge sums of money to politicians who then champion the doners' corrupt drive for even greater wealth. In the long run, the dominant wisdom ran, tax payers must foot the increasingly burdensome bill. Leading politicians have been responsive to the public's discontent. In 1993 President Bill Clinton urged Congress to curb the power of PACs, and in June of that year, the Senate passed a bill that would get rid of them.

But the issue was not settled. In the House of Representatives, most Democrats vowed to fight to keep PACs, arguing that these organizations created for the express purpose of meeting campaign expenses were an essential source of funding. Black members have been particularly committed.

The black caucus, which in 1993 was comprised of 38 House members, indicated that it must defend PACs because minority candidates are particularly dependent on them. Disproportionately representing poor districts, minority politicians generally lack white candidates' frequent access to wealthy schools and corporations that can be major funding sources. As Representative Eva Clayton, a first-term Democrat representing the district with the lowest per-capita income in North Carolina said, "If your district is poor, you're not wealthy and you're excluded from affluent circles; it's hard to raise money" (Donovan, 1993:2523).

Compared to whites, blacks are less inclined to oppose PACs, seeing these organizations not as potential sources of corruption but as useful means to counter wealthy interests. Reflecting the latter outlook, Representative Melvin Watt, another first-term member of the black caucus, noted, "The whole rationale for having PACs was to enable small contributors to have an influence. What is wrong with that?" (Donovan, 1993:2524).

Commenting on African American House candidates, Ronald Walters, the political scientist at Howard University cited earlier, said, "They're no different than anyone else. They're trying to protect their political base" (Donovan, 1993:2524). The difference is that in the case of black candidates, PACs serve a more central funding role than they do for many of their white colleagues.

While PACs are important for members of the black-caucus, they traditionally have received limited support from them. One reason for this disinterest has been that potential contributors have recognized that African American House members, who tend to have been recently elected to office, generally have lacked seniority on key committees. As a result, they did not possess the ability to influence the outcome of significant legislation that could benefit PAC sponsors, and so potential sponsors stayed away. That situation is starting to change. Three blacks now chair full committees, and ten head subcommittees. As major policy players, these senior black House members can steer PAC contributions not only toward themselves but toward junior members who might otherwise be overlooked. As a result PACs have started to show a true interest in black-caucus members.

For White House leaders, an alliance with the black caucus on the PAC issue permits them to sound like progressive legislators and not simply politicians concerned about the possible loss of a lucrative source of campaign funds. Thus House Speaker Thomas Foley declared, "I don't think it's a . . . reform to cut off the opportunity of women and African Americans and Hispanics and other minorities to seek office and be elected" (Donovan, 1993:2525). Certainly members of the black caucus will pursue this line of thought. Representative John Lewis noted that in spite of the corrupt uses of PACs that have occurred, people should remember that they were originally intended as part of a campaign-reform package. Lewis said, "They allow working people to pool their dollars so the millionaires and the big-money interests won't be in the game alone" (Donovan, 1993:2526).

While minority candidates for political office seek a leveling of the playing field, this goal becomes an urgent matter in the criminal-justice process.

RACIAL MINORITIES AND THE CRIMINAL-JUSTICE SYSTEM

In December 1990 American federal and state prisons contained about 774,375 people. About 369,485 were white, 367,122 African American, 103,065 Hispanic, 6,251 Indian or native Alaskan, and 2,806 Asian Americans (U.S. Department of Justice, *Correctional Populations in the United States, 1990,* Tables 5.6 and 5.9).

It is revealing to compare racial groups' representation in the prison population adjusted for their numbers in the overall American population: African Americans stand out. Blacks are 30 times more highly represented at state and federal prisons than Asian Americans; 6.3 times more than whites; 2.6 times more than Hispanics; and 3.75 times more than Native Americans. Furthermore black males are 6.6 more heavily represented in state and federal prisons than white males (*Correctional Populations in the United States, 1990,* Tables 5.6, 5.7, and 5.9; U.S. Bureau of the Census, *Statistical Abstract of the United States: 1993,* No. 18 and No. 23). With their members so heavily represented in the criminal justice system, many young black men are as inclined to consider prison an inevitable part of their life experience just as many young white men assume that they will go to college (Mauer, 1994:90). We need to consider why African Americans are disproportionately trapped in the criminal-justice system.

Alfred Blumstein (1982) and Patrick Langan (1985) sought to determine whether racial discrimination explains African American overrepresentation in prisons. Their studies of state prisons produced similar results, with both researchers concluding that the disproportionate number of blacks arrested, particularly for major crimes carrying severe penalties, largely explained their overrepresentation in the prison population. Thus Langan indicated that his study demonstrated that "even if racism exists, it might explain only a small part of the gap between the 11% [currently 12%] black representation in the United States adult population and the now nearly 50% black representation among persons entering state prison each year in the United States" (Langan, 1985:682).

Two comments on these studies seem appropriate. First, since both compare the number of individuals arrested with those who eventually end up in prison, they are not examining the issue of whether racism enters the criminal-justice process during the arrest phase.

Second, these investigations might have underestimated the extent to which racism exists throughout the entire criminal-justice system. Marjorie Zatz (1987) suggested that such investigations may concentrate on readily detectable measures of bias and overlook less obvious racist displays—for instance, a prosecutor's request for a long sentence for a black man not officially sought because of his race but because of his history of criminal activity. In addition, Zatz emphasized that participants in the criminal-justice system inevitably try to hide racist policies since such activities would cast doubt on the legitimacy and rationality of the entire system. Other researchers have indicated that most studies of racial discrimination in the criminal-justice system have focused at specific points—arrest, arraignment, sentencing, and so forth. Such studies tend to ignore or deemphasize that accused people's involvement in this system is a process. Thus seemingly trivial bits of information or commentaries that are racially discriminatory can remain in an individual's file or be transmitted verbally, appearing to have no impact in the early stages of the criminal-justice process but then impacting when individuals are sentenced or incarcerated (Bridges and Crutchfield, 1988; Swigert and Farrell, 1977).

Some experts, in fact, have become convinced that quantitative data assessing racism at discrete points in the criminal-justice process are invariably superficial, even misleading. Instead they are much more inclined to favor participants' detailed observations of the criminal-justice process. This qualitative information, they contend, can supply a much fuller sense of the extent to which racism resides in a given criminal-justice system (Mann, 1994).

In 1991 the 17-member New York State Judicial Commission on Minorities composed of judges, lawyers, law professors, and an official from the State Education Department concluded that the state-court system is "infested with racism." The Commission concluded that minority-group members are less likely than whites to receive favorable actions from the courts; that judges and prosecuting attorneys are more hostile and racially biased toward minorities than are other court employees; that minority lawyers are often subjected to opposing attorneys' racial stereotyping and racist jokes (Gray, 1991).

In short, there is the distinct possibility that racism is more prevalent within the criminal-justice system than the Blumstein and Langan investigations concluded. Blacks and Puerto Ricans, whose incarceration rate is closest to blacks, are the most likely victims. Let's consider why racism permeates this system.

Sense of Threat: Key to Racism in the Criminal-Justice System

Several years ago sociologist Darnell F. Hawkins (1987) wrote about the relationship between race and the criminal-justice system. Hawkins made a specific point reminiscent of a more general issue discussed within the first chapter's introduction of internal colonialism—that conflict theorists have tended either to ignore the role played by race in relation to criminal justice or have subordinated its significance to social class. The result, Hawkins indicated, is that conflict theorists have simply lumped all poor together, whether members of racial minorities or white, assuming that people's socioeconomic class is the major factor determining their treatment in the criminal-justice system. For this issue, however, race appears to play a critical role.

Hawkins concluded that a sense of threat is the key factor encouraging racial discrimination in the criminal-justice process. When whites see blacks' criminal behavior as threatening, they are likely to deal with them harshly. On the other hand, when whites do not see blacks' crimes as threatening, they will not subject them to discriminatory treatment (Hawkins, 1987). Other research has produced similar evidence. Thus investigators calculated relative arrest rates for blacks and whites; the percentage of blacks arrested for a given crime out of the total number known to have committed that crime was compared to the percentage of whites arrested for the same crime out of the number known to have committed that crime. One study found that for robbery the arrest percentage for blacks and whites was nearly identical. However, in the cases of assault and rape, the black arrest rate was distinctly higher than the white one (Yu and Liska, 1993).

This evidence seems consistent with the internal-colonialist perspective, suggesting that whites fixate on controlling racial minorities' activities. A sense of threat emerges when whites believe that blacks' actions would loosen their controlling grip, and often criminal behavior, particularly violent criminal behavior can produce that sense.

Hawkins's thesis also receives support from other studies examining arrest rates. In an investigation of 77 American cities with populations of over 100,000 people, there was no relationship between cities' proportion of poor and their arrest rates. On the other hand, the proportion of racial minority-group members and the extent of racial segregation within cities correlated to minority individuals' arrest rates. Thus the higher the proportion of minority-group members and the more extensive racial segregation, the higher the arrest rate, both for minority-group members and whites. Why did this result occur? The researchers reasoned that with the combination of a high percentage of minority-group members and a low level of racial integration, whites' perceived threat of crime grew. These perceptions increased pressure on police to control crime, and the result was an accelerated rate of arrests for both racial minorities and whites (Liska, Chamlin, and Reed, 1985).

A study drawing its data from a representative sample of American 11- to 17-year-olds concluded that for serious offenses (in particular, felony theft, felony assault, robbery, hard drug use, and fraud) African Americans were two to three times more likely to be arrested and charged than whites. But this finding does not mean that racial discrimination definitely occurred. Perhaps black and white youths differed in some other significant respect besides race. Investigators examined several of the most likely possibilities. Did the youthful blacks have a more extensive history of delinquencies? No! Perhaps the blacks were more likely to have committed crimes involving either greater physical injury or the use of guns? Once again, no! The researchers concluded that young African Americans "appear to be at greater risk for being charged with more serious offenses than whites involved in comparable levels of delinquent behavior, a factor that may eventually result in higher incarceration levels" (Huizinga and Elliot, 1987:221).

Another study found that black youths were not only more likely to be arrested than whites but also were more frequently held, charged, sentenced, and incarcerated. The researchers suggested that when black youths "discern differential and more lenient treatment for their Anglo counterparts, a bitter and ironic form of accountability is taught" (Fagan, Slaughter, and Hartstone, 1987:253). A self-fulfilling prophecy develops. Motivated by their perception that young African Americans represent a greater threat than white youth, police, judges, and other court officials treat them more harshly. The black youths perceive their biased treatment, and, indeed, are likely to become a more substantial threat than they would have been without exposure to racism in the criminal-justice system.

A number of other studies demonstrate racial bias in sentencing, with the relationship between threat and race apparent once more. An investigation done in 39 states found that blacks typically served longer sentences than whites for robbery, rape, and murder (Hacker, 1988). A growing body of research indicates that in many cases the key factor is the race of the victim. Evidence suggests that when the victim of rape or robbery is white, the sentence is likely to be more severe (LaFree, 1980; Thomson and Zingraff, 1981).

A related conclusion appears in murder cases. Researchers have found that when the level of seriousness is controlled—that is, when four possible racial combinations of offender and victim are compared for similar degrees of severity, such as whether only one person was killed or whether multiple killings were involved—prosecutors and juries are more likely to demand the death penalty if the victim is white and the offender is black than in any of the other three possible racial combinations—white offender/black victim, black offender/black victim, or white offender/white victim (Ekland-Olson, 1988; Jaynes and Williams, 1989:488–489; Keil and Vito, 1989). Once again the concept of threat seems relevant. When a black person kills a white person, he or she is not only offending the individual whom the state has an obligation to protect but also the state itself by challenging whites' control of the social order. African Americans killing whites present the spectre of insurrection. White murderers generally create a similar sense of threat only if they kill public officials or law-enforcement personnel (Hawkins, 1987:726).

In a study of state prisons in 48 states, George S. Bridges and Robert D. Crutchfield (1988) found that African Americans were disproportionately imprisoned in states where the black citizenry was relatively poor compared to whites, primarily urban, and a fairly small percentage of the overall population. North-central states had the disproporionately highest number of black prison inmates and southern states the lowest. The researchers decided that while racial differences in arrest rates was a factor in the disproportionate imprisonment of blacks, it was a much less significant factor than indicated in the Blumstein and Langan studies.

Bridges and Crutchfield hypothesized that one factor that might have contributed to the high proportion of African Americans in the prison population in states where blacks were poorer and concentrated in urban areas might have been longer criminal records among blacks. But blacks' records were not longer than whites'. Like Darnell Hawkins these researchers eventually endorsed the idea of threat, suggesting that an effective analysis of their findings needed to consider that disproportionate punishment is the dominant white group's means of signaling its determination to maintain control over African Americans and other racial minorities in a situation where they consider the stable social order threatened (Bridges and Crutchfield, 1988:719).

But why, one might ask, do people in the north-central states—in particular Minnesota, Nebraska, Wisconsin, and Iowa, according to the Bridges and Crutchfield data—appear to feel the strongest sense of threat from blacks? One possibility is that in such states many whites find racial confrontation a horrifying abstraction. They have had little or no contact with blacks but are painfully aware that not far away—in Minneapolis, Omaha, Milwaukee, or Des Moines—there is a heavy concentration of poor blacks who, their television-news programs and newspapers daily inform them in gruesome detail, are heavily engaged in crime, much of it violent. As a result these people are frightened, and they react by pressuring their politicians, police, sheriffs, prosecutors, and judges to crack down on African Americans and other minorities.

In the late 1960s, I recall watching a news program during which a reporter standing in a remote corn field in one of the north-central states reported that where he was, 100 miles from the nearest city, people were far more terrified of being victims of rioting inner-city blacks than any urban residents he had ever encountered.

For individual minority-group members, the patterns discussed here have often come home to roost. In some cases they see that compared to whites who have committed comparable crimes, they received stiffer sentences. Or, the relevance of threat against whites can become apparent when they assess the penalties imposed for their own crimes. As an adolescent, Nathan McCall faced charges for two felonies, with very different results. In *Makes Me Wanta Holler,* he explained:

> I shot and nearly killed Plaz, a black man, and got a thirty-day sentence; I robbed a white business and didn't lay a finger on anybody, and got twelve years. I got the message. I'd gotten it all my life: Don't fuck with white folks. (McCall, 1994:144)

Some observers might conclude that whites' sense of threat is regrettable but that, after all, blacks represent a significant threat to whites' sense of security. However, consider a sobering comparative reality: In the course of an average hour, two Americans will be murdered, but four U.S. citizens will die of unhealthy or unsafe conditions in the workplace—events that were also precipitated by major criminal violations (Reiman, 1994:294). In the latter situation, people end up just as dead, and the misery and suffering is similar. Yet while also illegal, the conditions causing those deaths are often not perceived as crimes and when considered crimes, the sense of threat is much less compelling for the general public. Undoubtedly the combined race and class factors help produce the difference: It remains difficult for most white Americans to consider wealthy white executives as a threat while poor black individuals readily qualify.

Judges are well aware that prisons are disproportionately filled with minority-group members, representing a special level of threat to the numerical minority— white inmates. For this reason they are often more inclined to give whites than blacks probation instead of incarceration. One judge explained:

> This [consideration] is becoming more important all the time—especially with the prisons so overcrowded—you are reluctant to send white offenders especially younger ones, to a prison that is largely black. It seems the prisons are becoming more and more black and Hispanic, so judges are leery because they have heard horror stories about what has happened. (Kramer and Steffensmeir, 1993:371)

While the injustices described in this section are not about to disappear, some of them are under siege. In May 1994 a federal judge ordered the Justice Department to explain something normally not requiring explanation—why it was seeking the death penalty against an African American defendant in a murder case. Although the vast majority of homicide cases are tried in state court, the order could be precedent-setting, forcing prosecutors to reveal the basis for decisions that could be racially biased. In some cases this requirement could provide critical evidence since a crime bill in the House would permit defendants to appeal capital-punishment decisions if they can demonstrate that they were the victims of racial bias. Richard Dieter, an expert on capital punishment, observed, "If this information comes out fairly soon, it might influence a major piece of legislation" (Quoted in Holmes, 1994a:A18).

The sense of threat also seems to be a factor encouraging racial violence.

VIOLENCE AGAINST RACIAL MINORITIES AND THE CONDITIONS ENCOURAGING IT

In his well-known study of a southern town in the 1930s, John Dollard (1937) summed up his perception of whites' motivation for aggression against African Americans with the following statement. He wrote:

> In the end it seems . . . [most accurate] to say that white people fear Negroes. They fear them, of course, in a special context, that is, when the Negro attempts to claim any of the white prerogatives or gains. . . . By a series of hostile acts and social limitations the white caste maintains a continuous threatening atmosphere against the possibility of . . . demands by Negroes; when successful, . . . the effect is to keep the social order intact. (Dollard, 1937:316–317)

Sometimes whites' violence against racial minorities has served to keep the social order intact, and sometimes it has been a means of winning control over minorities.

From the seventeenth through the nineteenth centuries, white invaders battled Native Americans in the continuous effort to take over their land and their lives. Broken treaties and the slaughter of defenseless Indian women, children, and elderly people were common practices. Richard Maxwell Brown indicated that the effect of whites' dealings with Indians "has not been a healthy one; it has done much to further our proclivity to violence" (Brown, 1979:34).

One could make the same point about whites' violent treatment of blacks. With the end of slavery, some southern whites developed a special organization for dealing with African Americans—the Ku Klux Klan, which was discussed in Chapter 1. Three phases have occurred. In the 1860s under the direction of Nathan Bedford Forrest, a former slave trader and Confederate general, the Klan developed as a central organization in the effort to restore the Confederacy. During the 1920s the Klan appeared once more, largely outside the South, as a white-supremacist structure intent on assuming political control. In some political districts, its influence was strong because candidates for office either needed to be Klan members or to receive the organization's endorsement. Finally since the

1960s, the Klan has revived once again, using the Confederate battle flag as its symbol and emphasizing the grandeur of the institutions of the segregated white South. At times the modern Klan has united with the American Nazi Party and other fascist groups (Lawrence, 1994:23–24).

Even before the development of the Klan, racial riots served to intimidate blacks. Antiblack riots, which occurred in the North in the 1820s and 1830s and continued in both the South and North for about four decades after the Civil War, were one-sided attacks on blacks by whites. From about 1915 through the 1940s, whites still initiated riots, but blacks began to develop their own counter-rioting gangs. From 1964 through 1967, certain circumstances encouraged some inner-city residents to initiate riots. Generally the rioters were infused with black pride, frustrated by limited economic opportunities available to them, and mobilized by local incidents, such as a white policeman's beating or killing of a black resident.

Other racial minorities have also encountered extensive violence. For instance, in the 1870s and 1880s, Chinese workers competing with whites for jobs were often run out of town, beaten, or even killed. In Los Angeles in 1871, between 18 and 21 Chinese men were hanged or burned to death, and in 1887 in desolate Hell's Canyon on the Idaho-Oregon border, 31 Chinese gold miners were robbed and murdered (Kitano and Daniels, 1988:22).

In the 1990s, to be sure, those who want to control racial minorities' advancement are no longer "successful" in Dollard's 1930s sense. The relationship between threat and violence, however, is probably similar—with whites who want African Americans or other racial minorities "kept in their place" using violence as a means of intimidation.

One issue that has received considerable attention has been the number of blacks killed by the police. In any given year, a disproportionate number of blacks will be killed by police—about a fourfold greater number than one would expect by their overall proportion of the population. However, some researchers suggested that violence is more likely to develop when police arrest or attempt to arrest individuals for serious offenses. They pointed out that when analysts consider not only offenders' race but the seriousness of the crimes with which they are charged, the number of African Americans killed is not disproportionate (Jaynes and Williams, 1989:477–478).

The same statistical murkiness discussed in the previous section develops once more: Since researchers do not systematically observe law-enforcement officials on the job, they cannot determine to what extent racial bias enters at the arrest stage—either in the decision to arrest or to use deadly force.

What is known is that in inner-city areas, typical white police officers are modestly educated individuals, most likely high-school graduates who had never previously set foot in the districts they now patrol. Frequently they appear to judge individuals first and foremost by their color, and because of the ongoing barrage of poverty and crime with which they have to deal, many have become so disillusioned that they view even law-abiding African Americans as belonging to "the other side" (Hacker, 1992:190).

Sociologist William B. Waegel did a study that gets at least some relevant, behind-the-scenes information. Waegel spent about ten months as a participant-observer in a police department in a northeastern city. He concluded that politicians' calls for the harsh treatment of criminals along with victims', friends', or family members' demands for revenge create a moral climate encouraging violence against offenders. Widespread racism, Waegel believed, plays into the process. In urban areas, where minorities are overrepresented in serious crimes, police are likely to feel that race itself is a major cause of crime. Frequently Waegel heard comments supporting such a position. For instance, during the investigation of a homicide involving a member of a racial minority (Waegel did not specify which group), the researcher heard one detective tell another, "Maybe Hitler was right, he just had the wrong group." And during another investigation in which all the parties involved were black, a veteran officer told Waegel, "You've got to understand, these people are animals, and we're here to keep peace among animals." In the aftermath of a police shooting, a colleague approached the officer responsible and asked what happened. The officer described the circumstances, which included shooting the suspect while he was lying unarmed on the ground, and then concluded, "What was I supposed to do?" Without hesitation the other policeman replied, "What's another dead nigger anyway?" (Waegel, 1984:148)

In March 1991 in Los Angeles, the most celebrated recent incident of police violence against a minority-group member occurred. Two police officers kicked and beat Rodney G. King, a local African American, for two minutes while 13 other officers and 20 local residents watched. What was unique about the incident was that one of the local residents filmed the beating, and it was widely shown on national television. The large number of police present during the beating and transcripts of squad-car communications, which indicated that such incidents occurred frequently, supported the widespread belief in the Los Angeles area that police violence against black and Chicano citizens is commonplace. Jerome Skolnick, a sociologist specializing in police behavior, indicated, "This is going to be the defining incident in police brutality; it's going to be the historical event for police in our time" (Mydans, 1991:B7).

Sometimes juries take police violence against minorities into account. In 1987 Larry Davis, a black drug dealer in the Bronx, was sought by the police for several felonies. Eventually he was tracked to an apartment where a shootout occurred. At Davis's trial for attempted murder, witnesses differed about which side shot first. Davis's attorneys conceded that he had shot at the police—it would have been difficult to argue otherwise since several officers were wounded—but the attorneys explained that Davis sincerely believed that these white police officers had no intention of letting him live and that his only hope for survival was to defend himself. Thus the attorneys plead self-defense. While it is not unusual for a defendant to claim that he or she acted in self-defense, this was the first time that such a plea had been employed to justify firing at the police. Nonetheless the Bronx jury of African American and Hispanic citizens voted unanimously to acquit Davis on the charge of attempted murder. These law-abiding citizens had no particular use for Larry Davis, but they felt compelled to accept his explanation about the police squad's deadly intention toward an armed black man (Hacker, 1992:190–191).

Overall inner-city residents, like residents elsewhere, appreciate police protection. Sometimes, in fact, local violence becomes so extensive that some citizens are willing to have some rights suspended in exchange for increased protection. In the Robert Taylor Homes, a gang-ridden public housing project in Chicago, residents have been divided about whether local police without warrants should be allowed to make sweeps through the project looking for weapons. In an area where 300 reports of gunshots occurred in one three-day period, a number of residents indicated that they supported the sweeps. On the other hand, an attorney representing a tenant's group opposing the sweeps asserted that the sweeps will have no long-term effect, representing a Band-Aid on a serious wound (Terry, 1994). Furthermore if constitutional limitations on the police are suspended, their opportunities to engage in violence against citizens are increased.

Besides racist violence by police, ordinary citizens sometimes engage in it. In the past decade, analysts of racism have emphasized the apparent rise in white citizens' initiation of violence, particularly on college campuses. For instance, the Justice Department indicated that the number of campuses in which race-related incidents occurred rose from 48 in 1986 to 76 the following year.

Commenting on a racial killing that occurred in New York City and will presently be discussed, sociologist Bob Blauner noted, "We're not used to seeing incidents of racial violence spearheaded by the young—this is something new and it cuts across class lines" (Johnson, 1989:section 1, p. 32).

Janet Caldwell, a member of the Center for Democratic Renewal, an Atlanta-based research group that monitors the Ku Klux Klan and other white-supremacist groups, suggested that in the modern world, a white skin no longer translates to automatic privilege. Caldwell said "Young whites are facing things they never had to face before" (Johnson, 1989:section 1, p. 32). No longer do whites monopolize high-paying, prestigeous jobs. Many resent the situation, and they can find support from various media sources, notably white-power rock-and-roll groups such as Guns N' Roses, whose debut album sold 9 million copies and included vicious put-downs of African Americans and other racial minorities (Pareles, 1989).

In a study of the Ku Klux Klan, researchers found extensive evidence of youthful racism, learning to their surprise that even though Klan membership had been greater in the past, support was unrelated to age—that "favorable attitudes toward the Klan are not dying out in the younger generation" (Seltzer and Lopes, 1986:96). The investigators discovered that the social variable that most predicted support for the Klan was education, actually the lack of it: The less formal the education, the greater the expressed support. The researchers did not know whether this relationship resulted because better-educated people have learned to tone down their racist expression or actually are less inclined to be racist (Seltzer and Lopes, 1986:98).

Another study conducted in Wilkes-Barre, Pennsylvania, illustrated how Ku Klux Klan members have learned to exploit whites' fears. When new owners of the local newspaper anticipated a workers' strike, they hired a security company, which deployed guards throughout the building—in rest rooms, on the shop floor, in most work areas, and in the places where workers gathered to talk or eat lunch. The workers deeply resented the guards' presence, feeling that the company was trying to intimidate them into not striking. The fact that the guards were primarily black while the newspaper workers were mainly white compounded the tension, and in the weeks that preceded the strike, the workers' frustration centered on the guards, whom they constantly threatened and insulted with racial slurs.

Eventually the strike occurred, and workers began mass picketing in front of the newspaper headquarters. At this point built-up frustrations were released on the guards, with many spat upon, hit by objects, and punched.

After the outbreak of violence, Klan organizers approached the strikers, suggesting that their fury toward the black guards should extend to the entire black community of Wilkes-Barre. What was particularly disturbing to local African American leaders was that few whites expressed alarm or even concern about the Klan actions. Eventually the security company was replaced with one using exclusively white guards. Tensions lessened, and finally the strike was settled. It appeared, however, that the events described placed a long-term strain on race relations in Wilkes-Barre (Keil, 1985).

When jobs are on the line in interracial situations, there is likely to be racially targeted resentment, which can turn violent. Visitors to Detroit-area auto plants have found racist anti-Japanese posters and graffiti very prevalent. Some United Auto Worker locals have ordered and distributed bumper stickers reading "Toyota-Datsun-Honda = Pearl Harbor" and "Unemployment—Made in Japan." A number of auto executives have been equally unrestrained. In particular, Bennett E. Bidwell, Chrysler's executive vice president for sales and marketing, suggested that the most effective means of limiting car imports would be to charter the *Enola Gay* (the airplane that dropped the first atomic bomb on Japan) (Daniels, 1988:342–343).

The most celebrated violent incident emerging from this situation occurred on June 19, 1982. Vincent Chin, a Chinese American, went with three friends to a topless bar, where a white automobile-industry foreman mistook him for Japanese and started making racial slurs, suggesting that Chin was responsible for his unemployment. A scuffle developed, and all participants were thrown out of the bar. Later that evening the white foreman and his stepson saw Chin at a restaurant, waited for him to leave, and then, while the stepson held Chin, the older man beat him with a baseball bat. Chin died four days later. Originally charged with second-degree murder, the whites were allowed to plead guilty to manslaughter; they were fined $3,780 each and put on three years probation. The local Asian American community was outraged, charging that a racist deevaluation of Asian Americans led to the light sentences. Eventually their protests produced a federal investigation and a federal indictment of the older man, who was found guilty of depriving Chin of his civil rights. In September 1984 he received 25 years in prison, but upon appeal, witnesses' conflicting and vague testimony produced an acquittal (Kitano and Daniels, 1988:189).

The Chin murder was hardly an isolated incident. Asian Americans have increasingly become the target of hate groups, with Navroze Mody killed in 1987 by eleven youths belonging to a gang whose stated purpose was to rid Jersey City of Asian Americans and Sam Nang Nhem kicked and beaten to death in 1993 in Fall River, Massachusetts, simply because he had the ill-timed misfortune of walking by a group of brawling young white men who instantly decided "to knock that gook out." The perpetrators of anti-Asian bigotry and violence are usually members of the racial or ethnic group living in the area where a given Asian American group has settled and started establishing an economic foothold in a variety of businesses. Thus in Texas those responsible have been whites and Chicanos, in Seattle and Tacoma African Americans and Hispanic Americans, in Boston whites, and in Philadelphia whites and blacks (*New York Times*, 1994; Wong, 1994).

Modern Native Americans sometimes are victims of violence when they use the court system to obtain illegally removed tribal rights. After the Ojibway of northern Wisconsin sued for return of traditional fishing rights, hundreds of whites gathered on different occasions to protest. During the 1987 fishing season, 12 Ojibway spearers were trapped on a small point of land by about 500 whites, who hurled rocks and racial insults and blocked escape until a tactical squad arrived and dispersed the mob. In the spring of 1989, several anti-Indian organizations with such names as Protect Americans' Rights and Resources and Stop Treaty Abuses organized against Ojibway fishermen, throwing rocks, shooting ball bearings from high-powered slingshots, shouting racist vulgarities, and taking to the water to swamp the Indians' boats. Over 200 of the members of these anti-Indian organizations were arrested during a 12-day span. It is not readily apparent why the return of Ojibway fishing rights so angered whites. Did they feel threatened? One Native American writer stated:

> It seems to enrage white people whenever Indians manage to hold onto any vestige of their land, their heritage, their rights. The racist resentment unleashed in northern Wisconsin is never far from the surface in areas with an Indian presence. The thin veneer of civilization is easily stripped away. (Harjo, 1989:25)

For racial minorities negative living conditions can encourage violence. In a study conducted in Baltimore, Taylor and Covington (1990) found that murder and assault rates rose rapidly in largely black neighborhoods in which rapid growth of poverty indicated that residents' quality of life was declining.

James W. Balkwell provided consistent findings. In research done in 150 urban areas each containing 50,000 or more inhabitants, Balkwell (1990) learned that what he called "ethnic inequality" was the social factor best predicting the homicide rate. Balkwell obtained income data from five ethnic categories—non-Hispanic whites; African Americans; Native Americans, Eskimos, or Aleuts; Asian Americans; and Hispanic Americans. He found that the greater the proportion of poor racial minority-group members, the higher the homicide rate. Balkwell suspected that a version of the frustration-aggression theory applied here: Frustrated and angered by restrictions for achieving economic success and unable to confront the true sources of their frustration, poor members of racial minorities sometimes lashed out at the people at hand, who served as scapegoats.

Native American women, in particular, have been victims of this pattern. Evidence from a regional psychiatric center for women serving a five-state area in the Southwest suggested that at least 80 percent of the female patients had been victims of sexual assault, with a substantial number having suffered gang rape. Deprived of respect and self-respect in a world where they were systematically stripped of their traditional culture, Indian men were taught that emulation of the white man was the route to follow. That emulation included the brutalization of women—an act conspicuously missing from their traditional cultures (Allen, 1995).

Journalist and former gang member Nathan McCall experienced a similarly deprived upbringing. Growing up in a working-class, African American neighborhood, he and his friends knew that in the wider society, they had little or no respect. For that reason, McCall argued, the young blacks he knew "viciously protected what little morsels of self-respect they thought they had left" (McCall, 1994:52). Seemingly petty issues could generate vicious, even deadly fights if one of the participants felt that his self-respect had been challenged. Furthermore McCall and his friends often committed gang rape, with these violent acts helping to create cohesion in their gang (McCall, 1994:39–49).

Nonetheless the single dominant factor linked to violence is economic condition, and that linkage also occurs with violent crime. Research based on arrest rates in New York City found that black males and females had higher arrest rates for homicide, robbery, assault, and burglary than both their white and Hispanic counterparts. The investigators concluded that backgrounds featuring poor schools, a lack of legitimate job opportunities, and weak community organizations pushed young black men and women away from the mainstream job world and pulled them toward the criminal underworld, where violence is widespread. While many studies have analyzed how black males' disadvantaged status has promoted their disproportionate involvement in violent crime, little attention has been paid to the fact that a comparable pattern has developed for young black females (Sommers and Baskin, 1992).

Examining the 26 cases of youths awaiting trial for murder in May 1994 in New York City, a journalist found the following pattern:

- That they are minority-group members, with 21 of 26 black teenage boys. In their minority status, these young people have faced the debilitating effects of institutional racism in such areas as education, work, and housing.
- That 21 of 26 lived with a single parent, aunt, or grandmother, half of whom were employed. While conclusions suggesting that young people who kill invariably grow up in a welfare-dependent, drug-abusing underclass are simplified, these youths' family bonds and supervision tended to be weak. As a result the children tended to skip school and spent most of their time hanging out on the street.
- That handguns, particularly semiautomatic weapons, were readily available and were used in 20 of the murders. Guyce Hayes said he bought a .32-caliber handgun from a neighborhood crack addict for $40 when he was 14 years old. He explained, "I just bought it to be buying it because I had the money at the time" (quoted in Dugger, 1994:B6). A year later he used it to shoot two men.
- That the killings occurred in the course of robberies and disputes and that frequently the shooter was high at the time.

A black police officer working in inner-city Chicago commented on children's frequent exposure to violence and death in a world where drug dealers' fight for control of turf is the dominant cause of violent activity. He said:

> The little children growing up in in our inner city have experienced more violence than many of our veterans of wars. Working in the projects, I can recall the children as somebody was shot on a playing field. By the time the ambulance arrived, there are all these children looking at a dying person. It's a hot day, everybody out playing. You see these little kids just looking. Most Americans never experience this. I didn't until I was an adult. It's just so ordinary, so everyday with them, seeing death. (Terkel, 1992:253)

The officer went on to explain that several years earlier in a nearby upper-middle-class suburb a disturbed woman killed several school children. For the surviving children, the school provided extensive psychiatric counseling. For inner-city children, in contrast, no psychiatric care is available to respond to their frequent encounters with violence. They simply must deal with such harsh realities the best they can.

The following situation involves a highly publicized incident of racial violence.

A Killing in Bensonhurst

On the evening of August 23, 1989, four young black men came to an all-white neighborhood in Bensonhurst, a section of Brooklyn, to sell a used car. Unknown to these four men, they were watched by a group of young white men carrying baseball bats and, in one case, a .32-caliber handgun. A witness said that the whites approached the African Americans, and one suggested that they club them. No, they should kill one of them, another said. A moment later one of the young white men shot Yusuf K. Hawkins twice in the chest, and he died.

Within a few days, the public learned about circumstances behind the killing. Bensonhurst is a closed, protected world primarily inhabited by Italian immigrants. As one resident said, "This neighborhood, it's like a family." Like a family, neighbors knew one another's problems and often became involved in one another's disputes and feuds.

An 18-year-old woman named Gina Feliciano was the former girlfriend of 19-year-old Keith Mondello. She was no longer interested in him and emphasized her disinterest by telling him that she was going to bring a bunch of her African American and Puerto Rican friends to the neighborhood for a party. Feelings against Feliciano were already negative because she violated neighborhood norms by dating blacks and dark-skinned Puerto Ricans. Her statement served as a threat, and when Hawkins and his friends showed up, they were mistaken for Feliciano's friends.

The issue of threat, that has been so prominent in this section and in the discussion of the criminal-justice system, seems relevant here. Residents of Bensonhurst felt a strong sense of threat from black outsiders, and they endorsed norms consistent with that sense of threat, norms invoking a sense of caste: One should date and associate only with "one's own kind." Gina Feliciano violated this norm by dating members of racial minorities. She further betrayed her own people by threatening to bring in minority-group members to her own neighborhood. Sociologist Gerry Krase, who has studied Bensonhurst, indicated that residents' sense of threat from blacks produced the feeling "that they have to defend the family, the neighborhood against incursion" (Kifner, 1989:B4).

Comments from Bensonhurst residents were consistent with this theme. Many residents expressed the idea that the killing "was being blown out of proportion"—that African Americans simply entering their neighborhood represented a physical threat even though Gina had never suggested that her friends would be coming in to engage in violence. Carolyn Scalici, a young woman who was interviewed leaning against the candy store where the youths charged in the killing regularly gathered, said, "Keith was in trouble and his friends came to help. The same thing would have happened if it was white guys came in. He was defending himself." One young woman provided an interesting view of racism. In a contradictory statement, she declared, "This wasn't racial and I've never been racial in my life. But white people should stick together for ourselves" (Kifner, 1989:B4).

The Bensonhurst killing shows how savage racial confrontations can become when people perceive a sense of threat. In this case an isolated, racist white group felt threatened by blacks and killed an innocent black man, who was viewed as a threatening outsider.

While most white Americans are less isolated than Bensonhurst residents, it appears that the sense of racial threat found in that community thrives widely.

REFERENCES

Allen, Paula Gunn. 1995. "Angry Women Are Building: Issues and Struggles Facing American Indian Women Today," pp. 32–36 in Margaret L. Andersen and Patricia Hill Collins (eds.), *Race, Class, and Gender: An Anthology.* Belmont, CA: Wadsworth. Second edition.

Awanohara, Susumu. 1993. "Spicier Melting Pot," pp. 112–117 in John A. Kromkowski (ed.), *Race and Ethnic Relations 93/94.* Guilford, CT: Duskin Publishing Group. Third edition.

Balkwell, James W. 1990. "Ethnic Inequality and the Rate of Homicide." *Social Forces* 69 (September):53–70.

Baron, Harold M. 1968. "Black Powerlessness in Chicago." *Trans-Action* 6 (November):27–35.

Blumstein, Alfred. 1982. "On the Racial Disproportionality of United States' Prison Populations." *Journal of Criminal Law and Criminology* 73 (fall):1259–1281.

Branch, Taylor. 1988. *Parting the Waters: America in the King Years, 1954–1963.* New York: Simon and Schuster.

Bridges, George S., and Robert D. Crutchfield. 1988. "Law, Social Standing and Racial Disparities in Imprisonment." *Social Forces* 66 (March):699–724.

Brown, Richard Maxwell. 1979. "Historical Patterns of American Violence," pp. 49–76 in Hugh Davis Graham and Ted Robert Gurr (eds.), *Violence in America: Historical & Comparative Perspectives*. Beverly Hills, CA: Sage. Publications. Revised edition.

Browning, Rufus P., Dale Rogers Marshall, and David H. Tabb. 1986. "Protest Is Not Enough: A Theory of Political Incorporation." *PS* 19 (summer):576–581.

Churchill, Ward. 1990. "The Black Hills Are Not for Sale: A Summary of the Lakota Struggle for the 1868 Treaty Territory." *Journal of Ethnic Studies* (spring):127–142.

Cornacchia, Eugene J., and Dale C. Nelson. 1992. "Historical Differences in the Political Experiences of American Blacks and White Ethics." *Ethnic and Racial Studies* 15 (January):102–124.

Daniels, Roger. 1988. *Asian Americans: Chinese and Japanese in the United States since 1850*. Seattle: University of Washington Press.

Dollard, John. 1937. *Caste & Class in a Southern Town*. New Haven: Yale University Press.

Donovan, Beth. 1993. "Black Caucus: PAC Funds a Must for Minorities." *Congressional Quarterly Weekly Report* 51 (September 25):2523–2526.

Dugger, Celia W. 1994. "Youthful, Impressionable and Accused of Murder." *New York Times* (May 17):A1+.

Ekland-Olson, Sheldon. 1988. "Structured Discretion, Racial Bias, and the Death Penalty: The First Decade after *Furman* in Texas." *Social Science Quarterly* 69 (December):853–873.

Fagan, Jeffrey, Ellen Slaughter, and Eliot Hartstone. 1987. "Blind Justice? The Impact of Race on the Juvenile Process." *Crime & Delinquency* 33 (April):224–258.

Feagin, Joe R., and Clairece Booher Feagin. 1993. *Racial and Ethnic Relations*. Englewood Cliffs, NJ: Prentice-Hall. Fourth edition.

Gray, Jerry. 1991. "Panel Says Courts Are 'Infested with Racism.'" *New York Times* (June 5):B1+.

Gutiérrez, Ramon A. 1993. "Community, Patriarchy, and Individualism: The Politics of Chicano History and the Dream of Equality." *American Quarterly* 45 (March):44–72.

Hacker, Andrew. 1988. "Black Crime, White Racism." *New York Review of Books* 35 (March 3):36–41.

Hacker, Andrew. 1992. *Two Nations: Black and White, Separate, Hostile, Unequal*. New York: Charles Scribner's Sons.

Hagan, William T. 1986. "Tribalism Rejuvenated: The Native American since the Era of Termination," pp. 295–304 in Roger L. Nichols (ed.), *The American Indian: Past and Present*. New York: Alfred A. Knopf. Third edition.

Harjo, Suzanne Shown. 1989. "Rights of Spring: Racism in Wisconsin." *Daybreak* 3 (spring):24–25.

Hawkins, Darnell F. 1987. "Beyond Anomalies: Rethinking the Conflict Perspective on Race and Criminal Punishment." *Social Forces* 65 (March):719–745.

Hero, Rodney E., and Kathleen M. Beatty. 1989. "The Elections of Federico Pena as Mayor of Denver: Analysis and Implications." *Social Science Quarterly* 70 (June):300–310.

Holmes, Steven A. 1994a. "U.S. Ordered to Tell How It Decides to Seek Executions." *New York Times* (May 11):A18.

Holmes, Steven A. 1994b. "Uncharted Change at the N.A.A.C.P." *New York Times* (May 16):6.

Holmes, Steven A. 1994c. "N.A.A.C.P. Leader Ousted by Board, Hints He Will Sue." *New York Times* (August 22):A1+.

Huizinga, David, and Delbert S. Elliott. 1987. "Juvenile Offenders: Prevalence, Offender Incidence, and Arrest Rates by Race." *Crime & Delinquency* 33 (April):206–223.

Jaynes, Gerald David, and Robin M. Williams, Jr. (eds.). 1989. *A Common Destiny: Blacks and American Society.* Washington, DC: National Academy Press.

Jehl, Douglas. 1994. "Clinton and Indians Meet to Underline New Stature." *New York Times* (April 30):10.

Johnson, Kirk. 1989. "Racism and the Young: Some See a Rising Tide." *New York Times* (August 27):32.

Johnson, Kirk. 1994. "Pequots Invest Casino Wealth in a New Game: Party Politics." *New York Times* (August 30):A1+.

Keil, Thomas J. 1985. "Capital, Labor, and the Klan: A Case Study in the Deterioration of Local Racial Relationships." *Phylon* 46 (winter):341–352.

Keil, Thomas J., and Gennaro F. Vito. 1989. "Race, Homicide Severity, and Application of the Death Penalty: A Consideration of the Barnett Scale." *Criminology* 27 (August):511–531.

Kifner, John. 1989. "Bensonhurst: A Tough Code in Defense of a Closed World." *New York Times* (September 1):A1+.

Kitano, Harry H. L., and Roger Daniels. 1988. *Asian Americans: Emerging Minorities.* Englewood-Cliffs, NJ: Prentice-Hall.

Kramer, John, and Darrell Steffensmeir. 1993. "Race and Imprisonment Decisions." *Sociological Quarterly* 34 (May):357–376.

LaFree, Gary. 1980. "The Effect of Sexual Stratification by Race on Official Reactions to Rape." *American Sociological Review* 45 (October):842–854.

Langan, Patrick A. 1985. "Racism on Trial: New Evidence to Explain the Racial Composition of Prisons in the United States." *Criminology* 76 (fall):666–683.

Lawrence, Ken. 1994. "Klansmen, Nazis, and Skinheads: Vigilante Repression," pp. 21–37 in Richard G. Majors and Jacob U. Gordon (eds.), *The American Black Male: His Present Status and His Future.* Chicago: Nelson-Hall Publishers.

Liska, Allen E., Mitchell B. Chamlin, and Mark D. Reed. 1985. "Testing the Economic Production and Conflict Models of Crime Control." *Social Forces* 64 (September):119–138.

Longoria, Thomas, Jr., Robert D. Wrinkle, and J. L. Polinard. 1990. "Mexican American Voter Registration." *Social Science Quarterly* 71 (June):356–361.

Maharidge, Dale. 1993. "Did 1992 Herald the Dawn of Latino Political Power?" *California Journal* 24 (January):15–18.

Mann, Coramae Richey. 1994. "The Reality of a Racist Criminal Justice System," pp. 249–253 in Richard C. Monk (ed.), *Taking Sides: Clashing Views of Controversial Issues in Race and Ethnicity.* Guilford, CT: Dushkin Publishing Company.

Marquez, Benjamin. 1989. "The Politics of Race and Assimilation: The League of United Latin American Citizens, 1929–40." *Western Political Quarterly* 42 (June):355–375.

Mauer, Marc. 1994. "A Generation behind Bars: Black Males and the Criminal Justice System," pp. 81–93 in Richard G. Majors and Jacob U. Gordon (eds.), *The American Black Male: His Present Status and His Future*. Chicago: Nelson-Hall Publishers.

McCall, Nathan. 1994. *Makes Me Wanna Holler: A Young Black Man in America*. New York: Random House.

Mydans, Seth. 1991. "Videotape of Beating by Officers Puts Full Glare on Brutality Issue." *New York Times* (March 18):A1+.

Mydans, Seth. 1994. "A Vietnamese American Becomes a Political First." *Migration World Review* 21 (September/October):44.

New York Times. 1994. "Guilty Verdict in Slaying Linked to Racial Hatred." (September 19):A12.

Pareles, Jon. 1989. "There's a New Sound in Pop Music: Bigotry." *New York Times* (September 10) Sec. 2, p. 1+.

Reiman, Jeffrey. 1994. "A Crime by Any Other Name," pp. 294–302 in Kurt Finsterbusch and George McKenna (eds.), *Taking Sides: Clashing Views on Controversial Social Issues*. Guilford, CT: Dushkin Publishing Group. Eighth edition.

Seltzer, Rick, and Grace M. Lopes. 1986. "The Ku Klux Klan: Reasons for Support or Opposition among White Respondents." *Journal of Black Studies* 17 (September):91–109.

Skerry, Peter. 1994. "Not Much Cooking: Why the Voting Rights Act Is Not Empowering Mexican Americans," pp. 107–109 in John A. Kromkowski (ed.), *Race and Ethnic Relations 94/95*. Guilford, CT: Dushkin Publishing Group. Fourth edition.

Sommers, Ira, and Deborah Baskin. 1992. "Sex, Race, Age, and Violent Offending." *Violence and Victims* 7 (fall):191–201.

Swain, Johnnie Dee, Jr. 1993. "Black Mayors: Urban Decline and the Underclass." *Journal of Black Studies* 24 (September):16–28.

Swigert, Victoria, and Ronald A. Farrell. 1977. "Normal Homicides and the Law." *American Sociological Review* 42 (February):16–32.

Taylor, Ralph B., and Jeanette Covington. 1990. "Ecological Change, Changes in Violence, and Risk Prediction." *Journal of Interpersonal Violence* 5 (June):164–175.

Terkel, Studs. 1992. *Race: How Blacks & Whites Feel about the American Obsession*. New York: New Press.

Terkildsen, Nayda. 1993. "When White Voters Evaluate Black Candidates: The Processing Implications of Candidate Skin Color, Prejudice, and Self-Monitoring." *American Journal of Political Science* 37 (November):1032–1053.

Terry, Don. 1994. "Chicago Project in Furor about Guns and the Law." *New York Times* (April 8):A12.

Thomson, Randall J., and Matthew T. Zingraff. 1981. "Detecting Sentence Disparity: Some Problems and Evidence." *American Journal of Sociology* 86 (January):869–880.

U.S. Bureau of the Census. 1989. *Statistical Abstract of the United States: 1989*. Washington, DC: U.S. Government Printing Office. 109th edition.

U.S. Bureau of the Census. 1993. *Statistical Abstract of the United States: 1993*. Washington, DC: U.S. Government Printing Office. 113th edition.

U.S. Department of Justice. 1990. *Correctional Populations in the United States, 1990*. Washington, DC: U.S. Government Printing Office.

Vanderleeuw, James M. 1990. "A City in Transition: The Impact of Changing Racial Composition on Voting Behavior." *Social Science Quarterly* 71 (June):326–338.

Waegel, William B. 1984. "How the Police Justify the Use of Deadly Force." *Social Problems* 32 (December):144–155.

Wager, Linda. 1993. "Reclaiming Tribal Lands," pp. 74–75 in John A. Kromkowski (ed.), *Race and Ethnic Relations 93/94.* Guilford, CT: Dushkin Publishing Group. Third edition.

Wong, Morrison G. 1994. "Rise in Anti-Asian Activities in the United States," pp. 417–422 in *Sociological Footprints.* Belmont, CA: Wadsworth. Sixth edition.

Yu, Jiang, and Allen E. Liska. 1993. "The Certainty of Punishment: A Reference Group Effect and Its Functional Form." *Criminology* 31 (August):447–464.

Zatz, Marjorie S. 1987. "The Changing Forms of Racial/Ethnic Differences in Sentencing." *Journal of Research in Crime and Delinquency* 24:69–72.

Chapter
5

Knowing Your Place: Work and Housing

On January 13, 1994, federal marshals and the police kept watch as four black families moved into an all-white housing project called Vidor Village in the Texas town of Vidor. These families were the first African Americans to live in Vidor in more than 60 years.

This occasion was the first time since the mid-1960s that the federal government had used an armed escort to enforce the integration of a housing project. In 1993 four African American families had moved out after enduring what they reported to be unrelenting hostility from some whites. One of the former black residents said that whites often directed racial epithets at her, and another reported that he simply got tired wondering what abuse he would hear from a passing car. Some testimonies obtained by a reporter indicated that whites from outside the project inflicted the worst abuse. In fact, when the last black resident moved out in September 1993, it was a white-supremacist group from Mississippi called the

Nationalist Movement that led a "Victory in Vidor" parade down the city's main street.

Early in 1993 more than 1,300 blacks were on a waiting list to enter Vidor Village, but after the intimidation against the first set of black families, only the four families that entered in January 1994 remained.

Among white residents in Vidor Village, the reaction to integration varied. Several told a reporter that they were tired of portrayals of Vidor as a bigoted town and that they wanted integration to work. Ilene Pierce indicated that she had gone over to welcome one of the new families. Pierce said that they "all seemed like anybody else, trying to make a living and getting on with their lives and raising children" (Verhover, 1994:A20). In contrast, a man who declined to give his name stated that integration was unfortunate but that "[t]here isn't anything we can do about it anyway. This is the future. This is the way the government says it's going to be" (Verhover, 1994:A20).

The internal-colonialist perspective fits all too effectively here—the idea of racial minorities' restricted freedom of movement. Certainly minority-group members' limited right to choose where they live is a clear case in point. In the discussion of housing, we see that this principle applies, albeit usually more subtly than in the Vidor Village situation.

In the first portion of the chapter, the relevance of internal colonialism is also apparent. As we saw in the opening chapter, one of the theory's basic ideas is the colonial-labor principle, which indicates that racial minorities must serve white controllers' interests and needs. We consider its relevance in the upcoming discussion of work.

RACIAL MINORITIES' WORK WORLD

At the end of the nineteenth century, Horatio Alger wrote a series of best-selling novels about hard-working, clean-living boys whose perseverance paid off. Their virtuous efforts produced a rise from poverty and obscurity to wealth and fame. Horatio Alger never bothered to emphasize that all his young heroes were white. For racial minorities of that era, the road to economic and social success was virtually nonexistent.

Before World War II, African Americans still largely lived in the rural South. With the outbreak of war, they started moving to both southern and northern cities, where wartime industrial jobs paid much higher wages than they had previously received. The labor-force transformation continued after the war, as we see examining job categories in which African American men and women made their statistically largest shifts.

In 1939, 41 percent of black men were farmers or farm workers; by 1984 the figure had dropped sharply to 5 percent. Meanwhile the proportion in clerical and sales, machine operation, and crafts rose from 19 to nearly 52 percent. During that period the proportion of women providing domestic service shifted from 60 to 6 percent while clerical and sales, machine operation, and crafts went from less than 8 to nearly 48 percent.

The transition from rural to urban living also gave African Americans increasing access to American consumer technology—inside plumbing, electricity, automobiles, refrigerators, telephones, radios, and eventually television. They also benefitted from improved medical care, especially in the late 1960s after the establishment of government-subsidized health care for the poor (Medicaid) and for the elderly (Medicare).

Overall, however, African Americans' economic advancement in the past half-century has been at best mixed. Through the 1970s and the 1980s, blacks' wages rose relative to whites, but African Americans experienced higher unemployment rates than whites, with the least educated workers most adversely affected. Poverty among African Americans has become increasingly evident. For instance, keeping the dollar's buying power at the 1984 level, we find that in 1984 about 40 percent of black men earned less than $10,000, up from 25 percent in 1969. For white men the respective percentages were 20 and 10 (Jaynes and Williams, 1989: 272–275).

Why have African Americans historically had lower incomes than whites? Differences of opinion exist. Wacquant and Wilson concluded that the dominant factors are the flight of manufacturing jobs out of northern and midwestern cities and the general economic shift toward service industries and occupations. When these conditions occur, they suggested, "even mild forms of racial discrimination—mild by historical standards—have a bigger impact on those at the bottom of the American class order" (Wacquant and Wilson, 1989:11). For these observers poor blacks' poverty is largely the result of impersonal, color-blind factors, primarily affecting low-income people.

Many scholars more strongly emphasize the impact of racism, offering recent evidence that racial discrimination has been a significant factor affecting African Americans at all income levels: limiting them in management (Morrison and Von Glinow, 1990; Larwood, Szwajkowski, and Rose, 1988) and male-dominated professions (Sokoloff, 1988); pushing them into low-skill as opposed to high-skill work (Kaufman, 1986); holding down salary levels (Geschwender and Carroll-Seguin, 1990; Killian, 1990; Thomas, 1993; Tomaskovic-Devey, 1993) and advancement from low-paying jobs (Beauregard, 1990; Pomer, 1986); and increasing the likelihood of unemployment or underemployment (Burstein and Pitchford, 1990; Farley, 1987; Johnson, 1990; Killian, 1990; Lichter, 1988; Tigges and Tootle, 1993).

Furthermore as we noted in Chapter 3, racial segregation has played a major role in the creation of a black underclass. Forced to live in restricted urban areas, poor African Americans find their residential districts particularly hard hit by such economic downturns as the one occurring in the early 1970s, especially when segregation policies make it likely or inevitable that large numbers of poor blacks from other districts are funnelled into them. Businesses leave; vital services, including medical care and schooling deteriorate, and crime and violence sharply increase (Massey, 1990). These are prime conditions fostering the **vicious cycle of poverty**—a pattern in which parents' minimal income significantly limits children's educational and occupational pursuits, thereby keeping them locked into the same low economic status. It is being argued here that in modern times, a poor minority member's residential area contributes significantly to the perpetuation of poverty.

Table 5.1   MINORITY GROUPS' POVERTY[1]

Percentage of Members of Different Racial Groups below the Poverty Level:
1991 (percent)

Puerto Ricans	40.6%
African Americans	31.9
American Indians	30.9
Mexican Americans	28.1
Asian Americans	12.2
Whites	10.7

Percentage of Black and White Individuals' Poverty: 1959 to 1992 (percent)

	Blacks	Whites
1959	55.1%	18.1%
1966	41.8	12.2
1970	33.5	9.9
1975	31.3	9.7
1980	32.5	10.2
1985	31.3	11.4
1990	30.6	10.0
1992	32.7	11.3

[1]The poverty index, which is updated each year, is an estimate of the money necessary to purchase basic consumer products and services. Individuals falling below the poverty line simply possess insufficient funds to make these purchases.

Note: While poverty has been an unrelenting American problem, data in this table make it clear that it has been a consistently greater threat to blacks than to whites.

Sources: U.S. Bureau of the Census, *Current Population Reports,* "Characteristics of the Population Below the Poverty Level: 1980," Table 38; U.S. Bureau of the Census. *Statistical Abstract of the United States: 1992,* No. 41; U.S. Bureau of the Census, *Statistical Abstract of the United States: 1992,* No. 42 and No. 53.

Given these conditions it is not surprising that in 1992 the proportion of African Americans living below the poverty level was nearly three times greater than the white proportion—32.7 percent compared to 11.3 percent (U.S. Bureau of the Census, *Statistical Abstract of the United States: 1993,* No. 49). Table 5.1 provides more information on racial minorites' poverty.

Research has also indicated that housing segregation affects middle-class blacks' job prospects. Often prevented from living in primarily white suburbs, which have become prominent sites for retail and service-trade industries in the last couple of decades (Darden, 1990; Schneider and Phelan, 1990), middle-class African Americans often have much less immediate physical access to good-paying jobs than whites.

Like African Americans other racial minorities have historically suffered job discrimination. For instance, during the 1950s and 1960s, increasing numbers of Japanese and Chinese Americans graduated from college and obtained jobs outside their ethnic locales, but they tended to be denied supervisory and higher administrative positions. The most formidable barrier to their advancement seemed to be white employers' reluctance to put Asian Americans into positions where they could hire and fire whites (Daniels, 1988:315–316).

To many white Americans, Asian Americans' occupational success is impressive, and, in fact, the success image has often become the dominant element in modern whites' stereotype of Asian Americans. Like any stereotype, however, this one provides a disservice for the group in point. Asian Americans' success image often overshadows significant amounts of underemployment, poverty among the elderly, mental illness, divorce and family disorganization, and juvenile delinquency even in the most accomplished Asian American groups. Some recently arrived Asian Americans, especially those from the Philippines, Vietnam, and Cambodia, tend to arrive poor and, in the case of the Vietnamese and Cambodians, carrying the traumatic psychological burdens produced by extensive exposure to warfare. Because of the simplistic success image, however, government agencies, educational institutions, and private corporations have been less likely to address the often pressing problems among Asian Americans than among other racial minorities (Chua-eoan, 1993; Crystal, 1989; Hurh and Kim, 1989).

Historically Mexican Americans have also suffered job discrimination, with workers in farming, oil, mining, and manufacturing jobs often classified as "nonwhites" and systematically paid less than their white counterparts. Many current employers have selectively hired illegal Chicano immigrants, who could be forced to accept subminimum wages and oppressive working conditions to avoid being turned over to government authorities. Studies conducted primarily on Mexican Americans living in the southwestern states indicated that they are more likely to be successful occupationally if they speak English, live in areas where they represent a substantial proportion of the population, and have elected representatives in local government (Mladenka, 1989; Stolzenberg, 1990).

Those without these attributes often find themselves at the mercy of the internal-colonialist system. In 1994 California passed Proposition 187, a referendum which denied education and health services to illegal migrants and their families. Still desperately needing work, impoverished Mexicans continued to arrive in the state, providing somewhere between about one-third and two-fifths of workers tending and harvesting the fields of lettuce, broccoli, mustard greens, grapes, and other crops. For growers, who have always given their illegal workers below-minimum wages, the steadily increasing pool of Mexican workers has made it possible to pay their employees about 15 percent less than a decade ago, thus fattening their profits (Chavez, 1994).

Research has indicated that besides blacks, Puerto Ricans are the only major racial group suffering racial segregation so severe that they are locked into residential areas that have been steadily deteriorating since the advent of the 1970s economic downturn (Massey and Eggers, 1990). In other words besides blacks, Puerto Ricans have been the only other major racial group in which an underclass has been rapidly expanding. About two-fifths of the Puerto Rican population in the United States—40.6 percent in 1991—falls below the poverty line (U.S. Bureau of the Census, *Statistical Abstract of the United States: 1990*, No. 53).

For Puerto Ricans institutional racism has also been a common barrier. In New York City, for example, applicants for many low-level service jobs such as trash collection have been required to take tests written in English that are not job-related and that, besides, could be translated easily into Spanish. Another illustration of institutional racism is that Puerto Ricans, who tend to be smaller than average American citizens, find that height and weight requirements for police and fire-department jobs can rule them ineligible (Feagin and Feagin, 1993:306).

Research on Puerto Rican women in the New York City area indicated that respondents with 11 or more years of formal education, good ability to speak English, no children under five, and previous work experience were considerably more likely to be employed than women without all or most of these characteristics. A related pattern applied to higher-level positions. Puerto Rican women with advanced educational credentials (some college credits or college graduation), English-language proficiency, and delayed childbearing (until the middle or late 20s) were more likely to be in white-collar positions than those without these qualities. About 30 percent of the women studied lacked the traits making employment likely, and as education and English-language skills become increasingly required for employment, such women's chances of getting a job will grow even more remote (Falcon, Gurak, and Powers, 1990; Madamba and De Jong, 1994).

A number of state and national studies indicated that Native Americans frequently suffer discrimination in employment in towns located near reservations. Indians' work difficulties have been compounded by limited amounts of formal education and on reservations by the fact that a surplus of potential workers has tended to keep wages for such positions as laborer, truck driver, and typist scarcely half what they would be off the reservation (Olson and Wilson, 1984: 186–187).

Do most Americans appreciate the conditions just discussed? When asked in July 1989 which is more often to blame if a person is poor—lack of effort or circumstances—38 percent of a national sample indicated lack of effort, 42 percent opted for circumstances, 17 percent selected both, and 3 percent had no opinion. For whites, 39 percent chose lack of effort compared to 32 percent for members of racial minorities; among whites, 41 percent selected circumstances while 48 percent of racial-minority members chose that option (Gallup, 1989). Clearly whites were more inclined than minority members to focus on individuals' failure and hold them responsible—"blame the victim" in the phrase introduced in Chapter 3—while members of racial minorities were more likely to take a sociological perspective, focusing on conditions promoting poverty in people's lives. Why the difference? While the survey did not examine this issue, it seems probable that racial minorities' more intimate contact with poverty, and, perhaps in particular, their knowledge of the role racism plays, encourage them to be aware of social conditions producing poverty.

Abundant evidence suggests that racism affects racial minorities in the economy. One way to examine the situation systematically is to analyze employment as a process involving three phases.

RACIAL MINORITIES AND THE EMPLOYMENT PROCESS

When a national survey team asked Americans whether or not blacks in their community have as good a chance as whites to receive any job for which they are qualified, seven out of ten (70 percent) agreed that they did. Respondents' race was a significant factor. Compared to 73 percent of whites, only 43 percent of blacks replied affirmatively (Gallup and Hugick, 1990).

At each stage of racial minorities' work experience, evidence of racism is prevalent. We examine the job-candidate stage, the job-screening stage, and the job-promotion stage. Then we consider black managers' experience.

Job-Candidate Stage

Research has indicated that African Americans are excluded from entire job areas, especially well-paid positions requiring minimal education and experience. For instance, African Americans who seek jobs in large restaurants are usually kept out of such positions as waiter and cook that lead to promotion and supervisory roles. Instead they are pushed into low-paying, dead-end jobs—dishwasher and busboy. A 1985 study done in New York City found blacks were virtually unrepresented in 130 of 193 private-sector industries, and the few working in these industries were primarily in clerical positions (Steinberg, 1989:49). Individual racism helps produce this outcome, but social networks, rather the lack of such networks, also contribute significantly.

In a society where racial segregation permeates all major structures, members of different races are primarily involved in social networks—composed of friends, neighbors, colleagues, and other work-related associates—containing members of their own race. This situation has a significant impact on job applicants. At the job-candidate stage, there are fertile possibilities for institutional racism: Members of racial minorities are indirectly discriminated against because frequently they lack access to whites' social networks, which generally provide better leads and informal recommendations for jobs than their own.

When social networks are a chief means of job recruitment, minority members are more likely than whites to be denied employment or to receive low-paying jobs. For poor, young members of racial minorities, who live in residentially segregated areas, have limited schooling, and modest or no work histories, social networks helping to obtain employment are deficient (Jaynes and Williams, 1989: 320–321). For this reason alone, they are at a distinct disadvantage to other groups competing for jobs.

As the prestige and pay of jobs increase, use of social networks for locating candidates declines. For positions requiring college degrees, employers are much more likely to place advertisements in the local mass media than they do when hiring people for lower-level slots.

Nonetheless social networks are also used for higher-level jobs. In a study of 4,078 employers, when respondents indicated that they relied on social networks as a chief means of recruitment for college-degree jobs, their openings were more likely to be filled by whites than when they indicated limited reliance on these networks.

Besides determining whether individuals will be hired, access to social networks appears to affect job candidates' income. In the same investigation, black high-school graduates who used segregated networks averaged $5.69 per hour, those who did not use networks averaged $5.74 per hour, and, in contrast, those who had access to desegregated networks averaged $6.45 per hour (Braddock and McPartland, 1987).

Sometimes by choice and sometimes because of legal pressure, government agencies, most major companies, and many smaller businesses have initiated formal written policies to recruit minorities. These affirmative-action standards have produced major gains for African American job-seekers, with the percentage of blacks in the work force increasing by 50 percent between 1965 and 1990. For blacks and some other minority groups, however, there remains a long way to go. For instance, while blacks represent nearly 13 percent of the U.S. population, they represent only 5 percent of all professionals. Furthermore when economic hard times hit a company, the distinct danger exists that executives will either ignore or downplay their affirmative-action commitment (Gleckman et al., 1993).

Job-Screening Stage

When employers confront a pool of job candidates, they usually have certain desirable traits in mind. First, they are likely to set a minimum educational standard, and this practice represents institutional racism when it is irrelevant to on-the-job performance and yet disproportionately eliminates racial minorities, whose members are on the whole less educated than whites. A study of equal-employment-opportunity cases brought to federal appellate court showed that employers were usually unable to demonstrate that educational credentials and test scores related to productivity (Burstein and Pitchford, 1990).

Screening candidates also involves an evaluation of individuals, and individual racism can appear at this time. In some job categories, minorities still are largely screened out. Political scientist Andrew Hacker suggested that perhaps the reason why blacks have largely been excluded as dental hygienists is that whites are probably unwilling to accept African Americans' fingers in their mouths (Hacker, 1992: 110).

One study found that many companies frequently eliminated 30 to 40 percent of applicants by a screening interview. In such situations employers did not need to make direct reference to race, even among themselves. They could discuss impressions of candidates' "intelligence," "appearance," "vigor," and "self-confidence," with such references intentionally or perhaps unintentionally playing into interviewers' racial stereotypes (Lopez, 1976).

In the previously cited study of 4,078 employers, investigators found that whites were more likely to be chosen for jobs when employers valued such traits as quick learning, advanced reading skill, math excellence, and good judgment. This trend was most apparent for jobs requiring high-school certificates and less though still evident for jobs needing some college or a college degree (Braddock and McPartland, 1987). With such stereotypes prevalent, blacks seeking jobs which possess a distinct intellectual component have little hope of getting them unless they are fully qualified or overqualified educationally while for whites educational criteria might be applied less stringently.

It is sobering to learn that when researchers asked members of the college class of 1957 from three Ivy League colleges, which have traditionally supplied about two-fifths of America's business elite, whether they agreed with the conclusion that blacks are as intelligent as whites, just 36 percent of the Princeton class, 47 percent at Yale, and 55 percent at Harvard agreed (Jones, 1986:88). If a similar mind set exists throughout the business world, it is hardly surprising that blacks face widespread job discrimination.

For Asian Americans there is underrepresentation in such occupations as journalism, law, and social sciences as well as administrative positions in management. When interviewed about this pattern, Asian American job candidates say that they tend to avoid applying for positions requiring language skills and extensive person-to-person contact because they believe white employers feel they will only succeed in positions requiring technical knowledge (Chun, 1993). Whether or not this self-screening process reflects prospective employers' perception, its operation is widespread.

At the screening stage, Asian American women are likely to encounter stereotypes that can block their access to job opportunities. The most prominent pair of stereotypes are that Asian American women have manual dexterity along with endurance for routines and thus are well suited for assembly-line work; and that they are diligent, loyal, and attentive to detail and thus makes good subordinates in clerical and service work but are ill-suited to function as supervisors (Lai, 1995).

Even over the telephone, employers sometimes screen out minority candidates. In an experimental study in which white and Hispanic pairs of applications responded to randomly sampled job vacancies listed in the newspapers and employment agencies in Washington, D.C., and its surrounding suburbs, discrimination occurred. Although the qualifications provided were similar between the white and Hispanic applicants, the latter group, whose members displayed a slight Spanish accent and Spanish surnames, received a less favorable response in 22.4 percent of the calls; in particular, the Hispanic applicants were less likely to be asked to appear for a job interview (Bendick, Jackson, Reinoso, and Hodges, 1993).

Another study produced a consistent result, discovering that Mexican Americans with distinct accents consistently earned less money than Mexican Americans without foreign accents—that in fact the accent "penalty" was distinctly greater for Mexican Americans than either German Americans or Italian Americans; the reason, the researchers suspected, was that employers might be particulary suspicious that heavily accented Mexican Americans were illegal aliens who could be forced to work for low wages (Davila, Bohara, and Saenz, 1993).

Job-Promotion Stage

The national study of 4,078 employers indicated that for promotion African Americans' chances were closer to whites' if candidates came from within instead of outside an organization. Nonetheless blacks were not as likely to be promoted as whites when only internal candidates were involved; the researchers learned that within organizations when workers' qualifications were held constant, blacks' salaries tended to be distinctly lower than whites' (Braddock and McPartland, 1987:23).

On the job African Americans and members of other racial minorities tend to face "a triple jeopardy"—racial stereotyping, the solo role of being the only member of a racial minority at the work site, and the token role, where whites consider them inferior if they obtained their positions through affirmative action. The impact of these three factors is likely to affect blacks negatively when they apply for promotion (Pettigrew and Martin, 1987).

Individuals who are the only or nearly the only representatives of racial minorities in an organization frequently encounter stereotypes. If an African American employee does something that an observer can interpret negatively, such as speaking somewhat harshly to a colleague, then that behavior is more likely attributed to a basic deficiency in the person's character than in the case of a white person who acted similarly. In the latter instance, the white colleague would probably attribute the harsh statement to a situational factor, saying, "Oh, she's just having a bad day."

On the other hand, when minority workers perform effectively, stereotypes rationalize the situation. Of an employee belonging to a racial minority, white colleagues might say, "He works so hard because he has to compensate for his lack of intelligence." Or they might claim that this person's success was the result of favoritism from a boss sensitive to pressures to incorporate minority individuals in high positions.

The second element in the triple jeopardy is the solo role. As the only or almost only member of their own group, African Americans or members of other racial minorities are likely to experience unrealistic evaluation from whites who have had little or no previous contact with racial minorities. White workers often expect poor performances from African Americans. One solo black worker reported, "They were astonished to find that I could write a basic memo. Even the completion of an easy task brought surprised compliments" (Pettigrew and Martin, 1987:55). Sometimes minority solo employees find the opposite—that expectations are unrealistically high. In either case the situation is not useful for them. Considered different from whites, they are not evaluated realistically and thus do not receive substantive feedback that provides a helpful evaluation of their progress on the job.

The third factor is the token role. If fellow workers or supervisors feel that a member of a racial minority received a position because of affirmative action, then these people are likely to assume the individual is incompetent, only able to obtain the job when given unfair advantage because of race.

It appears likely that the triple jeopardy is a major reason why the greatest disparity in income between black and white males occurs between the ages of 30 and 50. A study using national samples of black and white men found that in the 1980s black men in their 30s and 40s obtained 86.6 and 86.7 percent, respectively, of white men's earnings—a smaller percentage than in both younger and older age categories. A similar pattern was apparent for each decade back to the 1930s. The researchers concluded that their data suggested support for the conclusion that discrimination against black men accumulated through the different stages of the work process. By the way, for black and white men in their 50 and 60s, income differences started to decline because white men were more inclined to move toward partial or total retirement, depending to a greater extent than blacks on their relatively greater amount of accumulated wealth (Thomas, Herring, and Horton, 1994).

It should not be surprising to learn that research has shown little movement of minorities into top executive positions. A national survey of senior executives found that during the 1980s African Americans increased their miniscule percentage of top corporate positions from 0.2 to 0.6 percent and Hispanics (three-quarters of whom are either Mexican American or Puerto Rican) expanded from 0.1 to 0.4 percent (Sklar, 1995). The barrier faced by minorities and women seeking to move into top management has sometimes been called a "glass ceiling"—so subtle that it is nearly invisible but also strong enough to block candidates from moving to the top rungs of the corporate ladder (Morrison and Von Glinow, 1990).

Perhaps no situation portrays racial minorities' special job pressures better than black managers' experiences.

Black Managers: The Dream in Jeopardy

As black managers move into the white corporate world, they must make major adjustments. Often they have come from very different backgrounds than their white colleagues. To be able to survive, they must learn norms governing behavior in what often feels like an alien world and make the necessary adjustments. Whites' stereotypes or discriminatory practices can complicate such adjustments.

Few if any people encounter business management as an easy, tension-free experience. All executives must work hard and produce tangible results that lead to increased company profits. If unsuccessful, they will not advance and might lose their jobs. This issue alone is a source of considerable stress to many executives, both black and white. We see, however, that blacks face additional stresses.

Because African Americans entering executive positions often have very different backgrounds from whites', they are frequently unsure about standards of conduct and feel nervous and confused about interracial relations. As the solo African American management trainee in a department with over 8,000 employees, Edward Jones faced such problems. In a detailed account of his opening months on the job, Jones indicated that he worked very hard and did everything he could imagine to receive good evaluations, and yet he was nearly fired, astonished to be told that he lacked tact and was constantly rocking the boat.

In his evaluation of this experience, Jones concluded that his style of relating to coworkers and bosses was sometimes inappropriate—that the world of white business required a low-key behavioral style with which he was unfamiliar.

But, according to Jones, there was another issue. He was convinced that his

peers and supervisors were unable to perceive me as being able to perform the job that the company hired me for. Their reaction to me was disbelief. I was out of the "place" normally filled by black people in the company, and since no black person had preceded me successfully, it was easy for my antagonists to believe I was inadequate. (Jones, 1973:114)

As the colonial-labor principle emphasizes, blacks have traditionally been assigned menial jobs, and Jones's placement in a management position opposed whites' expectations. White colleagues responded to the confusing situation by unleashing their racial stereotypes on their solo black manager.

Entering corporations, black managers often find that the unrelenting emphasis on making profits means that corporate leadership often fails to establish clear standards about racial issues. To survive and do well, African American executives usually try to conform, but to what standards, in fact, are they supposed to conform? Sometimes top leaders within a corporation try to pretend that race is not an issue, and so all employees, regardless of race, are expected to support such a position. Moreover some white managers become defensive if racism is ever mentioned. Jones wrote, "After all, it's un-American to be prejudiced, and who wants to be un-American? So white and black managers, fearful of confronting the issue, take part in a charade" (Jones, 1986:90). The result is that communications between African Americans and whites become highly strained.

The isolated, confusing circumstances in which black managers often find themselves are special problems when they seek promotion, which requires effective relations with coworkers and superiors. A black middle manager described a situation in which a black manager working for her demanded an overdue merit raise. Convinced that he deserved it, the middle manager gathered relevant documentation and went to the appraisal meeting. That meeting involved several white male colleagues who spoke without documentation of their respective candidates, voted down her nominee, and awarded merit raises to several of their own people. According to the black middle manager, a "buddy system" existed. She explained, "It turned out to be a matter of 'Joe, you did a favor for me last week, so I'll support you in getting your person in this week. You owe me one, old buddy'" (Jones, 1986:89). Within this system African Americans, who are new arrivals and widely considered "different" or inferior, are often victims of severe discrimination.

In business, high-level executives often become sponsors of younger subordinates, but a prominent white consultant told Edward Jones that white managers are usually uncomfortable sponsoring African Americans, fearing negative reactions from other whites (Jones, 1986:89). As a result, black executives often find themselves shunted into slots out of the corporate mainstream—into community relations, personnel, or anything to do with minorities. Furthermore many black executives claim that their superiors withhold more strategic information from them than from their white colleagues. As a result African Americans claim that they can be much less effective than white colleagues (Campbell, 1982).

Most black executives believe that to obtain promotion they must demonstrate competence and loyalty in ways not required of whites. What happens, a black executive wonders, if he hires a black secretary? He is likely to decide against it, realizing, as one black manager noted, that peers and superiors might say "that's a black operation over there, so it can't be too effective" (Jones, 1986:90). Or consider the case of Charlie, a junior executive who was straightforward and honest if not militant about racial issues. One day several lower-level black managers approached him, expressing concern about what they saw as a pattern of discrimination limiting their careers. Charlie felt that the top officers ought to hear their account and arranged a meeting with them. Two days before that meeting, the president took Charlie aside and said, "Charlie, I'm disappointed that you met with those people. I thought we could trust you" (Jones 1986:90). Certainly this statement made it clear that Charlie's superiors were giving him little maneuvering room: If he were going to keep rising in the company, he would need to reject racial loyalties, making loyalty to his white superiors and the company his only concern.

An additional challenge now seems to confront black managers. A study of 76 high-ranking African American executives working in Chicago-based Fortune 500 companies found that about two-thirds have been in racialized jobs, focusing on black consumers or personnel, or on civil-rights issues like affirmative action or the development of minority business. Such narrow experience is a disadvantage for these executives when they seek promotion. Typically one African American manager commented:

> I talked to [people] in various divisions that I was interested in, and I got the lip service that they would keep [me] in mind if something opened up. As it happened, that just did not develop. I can never remember being approached by anyone. Nothing [happened] that I can hang [onto] as an offer. People would ask, "Have you ever run a profit and loss operation?" (Collins, 1993:442)

Black managers not only face the possibility of dead-end jobs, but there is also the distinct danger of losing those they have. In an era of business retrenchment and deteriorating national concern about minorities' advancement, job slots dealing with African Americans' needs and interests are likely to be eliminated or reduced.

For African Americans the move into the alien corporate world offers the same rewards of wealth, power, and prestige whites receive. It is a journey, however, that promises special difficulties and tensions: Often they need to learn new rules and to adjust to special, race-related demands made on them. Even when they adjust successfully, their rewards are likely to be less extensive than whites'.

Besides seeking work in the mainstream economy, members of racial minorities have pursued some unique approaches.

MINORITIES' SPECIAL STRATEGIES

One special strategy is to establish businesses that offer select products or services not provided by the mainstream economy—Japanese Americans in farming or Native Americans in casino gambling—and the other is to seek employment in areas where minorities' participation has traditionally been encouraged—blacks in professional sports, for instance.

Japanese Americans in Farming

How can a racial minority survive in a repressive, racist society? While there is no foolproof answer to this question, many Asian immigrants developed a response:

Find a business that provides a potentially profitable product or service that is minimally competitive with those supplied by established whites. Chinese opened restaurants, laundries, and garment factories (Sanders and Nee, 1987; Wong, 1987). Japanese produced a variety of agricultural products. The Japanese experience in California serves to illustrate this strategy for seeking economic success (Jiobu, 1988a).

In the 1890s Japanese immigrants, many of them with a background in farming, began to work as farm laborers. In the next two decades, government officials became concerned that the hard-working Japanese would dominate agriculture, and so their immigration was restricted, their political rights were removed, and, if not citizens, they were prevented from owning land.

Still Japanese farmers prospered. Often the laws prohibiting land ownership were poorly enforced, and white land owners and bankers were generally eager to do business with the Japanese, selling them marginal land at high prices. The Japanese approach to farming was to concentrate on crops that required intensive labor and specialized care and that could be grown in profitable amounts on fairly small plots of marginal land. Besides their farming expertise, Japanese efforts benefitted from an ancient cultural tradition emphasizing hard work, sacrifice for the future, and patience in the face of adversity. Their efforts paid off. In the early 1920s, in the Sacramento area, for instance, Japanese farmers grew 80 percent of the tomatoes, 61 percent of the asparagus, and 78 percent of the spinach. By the outbreak of World War II, estimates indicated that throughout the state Japanese Americans, who were about 2 percent of the population, were producing over 90 percent of snap beans, strawberries, and celery and about 50 percent of artichokes, cauliflower, cucumbers, and tomatoes.

Forced relocation of all Japanese Americans living on the West Coast during World War II produced significant economic losses for farmers, but their overall capital investment was fairly modest, and thus the majority managed to reestablish themselves in the farming business after the war.

In the past 20 or 30 years, there has been a steady decline in the proportion of Japanese Americans entering agriculture. But early success in farming seems to have served several important purposes: It provided funding that subsidized the education and training of many members of the next generation of Japanese Americans; it also established Japanese Americans as a hard-working, reputable people in the eyes of the majority group, thus making it easier for youthful Japanese Americans to enter the mainstream economy.

Native Americans in Casino Gambling

Unlike Japanese in farming, Indians involved in casino gambling have enjoyed a favored status. Two specific legal conditions have promoted casino gambling. First, the U.S. Supreme Court has supported Indian tribes' right to negotiate business deals as sovereign nations. Then the Indian Gaming Regulatory Act of 1988 required that states negotiate agreements to build casinos with tribes living on reservations. Since that time Native Americans have opened about 170 casinos, and dozens more are planned. More than 150 tribes, about half of those in the continental United States, are either involved in this business or in the near future plan to enter it (Clines, 1993; Meier, 1994; Schaefer, 1993:167).

The largest of all the Indian gambling establishments, the Foxwoods High Stakes Bingo & Casino, is on the reservation of the Mashantucket Pequots in Ledyard, Connecticut. By the end of 1993, Foxwoods, which opened in February 1992, had 9,200 workers, making it one of the largest employers in the state. In the summer of 1994, the estimate was that Foxwoods was bringing in revenues of about $800 million a year, clearing over $400 million a year in profit. Because of its ready access to a large, fairly affluent clientele as well as the absence of nearby competition, Foxwoods appears to be the most profitable casino in the world. When in September 1993, Foxwoods opened a new building, the size of the operation doubled, and it became the largest gambling operation in the Western hemisphere, edging out the Taj Mahal in Atlantic City. Like all Indian gambling operations, Foxwoods is exempt from federal and state taxes. However, deals can produce state revenues. Thus in May 1993, Governor Lowell Weicker agreed to give the Pequots monopoly control of slot machines in the state in exchange for $113 million a year of aid to the state's cities (*Economist,* 1993; Johnson, 1993; Passell, 1994).

A major issue tribes involved in casino gambling must face is the extent to which they operate on their own or, in various ways, seek outside help. Richard (Skip) Hayward, the Mashantucket Pequot chief now widely regarded as a genius at casino development, hired as his chief executive G. Michael Brown, the former director of New Jersey's Division of Gaming Enforcement. Brown, a former prosecutor who forced the Atlantic City casinos to cut their ties with the underworld, has eased back on the absolute sovereignty so cherished by other tribes and sought to cooperate with state and federal law-enforcement experts to keep out organized crime and other outsiders' illegal efforts to make money at Foxwoods.

It is one thing to bring in a single expert like G. Michael Brown, but it quite another thing to permit outside casino businesses to run their operations. Some tribes, such as the St. Regis Mohawks in upstate New York and the Ak-Chin of Arizona, have already signed agreements with such companies permitting them to build and run their casinos for a share of their revenues. While federal regulators must review all these agreements, there is no guarantee that they will be run honestly or effectively. The Wisconsin Winnebago tribe, for instance, nearly went bankrupt after a corrupt businessman ran its casino for 20 months.

Clearly Native Americans are finding that the casino business can be precarious. Some opponents like Donald Trump have lobbied Congress to curtail the Indians' billion-dollar tribal power. They argued that tribes' designation as sovereign states, which permits them to escape normal governmental regulation of business and exemption from state and federal taxation, provide an enormous competitive advantage. In addition, the Indians recognize that these are perilous times—that if any major casino scandals occur, their future in this business could be jeopardized (Clines, 1993; Meier, 1994).

Success also produces significant growing pains. In the area around the Foxwoods Casino in Connecticut, many local residents are disturbed by the noise, traffic congestion, crowds, and crime the large influx of outsiders has brought to the area. They are hardly comforted by the Mashantucket Pequots' plan to use some of their profits to buy 8,000 acres of adjoining land and annex it to the reservation, quintupling its size and encircling the towns of Ledyard and Preston. If this purchase occurs, officials in those two towns would lose political control over that land, and as soon as it became part of the reservation, there would be no more payment of property tax. Thus many whites living near Foxwoods tend to strongly oppose the annexation (*Economist,* 1993; Johnson, 1993).

In spite of the economic gains casino gambling can mean for Indians, financial problems can occur. The pie appears to be shrinking. While casino gambling is a huge business, the number of tribes starting their own operations has sharply increased in recent years. In some places the intake of revenues has already been adversely affected. The larger operations are probably firmly established, but some of the newer ventures are likely to find that the pieces of pie left for them are simply too thin to sustain them (Meier, 1994). Furthermore in some remote reservation areas, the primary customers are likely to be poor Indians. Duane Beyal, the assistant to the president of the Navaho Nation, asked a troubling question. "When you have such a large population with high unemployment, all kinds of poverty and related problems like alcoholism, and you put a casino in the middle of it, what kind of problems do you have?" (Judson, 1994:5).

Blacks in Sport

For African Americans two avenues to possible financial success have traditionally been open: entertainment and sports. The openness of entertainment and sports suggests the internal-colonialist issue mentioned in the chapter title—knowing one's place. In the realm of the physical, whites experienced little sense of threat from blacks as long as blacks were merely strong or physically capable. The key issue for whites was maintaining control. In the well-known book *Soul on Ice,* Eldridge Cleaver analyzed racism in American society, classifying white men "Omnipotent Administrators"—all mind and no body—and labelling black men "Supermasculine Menials"—all body and no mind (Cleaver, 1970:166). According to Cleaver, the reality of modern sport in which large numbers of black professional athletes perform impressive physical feats for primarily white audiences simply confirms in the racist's mind the natural order of things.

But while blacks have found the world of professional sport open to them, the question remains whether they have experienced racial discrimination within it. We consider, examining research involving professional baseball, football, and basketball.

Writing about major-league baseball, Robert M. Jiobu (1988b) suggested that for a number of reasons related to the game itself, one would expect baseball to be relatively free of racial discrimination. First, major-league baseball, which has been voluntarily integrated since 1947, has a longer history of integration than most American activities. Second, with constant exposure to the mass media, baseball officials are fully aware that incidents of racism will be exposed. Third, widespread agreement exists about the basis for evaluating good performance, and major statistics on batting, pitching, and fielding are well publicized. Fourth, the goal of winning dominates professional baseball, and there is general acceptance that regardless of race, the best players are the ones that most effectively help a team to win. So these four reasons would discourage racial discrimination in baseball.

To find out whether racism occurred in the game, Jiobu looked at the records of major-league baseball players involved in at least 50 games between 1971 and 1985. He learned that African Americans' performance levels were higher than those for either Hispanics or whites. Blacks' lifetime slugging average (total bases per thousand times at bat) was .381 contrasted to .337 for Hispanics and .348 for whites, and blacks' lifetime batting average (hits per thousand times at bat) was .258 compared to .245 for Hispanics and .241 for whites.

Because of their superior performances, African Americans last longer in the major leagues than the other two groups. For blacks the median survival time is 11.8 years while for whites and Hispanics it is 10.0 years.

So far there has been no evidence of racism. According to the data, African Americans perform better and as a result maintain longer careers in major-league baseball. But Jiobu realized that another issue required analysis. What happens if performance levels among the three groups are controlled (kept constant)? When this occurs, it turns out that African Americans' careers are shorter than either Hispanics' or whites'. Jiobu concluded that blacks are "simultaneously rewarded for their performance and penalized for their race" (Jiobu, 1988b:532).

Why are African Americans penalized for their race? Jiobu speculated that a major factor might be owners and management's concern that the predominantly white fans will not support a largely black team. To prevent such a result and yet to produce a winning team, owners and managers appear to place a distinct limit on the number of black players, cutting African Americans as soon as their skills start to decline while keeping a certain number of white players of comparably marginal ability. Many prominent writers and academics have suggested that there is no activity more typically American than baseball. In contrast to those positive commentaries, Jiobu's findings suggest a strictly negative side to the observation.

Research on football players in the National Football League, the second major professional sport, has examined another racism issue—whether or not a player's race affects his position. Investigators' basic assumption is that more central positions in a football formation—on offense centers, quarterbacks, and guards—are not only central physically but also socially and politically: These positions are central to communication and leadership, and players at the seven other positions simply must follow orders. If professional football reflects the racial-stratification system prevailing in American society, then one would expect that whites would dominate the central positions and African Americans the less central ones. Let's consider whether this process, which is called stacking, has occurred.

Between 1975 and 1985, the percentage of black players in the National Football League increased from 41.6 to 51.3 percent. Nonetheless during that time period, stacking remained disproportionately high on both offense and defense, with some impressive statistical increases in the offensive pattern. Most notably among quarterbacks, whose position is the most cerebral and most involved in decision making, whites' score went from 95.5 to 97.1 percent. While the researchers unfortunately did not distinguish centers and guards, the most central of offensive linesmen, from the other offensive linesmen, they did indicate that during the same ten-year span, the percentage of white offensive linemen increased from 76 to 89 percent. (Since on a given team, the guards and center represent about 43 percent of the offensive line—it varies with the formation—one can guess that between 1975 and 1985, the proportion of central linemen who were white increased.) In contrast, African Americans' participation rose in noncentral positions. The proportion of black running backs increased dramatically from 65 to 86 percent, and the proportion of black receivers went from 55 to 62 percent. The authors concluded, "The positions requiring leadership and thinking ability have become even more 'white' and the positions necessitating speed, quickness, and 'instinct' have become even more 'black'" (Schneider and Eitzen, 1986:260).

Research conducted in major-league baseball reached a similar conclusion about stacking. Between 1960 and 1988, blacks were most highly represented in the outfield, the least central positions, and least represented at pitching and catching, the most central positions. It appears that the major factor contributing to stacking in professional baseball has been the influence of white coaches, who have often encouraged developing black ball players to move to the less central positions (Lavoie and Leonard, 1994). Current research has not addressed what motivates white coaches' actions. Do they believe that black players are less capable of communicating than white players, do they feel less comfortable communicating with black players and thus locate blacks far from themselves, or do both issues apply?

In basketball, the third major professional sport, a study found that as a group African American players outperformed white players and as a result were better paid. Discrimination was apparent when performance statistics were held constant for the 1984–85 professional season: Researchers learned that blacks as a group averaged about $26,000 less per year than whites (Koch and Vander Hill, 1988). The authors suggested that while it "is difficult to avoid the conclusion that race discrimination . . . is the cause" (Koch and Vander Hill, 1988:92), other factors such as the possibility that upon entering professional basketball blacks are less knowledgable or aggressive bargainers than whites might also be relevant.

Besides athletes, management personnel are significant participants in the world of professional sport. Although black management personnel in professional basketball, baseball, and football remain considerably below the proportion of black athletes in their respective sports, their numbers have been slowly increasing. Since the 1970s there have been a few black managers in major-league baseball and head coaches in the National Basketball Association. In 1989—finally—the Oakland Raiders became the first team in the National Football League to hire a black head coach.

Commenting on major-league baseball, Hank Aaron, a senior vice president for the Atlanta Braves and baseball's all-time home-run champion, indicated that blacks' involvement in baseball management has been minimal. Aaron cited the impact of social networks discussed earlier. He concluded, "Baseball was and continues to be a good-old-boy network." Aaron added that the commissioner of baseball and the president of the United States should push for significant change (Araton, 1991).

Whether it is baseball or some other professional sport, minorities seeking to enter management often find themselves subjected to a distinct double standard.

Analyzing the characteristics of black men who have been head coaches in the National Basketball Association, journalist Harvey Araton (1992) noted that while many white coaches have been outspoken and aggressive, their black counterparts have consistently been "low-key, unthreatening personalities." The colonial-labor principle suggests that minority-group members are supposed to "know their place," accepting a subordinate role in the world. An outspoken black coach defies the image racists find comfortable.

Recently Drew Pearson, a former all-pro wide receiver for the Dallas Cowboys and now the president of a successful sportswear manufacturing company, has raised another issue involving blacks' participation in professional sport. Black athletes, Pearson argued, have been restricted in their range of roles. For example, while top black athletes have made large sums of money doing endorsements for athletic products, they could make more money and even provide jobs for poor, inner-city African Americans if they started their own companies. Black athletes have not pursued this course of action because since their first years in organized sports, they have been brought up to see themselves narrowly—as just athletes. Pearson said:

> You don't really see yourself as a coach or as someone running these concession stands that generate money. Power people see us as being participants, not the ones that set up these leagues, not the ones making any decision concerning the welfare of the league. (Rhoden, 1990:B7)

According to Pearson, black athletes need to recognize both for their own good and for the benefit of young, struggling African Americans that they should consider trying to become major players in the commercial and administrative areas of professional sport.

In professional basketball Isiah Thomas has had an opportunity to take a significant step in that direction, becoming part owner of the new Toronto team in the NBA. As a five-year president of the NBA Players Association, Thomas had extensive administrative experience that undoubtedly prepared him to function in his new capacity. Journalist Harvey Araton indicated that while Thomas is tough and controversial, his new position is one that "even those who don't like Thomas should applaud. Black leaders in sports have said that executive entrenchment and ownership are the only true means of obliberating quotas and old-boy networks" (Araton, 1994:5). He added that basketball's black superstars have sufficient power to demand access to such top positions.

As we shift from jobs to housing, we once again find ample evidence of racism.

RACIAL MINORITIES AND HOUSING

One of the basic points in the internal-colonialist perspective involves freedom of movement. To what extent are members of racial minorities restricted in where they go and, in particular, where they live?

Since the 1920s sociologists have been interested in residential segregation. As they watched various European groups settling in this country, they predicted that as groups' socioeconomic status rose, residential restrictions would disappear. For white groups this proved true, and it has been generally accurate for Native Americans, Asian Americans, and Mexican Americans (Darden, 1990; Massey and Eggers, 1990; White, Biddlecom, and Guo, 1993).

For African Americans the pattern has been different. At the end of the nineteenth century, the perhaps 200,000 blacks living in northern and midwestern cities were well integrated, with the typical black resident living in an area that was 90 percent white. But then starting in the 1890s and carrying through the 1920s, the migration of southern blacks to northern cities sharply increased. Many whites became hostile, and between 1900 and 1920, riots occurred in a number of northern and midwestern cities. African Americans who lived outside what were considered "black" areas often had their houses burned or ransacked. To blacks the message was clear: To stay healthy, one needed to live in what were called "black belts," "darkytowns," or "bronzevilles." In subsequent decades the progressive segregation of blacks continued, and by 1940 the boundaries of the modern black ghetto were established in nearly every northern city (Massey and Denton, 1993: 29–31).

Following World War II, a major movement to the suburbs occurred. It was, however, a "whites only" movement. Bowing to local pressure, the federal government permitted suburban towns and cities to zone their own land, and invariably under the guise of promoting health and safety, these municipalities prevented the entrance of public housing, which might have brought poor people, particularly poor minorities into their midst. Furthermore authorities for the Federal Housing Authority believed that racial segregation would establish neighborhood stability and housing values, and so they prevented blacks from receiving mortgages insured by the Federal Housing Authority—a major source of low-interest loans in those years (Weir, 1994).

In the modern era, many whites have continued to support housing discrimination against blacks. Nancy Denton and Douglas Massey, a pair of sociologists specializing in housing discrimination, wrote, "Blacks represent a major exception to the pattern of declining segregation with rising socioeconomic status" (Denton and Massey, 1988:798).

Denton and Massey found that this conclusion about residential segregation for blacks held across different socioeconomic levels. For metropolitan areas with the largest black populations, they calculated the **index of dissimilarity,** which indicates the proportion of a particular racial group that would need to change residential location in order to achieve racial evenness—a condition in which that racial group's representation throughout a city's census districts would be dispersed proportionate to its overall representation in the city. Thus high indexes of dissimilarity demonstrate high levels of housing segregation: Large numbers of blacks would need to relocate to establish racial evenness.

In the metropolitan areas with the 60 largest black populations, the index of dissimilarity for African Americans with none to 4 years of schooling completed was 83 percent, for those with 12 years of schooling 71 percent, and for those with 17 or more years of schooling (schooling beyond college) 68 percent. There was, in short, only a slight decline in the index of dissimilarity as African Americans' education increased. When the researchers calculated the index of dissimilarity for income in those same 60 metropolitan areas, a similar pattern emerged. For blacks making under $2,500 per year, the dissimilarity index was 80 percent, dropped to

Table 5.2   BLACKS' RESIDENTIAL SEGREGATION

	Index of Racial Dissimilarity for Years of School Completed (percent)				
	0–4	8	12	16	17+
Mean, metropolitan areas with 10 largest black populations	84%[1]	84%	78%	72%	73%
Mean, metropolitan areas with 20 largest black populations	80	80	75	70	70
Mean, metropolitan areas with 60 largest black populations	83	81	70	68	68

	Index of Racial Dissimilarity for Yearly Income (percent)				
	$2,500	$5,000	$10,000	$20,000	$50,000+
Mean, metropolitan areas with 10 largest black populations	84%	82%	79%	76%	79%
Mean, metropolitan areas with 20 largest black populations	81	79	76	74	77
Mean, metropolitan areas with 60 largest black populations	80	78	74	73	80

[1]Figures are rounded off to the nearest percentage.

Note: This table concerns two measures of blacks' indexes of dissimilarity—the percentage of blacks that would need to change residential areas to achieve a racially balanced outcome in a given city. Two distinct trends are apparent. First, as blacks' years of schooling and income increase, there is little change in the index of dissimilarity; in fact, in all three classifications of metropolitan areas, the highest income group scored a higher index of dissimilarity than the second highest income group. Second, the larger the black populations of metropolitan areas, the higher the indexes of dissimilarity across educational and income levels.

Source: Adapted from Nancy A. Denton and Douglas S. Massey. "Residential Segregation of Blacks, Hispanics, and Asians by Socioeconomic Status and Generation." *Social Science Quarterly,* 69 (December 1988): pp. 797–817.

73 percent for those with income of $15,000 or $20,000 per year, but then rose to 80 percent for those with income of $50,000 per year or more (Denton and Massey, 1988:803). Table 5.2 presents blacks' indexes of dissimilarity for education and income in three sets of metropolitan areas.°

Another factor affecting blacks' residential segregation is the population density of the area in which they live. African Americans living in the suburbs do experience more segregation than other groups but less than blacks in large metropolitan areas (Massey and Denton, 1988). The most profound residential segregation

°One should emphasize that indexes of dissimilarity do not reveal residents' feelings about segregated housing. While many African Americans want to escape segregated housing areas, some undoubtedly have various reasons for wanting to remain in them.

experienced by African Americans occurs in the following large cities—Baltimore, Chicago, Cleveland, Detroit, Milwaukee, and Philadelphia. They are closely followed by Gary, Los Angeles, and New York. In these cities massive physical areas are exclusively black. As a result residents are likely to be largely or completely isolated from whites, most decisively affecting black citizens' opportunities for effective education and employment (Massey and Denton, 1989).

There is only one other major group that suffers a high level of residential segregation across all socioeconomic levels—black Puerto Ricans and other black Caribbean Hispanics who do not identify themselves as white. While white Puerto Ricans become increasingly integrated as their socioeconomic status rises, this is decisively not the case with black Puerto Ricans, whose most frequent non–Puerto Rican neighbors are African Americans. It seems clear that for many white Americans a powerful desire is not to live near black people (Denton and Massey, 1988; 1989; Massey and Fong, 1990).

In the opening chapter, we encountered William J. Wilson's thesis about the declining significance of race. Lower-class status is the dominant source of oppression for blacks, Wilson argued. But the data on residential location question this conclusion: For African Americans a high-educational or high-income level does little to overcome residential segregation.

For Asian Americans and Mexican Americans, the situation contrasts sharply. In metropolitan areas containing the heaviest concentrations of these two racial groups, their indexes of dissimilarity declined more sharply with rising socioeconomic status than blacks'. Well-educated Asian Americans and Mexican Americans are accepted as neighbors by most whites, even in metropolitan areas where they live in large numbers (Denton and Massey, 1988:810–812).

The least segregated Asian American group is Japanese, with the Chinese, Filipino, Korean, Indian, and Vietnamese following in that order. It appears that the proportion of immigrants in an Asian American group affects its residential integration: The smaller the proportion of immigrants, the higher the group's residential integration (Langberg and Farley, 1985). One team of researchers concluded that Asian Americans are able to "translate their socioeconomic achievements into residential assimilation" (White, Biddlecom, and Guo, 1993:93). As Asian Americans' income rises, they are more inclined to live in the suburbs. In fact, Asian American suburban households have income that is nearly a quarter greater than that of those living in central cities (O'Hare, Frey, and Fost, 1994).

Studies on Mexican Americans indicated that they are slightly less likely than Asian Americans but much more likely than blacks to share a neighborhood with whites (Darden, 1990; Massey and Fong, 1990).

An investigation of the suburbs surrounding New York City revealed a similar pattern. With rising income Asian Americans and Hispanics, particularly white Hispanics, are increasingly likely to live near whites. For African Americans, regardless of income, their race is a barrier to proximity to whites. It appears that while suburban whites are unconcerned about how many Asian Americans and white Hispanics live close by, they want a modest black presence (Alba and Logan, 1993).

Thus the dominant research finding is that African Americans' index of dissimilarity is much higher than other racial groups'. In the 10, 20, and 60 cities with the largest black populations, blacks with postgraduate schooling lived in more highly segregated areas than Asians with between no and four years of schooling. In addition, in those same three sets of cities, African Americans earning $50,000 or more per year resided in more highly segregated neighborhoods than Hispanic Americans earning between $2,500 and $5,000 a year (Denton and Massey, 1988).

A recent study found that once a certain minority dominates a given area, new inhabitants to that area are increasingly likely to be members of that group (Rosenbaum, 1994)—a particular problem for poor minorities. Forced to live in a deteriorating area, poor African Americans and Puerto Ricans suffer low-quality housing, dangers and tensions produced by high crime rates, substandard schooling for their children, and a physically unhealthy environment (Massey, 1990; Massey and Denton, 1993; Massey and Eggers, 1990). On the last point, residents affected have increasingly protested the occurrence of environmental racism—the distinct tendency to locate hazardous waste plants and other polluting industrial projects in poor, largely minority residential areas (Schneider, 1993).

A mildly optimistic point is that segregation rates have declined slightly over time. Examining the 232 metropolitan areas with substantial African American populations, a pair of researchers found a modest drop in the index of dissimilarity, thus indicating a slight decline in housing segregation. They concluded that areas with new housing construction, which tend to be less segregated than other locales, largely account for this development. In the Northeast and Midwest, where most suburbs have traditionally been hostile to blacks, the desegregation trend has been least apparent (Farley and Frey, 1994).

At this point we move from an analysis of housing-discrimination patterns to an examination of a process helping to produce them. As the focus shifts to acts of individual racism, a cautionary note seems necessary. While realtors and other key players sometimes discriminate against minorities, particularly African Americans, the impact of such institutional factors as poverty, joblessness, and inadequate schooling play a major, perhaps dominant role in perpetuating housing segregation (Clark, 1993).

Racist Tactics in Housing

We are now examining racism delivered with a smile, often with a distinct show of courtesy and even deference. A report issued by the Department of Housing and Urban Development estimated that realtors, bank officials, and personnel at other lending agencies have subjected African Americans and other minorities to about 2 million instances of housing discrimination annually (Minerbrook, 1994). Investigations have shown that realtors selling homes to blacks have often invested less time and energy with them or steered them to restricted locales.

Research on this topic has used what are called "fair housing audits," in which a black couple and a white couple with comparable incomes and credit ratings and seeking similar residence requirements contact the same set of realtors and are shown houses or apartments. Using this technique, investigators are able to determine whether or not differences occur in white and black couples' treatment. Robert Weink and associates (1979) pioneered this use of testers, studying real-estate activity in 40 large cities throughout the country and finding that discrimination against African Americans appeared in both rental housing and home sales. The investigation concluded that black clients had a 50 percent chance with houses and a 70 percent likelihood with apartments of encountering discrimination.

Realtors have discriminated against black clients in various ways. The body of research using testers seeking to rent has indicated that racial discrimination against African Americans occurred with respect to the number of available units, number of units offered for inspection, and length of waiting list. For home-buying black testers received less time, more limited information about houses in higher price ranges or more select neighborhoods, less discussion about financing, fewer house showings, and more discourteous or rude treatment such as cancelling appointments or showing up late for them (Leigh, 1989:74–75).

A major factor in housing discrimination has been the issue of steering clients toward particular residential areas (Galster, 1990a). Research in Boston indicated that the most significant consideration seemed to be the prospective residential section—in particular, whether or not it was currently an all-white area or undergoing racial transition. In the latter case, African Americans were much more likely to be shown housing. This research suggested that the primary cause of housing discrimination against blacks was agents' catering to their white clients' racism (Yinger, 1986).

Not surprisingly blacks are more attuned than whites to racial discrimination in housing. When in 1990 a national survey team asked Americans whether blacks have as good a chances as whites in their community to get any housing they could afford, 75 percent of whites answered affirmatively. Among blacks the figure was a much lower 47 percent (Gallup and Hugick, 1990).

Besides steering, realtors sometimes use a less subtle technique—"block busting." Once a few black families have moved into a residential area, a realtor can exploit homes owners' racial and financial fears, suggesting by telephone, mail, or visits that the neighborhood is starting to deteriorate rapidly, becoming a distasteful and dangerous place to live, and that they had better get out before their property becomes nearly worthless. Successful block-busting campaigns can transform an all-white to an all-black neighborhood in just a few years (Galster, 1990b).

The success of such tactics suggests that in order to avoid living near African Americans, many whites readily leave an area when blacks move into their neighborhood. One investigation concluded that two factors determined whites' departure—their desire to live in racial segregation and the percentage of African American residents in the district (Galster, 1990b). In a study conducted in Detroit, the most segregated U.S. city with a population of a million or more, evidence indicated a persistent if slowly declining white negative reaction to black neighbors. Thus when white respondents were asked if they would try to leave a neighborhood when 5 of 14 houses had black residents, 41 percent replied affirmatively in 1976 and 29 percent in 1992 (Farley and Frey, 1994:29).

Clearly many whites are deeply disturbed when forced to live in racially integrated areas. As a ten-year-old, journalist Brent Staples lived in a neighborhood where except for his African American family, everyone else was Polish or Ukrainian. Staples loved airplanes, and at home he made wooden models, which he flew outside the house. One day he was flying a plane in an open space next to a neighbor's house. The plane—a wooden spitfire with British Royal Air Force markings and a propeller powered by a rubbar band—took off nicely but landed in the neighbor's vegetable patch. The old man who was working there grabbed the plane, muttered words in Ukrainian, and hurried into the house. A few minutes later a grandson came out, paused at the door, and then red-faced walked to the fence, where he handed Staples the plane's remains. It had been dismembered into strips no wider than popsicle sticks with the rubbar band neatly wrapped around the wreckage. Staples held back the tears until he reached the alley. It was the deepest cruelty he had ever known. Grandfathers were supposed to be nice, especially to children. Staples wrote:

> I suspect that grandpa missed the days when black people were confined to small streets and alleys near the river; when the shipyard and the oil refineries were segregated, complete with supervisors for the colored; when the Poles and Ukrainians lived alone with their own, their schools, and their bakeries. Now black people were right next door. Grandpa needed someone to look down on. (Staples, 1994:61)

Along with many citizens and realtors, bank officials often support racist housing policies. A study by the Federal Reserve System indicated that banks and savings institutions in the Boston area were discriminating racially in the awarding of mortgages. After income, property values, and other nonracial factors were taken into account, a sharp difference remained between the percentage of mortgages granted in white and in African American neighborhoods. Other studies had found a similar pattern in Detroit and Atlanta (Gold, 1989).

However, evidence suggests that bankers might be changing their policies. In such major cities as New York, St. Louis, and Philadelphia, some bankers are deciding that providing mortgages for low-income, largely minority inner-city residents not only helps remove their organization's discriminatory image but also can provide the bank new business opportunities. Some banks work with housing advocacy groups like Acorn, which has 70,000, primarily African American members and two decades of active service. In Acorn's North Philadelphia office, counselors explain the program to people who call in or drop by, and applications are also filled out there. Applicants for mortgages never need to go beyond the Acorn office. Commenting on the organization, a federal banking official said, "Acorn is street-tough rough and they bedevil the bankers. But they've gotten banks to commit millions they otherwise would not have lent" (Wayne, 1992:50).

In the near future, banks might come under growing pressure to provide more loans to low-income residents. While the Community Reinvestment Act of 1977 required increased lending to individuals in low- and moderate-income areas, mounting evidence has suggested that most banks have avoided compliance. However, the Clinton administration has developed a plan to tighten the law's standards, and some banks are already starting to cooperate. For instance, in August 1993, CoreStates New Jersey National Bank opened a branch in Camden, New Jersey, the first new bank outlet in 22 years in that depressed city. Working with a credit union run by the Latin American Economic Development Association, the bank makes home-mortgage and home-equity loans to low-income, primarily minority residents (Scherreik, 1994).

Another factor which probably discourages discrimination in housing has been the punitive damages some participants in the housing industry have been forced to pay. Thus in New York City, over 2,000 African American and Hispanic individuals were awarded $20 million when a ruling found that they were the victims of discrimination in public-housing assignments (Zimmerman, 1992). In Washington, D.C., 40 real-estate and advertising firms faced a suit for using advertisements that steered both black and white buyers to selected neighborhoods. Most of the companies reached a financial settlement and changed their ads, but while altering its ads, Colonial Village, a major realty company, did not settle and ended up paying $850,000 in punitive damages (*News Media & the Law*, 1992).

The federal government can take other measures to reduce housing discrimination under existing laws. First, Housing and Urban Development (HUD) personnel could provide financial assistance to local fair-housing organizations to investigate and prosecute claims of discrimination. At present those organizations tend to be weak, and cases against violators of housing-discrimination laws are unlikely to be forcefully prosecuted. Second, housing-discrimination cases require evidence. HUD could establish a permanent testing program, identifying realtors engaging in housing discrimination and then turning over the evidence for prosecution (Massey and Denton, 1993:229–230).

Until such measures are taken, the likelihood exists that the kind of racist treatment described in the following section will keep occurring.

What Happened When a Puerto Rican Tried to Sell His House in an All-White Neighborhood

In *Stigma* Erving Goffman suggested that oppressed individuals often experience a "phantom acceptance," which means that the nonoppressed members of the society treat them as normal during superficial contacts as long as the latter support the charade by pretending that they are treated like everyone else. In order to establish the fantasy, oppressed people generally must keep their distance (Goffman, 1974:122) or, as the phrase goes in this chapter, know their place.

When African Americans or black Puerto Ricans, the two groups most likely to suffer housing discrimination, attempt to move into a white neighborhood, they are rejecting the phantom-acceptance game. If members of these minorities pursue this course of action, they are likely to encounter discriminatory tactics.

Piri Thomas, a black Puerto Rican, bought two houses on Long Island, New York, from Don Baldwin, his white brother-in-law, and moved into one of them. At first both he and his wife were very happy and proud to have moved from an inner-city neighborhood to the suburbs, and Thomas worked hard getting both houses into shape. Soon, however, he noticed that the neighbors would walk by and stare, often insolently, apparently suggesting that he shouldn't have dared to move into their neighborhood.

Once Thomas overheard a couple discussing the situation. The wife wondered "who could have sold that nigger a house in her community" (Thomas, 1973:199). The husband replied that it had been Don Baldwin and that the family was Puerto Rican, not black. Thomas was infuriated, noting that in their bigoted minds being Puerto Rican was a notch above being black. Thomas wrote:

> Who makes the damned rules of who's better than who? I looked back at the two so-called Christians walking with their child and just to get their attention, I let out a mighty yell. They looked back and I made a most exaggeraged bow and the gesture let them know I'd heard the bullshit that they, white Christian God-loving God-fearing [people], had put down. (Thomas, 1973:199)

Eventually the Thomases decided to move back to New York City. While local racism played some role, the primary reason was that Thomas was working in the City, and the commute on top of a long day's work was backbreaking. So deciding to sell the houses, Thomas went to see Paul Hendricks, a realtor.

As soon as Hendricks saw Thomas, he tried to steer him toward an area where he indicated some of the best African American families lived. No, Thomas indicated, he didn't want to buy a house but wanted to sell two of them. Hendricks was puzzled, not recalling what he believed was a black family in that locale. When Thomas mentioned that he had bought the houses from Don Baldwin, Hendricks's face lit up with recognition. "Oh . . . ha ha, of course, you're the Spanish family I've heard about" (Thomas, 1973:208). Puerto Rican, replied Thomas. They talked some more, and in spite of distinct reservations about Hendricks, Thomas decided to use him as a realtor.

Hendricks brought a few people to see the houses, but none of them were interested in buying. Eventually Thomas himself found a buyer. At first Hendricks was enthusiastic that a buyer had been found. But as soon as Thomas handed him a piece of paper on which the name and address were written, the enthusiasm faded. What was the matter? Thomas wanted to know. Was the family black? Mr. Henricks asked.

> "That's right. Why?" I asked knowing the why all the way.
> "Really, Mr. Thomas, I don't know quite how to say this, but you certainly must know that Silver View is a, er . . . white community and they wouldn't be happy there . . . and you bought your house from Mr. Baldwin, who's lived here many years and his parents before him, and, well, you being, er . . . Spanish is not like. . . ."
> My blood was tearing itself up into my eyeball.
> "Why don't you just come out with it, fella?" My eyes just stared into his.
> "Well, it's not that I mind, but the people, I mean their homes, they've worked hard and they do mind, ah . . . mixing, and well, Dammit, I have lived here all my life. Real estate is my livelihood and if I sold to a colored family property in Silver View, well . . . Can you understand? I mean, put yourself in my place?" (Thomas, 1973:210)

No, he wouldn't do that, Thomas replied. He got rid of the agent and prepared to sell the house directly to the black family, but threatened by members of the all-white Better Civic Improvement Committee, the prospective purchaser withdrew.

The Thomases moved back to New York City, still hoping to sell to whomever they wished. Returning during the winter, they found that the house in which they had been living had been broken into, many windows were smashed, water had been turned on in the unheated house, thereby bursting the pipes, and dog dung had been smeared throughout the house.

Piri Thomas challenged the phantom-acceptance game by attempting to sell his house to a black couple. Eventually he was defeated by the racist system he attempted to overcome. The couple to whom he planned to sell his house was intimidated and decided not to buy it, and Thomas was punished when his house was broken into and damaged.

REFERENCES

Alba, Richard D., and John R. Logan. 1993. "Minority Proximity to Whites in Suburbs: An Individual-Level Analysis of Segregation." *American Journal of Sociology* 98 (May): 1388–1427.

Araton, Harvey. 1991. "Aaron Speaks with Vincent on Remarks about Hiring." *New York Times* (May 15):B5+.

Araton, Harvey. 1992. "Beard Finally Showing His Stuff." *New York Times* (March 11):B13.

Araton, Harvey. 1994. "He Bargains as He Plays: Smartly." *New York Times* (January 9):5.

Beauregard, Robert A. 1990. "Tenacious Inequalities: Politics and Race in Philadelphia." *Urban Affairs Quarterly* 25 (March):420–434.

Bendick, Marc, Jr., Charles W. Jackson, Victor A. Reinoso, and Laura E. Hodges. 1993. "Discrimination against Latino Job Applicants: A Controlled Experiment," pp. 86–93 in John A. Kromkowski (ed.), *Race and Ethnic Relations 93/94.* Guilford, CT: Dushkin Publishing Group. Third edition.

Braddock, Jomills Henry, II, and James N. McPartland. 1987. "How Minorities Continue to Be Excluded from Equal Employment Opportunities: Research on Labor Market and Institutional Barriers." *Journal of Social Issues* 43:5–39.

Burstein, Paul, and Susan Pitchford. 1990. "Social-Scientific and Legal Challenges to Education and Test Requirements in Employment." *Social Problems* 37 (May):243–257.

Campbell, Bebe Moore. 1982. "Black Executives and Corporate Stress." *New York Times Magazine* (December 12):36–39+.

Chavez, Lydia. 1994. "More Mexicans, More Profit." *New York Times* (December 9):A33.

Chua-eoan, Howard G. 1993. "Strangers in Paradise," pp. 118–121 in John A. Kromkowski (ed.), *Race and Ethnic Relations 93/94.* Guilford, CT: Dushkin Publishing Group. Third edition.

Chun, Ki-Taek. 1993. "The Myth of Asian American Success and Its Educational Ramifications," pp. 175–185 in Young I. Song and Eugene C. Kim (eds.), *American Mosaic.* Englewood Cliffs, NJ: Prentice-Hall.

Clark, William A. V. 1993. "Measuring Racial Discrimination in the Housing Market." *Urban Affairs Quarterly* 28 (June):641–649.

Cleaver, Eldridge. 1970. *Soul on Ice.* New York: Dell Publishing.

Clines, Francis X. 1993. "Indian Tribes Close Ranks to Protect Casinos from Cheats and Competitors." *New York Times* (December 25):6.

Collins, Sharon M. 1993. "Blacks on the Bubble: The Vulnerability of Black Executives in White Corporations." *Sociological Quarterly* 34 (August):429–447.

Crystal, David. 1989. "Asian Americans and the Myth of the Model Minority." *Social Casework* 70 (September):405–413.

Daniels, Roger. 1988. *Asian Americans: Chinese and Japanese in the United States since 1850.* Seattle: University of Washington Press.

Darden, Joe T. 1990. "Differential Access to Housing in the Suburbs." *Journal of Black Studies* 21 (September):15–22.

Davila, Alberto, Alok K. Bohara, and Rogelio Saenz. 1993. "Accent Penalties and the Earnings of Mexican Americans." *Social Science Quarterly* 74 (December):902–916.

Denton, Nancy A., and Douglas S. Massey. 1988. "Residential Segregation of Blacks, Hispanics, and Asians by Socioeconomic Status and Generation." *Social Science Quarterly* 69 (December):797–817.

Denton, Nancy A., and Douglas S. Massey. 1989. "Racial Identity among Caribbean Hispanics." *American Sociological Review* 54 (October):790–808.

Economist. 1993. "Connecticut: A Tribal Dance." 328 (September 18):31.

Falcon, Luis M., Douglas T. Gurak, and Mary G. Powers. 1990. "Labor Force Participation of Puerto Rican Women in Greater New York City." *Sociology and Social Research* 74 (January):110–114.

Farley, John E. 1987. "Disproportionate Black and Hispanic Unemployment in U.S. Metropolitan Areas: The Role of Racial Inequality, Segregation and Discrimination in Male Joblessness." *American Journal of Economics and Sociology* 46 (April):129–150.

Farley, Reynolds, and William H. Frey. 1994. "Changes in the Segregtion of Whites from Blacks during the 1980s: Small Steps toward a More Integrated Society." *American Sociological Review* 59 (February):23–45.

Feagin, Joe R., and Clairece Booher Feagin. 1993. *Racial and Ethnic Relations.* Englewood Cliffs, NJ: Prentice-Hall. Fourth edition.

Gallup, George, Jr. 1989. *Gallup Report* (August).

Gallup, George, Jr., and Larry Hugick. 1990. "Racial Tolerance Grows, Progress on Racial Equality Less Evident." Gallup Poll Monthly (June):23–32.

Galster, George C. 1990a. "Racial Steering in Urban Housing Markets: A Review of the Audit Evidence." *Review of Black Political Economy* 18 (winter):105–129.

Galster, George C. 1990b. "White Flight from Racially Integrated Neighborhoods in the 1970s." *Urban Studies* 27 (June):385–399.

Geschwender, James A., and Rita Carroll-Seguin. 1990. "Exploding the Myth of African-American Progress." *Signs* 15 (winter):285–299.

Gleckman, Howard, et al. 1993. "Race in the Workplace: Is Affirmative Action Working?" pp. 152–159 in John A. Kromkowski (ed.), *Race and Ethnic Relations 93/94.* Guilford, CT: Dushkin Publishing Group. Third edition.

Goffman, Erving. 1974. *Stigma: Notes on the Management of Spoiled Identity.* New York: Jason Aronson.

Gold, Allan R. 1989. "Racial Pattern Is Found in Boston Mortgages." *New York Times* (September 1):A1+.

Hacker, Andrew. 1992. *Two Nations: Black and White, Separate, Hostile, Unequal.* New York: Charles Scribner's Sons.

Hurh, Won Moo, and Kwang Chung Kim. 1989. "The 'Success' Image of Asian Americans: Its Validity, and Its Practical and Theoretical Implications." *Ethnic and Racial Studies* 12 (October):512–538.

Jaynes, Gerald David, and Robin M. Williams, Jr. (eds.). 1989. *A Common Destiny: Blacks and American Society.* Washington, DC: National Academy Press.

Jiobu, Robert M. 1988a. "Ethnic Hegemony and the Japanese of California." *American Sociological Review* 53 (June):353–367.

Jiobu, Robert M. 1988b. "Racial Inequality in a Public Arena: The Case of Professional Baseball." *Social Forces* 67 (December):524–533.

Johnson, Gloria Jones. 1990. "Underemployment, Underpayment, Attributions, and Self-Esteem among Working Black Men." *Journal of Black Psychology* 16 (spring):23–43.

Johnson, Kirk. 1993. "Indians' Casino Money Pumps Up the Volume." *New York Times* (September 1):B1+.

Jones, Edward W., Jr. 1973. "What It's Like to Be a Black Manager." *Harvard Business Review* 51 (July/August):108–116.

Jones, Edward W., Jr. 1986. "Black Managers: The Dream Deferred." *Harvard Business Review* 64 (May/June):84–93.

Judson, George. 1994. "Some Indians See a Gamble with Future in Casinos." *New York Times* (May 15):Sec. 4, 5.

Kaufman, Robert L. 1986. "The Impact of Industrial and Occupational Structure on Black-White Employment Allocation." *American Sociological Review* 51 (June):310–323.

Killian, Lewis M. 1990. "Race Relations and the Nineties: Where Are the Dreams of the Sixties?" *Social Forces* 69 (September):1–13.

Koch, James V., and C. Warren Vander Hill. 1988. "Is There Discrimination in the 'Black Man's Game'?" *Social Science Quarterly* 69 (March):83–94.

Lai, Tracy. 1995. "Asian American Women: Not for Sale," pp. 181–190 in Margaret L. Andersen and Patricia Hill Collins (eds.), *Race, Class, and Gender: An Anthology.* Belmont, CA: Wadsworth. Second edition.

Langberg, Mark, and Reynolds Farley. 1985. "Residential Segregation of Asian Americans in 1980." *Sociology and Social Research* 70 (October):71–75.

Larwood, Laurie, Eugene Szwajkowski, and Suzanna Rose. 1988. "Sex and Race Discrimination Resulting from Manager-Client Relationships: Applying the Rational Bias Theory of Managerial Discrimination." *Sex Roles* 18 (January):9–29.

Lavoie, Marc, and Wilbert M. Leonard, III. 1994. "In Search of an Alternative Explanation of Stacking in Baseball: The Uncertainty Hypothesis." *Sociology of Sport Journal* 11 (June):140–154.

Leigh, Wilhelmina A. 1989. "Barriers to Fair Housing for Black Women." *Sex Roles* 21 (July):71–84.

Lichter, Daniel T. 1988. "Racial Differences in Underemployment in American Cities." *American Journal of Sociology* 93 (January):771–792.

Lopez, Felix. 1976. "The Bell System's Non-Management Personnel Selection Strategy," pp. 226–227 in Phyllis A. Wallace (ed.), *Equal Opportunity and the AT&T Case.* Cambridge, MA: M.I.T. Press.

Madamba, Anna B., and Gordon F. De Jong. 1994. "Determinants of White-Collar Employment: Puerto Rican Women in Metropolitan New York." *Social Science Quarterly* 75 (March):53–66.

Massey, Douglas S. 1990. "American Apartheid: Segregation and the Making of the Underclass." *American Journal of Sociology* 96 (September):329–357.

Massey, Douglas S., and Nancy A. Denton. 1988. "Suburbanization and Segregation in U.S. Metropolitan Areas." *American Journal of Sociology* 94 (November):592–626.

Massey, Douglas S., and Nancy A. Denton. 1989. "Segregation along Five Dimensions." *Demography* 26 (August):373–391.

Massey, Douglas S., and Nancy A. Denton. 1993. *American Apartheid: Segregation and the Making of the Underclass.* Cambridge, MA: Harvard University Press.

Massey, Douglas S., and Mitchell L. Eggers. 1990. "The Ecology of Inequality: Minorities and the Concentration of Poverty, 1970–1980." *American Journal of Sociology* 95 (March):1153–1188.

Massey, Douglas S., and Eric Fong. 1990. "Segregation and Neighborhood Quality: Blacks, Hispanics, and Asians in the San Francisco Metropolitan Area." *Social Forces* 69 (September):15–32.

Meier, Barry. 1994. "Casinos Putting Tribes at Odds." *New York Times* (January 13):D1+.

Minerbrook, Scott. 1994. "Home Ownership Anchors the Middle Class," pp. 157–161 in John A. Kromkowski (ed.), *Race and Ethnic Relations 94/95.* Guilford, CT: Dushkin Publishing Group. Fourth edition.

Mladenka, Kenneth R. 1989. "Barriers to Hispanic Employment Success in 1,200 Cities." *Social Science Quarterly* 70 (June):391–407.

Morrison, Ann M., and Mary Ann Von Glinow. 1990. "Women and Minorities in Management." *American Psychologist* 45 (February):200–208.

News Media & the Law. 1992. "Jury Awards $850,000 in Fair Housing Case." 16 (summer):6.

O'Hare, William P., William H. Frey, and Dan Fost. 1994. "Asians in the Suburbs." *American Demographics* 16 (May):32–38.

Olson, James S., and Raymond Wilson. 1984. *Native Americans in the Twentieth Century.* Provo: Brigham Young University Press.

Passell, Peter. 1994. "Foxwoods, a Casino Success Story." *New York Times* (August 8):D1+.

Pettigrew, Thomas F., and Joanne Martin. 1987. "Shaping the Organizational Context for Black American Inclusion." *Journal of Social Issues* 43:41–78.

Pomer, Marshall I. 1986. "Labor Market Structure, Intragenerational Mobility, and Discrimination: Black Male Advancement Out of Low-Paying Occupations, 1962–1973." *American Sociological Review* 51 (October):650–659.

Rhoden, William C. 1990. "The Man Who Has His Own." *New York Times* (May 25):B5.

Rosenbaum, Emily. 1994. "The Constraints on Minority Housing Choices, New York City, 1978–1987." *Social Forces* 72 (March):725–747.

Sanders, Jimy M., and Victor Nee. 1987. "Limits of Ethnic Solidarity in the Enclave Economy." *American Sociological Review* 52 (December):745–773.

Schaefer, Richard T. 1993. *Racial & Ethnic Groups.* New York: HarperCollins. Fifth edition.

Scherreik, Susan. 1994. "More Banks Taking Space in Ethnic Neighborhoods." *New York Times* (February 20): section 10, p. 7.

Schneider, John J., and D. Stanley Eitzen. 1986. "Racial Segregation by Professional Football Positions, 1960–1985." *Sociology and Social Research* 70 (July):259–261.

Schneider, Keith. 1993. "The Regulatory Thickets of Environmental Racism." *New York Times* (December 19):Sec. 4, p. 5.

Schneider, Mark, and Thomas Phelan. 1990. "Blacks and Jobs: Never the Twain Shall Meet?" *Urban Affairs Quarterly* 26 (December):299–312.

Sklar, Holly. 1995. "Imagine a Country," pp. 121–130 in Paula S. Rothenberg (ed.), *Race, Class, and Gender in the United States: An Integrated Study.* New York: St. Martin's Press. Third edition.

Sokoloff, Natalie J. 1988. "Evaluating Gains and Losses by Black and White Women and Men in the Professions, 1960–1980." *Social Problems* 35 (February):36–53.

Staples, Brent. 1994. *Parallel Time: Growing Up in Black and White.* New York: Pantheon Books.

Steinberg, Stephen. 1989. "The Underclass: A Case of Color Blindness." *New Politics* 2 (summer):42–60.

Stolzenberg, Ross M. 1990. "Ethnicity, Geography, and Occupational Achievement in Hispanic Men in the United States." *American Sociological Review* 55 (February): 143–154.

Thomas, Melvin E. 1993. "Race, Class, and Personal Income: An Empirical Test of the Declining Significance of Race Thesis, 1968–1988." *Social Problems* 40 (August): 328–342.

Thomas, Melvin E., Cedric Herring, and Hayward Derrick Horton. 1994. "Discrimination over the Life Course: A Synthetic Cohort Analysis of Earnings Differences between Black and White Males, 1940–1990." *Social Problems* 41 (November):608–628.

Thomas, Piri. 1973. *Savior, Savior, Hold My Hand.* New York: Bantam Books.

Tigges, Leann M., and Deborah M. Tootle. 1993. "Underemployment and Racial Competition in Local Labor Markets." *Sociological Quarterly* 34 (May):279–298.

Tomaskovic-Devey, Donald. 1993. "The Gender and Race Composition of Jobs and the Male/Female, White/Black Pay Gaps." *Social Forces* 72 (September):45–76.

U.S. Bureau of the Census. 1993. *Statistical Abstract of the United States: 1993.* Washington, DC: U.S. Government Printing Office. 113th edition.

Verhover, Sam Howe. 1994. "Under Armed Escort, Blacks Move into White Texas Housing Project." *New York Times* (January 14):A1+.

Wacquant, Loic J. D., and William Julius Wilson. 1989. "The Cost of Racial and Class Exclusion in the Inner City." *Annals of the American Academy of Political and Social Science* 501 (January):8–25.

Wayne, Leslie. 1992. "New Hope in Inner Cities: Banks Offering Mortgages." *New York Times* (March 14):1+.

Weink, Ronald E., et al. 1979. *Measuring Racial Discrimination in American Housing Markets*. Washington, DC: U.S. Government Printing Office.

Weir, Margaret. 1994. "Race and Urban Poverty: Comparing Europe and America," pp. 193–197 in John A. Kromkowski (ed.), *Race and Ethnic Relations 94/95*. Guilford, CT: Dushkin Publishing Group. Fourth edition.

White, Michael J., Ann E. Biddlecom, and Shenyang Guo. 1993. "Immigration, Naturalization, and Residential Assimilation among Asian Americans in 1980." *Social Forces* 72 (September):93–117.

Wong, Bernard. 1987. "The Role of Ethnicity in Enclave Enterprises: A Study of the Chinese Garment Factories in New York City." *Human Organization* 46 (summer): 120–130.

Yinger, John. 1986. "Measuring Racial Discrimination with Fair Housing Audits: Caught in the Act." *American Economic Review* 76 (December):881–893.

Zimmerman, Joseph F. 1992. "Housing Authority in New York City to Compensate Victims of Steering and Discrimination." *National Civic Review* 81 (fall/winter):515–516.

Chapter
6

Blocking the Gateway: Education

*F*ifteen-year-old Mark Jenkins lives with his mother and two of his three siblings in the all-black Cabrini-Green housing project in Chicago in a building that many feel looks like a prison. In 1987 he was caught in a crossfire between two gangs fighting outside his apartment building, and a bullet lodged in his left arm just below the shoulder, shattering the bone. Mark explained, "They sniped me. I couldn't get out of the way in time." It was an automatic rifle, Mark explained. He hears them every day.

Like thousands of young African Americans enclosed in the inner city, Mark finds himself surrounded by violence and frustration, and he is a member of a statistical category—poor black male teenagers—that is more likely to commit crimes and sell and use drugs than any other population group.

Mark, however, is determined to avoid such an outcome. He has not joined a gang; he goes to school regularly; he sells newspapers on weekends; and he often surprises his mother by cleaning the apartment and then complaining when his siblings mess it up. The violence around Mark, however, has affected him. In 1987 he spent two weeks in a juvenile-detention center on assault charges. Later the charges were dropped, with the probation officer reporting that Mark was wrongly accused.

So here is a young person struggling to survive and do well in an environment that makes his efforts difficult or perhaps futile. What role has schooling played? Early in elementary school, Mark earned good grades but then had to repeat the sixth grade when standardized tests revealed that he was reading at only a second-grade level. In the fall of 1987, he had to transfer to Lincoln Park High School, in spite of poor grades, because he had become too old for elementary school.

Mark labors at school work but does not do well. It would be miraculous if he did. All his life he has attended poorly financed, overcrowded inner-city schools. Seldom have teachers paid much attention to him; never have they systematically tried to overcome his lifelong educational disadvantage. The high school is little help in this regard. While it brings together students from varied backgrounds, Mark and other poor African American students with weak academic backgrounds tend to be separated in classes from students with stronger academic preparation. In the hallways Mark passes middle-class white and black students wearing teeshirts and sweatshirts representing top universities; he imagines that they live in nice homes where they don't need to dodge bullets and explained that they deserve a better life than he because "they're smarter than me." This, according to experts, is not an unusual analysis; while poor delinquents tend to blame society for their plight, poor nondelinquents are likely to blame themselves. Having grown up in an all-black housing project, Mark has had almost no contact with whites and is wary of them. He said that he has no white friends and added, "We don't have nothing in common."

Mark's goals in life are modest by many Americans' standards. He would like to graduate from high school and either go on to college or the Navy. He would also like to visit New York. But he is failing several of his courses; the circulation manager is cutting back the number of paperboys and so Mark is probably going to lose his job; and several of the local gangs are trying to recruit him (Wilkerson, 1988).

This is not a pleasant, inspiring account. It doesn't coincide with the American dream, emphasizing that hard-working, ambitious young men, in the Horatio Alger mold, are sure bets for success and glory. What that dream fails to recognize is that for people who are poor and belong to racial minorities, circumstances dictate that the dream either never exists or starts to fade rapidly at an early age. And schools, we find, play a significant role in the absence or death of that dream.

At this point let us consider the role of education in American society and then assess how racism links to educational policy. To begin, in preindustrial life, education had relatively little career significance for most individuals. They pursued a line of work, often that maintained by their parents—farming, a trade, some activity where expertise developed strictly out of experience and credentials were seldom an issue.

But as society industrialized, literacy and other educational skills became increasingly necessary, or—what was equally important—policy makers and employers perceived them as necessary. For a large proportion of modern jobs, American citizens must have formal educational credentials—high-school certificates, college degrees, and frequently graduate degrees.

Supposedly American society endorses equal opportunity for all citizens. However, given the link between education and job success, equal opportunity is nothing but an abstract principle unless all children, regardless of race and family income, have access to sufficiently high-quality schooling that they will be eligible for respectable, good-paying jobs. Absence of such schooling produces the opposite condition—a society in which the economic and social status quo is maintained.

In Chapter 5 we noted that the rapid build-up of the urban underclass has been produced by funnelling large numbers of black and Puerto Rican citizens into segregated, already poor inner-city areas, causing them to deteriorate much more rapidly. Education is one of the important areas seriously affected by this deterioration. In the American public-education system, local property tax is a prominent contributor to public education, and in poverty-stricken areas, such funding will be minimal, perhaps nearly nonexistent. Thus local funding for education in such areas will be very low, and the quality will suffer seriously. One can readily argue that institutional racism is embedded in the public-education system: The economic condition of a residential area affects the quality of education children receive, and racial minorities are disproportionately located in low-income districts, which receive inferior schooling. Figure 6.1 represents the relationship of factors described here.

A close relationship between racism and inferior schooling seems to exist. These are negative conditions that will be discussed frequently in this chapter. But as a foundation for this discussion, it seems necessary to convey some sense of the goals maintained in effective schooling. Consider, for instance, the following statement issued by Cold Spring School, a widely acclaimed elementary school in New Haven, Connecticut:

> The cornerstone of Cold Spring School's program for elementary age child is active, personally fulfilling learning with an emphasis on inquiry and problem solving. The program encourages self-awareness and creativity. This approach to learning challenges children to think as well as act, finding alternative ways to reach solutions. At Cold Spring, children experience school as a stimulating, nurturing extension of family life. Children learn not only cognitive skills but also independence, responsibility, and sensitivity. . . . The sense of community enables them to take the intellectual risks necessary to stretch academically. (Fiss, 1989)

The statement suggests that an effective school establishes a nurturing environment that develops for children both a highly positive image and understanding of themselves, and also the intellectual and emotional tools to do well in the modern world.

Figure 6.1
Factors Contributing to Inferior Inner-City Schools for Minority Children

Racial segregation→Rundown inner-city areas→Provision of limited→Inferior inner-city
                                            property tax for   schools
                                            school funding

Let's recall internal-colonialist theory, with its emphasis on dominant whites continuing a colonial system of control. One tenet of the internal-colonialist perspective is the colonial-labor principle, which asserts that racial minorities' work is menial and low-status, simply serving the dominant group's interest. If members of racial minorities are deprived of effective education, their opportunity for achieving good-paying, satisfying work is minimal. Then there is the internal-colonialist principle asserting that racial minorities' culture is invariably inferior. As we see at several places in this chapter, this tendency has appeared in the American education system as efforts to Americanize students, ignoring cultural traditions possessed by some of them.

In the next section, we survey the historical development of racial minorities' education in the United States. The second major part of the chapter assesses some of the complicated, contemporary issues involving the relationship between education and race—issues that demonstrate the relevance of internal colonialism to modern education.

A BRIEF HISTORY OF RACIAL MINORITIES' SCHOOLING

Most of the slave states passed laws prohibiting people from teaching slaves to read and write. Masters felt that if they became literate, they might read antislavery newspapers and become discontent or forge passes and escape (Rothenberg, 1988:191). Still some, like Frederick Douglass, learned how to read. In his autobiography Douglass indicated that while working in Baltimore, he traded bread to poor white boys for "that more valuable bread of knowledge" (Douglass, 1968:54).

In the mid-nineteenth century, northern public schools excluded African Americans. Many towns and cities made no provisions for blacks' education while others, including Boston and New York, supplied modest funding for segregated, highly inferior schools (Bailyn et al., 1977:503).

Educational discrimination carried into the twentieth century, with inequality greater in the South than in the North. In 1940, for example, data compiled by the U.S. Department of Education from a dozen southern states indicated that per-pupil expenditures for whites averaged over three times those for blacks, with white students in Mississippi receiving seven times the amount provided blacks (Jaynes and Williams, 1989:58). Clearly the southern states operating under a legally mandated "separate but equal" doctrine were providing educational facilities for African Americans that were far short of equal.

Through the 1940s and early 1950s, there was an accumulation of legal precedents challenging the "separate but equal" doctrine, but the decisions used cautious, narrow wording. Then in 1954 in *Brown* v. *Board of Education,* the Supreme Court took a bolder step, declaring separate educational facilities for different racial groups unequal and inhumane. The following year the Supreme Court stated that school desegregation should proceed "with all deliberate speed" (Bailyn et al., 1977:1219–1220).

But there was strong opposition from many southern whites. In 1957, in the first effort to desegregate southern public schools, Governor Orval Faubus of Arkansas ordered the National Guard to prevent nine African American students from enrolling in previously all-white Central High School. Each morning the students vainly tried to enter the school and were turned away by the Guard troops. An ever larger mob of angry whites gathered each day to make certain that the black students were stopped. Several times violence broke out, and one day two black reporters were beaten and schools' windows and doors were broken. President Eisenhower, a former general, saw the situation strictly in military terms—as an insurrection against the federal government. The solution, he decided, was to deploy a thousand riot-trained troops of the 101st Airborne Division. Through the school year, the troops occupied the school, and while violence declined, black students encountered countless incidents where they were mocked and ridiculed (Branch, 1988:223–224).

School desegregation proceeded very slowly in the South. White groups like the White Citizens' Councils threatened and intimidated African American students integrating schools, and many administrators resisted the law or simply closed their schools. In 1954 in 11 southern states, the proportion of African Americans attending classes with whites was less than one-tenth of 1 percent. Ten years later the proportion had only risen to about 2 percent. The factor producing a major increase in desegregated schooling was the 1964 Civil Rights Act, which stated that until compliance with desegregation laws occurred, there would be no federal aid to local school districts. As a result the proportion of black students in formerly segregated southern schools rose to 18 percent in 1968 and then 46 percent in 1973. Since that time, however, there has been little or no increase in southern school desegregation (Jaynes and Williams, 1989:75–76).

An analysis of this pattern seems instructive. Many southern school districts have been organized on a countywide basis, combining cities and suburbs, and thus a mandate to desegregate quickly produced a sharply increased racial mix of students even though whites are more inclined than African Americans to live in suburban areas. In some southern school districts, however, separation of cities and suburbs occurs, and as a result blacks, who are disproportionately located in cities, find themselves in largely segregated schools. In the North the latter pattern of school districting has dominated.

In the middle 1960s, the segregated nature of northern public schools became a publicized issue. As mandated by the Civil Rights Act of 1964, Congress ordered the federal Commissioner of Education to conduct a study of the availability of educational opportunities for Americans of different races, religions, and national origins, and sociologist James S. Coleman was put in charge. What became known as the Coleman Report was a massive study conducted throughout the country involving 600,000 children, 60,000 teachers, several thousand principals, and several hundred school superintendents. One major conclusion was that minority-group students from poor areas could frequently improve their academic performance when they attended schools with students living in affluent districts (Coleman et al., 1966). This conclusion led directly to the practice of busing.

The plan was that busing minority students from inner-city to suburban schools and white students from suburban to inner-city facilities would produce an educational atmosphere that would prove beneficial for racial minorities. Busing has provoked considerable controversy and even violence. Most white parents have not cited integrated classrooms as their reason for opposition. Instead they have claimed to be concerned about the inferiority of inner-city schools, their unfamiliarity with these facilities, lengthy schools days that result from long-distance busing, the danger their children face by entering high-crime areas, and the destruction to community spirit produced by the loss of neighborhood schools (Armor, 1989:26). One study concluded that nonracial factors like those just cited were at least as important as the racial composition of inner-city schools in predicting white students' refusal to be bused to inner-city schools (Rossell, 1988). Sixteen years after the Coleman Report appeared, James Coleman wrote about busing, acknowledging "the general unpopularity of this policy, greatest among whites, but also true for Hispanics and blacks" (Coleman et al., 1982:197).

A study of pioneers of school integration also revealed negative reactions. Sociologist Leslie Inniss (1993) interviewed 20 individuals who along with her were in the first group of black students to integrate elementary and high schools in a southern city. Thirty years later the negative impact of the name-calling, vandalism, and general intimidation the students had experienced was still apparent. Two of them had suffered nervous breakdowns at the time and never effectively recovered. The others felt like "guinea pigs who were sacrificed with little or no regard for what might happen to them in the long term." Inniss continued:

> One desegregated school attender reported that she often wonders "what I would have thought like and been like before all those people impinged what they think and are on me." Another female lamented that "we gave up so much and got so little in return." Finally, an extremely angry and bitter male stated that "forced integration was the worst thing that happened to our race." He went on to explain that during school desegregation, "we were forced to play their game by their rules, but now my goal is to extract all their knowledge to use it to beat them at their own game." (Inniss, 1993:9)

The current picture is hardly sanguine. Because of segregated housing patterns and white resistance to school integration, nearly 70 percent of black students currently attend segregated schools. The principal change that has occurred in the past quarter-century is that school segregation is now more likely to exist in the Northeast and the Midwest than in the South; in the 1960s the South led the nation in this area of dubious distinction (Celis, 1994; Molnar, 1993). Consider a typical northeastern city. In Philadelphia, which has 19 new public schools that have been expressly established with the idea of promoting more racially balanced student bodies, the school system remains just about as segregated as it was a quarter-century ago (Hinds, 1994b).

Like African Americans, early Asian Americans faced educational discrimination. In nineteenth-century California, the children of Chinese immigrants, the first Asians in the United States, were not permitted to enter public schools even though their parents, forced to pay extra taxes, contributed to them at a higher rate than most residents. To rectify the situation, Chinese immigrants sued to gain access to schools. In 1885 a judge in San Francisco ruled in favor of the Chinese, declaring that there was no legal basis for excluding Chinese children from the public-school system and requiring the city to establish a special school for Chinese children.

Two decades later Japanese immigrants to the San Francisco area were more difficult to satisfy. Compelled to send their children to the Asian school originally established for Chinese children, Japanese parents rebelled, rallying support against school segregation from the Japanese government, which at the time had considerable influence with top American leaders. In 1907 President Theodore Roosevelt temporarily resolved the situation by negotiating with the Japanese government a "gentleman's agreement" whereby the segregation policy would be removed if the Japanese government agreed to block the flow of immigrants competing with Californians for jobs (Hsia, 1988:11–12).

Since the second decade of the twentieth century, Asian Americans have been very successful educationally, surpassing whites in the number of years of schooling completed. Curiously racism contributed to this success. Beginning with the Chinese Exclusion Act of 1882 and continuing with the Immigration Act of 1924, restrictive legislation relieved pressure on local Asian American communities previously forced to absorb new immigrants, permitting funds that would have been used to help new arrivals to be invested in children's education. In addition, those Asian immigrants allowed to come to the United States were highly selected, with educational qualifications well above the national average.

Prevented from entering most professions and excluded from the relatively well-paid craft industries, Asian immigrants devoted themselves to an ethnic economy centered in agriculture, trade, and services. They strongly encouraged their children to obtain a good education either as a means of entering a profession or of preparing themselves to more effectively run the family business.

With declining discrimination Asian Americans' level of educational attainment has increased markedly, with a college degree becoming the standard. Continuing emphasis on education, particularly higher education, seems to be the rational response of people who are less involved in ethnic industries than in the past, cherish professional careers, and recognize that in modern times these positions are unobtainable without appropriate degrees (Hirschman and Wong, 1986).

Mexican Americans have been more victimized educationally. Early in this century, education officials classified Mexican immigrants as farm laborers and decided that for them and their children schooling was a low priority. Language also played an important role in impeding their educational advancement. With Spanish as their first language, young Mexican American children often found themselves falling rapidly behind children whose native language was English. Evaluated by IQ tests given in English, Chicano children were often classified EMR ("educable/mentally retarded") and were placed in lower tracks that prepared them for low-level jobs requiring minimal formal education. Mexican American children whose parents had a fairly high level of education and used English in the home were more likely to do well in school. Until at least the early 1970s, the principal response to this language problem made by many school officials was a victim-blaming action—establishing a "no-Spanish" rule for Mexican American students. Caught speaking Spanish at school, they were punished. As internal-colonialist theory indicates, such a move was a clear assertion of the inferiority of the Spanish language and created considerable resentment among Chicano students. Not surprisingly in 1974, the U.S. Commission on Civil Rights concluded that the curriculum in southwestern schools did not meet Chicano students' needs; it effectively served just one group—white, middle-class, English-speaking children (Simpson and Yinger, 1985:342–345).

For over three decades, Puerto Rican children have been having serious difficulties in the American public-school system. A 1958 study indicated that two major sources of children's difficulties were language handicaps and ineffective relationships between teachers and parents. The report concluded with 23 recommendations, many stressing closer personal attention to the individual child and much greater contact with children's parents. A decade later a nationwide conference on Puerto Rican education indicated that instead of improving, problems were worsening (Fitzpatrick, 1987:141–142). The trend has continued. Recent data have indicated that of all the groups discussed in this book, Puerto Ricans have the lowest Scholastic Aptitude Test (SAT) scores (*New York Times,* 1994) as well as the highest school-dropout rate (Fuentes, 1994).

From the early colonial era until well into the twentieth century, Native Americans have faced a relentless criticism highlighted by internal colonialism—that they have suffered from an inferior cultural tradition. Early schools were run by the Bureau of Indian Affairs or religious groups which received government financing. As we noted in Chapter 3, many officials believed that the most efficient means of Americanizing Indian children was to send them to boarding schools where they could be systematically "civilized" as preparation for becoming submissive domestic workers or manual laborers. Between 1890 and 1930 in the Southwest, for instance, about one-quarter of Indian children attended such boarding schools. This sometimes brutal, often humiliating practice was never particularly successful, and it ended during the 1920s.

By the mid–1930s, the emphasis was on public schools for Native Americans. Nonetheless after World War II, large proportions of Indian children were still not enrolled in school. Since the 1960s growing pressure from Native Americans has produced improved schooling and higher levels of attendance although widespread complaints persist about the quality of education and the emphasis on a curriculum which either ignores or denigrates traditional Indian cultures. A chilling reality is that after the tenth grade, about 36 percent of Native American pupils drop out of school—a figure twice that of whites.

Native American children generally fall below national averages on standardized tests. At the third-grade level, they are about one year below the national average, and that margin increases to two years for high-school students. What factors produce this result? Researchers have indicated that the environment in which Indian children develop plays a major role. Frequently their families offer limited effective preparation for school performance; many Native American parents are illiterate or minimally educated and speak little or no English. In addition, communities in which Indian children live provide mixed messages about doing well in school and seeking success in "the white world"

(Feagin and Feagin, 1993:200–201; Fuchs and Havighurst, 1972:118–135; Lomawaima, 1993; Schaefer, 1993:170–171; Simpson and Yinger, 1985: 348–351).

Recent figures show that among people over 25, Asian Americans obtain more schooling than any other major ethnic or racial group, including whites. In 1991 39.9 percent of Asian Americans completed four years of college or more while for whites the figure was 22.2 percent (U.S. Bureau of the Census, *Statistical Abstract of the United States: 1993*, No. 233). In the following section, we examine a number of topics involving race and education.

Table 6.1 provides information of different groups' number of years in school.

Table 6.1   WHITES' AND RACIAL MINORITIES' AMOUNT OF SCHOOLING

Group	*Number of Years in School for People Aged 25 or More (percent)*[1]		
	Less than 4 Years of High School	4 Years of High School but No College Degree	College Degree or More
Asian Americans	18.2%	42.7%	39.1%
Whites	20.1	57.7	22.2
African Americans	33.3	55.2	11.5
Puerto Ricans	42.0	47.9	10.1
Mexican Americans	56.4	37.4	6.2

[1] Figures in this table are for the year 1991.

Note: The higher a group appears in this table, the greater the proportion of the group with a college degree or additional education. Thus it is apparent that Asian Americans have been more successful in obtaining higher education than whites, who, in turn, have graduated a higher proportion from college than African Americans, Puerto Ricans, and Mexican Americans.

Source: U.S. Bureau of the Census. *Statistical Abstract of the United States: 1993,* Table 233.

CONTROVERSIAL ISSUES IN MINORITIES' EDUCATION: RACISM OR WHAT?

Recall the two points about the relationship between education and internal colonialism raised at the beginning of the chapter. Racial minorities have traditionally been forced to perform menial, low-status work and also been labelled culturally inferior. In this section both issues frequently arise as we examine racial minorities' access to education and organizational policies affecting schooling.

Opening the Gate: Racial Minorities' Access to Education

We analyze two policy topics here—affirmative action and school desegregation. In both areas people feel strongly and raise arguments to support their respective positions.

Affirmative Action in Education   Affirmative action is a government-supported directive requiring employers and schools to develop timetables and goals for increasing employment and educational opportunities for women and minority-group members. Roots of affirmative action appear in the Civil Rights Act of 1964, an executive order issued by President Lyndon Johnson in 1965, and a Labor Department statement produced in 1970.

Supporters of affirmative action stress that this policy is traditionally American, representing our culture's emphasis on equal opportunity by helping to remedy historical disadvantages suffered by racial minorities in access to education. One team of writers noted that until the Civil Rights Act of 1964, there was "a legally sanctioned and pervasive system of discrimination" against blacks and other racial minorities (Wigdor and Hartigan, 1990:12). African Americans and other racial minorities are especially disadvantaged because, unlike many of the white immigrant groups arriving in the nineteenth and early-twentieth centuries, they seek educational advancement in a highly competitive time period against majority-group members whose educational preparation has often been better than theirs.

Affirmative action can offset some subtle racist practice, the advocates emphasize. For example, interviewers for college or graduate programs might claim that certain personality factors are the basis for dismissing some minority candidates, but in many cases such observations are nothing but coded references to candidates' race.

A final point stressed by advocates is that goals and timetables for affirmative action are not rigid. Goals need not become quotas specifying that an exact number of a certain minority must enter an upcoming college class; affirmative-action procedures are flexible guidelines but nonetheless guidelines to be taken seriously.

Like proponents of affirmative action, opponents might begin by stressing that theirs is the traditionally American position because it emphasizes that individuals must succeed in a competitive situation on their own, without governmental intervention.

One issue opponents raise is that goals might not start out as quotas but that over time they inevitably harden into them, and a quota system favoring minority educational candidates represents reverse discrimination. The claim about reverse discrimination, in fact, is the central concern expressed by opponents of affirmative action. They feel that this policy establishes two classes—those who benefit from affirmative action and those who do not. According to opponents this arrangement presents two major problems. First, its two-part division is impractical. Why, for instance, should Chinese Americans and Japanese Americans, who in spite of discrimination have done very well educationally, benefit from affirmative-action programs? On the other hand, what about poor white males? They are judged solely on the basis of their ethnicity and sex, and no consideration exists for the fact that they are just as clearly victims of poverty as members of racial minorities. Second, the system undermines the time-honored American tradition of judging people by their individual level of success. Affirmative action reestablishes the infamous "separate but equal" doctrine of the *Plessy* v. *Feguson* case (Blits and Gottfredson, 1990:9–10). When people are judged as members of separate categories, opponents argue, inequality—in this case reverse discrimination—is inevitable.

Finally opponents of affirmative action indicate that not even the supposed beneficiaries gain from it. Since members of racial minorities receive an unfair advantage, their qualifications will always be suspect, and they might even have some doubts themselves.

Yet in spite of significant opposition, affirmative action has become widely established in education. Consider, for instance, the situation at the University of California, Berkeley. In 1973 an official plan recommended that each of the state colleges and universities should attempt to represent the general ethnic and racial composition of the recent high school classes. Eight years later, however, a study indicated that while the combination of African Americans and Hispanics totalled 27.2 percent of the statewide pool of high-school graduates, the Berkeley student body was only 8.2 percent black and Hispanic, thus falling two-thirds short of the earlier target.

It was not overt discrimination that caused the shortfall. The difficulty was that to be accepted at Berkeley and seven other selective California campuses, applicants had to rank in the top 12.5 percent of the state's high-school graduates as determined by an index combining grades and SAT scores. Because of educational disadvantage, few African Americans and Hispanics were in that 12.5 percent. To achieve the affirmative-action target, administrators had to loosen the entrance standards for those two groups.

Since the early 1980s, the percentages for major racial groups have remained fairly stable. In the 1988 entering class, black and Hispanic applicants together had about 31 percent of the positions. Asian Americans received 27.5 percent—three times their proportion among high-school graduates. The most striking result might have been that only 38.9 percent of the 1988 class positions went to whites, who represented 61.1 percent of the state's high-school graduates and had received two-thirds of the freshman places just seven years earlier.

Still it was unreasonable for whites to complain since their overall academic results were hardly impressive: A mere 15.8 percent of white high-school graduates across the state met Berkeley's entrance standards. On the other hand, while Asians were represented well beyond their proportion of the high-school population, a large number of Asians who met the minimum standard for Berkeley were rejected. In television interview and newspaper articles, frustrated Asian American applicants indicated that they had attained the academic criteria for entrance to Berkeley and still had been turned away (Hacker, 1992:136–138). Clearly the Berkeley situation was a ticklish one. In admitting different groups, admissions officials considered both affirmative-action criteria and academic performance, with the emphasis often on the former.

Conflict theory, the body of theory to which internal colonialism belongs, emphasizes that there will invariably be a struggle for scarce resources, and certainly limited student slots at a highly regarded university represents a clear case in point. While one might feel compassion for white students whose test scores and grades must be better than minority-group members to be accepted in select colleges or universities, one should fully appreciate historical conditions that produced the current underrepresentation of many racial minorities and recognize that justice demands compensation for those conditions.

A critical requirement, however, is that minorities meet the basic performance standards of the school they enter. Otherwise majority-group members will inevitably feel that they have been unfairly deprived, and minority-group individuals well might end up doing badly and feeling inadequate (Gleckman et al., 1993). If affirmative-action standards open up places in a college or university for minority students who drop out of college in disproportionately high numbers, then administrators have not established an effective policy, and everyone has lost. On the other hand, it would be justifiable to set lower SAT requirements for minorities, because these tests are poor predicators of academic performance in college.

Actually one major racial minority—Asian Americans—bears a unique relationship to affirmative action. Because of special historical conditions, some of which we have discussed, they have been unusually successful educationally. They have done so well, in fact, that in some high-level educational programs, a substantial portion of eligible Asian American students are rejected. In spite of very similar scores to whites' on the Standardized Aptitude Tests and comparable levels of participation in such nonacademic areas as sports and artistic activities, Asian Americans' acceptance rate at Brown, Harvard, Princeton, and Stanford have been only about 70 percent whites' rate (Bunzel and Au, 1987:53–56). At such colleges Asian Americans gain acceptance in greater proportion than their numbers in the population but in spite of comparable levels of achievement receive proportionately fewer places than whites.

Desegregation and Racial Equality   A review of the hundreds of studies on school desegregation suggested that modest gains in African Americans' performance on standardized tests and in school grades result from one to two years in interracial schools (Jaynes and Williams, 1989:373–374).

Braddock, Crain, and McPartland (1984) contended that the narrow relationship between school desegregation and blacks' academic performance has received too much attention. They examined ten major studies on the connection between segregation in schooling and segregation in other basic activities and concluded that besides short-term academic performance, segregated schooling affected students' lives in other important ways. Black students who attended integrated elementary or secondary schools were more likely to enroll in integrated colleges, to complete those programs, to have white social contacts and friends, to work in desegregated businesses, and to live in integrated housing areas. The researchers concluded that "desegregation puts majorities and minorities together so that they can learn to coexist with one another, not so that they can learn to read" (Braddock, Crain, and McPartland, 1984:260).

Gary Orfield, director of the Harvard Project on School Desegregation, has recognized the importance of integrated education. Orfield and his colleagues have been examining the different solutions to promote integrated schooling when intradistrict busing is not available. Perhaps the best course of action, the researchers found, was to remove many established faculty members from segregated schools and replace them with teachers dedicated to effectively educating low-income students in a racially segregated setting. If integration cannot be achieved, the investigators declared, then provide quality instruction (Berkman, 1994).

While integration offers distinct benefits, it sometimes produces difficult, even painful encounters for students brought together from different backgrounds. Consider a couple of illustrations. At Swarthmore College in Pennsylvania, Alexis Clinansmith, who is white, accused fellow student Ewart Yearwood, who is Hispanic, of stalking and intimidating her—a form of sexual harassment—after she had repeatedly refused to go out with him. Yearwood denied the claim of sexual harassment, saying that because of cultural differences, Clinansmith misinterpreted his behavior. Yearwood did admit that that he disobeyed a dean's order to stay away from Clinansmith, and for that violation a disciplinary committee recommended his suspension for the spring semester. The panel deadlocked on the charge of sexual harassment. Both parties appealed to the college president, who concluded that Yearwood had not engaged in sexual harassment but had severely frightened Clinansmith. The president proposed that if Yearwood would withdraw from Swarthmore for a semester, the college would pay his tuition at any other school and then reinstate him the following semester if he successfully completed a counseling program. Student reaction to this decision was diverse, with some supporting it and others feeling that the president's position had been either too punative or not punative enough. Many students indicated that the president's position was a compromise, and that while compromises were not popular on campus, this one permitted a resolution to a complicated issue that simultaneously involved claims about racism, sexism, and fairness. Afterwards campus life could return to normal (Hinds, 1994a).

Sometimes the issues involving racism on campus seem simpler to college administrators, and as a result they take decisive action. At Brown University an undergraduate shouted "nigger" and several other racial slurs in a well-trafficked part of campus. School officials declared that these words were not a "speech," which would be protected by First Amendment rights involving free speech, but an action that disrupted the campus atmosphere and threatened the maintenance of public order. The student was expelled (Hacker, 1992:150).

Frequently college and university officials do not prepare for issues involving racial bigotry. Then if an incident occurs, they are caught flat-footed, forced to react entirely after the fact. Better to be prepared for such occurrences, with a response plan featuring a predesignated, well-rehearsed "bigotry team" composed of the college president, appropriate deans, campus security officials, and faculty and student representatives. The president, in particular, should be prepared to make strong statements and take decisive actions indicating that racial bigotry has no place on that campus (Stern, 1993).

Minority students have their own sources of support. On many integrated campuses, there are now enough African Americans as well as members of other racial minorities to produce their own organizations and social centers. At the University of California at Berkeley, where minorities compose 55 percent of the enrollment, racial and ethnic organizations are highly specialized. For instance, if students have the appropriate combination of racial or ethnic status and career interest, they can join the Asian Business Association, the Black Sociology Student Association, or the Hispanic Engineering Society. Strong differences of opinion exist about whether separation is desirable (DePalma, 1991). On campuses people debate whether a largely separate existence strengthens minority students' self-image and performance or fosters suspicion and antagonism among different racial and ethnic groups. Can members of college and university communities establish a middle ground, nurturing both the solidarity of individual racial and ethnic groups and relations across racial and ethnic lines?

Sometimes whites are critical of blacks for sticking together, particularly at campus dining tables. Those who make such criticisms often fail to consider that whites also tend to prefer members of their own race. Moreover, were these critics to examine the situation further, they would learn that like whites, blacks do not habitually sit next to any members of their own race: Like whites they too have preferences based on shared outlooks and interests (Hacker, 1992:151).

Research has indicated that for African Americans optimal achievement results when they comprise at least 20 percent of the student body. With such a proportion, blacks have a fair-sized pool of friends as well as recognition and support from both students and the school administration (Hacker, 1992:166). It is very different for a small number of minority students forced to face a nearly all-white school.

Attending Alford J. Mapp, a previously all-white junior high school, Nathan McCall was the only African American in most of his classes. When he sat down in class, whites would get up and move away. The looks they gave each other made it crystal clear that they deeply resented his presence. The teachers were hardly any better, avoiding eye contact and refusing to acknowledge student hecklers. McCall wrote:

> It was too much for an eleven-year-old to challenge, and I didn't try. Instead, I tried to become invisible. I kept to myself, remained quiet during class discussions, and never asked questions in or after class. I kept my eyes glued to my desk, or looked straight ahead to avoid drawing attention to myself. I staggered, numb and withdrawn, through each school day and hurried from my last class, gym, without showering so that I wouldn't miss the only bus headed home. (McCall, 1994:18–19)

For many African Americans, whether or not to attend a mainstream college involves a process of weighing pros and cons. One consideration is that with less effective educational preparation often available to blacks, they are likely to rank higher academically at all-black colleges than at integrated campuses (Hacker, 1992:158). Such advantages, in turn, mean that students at all-black colleges are more likely to graduate and will obtain higher incomes than African Americans at predominantly white schools (Constantine, 1994; Love, 1993). Finally some African American students want to immerse themselves in black culture and study with black students and teachers. This outlook is particularly strong among some middle-class black students who attended largely white high schools. A senior at Howard University, an elite black school, stated, "My white friends from high school tried to talk me out of going to Howard. But I'd never had a black man teach me before, and when it happened, it made me feel kind of proud" (Alterman, 1989:63).

All-black colleges do have disadvantages. They tend to obtain less funding, possess fewer academic programs, and rank lower in prestige than their integrated counterparts (Hacker, 1992:158). An additional issue considered at the beginning of this section involves the basic nature of segregated education—that graduates of all-black colleges are less effectively prepared than African Americans from mainstream schools to function in the wider society.

In those mainstream schools, to be sure, racism frequently thrives.

The Terrible Twins: Racism and Alienation in School Policy

Florence Grier, a Sacramento community organizer, expressed frustration about school desegregation, noting that her all-black neighborhood had lost its junior high school. She observed, "I'm so frustrated and disillusioned with the whole integration bit. A lot of mothers are beginning to complain. Because what are the kids getting? They can't read. I have people coming to me saying, 'Let's organize and bring our kids back here and demand quality education. Quality teachers'" (Blauner, 1989:192).

As we have already noted, different opinions exist about the desirability of school desegregation, but everyone concerned about education recognizes the importance of high-quality schooling. Conditions that systematically prevent quality education for minority children are racist, or, at least, institutionally racist.

We examine two topics that involve race and racism and that significantly affect educational policy.

Minority Subcultures and Education   The internal-colonialist perspective emphasizes that dominant whites declare racial minorities' cultures inferior. As a specialist in curriculum and instruction and frequent observer of urban teachers, Carl A. Grant became convinced that white, middle-class students entering the teaching profession often have an unconscious belief in the superiority of white, middle-class cultural standards. For example, Grant observed a sixth-grade teacher, who was providing a lesson on topic sentences, telling his class of primarily African American students that having heard rap music, he was convinced that it wouldn't help them learn the English needed to get and keep good jobs. Grant wrote:

> The students silently tuned out this teacher and whatever instruction he might have offered on topic sentences. Had he introduced the lesson by using the words from rap songs to write a paragraph, the students would have remained interested. (Grant, 1989:766)

Language issues, of course, are central concerns for bilingual schools, some of which have been very successful. For instance, in New York City, Public School 84 has provided alternate-day immersion in Spanish and English for both Hispanic and non-Hispanic children. Language itself is not taught but learned through informal classroom activities encouraging social interaction (Morison, 1990). In the Rock Point school, located on a Navaho reservation, students encounter both languages in all grades, with children gradually exposed to increasing amounts of English to help prepare them for participation in the outside world. The amount of class time conducted in Navaho declines from about two-thirds in kindergarten to 10–15 percent in junior high and high school (Holm and Holm, 1990). Computer technology can aid such bilingual efforts. In one New Mexico school which the

Zuni tribe controls such computer innovations as interactive videodisc and hypertext technology have been successfully used to help children learn the Zuni language and obtain knowledge about the Zuni culture (*Futurist,* 1994).

Whether educators or not, Americans sharply disagree about racial minorities' right to seek cultural diversity in schools. Proponents suggest that keeping African American music or the Spanish language out of the curriculum represents a racist display—the assertion that these cultural traits are inferior. Opponents of cultural diversity disagree, saying that they are not being racist but simply focusing on elements of the mainstream culture.

Asian Americans' educational progress has hardly helped those arguing for cultural diversity. People of Asian Indian, Chinese, and Japanese heritage currently obtain higher percentages of high-school and college graduation, test scores, and prestigeous prizes (such as winners in the Westinghouse Science Talent Search to identify the top 40 science students in American high schools) than whites. These accomplishments have occurred with Asian American students "playing by the rules"—not insisting that educators consider their linguistic or cultural background. People who compare Asian Americans' and African Americans' academic accomplishments often conveniently overlook the fact that Asian Americans have distinct background advantages over African Americans, other racial minorities, and even many whites. Asian American students have been more likely than whites to have fathers that graduated from college, attained postgraduate degrees, and were employed in professional or managerial positions. Compared to whites, Asian American students have had higher educational expectations and aspirations and have been more likely to aspire to professional careers (Divoky, 1988; Wong, 1990).

Some researchers have argued that there are serious problems with an educational approach that makes no allowance for participants' varied cultural backgrounds. Janice Hale-Benson (1986) surveyed research on child development in Africa and black America, and concluded that behavioral similarities suggest that African American children grow up in a culture rooted in African tradition and that when attending school, they must adjust to a very different, often contradictory sets of demands.

Like Africans, Hale-Benson suggested, African Americans are born into an expressive cultural setting which emphasizes close, emotional contact. Use of language seems different in black culture. At home and in their communities, black children encounter a strong emphasis on black slang and extensive nonverbal communication, and their entire language experience builds around the idea of relationship—children interacting with adults and other children in a vibrant, emotionally and physically active environment. They master this body of skills and then, suddenly, they enter schools which primarily require analytic more than relational skills, written more than verbal expression, and much more constricted physical movement than previously experienced. What's the result? They are likely to receive such labels as "learning disadvantaged" or "hyperactive" and are destined to fail in the school system.

Black students, in essence, often face an educational process that stresses culturally "foreign" methods of teaching. Consider how this can hamper learning.

William F. Tate (1994), a college mathematics teacher, entered a classroom where a student teacher was working with five second-grade students—four white and one black. To illustrate the workings of addition, the teacher provided the following example: Joe has five pumpkin pies. Karen has six pumpkin pies. How many pumpkin pies do Joe and Karen have together? While the white children seemed excited about solving the problem, the black child sat quietly and seemingly uninterested. Tate asked the teacher about the African American student's behavior. "He's a good kid," the teacher replied. "He just doesn't like math." Asked about using pumpkin pies in her example, the teacher replied that Thanksgiving was arriving in two weeks, and she wanted a problem related to their holiday experience. Let's find out, Tate suggested, whether pumpkin pie is, in fact, a part of all the children's Thanksgiving experience. They asked the children, and it turned out that the four white children were expecting to have pumpkin pie but that for the black child sweet-potato pie would be the dessert of the day. Thus he approached this math problem at a distinct cultural disadvantage. While at Thanksgiving dinner not all white children have pumpkin pie nor all black children sweet-potato pie, the significant point raised here should be clear.

In a report entitled "A Curriculum of Inclusion" submitted to the Commissioner of Education in New York State, several prominent black educators reached a consistent conclusion, asserting that African American students have "been the victims of an intellectual and educational oppression" produced by the Eurocentric perspective that dominates most school curriculums. Such insensitivity, these educators contended, has a "terribly damaging effect on the psyches of young people," whose own "cultures are alienated and devalued" (Hacker, 1992:167).

This position seems distinctly consistent with the principle of cultural inferiority contained in internal colonialism. Educators battle over this issue. Some focus on the supposedly oppressive Eurocentric nature of American schools while others feel that the proponents of this position fail to consider that to succeed in mainstream society, a child must obtain both an appreciation and a knowledge of the dominant culture (Macedo, 1994; Ravitch, 1994). Furthermore, the latter group asserts, Hale-Benson and other critics of American education are not grasping the intellectual and personality diversity among African Americans or, in fact, within any racial group. Dorothy S. Strickland, a professor of education at Teachers College, Columbia University, declared, "We may be pushing an Asian child too hard simply because we expect him to excel in science and he may be drawn to poetry and music while the black child may be the budding scientist" (Berger, 1988:B4). Controversy reigns on this topic. There is disagreement about the effects of special school programs on different racial minorities and also diverse opinions about racial minorities' right to make such a demand.

On the last point, African Americans and members of other racial minorities who want quality schools which prepare them for effective participation in the mainstream economy and simultaneously want some of their own cultural elements—for instance, their literature, poetry, and music—featured in the education system are simply seeking full cultural equality with whites. After all, many whites are able to experience a combination of both integration is some spheres of life and self-segregation in others—choosing where to work, live, and play. As the dominant group, whites have had more personal options and have also possessed the power to control racial minorities' range of choices, including the content of school programs (Hacker, 1989:68).

Hopefully an increasing number of Americans now realize that a nation that incorporates cultural contributions of various racial and ethnic groups into its educational programs not only acknowleges its diverse membership but in the process enriches all students.

Leaks in the Pipeline   At critical points in the educational pipeline, African American, Mexican American, Puerto Rican, and Native American students drop out. Smaller proportions of these groups than either whites or Asian Americans complete high school, enter college, complete college, enter graduate school, attain graduate degrees, and enter the teaching profession at all levels (Blackwell, 1989; Haberman, 1989; Lang, 1988). Marvel Lang, a specialist on minority participation in higher education, pointed out that while equal educational opportunity has been a national policy since the late 1960s, most primarily white colleges and universities did little until the 1980s to ensure equitable access and retention of black students. Lang noted, "Thus, the burden of historic exclusory and discriminatory racial practices are still being felt by black students attending predominantly white institutions. In practice, too few black students are being enrolled and too few graduating from these institutions" (Lang, 1988:8). This position asserts that the failure of administrators at white-dominated colleges and universities to take necessary steps to recruit and graduate a substantial number of African American students represents a clear illustration of institutional racism.

Institutional racism in higher education is a major issue. In the past two decades, changing governmental policies toward educational aid have disproportionately affected racial minorities, notably African Americans. Between 1975 and 1986, outright grants as a percentage of total financial aid declined from 80 to 46 percent of financial aid while loans increased from 17 to 50 percent of the financial-aid package. For two reasons the change has probably reduced African Americans' college-going chances more than whites'. First, the reduction in outright grants seems to have had a greater impact on African Americans, because at an equal level of family income, black families are more vulnerable to unemployment and have fewer sources of wealth (economic assets such as stocks, bonds, and real estate). Second, African Americans are less likely than whites of comparable family income to seek government loans for education. It is probable that a major factor contributing to this greater reticence is that African Americans perceive more economic vulnerability than whites—because of the history of discrimination against them, their more limited chances of obtaining good jobs, and their smaller probability for promotion—and so they are less inclined than whites to take a chance and seek a government loan (Jaynes and Williams, 1989:343). On the surface federal government cuts in grants and increased emphasis on loans to college students would appear to be color-blind developments, but with a little investigation it becomes apparent that these funding cuts disproportionately discriminate against blacks—thus another case of institutional racism.

Consider an additional condition encouraging leaks in the pipeline. When colleges and universities have a small proportion of minority faculty, two reasons suggest an arid climate for minority attendance. First, since minority faculty members are among the major recruiters of minority students, their absence deprives a school of this important recruiting resource. In addition, minority students are less inclined to apply to a college with few minority faculty, because students recognize that a small number of minority faculty suggests that the particular school is no more than modestly committed to equal opportunity for minority groups (Epps, 1989:24). Thus the following statistics are instructive. In American higher education, whites represent about 90 percent of the teaching force. Asian Americans comprise about 3.9 percent, African Americans about 1.7 percent, Hispanic Americans 1.7 percent, and Native Americans about 0.3 percent (Blackwell, 1989:8).

To obtain college and university faculty positions, candidates often need doctorates. Thus recent figures about minorities' achievement in this area are instructive, and the situation does not bode well for blacks. Between 1982 and 1992, the number of African Americans earning doctorates declined by 9 percent. In contrast, for Native Americans, Asian Americans, and Hispanic Americans, increases occurred—by 92 percent, 83 percent, and 41 percent, respectively. While it is difficult to know exactly why blacks' number has been declining, sociologist Elijah Anderson suggested that

> there is a subtle backlash against affirmative action and special treatment. The result is a whole complicated series of things. But the fact is that there are very few mentors. And the fact is that young blacks have no real role models. (Manegold, 1994, A14)

Without question mentoring is a significant issue.

James Blackwell (1989), a leading authority on the subject, indicated that **mentoring** is a process by which people of higher rank and achievement instruct and guide the intellectual or career development of less experienced individuals outside of classrooms. Through mentoring, students obtain extensive knowledge of the mentor's field and also receive emotional support and stimulation to consider entering the field. Mentoring, actually the lack of it, is relevant to black students from the moment they become involved in the educational process. A government official who regularly visited inner-city schools indicated that he rarely met a black male teacher, especially in elementary schools, and that teachers and administrators regularly reported to him that the absence of black male role models is a major contributor to young black males' educational failure (Brooks, 1994:268).

Blackwell's impression is that faculty members seeking to become mentors often want to reproduce themselves, thus subconsciously or even consciously choosing individuals whose social characteristics, including race, ethnicity, and sex, are similar to their own (Blackwell, 1989:11). With small or even tiny percentages of minority faculty at most colleges, minority students have little or no opportunity to benefit from the unique opportunity provided by mentoring.

Does the absence of mentoring represent racism? The answer, it seems, depends on one's perspective. Certainly it would be difficult to accuse a white person of racism because he or she chooses to serve as mentor to an individual who happens to be white. On the other hand, one can argue that the entire higher-education structure is institutionally racist, continuously failing in various ways, including mentoring, to offer equal opportunity to racial minorities.

How can faculty members of a college or university respond to their school's underrepresentation of minority-group members? In the spring of 1990, Derrick Bell, Jr., an African American professor at Harvard Law School, took a decisive position on this issue. Bell noted that at the time he was one of sixty-one tenured faculty at the Law School, including three African American men and five women: There were, however, no African American women. Until Harvard Law School offered a tenured position to a black woman, Bell declared, he would take a leave without pay. He couldn't afford a year without salary, Bell said, but added, "I cannot continue to urge students to take risks for what they believe if I do not practice my precepts" (Butterfield, 1990:A1).

Another approach is the establishment of programs that meet minority students' needs. Olivia Castellano is a Mexican American woman who has always loved education but felt isolated and intimidated in high school and college, where none of the teachers and few of the students shared her background and experience. Then after two years of high-school teaching, she entered a master's program called the Mexican American Experienced Teachers' Fellowship at the University of California at Sacramento. Castellano wrote:

> The program brought me face to face with nineteen other Chicano men and women, all experienced public school teachers like myself, with backgrounds like mine. The program challenged every aspect of my life. Through group counseling, group encounter, classroom interaction, course content and community involvement, I was allowed to express my rage and to examine it in the company of peers who had a similar anger. Most of our instructors, moreover, were Chicano or white professors sensitive to Chicanos. For the first time, at 25, I had found role models. I vowed to do for other students what these people had done for me. (Castellano, 1995:308)

Now after 18 years of college teaching, Castellano sees herself less as a teacher and more as a "cultural worker, struggling against society to undo the damage of years of abuse" created by the combination of racism and sexism (Castellano, 1995:308).

From discussing upper-levels of education, we shift to opposite end of the age continuum and finish the chapter with a crucial issue—alienation and race in minority children's education.

Ghosts in the Classroom

In this section we take a detailed look at how minority children suffer institutional racism in the schools and often become victims of a self-fulfilling prophecy designating them inferior. We also examine some more optimistic material, which indicates successful schools or programs educators, parents, and children have sometimes produced.

For minority children going to schools where the learning process is ineffective, the point about the self-fulfilling prophecy is particularly relevant: It is hammered home to the majority of them that they are "disadvantaged"—that it is unlikely that they will do well in school and that, even if they do graduate from high school, there is little likelihood that they will be able to obtain good jobs. So many of them begin to withdraw emotionally from life at school. They participate minimally in classroom activity, are barely known by their teachers, start skipping school, and eventually drop out entirely—in Nat Hentoff's haunting term become "ghosts" (Hentoff, 1989:138).

Ineffective public education is a problem throughout the country, in the primarily white suburbs as well as the heavily minority inner-city areas, and inner cities contain white as well as minority students. However, the most overcrowded, poorly funded schools tend to have a high proportion of minority students. With these children the process of stereotyping most readily comes into play. Cultural inferiority and perhaps even limited intellectual capacity are reasons given for early failures in school. These children often become trapped in a self-fulfilling prophecy.

We consider some of the major components affecting the production of ghosts—physical structure of the school, parents' role, teaching policy, and, finally, the children themselves.

The Physical Structure of Schools   It might be possible to produce effective schooling in almost any environment, but pleasant, spacious surroundings certainly help. Often poor, inner-city schools are old, deteriorated buildings that look like fortresses, with chunks of missing ceiling, broken windows, nonfunctioning toilets, collapsing desks, outdated texts, chronic shortages of pencils, chalk, and erasers, and, inevitably serious overcrowding (Hentoff, 1989:141; Lukas, 1985:100–102). One writer observed, "Students in those schools hardly get the sense that education is valued or that *they* are valued. And the same message, of course, is delivered to the parents" (Hentoff, 1989:141). The physical structure, in short, can help convey a negative sense of self to students.

While destroying many current buildings and replacing them with smaller, brighter, less intimidating structures might be ideal, sometimes carefully planned program-oriented changes can compensate for physical disadvantages. If school administrators in old buildings can put the structures in running order and provide teachers up-to-date books and other basic supplies, schools can be effective environments for learning. Rafael Hernandez School uses an early twentieth-century building in an inner-city neighborhood. It is a so-called "school of choice," to which parents from different parts of the greater Boston community can send their children. Given the age of the building and the neighborhood, one might suspect that it would be unpopular. Quite the opposite. Its highly successful program, where African American, Puerto Rican, and white children are thoroughly integrated in all programs and expected to learn both Spanish and English, has produced a waiting list of children from all three groups (Glenn, 1989).

Parents   When minority parents examine their children's schools, they are likely to be deeply concerned but feel powerless to do anything to improve the situation. For instance, a black man who had been a school dropout in the South had come to New York City, where he had worked various menial jobs and was earning $90 a week. He had a daughter, and he was disturbed to see that each year her test scores were falling farther and farther behind the average for her age. He could visualize his daughter's future being as bleak as his own, and so in frustration he stood up at a Board of Education meeting to speak:

The father stared at the variously attentive members of the school board. "You people," he said, "operate a goddamn monopoly, like the telephone company. I got no choice where I send my child to school. I can only send her where it's free. And she's not learning. Damn it, that's *your* responsibility, it's the principal's responsibility, it's the teacher's responsiblity, that she's not learning."

There was no answer from the board.

"When you fail, when everybody fails my child," the father's voice had become hoarse with grief and frustration, "what happens? Nothing. Nobody gets fired. Nothing happens to nobody except my child." (Hentoff, 1989:142)

Since parents are not the ones most responsible for education, they seldom are the prime movers. However, they can make a positive contribution when a school is effective. One elementary school in Brooklyn now stays open into the early evenings. As a result working parents who normally are unable to pick up their children come into the school and chat with the teachers. Because of the extra effort produced by school administrators and teachers, parents are also willing to make a greater commitment. Visiting the Brooklyn school, the state Commisioner of Education was very impressed, and partly as a result of this experience, he decided to launch a pilot project in which ten elementary schools in poor areas would become year-round centers of education open from early in the morning into the evening seven days a week (Hentoff, 1989:145).

Psychiatrist James P. Comer's program provides a similar approach. After 22 years of research with black and Puerto Rican children in inner-city New Haven schools, Comer became convinced that such children "are in foreign territory" and that teachers and administrators are seldom aware precisely how students' cultural backgrounds make their adjustment to school life difficult. In New Haven, Comer established an inner-city educational program in which parents can provide significant assistance to their children, becoming classroom aides or tutors or joining school-governance committees. With parental participation students' needs can be more effectively identified and addressed, and as a result children are more likely to feel a welcome part of the school and confident about their activities in school. In recent years Comer's program has become nationally recognized and has been adopted by over 100 schools in eight states (Marriott, 1990).

The key to Comer's program has been effective parental involvement. Sometimes the key to eliciting it is quite simple. At Rock Point, the Navaho school mentioned earlier, the fact that the Navaho language played a prominent part in the school demystified the education process for parents who could speak little or no English and made them much more likely to participate in school-board activities or join parents' committees (Holm and Holm, 1990:183).

Parents, of course, can take the initiative to promote their children's educational success. A study of intergenerational relations revealed that when Mexican American mothers had high aspirations for their daughters, their daughters had a positive sense of maternal support, and this sense of support promoted both an optimistic outlook about the personal benefit of education and effective performance in school (Hernandez, Vargas-Lew, and Martinez, 1994).

For many minority parents, however, efforts to influence their children's approach to schooling fail to yield positive results. According to John O. Ogbu

(1990), poor black parents stressing the importance of education to their children often find themselves confronted by the harsh realities of an oppressive world, making it difficult to convey this message. These parents emphasize that success in school is a prerequisite to success in modern society, but children often see little evidence of such success. They observe parents struggling with low-level jobs, underemployment, and unemployment, and in their children's presence, parents are likely to complain to friends and relatives about "the system" they are encouraging their children to enter. Meanwhile in their neighborhoods, these young people learn about such survival strategies as stealing, drug dealing, and pimping: Norms supporting these strategies emphasize that success is possible without schooling, which is considered part of "the white man's thing" (Ogbu, 1990:158–159).

Teaching Policy   A key—one might argue *the* key—to effective education is teaching policy. A positive, student-supporting policy makes a good teacher more effective. For both the policy and the individual teacher, the goal is to provide children an opportunity to develop a positive self-image and the emotional and intellectual tools that permit them to be successful in the modern world. Educational policies frequently discriminate against minority children's pursuit of these goals.

In American public education, the "graded school" remains prominent. Students are expected to master a certain amount of material in a given year. Those who succeed are passed on to the next grade; those who don't will be held back. Since the widespread use of standardized tests began in the 1920s, the system of classification has become more precise: Testers obtain numerical scores representing intelligence and achievement levels, and as a result students can be classified gifted, superior, average, below-average, defective, dull, or whatever. Because of general cultural or language backgrounds that have left them relatively unprepared to do well in the American education system, many minority-group members tend to score lower on these tests than whites and thus receive the less exalted, more stigmatized labels. As one educator wrote, "Their labels . . . [become] badges—filed away in cumulative folders to follow them every step of the way through public school" (Cuban, 1989:783). A self-fulfilling prophecy has been set in motion, and the impact for many minority students is negative.

But as Robert Rosenthal and Lenore Jacobson (1968) demonstrated, self-fulfilling prophecies also can produce positive results. The researchers conducted an experiment at Oak School, a public elementary school in a low-income section of a medium-sized city. The first step was to give all of the 650 children a standard nonverbal test of intelligence. Rosenthal and Jacobson told the teachers that the test would predict intellectual "blooming" or "spurting"—students' rapid intellectual growth. Then at the beginning of the following year, each of the 18 teachers of grades one through six received names of students who would supposedly be bloomers in the year ahead. While the researchers claimed that the list of names reflected test results, names actually had been chosen at random. Thus at first differences between designated bloomers and the remaining children existed only in teachers' minds.

Eventually, however, teachers produced a self-fulfilling prophecy: They believed the bloomers were superior, treated them as such, and thereby encouraged superior performances from them. After a year these children scored higher on an IQ test than the other children. The difference was especially pronounced among first and second graders. While 19 percent of the regular children gained 20 or more IQ points, 47 percent of the "special" children produced such a gain. For the follow-up year, during which the supposed bloomers no longer had teachers who believed that they were superior, "special" first and second graders lost any advantage shown over their peers. The expected bloomers in grades three through six, however, showed higher scores compared to other children. Thus the impact of the self-fulfilling prophecy took effect more slowly on the older children but lasted longer.

This process unfolds in effective schools. Nat Hentoff, a well-known writer, visited Clara Barton High School in Brooklyn, where the school body is predominantly African American, Puerto Rican, and Asian American. He was immediately struck with the way the students carried themselves and spoke, especially to their teachers. At Clara Barton, Hentoff indicated that

> students looked directly at the teachers when they talked, and whether they were joking or in serious negotiation about an assignment, they were fully involved in the conversation. Their bearing showed considerable self-respect, not arrogance. They were comfortable with themselves, and so they were with others, including adults. (Hentoff, 1989:137)

A consistent eductional policy occurs in the Rafael Hernandez School, which was mentioned earlier. Throughout this school, children of diverse racial, ethnic, and linguistic backgrounds are put together and expected to develop verbal and written proficiency in both Spanish and English. By state law the school can exempt from state testing those students who require bilingual education or special-education services, but because of its policy emphasizing students sharing all activities, school officials have not done it. As a result the average test scores are fairly low, but the children are thriving emotionally and intellectually, building an understanding of each others' cultural backgrounds and with all three major groups—African Americans, Puerto Ricans, and whites—finding their own cultural experiences objects of positive, thorough inquiry, no students feel stigmatized or isolated (Glenn, 1989).

Students: Ghost-like or Alive?   In sociology a prominent concept related to socialization is Charles Horton Cooley's **looking-glass self**—individuals' understanding of what sort of person they are is based on how they think they appear to others. Members of racial minorities in inner-city schools have often received limited positive response from teachers, and thus their sense of self as students is diminished.

In ineffective schools most of class time involves teachers' telling students what to do. For many inner-city students, like Alicia in an all-black Harlem school, classroom knowledge becomes something to which they do not relate. Alicia said, "I'm wise, not smart. I knows what people are thinkin' and what's goin' down, but not what he be talkin' about in history" (Fine, 1985:47).

Once Hentoff read and discussed poetry with the primarily minority-group children in an inner-city high school, acting against the advice of the regular teacher who had explained that the children weren't interested in reading. At the end he was approached by an extremely shy young woman who asked if he could tell her something more about this Emily Dickinson. Later she told Hentoff that while it was weird, she felt some of the same things that Emily Dickinson had felt so long ago. Then very hesitantly she handed Hentoff some of her poems, indicating that she had never shown them to anyone because she had suspected that nobody would believe she could write poetry. It was the first time that anyone in the classroom had communicated with this young woman in a way that suggested the possibility of interest in her work and, as a result, drew her out of the ghost world.

John Simon is a teacher who regularly accomplishes such tasks. He has taken tough, often delinquent, inner-city, primarily minority-group children and turned them into effective readers, writers, and sometimes college students. Simon indicated that there is nothing special about his approach. It is neither revolutionary, nor does it require a charismatic personality, but it does take time. Simon told Hentoff:

> "First of all, . . . you have to listen. When I start working with a child I don't know too well, I spend a lot of time listening to him before I try to suggest a course of study. I have never fallen in with that dumb notion that you have to start 'teaching' from the very first day of class—as if teaching is something that happens in a vacuum without having to take account of where each student is, in his head, on that first day." (Hentoff, 1989:145)

Such an approach not only provides useful practical information to teachers about their students, but it has the added value of reflecting back to the child an enhanced sense of personal worth as the teacher acknowledges the worthiness of what the child says.

The Georgia Institute of Technology (Georgia Tech), in essence, has grappled with the looking-glass-self issue. In the 1970s this engineering school developed several programs to assist minority students' development of math and science skills as well as their social adjustment. While these efforts helped produce less isolated and better adjusted black and Hispanic students, they did little to improve their academic performance or to keep them in school. The problem, according to President John Patrick Crecine, was that "in the past we told them they were dumb, that they needed fixing, and we had them in remedial programs" (Smothers, 1994:A21). As the looking-glass-self concept suggests, the students were affected by the negative image imposed on them; often their behavior supported that image.

In 1989 the program was changed, making it a five-week mandatory introduction for all minority students. Now they take five demanding weeks of freshman math and chemistry with the same professors they will have in the fall, along with the option of a freshman psychology course to lighten the fall load. Perhaps most notable is the spirit of the program. Desi Bellamy, a senior from Athens, Georgia, said that its main strength "made it cool to be smart." He added, "You don't get the sense that they believe you need remediation coming in. And they tell you that you are the best of the best" (Smothers, 1994:A21).

With the looking-glass-self process altered, the results have been indisputable. Minority students' grade-point average has risen to 3.0 from 2.5, and retention has risen to nearly 100 percent. The results have been so dramatic that two other engineering colleges in the area have developed their own two-week program, and Georgia Tech will soon require a similar course of study for all entering freshmen.

Some teachers effectively fight the stigma of racism. Now how does one bottle the prescription for eliminating ghosts in the modern classroom?

CONCLUSION

One possibility is to develop a new conception of schools. Certainly such an approach was apparent in James Comer's emphasis on parental involvement, but educators must go farther.

In San Diego's Hamilton Elementary School, there is a program called "New Beginnings." Establishing the new program in 1991, the developers recognized that many children in this poor district, which contains African American, Mexican American, and white children, arrived at school with a variety of problems: They needed food, medical treatment, mental-health counseling, or sometimes a place to live. On specific cases staff members would meet, usually with a parent or parents present, and brainstorm about possible steps to take. In particular, the program developers recognized that all assistance should be provided in a caring, supportive way—not with the impersonal sense of superiority welfare and other agency bureacrats often display.

So far the fledgling program seems to be working well. Pam Dowling, an African American woman with two sons in the school, consulted with a family worker who served as her broker with other agency personnel. Dowling's sons received help after school, and staff officials made certain that she had sufficient funding to cover her food, gas, and electric expenses. In addition, New Beginnings has made it possible for Dowling to pursue her high-school certificate. Dowling considered the program "a godsend. Otherwise I would have gone into a little shell and said, 'What do I do next?'" (*MacNeil/Lehrer Report*, 1993). A preliminary report has suggested that the Dowling family's positive results are quite typical.

The organization of New Horizons is another asset: Its diverse services, which were previously diffused throughout the city, promote efficient, economical treatment. A challenge facing the development of such a program elsewhere is that many agency personnel are likely to resist giving up their autonomous status: Now staff members at a given agency need to work closely, sometimes in their perception too closely, with other service organizations.

Still the program is very promising. Carrie Parry, the principal at Hamilton Elementary, concluded:

> There's an old African proverb that says it takes a whole village to raise a child, and what we're trying to do is just that—have the whole village raise these children in our school. The more we do that, the more we'll get the outcomes we want. (*MacNeil/Lehrer Report*, 1993)

REFERENCES

Alterman, Eric. 1989. "Black Universities in Demand and in Trouble." *New York Times Magazine* (November 5):60–63+.

Armor, David J. 1989. "After Busing: Education and Choice." *Public Interest* (spring): 24–37.

Bailyn, Bernard, et al. 1977. *The Great Republic*. Lexington, MA: D.C. Heath.

Berger, Joseph. 1988. "What Do They Mean by 'Black Learning Style'?" *New York Times* (July 6):84.

Berkman, Harvey. 1994. "Professor Studies, Acts on Equality/Reality Gap." *National Law Journal* (May 23):A12.

Blackwell, James E. 1989. "Mentoring: An Action Strategy for Increasing Minority Faculty." *Academe* 75 (September–October):8–14.

Blauner, Bob. 1989. *Black Lives, White Lives*. Berkeley: University of California Press.

Blits, Jan H., and Linda S. Gottfredson. 1990. "Equality or Lasting Inequality?" *Society* 27 (March/April):4–11.

Branch, Taylor. 1988. *Parting the Water: America in the King Years 1954–63*. New York: Simon and Schuster.

Braddock, Jomills Henry, II, Robert L. Crain, and James S. McPartland. 1984. "A Long-Term View of School Desegregation: Some Recent Studies of Graduates as Adults." *Phi Delta Kappan* 66 (December):259–264.

Brooks, William C. 1994. "Black Males in the Work Force in the Twenty-First Century," pp. 263–270 in Richard G. Majors and Jacob U. Gordon (eds.), *The American Black Male: His Present Status and His Future*. Chicago: Nelson-Hall Publishers.

Bunzel, John H., and Jeffrey K. D. Au. 1987. "Diversity or Discrimination? Asian Americans in College." *Public Interest* (winter):49–62.

Butterfield, Fox. 1990. "Harvard Law Professor Quits until Black Woman Is Named." *New York Times* (April 24):A1+.

Castellano, Olivia. 1995. "Canto, Locura y Poesia," pp. 304–313 in Margaret L. Andersen and Patricia Hill Collins (eds.), *Race, Class, and Gender: An Anthology*. Belmont, CA: Wadsworth. Second edition.

Celis, William, III. 1994. "40 Years after Brown, Segregation Persists." *New York Times* (May 18):A1+.

Coleman, James S., et al. 1966. *Equality of Educational Opportunity*. Washington, DC: U.S. Government Printing Office.

Coleman, James S., et al. 1982. *High School Achievement*. New York: Basic Books.

Constantine, Jill M. 1994. "The 'Added Value' of Historically Black Colleges." *Academe* 80 (May/June):12–17.

Cuban, Larry. 1989. "The 'At-Risk' Label and the Problem of Urban School Reform." *Phi Delta Kappan* 70 (June):780–784+.

DePalma, Anthony. 1991. "Separate Ethnic Worlds Grow on Campus." *New York Times* (May 18):1+.

Divoky, Diane. 1988. "The Model Minority Goes to School." *Phi Delta Kappan* 70 (November):219–222.

Douglass, Frederick. 1968. *Narrative of the Life of Frederick Douglass.* New York: Signet Books. Originally published in 1845.

Epps, Edgar R. 1989. "Academic Culture and the Minority Professor." *Academe* 75 (September–October):23–26.

Feagin, Joe R., and Clairece Booher Feagin. 1993. *Racial and Ethnic Relations.* Englewood Cliffs, NJ: Prentice-Hall. Fourth edition.

Fine, Michelle. 1985. "Dropping Out of High School: An Inside Look." *Social Policy* 16 (fall):43–50.

Fiss, Irene. 1989. "Why Cold Spring School?"

Fitzpatrick, Joseph P. 1987. *Puerto Rican Americans: The Meaning of Migration to the Mainland.* Englewood Cliffs, NJ: Prentice-Hall. Second edition.

Fuchs, Estelle, and Robert J. Havighurst. 1972. *To Live on This Earth: American Indian Education.* Garden City, NY: Doubleday.

Fuentes, Luis. 1994. "Educating Puerto Ricans in the U.S.: The Struggle for Equity." *Equity and Excellence in Education* 27 (April):16–19.

Futurist. 1994. "Tribes Go High Tech." 28 (January/February):48–49.

Gleckman, Howard, et al. 1993. "Race in the Workplace: Is Affirmative Action Working?" pp. 152–159 in John A. Kromkowski (ed.), *Race and Ethnic Relations 94/95.* Guilford, CT: Dushkin Publishing Group. Third edition.

Glenn, Charles L. 1989. "Just Schools for Minority Children." *Phi Delta Kappan* 70 (September):777–779.

Grant, Carl A. 1989. "Urban Teachers: Their New Colleagues and Curriculum." *Phi Delta Kappan* 70 (June):764–770.

Haberman, Martin. 1989. "More Minority Teachers." *Phi Delta Kappan* 70 (June): 771–776.

Hacker, Andrew. 1989. "Affirmative Action: The New Look." *New York Review of Books* 36 (October 12):63–68.

Hacker, Andrew. 1992. *Two Nations: Black and White, Separate, Hostile, Unequal.* New York: Charles Scribner's Sons.

Hale-Benson, Janice E. 1986. *Black Children: Their Roots, Culture, and Learning Styles.* Baltimore: Johns Hopkins University Press. Revised edition.

Hentoff, Nat. 1989. "Anonymous Children/Diminished Adults." *Proceedings of the Academy of Political Science* 37:137–148.

Hernandez, Arthur, Linda Vargas-Lew, and Cynthia L. Martinez. 1994. "Intergenerational Academic Aspirations of Mexican-American Females: An Examination of Mother, Daughter, and Grandmother Triads." *Hispanic Journal of Behavioral Sciences* 16 (May):195–204.

Hinds, Michael deCourcy. 1994a. "Semester Starts at Swarthmore on Stormy Note." *New York Times* (January 18):A14.

Hinds, Michael deCourcy. 1994b. "Judge Orders Desegregation of Schools in Philadelphia." *New York Times* (February 5):6.

Hirschman, Charles, and Morrison G. Wong. 1986. "The Extraordinary Educational Attainment of Asian-Americans: A Search for Historical Evidence and Explanations." *Social Forces* 65 (September):1–27.

Holm, Agnes, and Wayne Holm. 1990. "Rock Point: A Navaho Way to Go to School: A Valediction." *Annals of the American Academy of Political and Social Science* 508 (March):170–184.

Hsia, Jayjia. 1988. *Asian Americans in Higher Education and at Work.* Hillsdale, NJ: Lawrence Erlbaum Associates.

Inniss, Leslie. 1993. "School Desegregation: Too High a Price?" *Social Policy* 24 (winter): 6–16.

Jaynes, Gerald David, and Robin M. Williams, Jr. 1989. *A Common Destiny: Blacks and American Society.* Washington, DC: National Academy Press.

Lang, Marvel. 1988. "The Black Student Retention Problem in Higher Education: Some Introductory Perspectives," pp. 3–11 in Marvel Lang and Clinita A. Ford (eds.), *Black Student Retention in Higher Education.* Springfield, IL: Charles C Thomas.

Lomawaima, K. Tsianina. 1993. "Domesticity in the Federal Indian Schools: The Power of Authority over Mind and Body." *American Ethnologist* 20 (May):227–240.

Love, Barbara J. 1993. "Issues and Problems in the Retention of Black Students in Predominantly White Institutions of Higher Education." *Equity & Excellence in Education* 26 (April):27–36.

Lukas, J. Anthony. 1985. *Common Ground.* New York: Alfred A. Knopf.

Macedo, Donaldo. 1994. "English Only: The Tongue-Tying of America," pp. 135–144 in Richard C. Monk (ed.), *Taking Sides: Clashing Views on Controversial Issues in Race and Ethnicity.* Guilford, CT: Dushkin Publishing Group.

McCall, Nathan. 1994. *Makes Me Wanna Holler: A Young Black Man in America.* New York: Random House.

MacNeil/Lehrer Report. 1993. (June 30).

Manegold, Catherine S. 1994. "Fewer Men Earn Doctorates, Particularly among Blacks." *New York Times* (January 18):A14.

Marriott, Michel. 1990. "A New Road to Learning: Teaching the Whole Child." *New York Times* (June 13):A1+.

Molnar, Aleex. 1993. "Facing the Racial Divide." *Educational Leadership* 50 (May):58–59.

Morison, Sidney H. 1990. "A Spanish-English Dual-Language Program in New York City." *Annals of the American Academy of Political and Social Science* 508 (March):160–169.

New York Times. 1994. "Gender Gap Continues to Close on S.A.T.'s." (August 25):A12.

Ogbu, John U. 1990. "Minority and Literacy in Comparative Perspective." *Daedalus* 119 (spring):141–168.

Ravitch, Diane. 1994. "Politicization and the Schools: The Case of Bilingual Education," pp. 126–134 in Richard C. Monk (ed.), *Taking Sides: Clashing Views on Controversial Issues in Race and Ethnicity.* Guilford, CT: Dushkin Publishing Group.

Rosenthal, Robert, and Lenore Jacobson. 1968. *Pygmalion in the Classroom.* New York: Holt, Rinehart and Winston.

Rossell, Christine H. 1988. "Is It Busing or the Blacks?" *Urban Affairs Quarterly* 24 (September):138–148.

Rothenberg, Paula S. (ed.). 1988. *Racism and Sexism: An Integrated Study.* New York: St. Martin's Press.

Schaefer, Richard. 1993. *Racial and Ethnic Groups.* New York: HarperCollins. Fifth edition.

Simpson, George Eaton, and J. Milton Yinger. 1985. *Racial and Cultural Minorities.* New York: Plenum Press. Fifth edition.

Smothers, Ronald. 1994. "To Raise the Performance of Minorities, a College Increased Its Standards." *New York Times* (June 29):A21.

Stern, Kenneth S. 1993. "Battling Bigotry on Campus," pp. 236–240 in John A. Kromkowski (ed.), *Race and Ethnic Relations 93/94.* Guilford, CT: Dushkin Publishing Group. Third edition.

Tate, William F. 1994. "Race, Retrenchment, and the Reform of School Mathematics." *Phi Delta Kappan* 75 (February):477–480+.

U.S. Bureau of the Census. *Statistical Abstract of the United States: 1993.* Washington, DC: U.S. Government Printing Office. 113th edition.

Wigdor, Alexandra K., and John A. Hartigan. 1990. "The Case for Fairness." *Society* 27 (March/April):12–16.

Wilkerson, Isabel. 1988. "'Separate and Unequal': A View from the Bottom." *New York Times* (March 1):A12.

Wong, Morrison G. 1990. "The Education of White, Chinese, Filipino, and Japanese Students: A Look at 'High School and Beyond'." *Sociological Perspectives* 33 (fall):355–374.

Chapter
7

All God's Children?: Minority Families

On January 25, 1986, Bill Moyers, a well-known newsman, hosted a prime-time, two-hour CBS Special Report titled *The Vanishing Black Family—Crisis in Black America.* Viewers were taken into a Newark, New Jersey, housing project for an intimate look at the supposed crisis in the modern African American family. They saw black teenage welfare mothers with their babies and children, with young fathers sometimes located on the fringe. When asked about their lives, some conceded that if it weren't for welfare, they wouldn't keep having children. One young man who had fathered six children by four women and supported none of them said, "So what I'm not doing the government does." While interviewing, Moyers generally appeared reasoned and nonjudgmental, but several times statements seemed to bring him close to losing his temper (Corry, 1986).

Jewell Handy Gresham suggested that beyond the already well-established conclusion that poor African American families have significant problems, two themes emerged. First, "a picture of 'jungle' immorality and degeneracy" was reinforced. Middle-class, white viewers could look with horrified fascination at these blacks, readily forgetting many political and economic leaders' well-publicized corruption and immorality, and conclude that these young people were alien and inferior. Second, there seemed to be such "pervasive pathology" that realistically it appeared no intervention could alter the situation. Contributing to this conclusion was a significant omission—the failure to consider the economic and political sources of family crisis among poor blacks. The difficulty, Moyers and others on the program suggested, lay within the African American family itself. At the end of the program, an older African American woman delivered the clincher when she said, "If Martin Luther King were alive, he would not be talking about the things I think he was talking about—labor and all that. He would be talking about the black family" (Gresham, 1989:119).

For many observers of race and poverty in the United States, this CBS program produced a powerful sense of deja vu. In this chapter we see that a celebrated government-sponsored report in 1965 offered similar conclusions. Neither then nor now have the facts cited about the black family been incorrect. Statistics and studies to be sure indicate that serious problems of poverty and fragmentation exist. An effective sociological approach, however, needs to provide a thorough analysis of the sources of these problems.

Treatises that focus on the degenerate quality of black families or other minority-group families are racist in the tradition described by internal colonialism since they emphasize cultural inferiority of blacks' family structure and as we see fail to propose practical economic programs that would alleviate or eliminate the problems. The second major part of this chapter indicates that racism lies in both the dominant culture's outlook on racial minorities' families and in the steps taken to overcome crises associated with them.

But before confronting these issues, we briefly examine the history of minority-group families, which begins to reveal why current problems exist.

HISTORY OF RACIAL MINORITIES' FAMILIES IN THE UNITED STATES

Slaves could not enter into binding contractual relationships, and since marriage is a contract, so-called slave marriages were not marriages in a legal sense. These arrangements required masters' approval, and masters could also dissolve them. They preferred marriages between their own slaves. The primary reason masters encouraged these unions was to perpetuate the slave population, and an owner considered it a waste if his male slave impregnated a woman on another plantation. In addition, if slave marriages involved workers on different plantations, then valuable working time was lost as slaves spent time away from their home plantations. Thus slaves were encouraged to marry individuals on their own plantations, and when this was not possible, masters often sought to purchase the spouse or sell their slave to the spouse's owner.

Frequently slaveholders' economic situation, such as bankruptcy or need for funds, promoted the sale of a slave spouse or child. However, even some owners who were indifferent to slaves' interest felt that if the family stayed intact, the male slave would remain concerned about his family's welfare and was less inclined to rebel or attempt to escape.

The bearing of children was particularly difficult for slave women, who had little or no medical care during pregnancy, childbirth, and afterwards. Furthermore they were required to work up to the moment they gave birth. During the week before childbirth, pregnant women picked three-quarters as much cotton as slave women of the same age who were neither pregnant nor nursing. Not surprisingly over half of slave infants died during the first year—about twice the mortality rate for southern white infants. Survivors received little care from mothers who were kept busy in the fields or household. Until the age of 14, the death rate for slave children remained twice that of white children. In spite of brutal conditions, slave mothers did what they could to stabilize the family, and its division was fiercely resisted. J. W. Loguen's mother, for instance, had to be tied to a loom when her children were taken from her to be sold.

In slave families men also encountered many restrictions. Unlike free men they could not economically support or protect their families. Frequently masters physically or sexually abused slave wives, and a husband's effort to intervene invariably produced dire consequences, including the possibility of death. In spite of the danger, slave narratives indicate that husbands intervened on behalf of their wives many times.

During the slave era, there were about half a million free blacks. Because they could own property and enter a variety of jobs, including skilled positions, their economic prospects were fairly good and their families tended to be stable. While some of them owned slaves, most of the men were former slaves who had purchased their wives and children. From this group the African American middle class began to develop.

Some historians suggested that slavery weakened the value of marriage for African Americans. Once freed, however, they began to marry in large numbers, and in 1917 90 percent of all black children were born in wedlock.

In the late-nineteenth century, racial discrimination made it difficult for most black men to find jobs. For black women, however, less restriction existed, and so even though it was considered a mark of slavery for them to work, many did. In 1900 about 41 percent of African American women were in the labor force compared to 16 percent of white women. In spite of their poverty, black families in the late-nineteenth and early-twentieth centuries tended to be stable, with men, especially unemployed men taking a significant role in domestic tasks (Franklin and Moss, 1988:127–128; Genovese, 1994; Johnson, 1989:53–54; Staples, 1984:218–221). At all income levels, African Americans have endorsed stable, economically self-sufficient families (Furstenberg, Morgan, Moore, and Peterson, 1987; Parker and Kleiner, 1977).

For African American families, the impact of racism has extended beyond the economic dimension into the psychological arena. Writing about the middle-class black family in the post–World War II era, E. Franklin Frazier indicated that sometimes these parents tried to shield their young children from awareness of segregation in various public facilities, including schools. Frazier concluded that because of the persistence of racism "the children of the black bourgeoisie can not escape the mark of oppression" (Frazier, 1957:214).

Frazier's study of the black bourgeoisie is a prominent example of African Americans' long tradition of research on their own racial group—research that has often featured the black family. From W. E. B. DuBois's (1967) *The Philadelphia Negro,* which was originally published in 1899, this tradition extends to Andrew Billingsley's (1968) work and the current writings of Robert Staples (1994) and Charles V. Willie (1991; 1993).

Like blacks, Native Americans were the victims of whites' racism, which also drastically altered their family life. The Native Americans whom early settlers encountered often had considerable tolerance for diverse forms of marriage. Monogamy, polygyny (one man with two or more wives), and polyandry (one woman with two or more husbands) were all acceptable forms of marriage in many societies. Generally polyandry occurred because of unusual circumstances, such as the crippling of an older brother encouraging that man's wife to form an additional marriage with her husband's younger brother, who then served as her chief means of economic support. Polygyny, on the other hand, was fairly common, with more than 20 percent of the Indians of the Great Plains and the Pacific coast engaging in the practice.

Another significant difference between Native Americans and whites was their relationship to the kinship structure, with this factor playing a much larger part in Indians' lives. When Native Americans married, the union was more a contract between two kinship groups (clans) than between two people. In addition, the type of kinship system determined significant relatives in an individual's life. Among the Crow, Hopi, and Choctaw Indians, there was a matrilineal system, in which people traced descent through the mother's kinship structure and the mother's relatives were recipients of prominent obligations and rights. Thus within this system, a boy's father was not considered a significant relative. His mother's brother was his source of discipline and instruction, and this man provided food, clothes, shelter, and eventually inheritance.

When European settlers encountered Indians, they readily adopted an internal-colonialist standard, designating their customs barbaric and inferior, seldom taking them seriously, and thus not understanding why Native Americans continued to follow cultural patterns that were distinctly non-European. For instance, nineteenth-century missionaries, teachers, and government agents were disturbed that among the Choctaw tribe, fathers seemed unconcerned about providing materially for their own children. When the whites learned that the source of fathers' outlook was the matrilineal system, in which fathers' were not economically responsible for their own children but for their sisters', they simply abolished that system. Clans were broken down or eliminated, and the nuclear family became the dominant kinship unit. In addition, a patrilineal system of obligation and inheritance replaced its matrilineal predecessor.

A law that helped impose these changes on Native Americans was the Indian Allotment Act, commonly known as the Dawes Act. Passed in 1887 it provided 160 acres of land to nuclear families and smaller amounts to individuals. Now the American government had made the nuclear family, not the extended family or the tribe, the dominant unit in Indians' lives. Alien standards abruptly replaced kinship patterns that had existed for hundreds, even thousands, of years. Christian morality became the norm for assessment: Government officials did not consider whether or not a custom had historically contributed to individuals' welfare and a tribe's stability. Thus all forms of plural marriage were eliminated even though polyandry often provided economic provision for a woman or family that otherwise would have had no economic support. On the Pacific coast, the potlach ceremonies, in which a lavish exchange of gifts occurred, were considered wasteful, heathen activities and were abolished even though these practices validated kinship titles and produced order among these groups (Kivisto, 1995:265–266; Price, 1984:246–252).

Unlike African Americans and Indians, Asian Americans did not suffer forced change in family practices. They were neither slaves nor invaded people. Their situation to be sure was often not easy.

The Chinese Exclusion Act of 1882, which restricted Chinese laborers who were competing against whites for jobs, also prevented Chinese men from bringing their wives and children to the United States. The Immigration Act of 1924 further contributed to the problem, making it impossible for Chinese American men to have their spouses naturalized. Consequently Chinese men in the United States remained separated from their wives and children for many years (Daniels, 1988:95–97; Li, 1982:306).

In the early years of prejudice and isolation, the limited number of Chinese women meant that American Chinatowns largely contained single males. This situation remained until the 1940s when officials permitted Chinese to enter the country in larger numbers than during the previous 60 years.

In Chinese communities individuals or families did not have isolated lives. Most immigrant Chinese belonged to a family association (clan), which had been village-centered in China and originally involved real blood relationships. When Chinese moved oversees, however, clans tended to broaden their membership, and in the Chinese communities of many American cities, a single clan tended to dominate, with most residents obtaining membership in that clan and maintaining loyalty to it in exchange for protection and assistance at difficult or dangerous times. While other ethnic groups had organizations for their members, Chinese clans were more intense: Even though members were usually unrelated to each other, they considered these groups to be extended families, and all who belonged to an individual's association were designated "clan cousins" (Kitano and Daniels, 1988:25–26). In an often violent new land, Chinese immigrants found their clans a major source of both psychological and practical support.

Modern immigrants continue to rely heavily on their families. A recent study indicated that foreign-born Chinese American women are considerably more inclined than their American-born counterparts to maintain extensive contact with their parents. The latter group are more likely to move out of the parental home before marriage, depart more sharply from the traditional close-knit parent-child relationships, and form significant relationships with nonfamily members (Ying, 1994).

Like the Chinese, early Japanese immigrants suffered discrimination, with a number of California newspapers agitating in 1905 for laws against their settlement in the United States. Three years later President Theodore Roosevelt negotiated the so-called "gentlemen's agreement" whereby the Japanese government agreed not to issue any more passports to laborers if Japanese American children in San Francisco could enter local public schools. The agreement between the two governments was deceptive in its representation of what was supposedly American citizens' interest. In public statements Roosevelt had claimed that the result would be almost complete blockage of further Japanese immigration. Actually for the next 16 years, female Japanese continued to enter the United States, and by 1930 the female Japanese population, which in 1900 had been 3.9 percent of the Japanese total in the United States, had become 41.1 percent of that total (Kitano and Daniels, 1988:55–57). As a result compared to early Chinese communities, Japanese settlements had a smaller percentage of bachelors.

The Japanese to be sure suffered intense hardships. In the twentieth century, no other American ethnic or racial group experienced forcible relocation, which occurred to Japanese Americans when they were removed from the West Coast in 1942 and placed in ten so-called relocation centers (concentration camps) during the remainder of World War II. While research did not document systematically the impact of living in the camps on family life, it must have been considerable. Quarters were cramped, and centers were surrounded by barbed wire and patrolled by armed soldiers who in several cases shot and killed individuals they were guarding (Kitano and Daniels, 1988:61–62).

One eloquent indication of the impact of camp life on individuals occurs when elderly Japanese Americans living on the West Coast meet each other for the first time. Conversation often begins with the question "What camp were you in?" and the discussion then proceeds with exchanges of personal camp experiences that are so intimate and detailed that all those who were not in the camps feel excluded (Ima, 1982:266).

Recent Asian families arriving in the United States, particularly those entering the country with few economic resources, contacts, and education, find themselves mired in poverty. Refugee families from Cambodia, Laos, and Vietnam tend to be poor, with about a third of the approximate million Southeast Asians on welfare. The stereotype of Asians as a model minority has excluded them from consideration in national-policy debates on issues like poverty, economic development, and health care. Paul M. Ong, a professor of urban planning at UCLA, contended that this exclusion has been part of a larger pattern of failure. He noted, "The country has not dealt very well with those on the margins. It's a tragedy and it affects us all" (Dunn, 1994:A23).

Like Asian Americans, the majority of Mexican American families entered this country under harsh conditions. Spurred by poverty and political instability, about a half-million Mexicans immigrated to the United States between 1900 and 1930. Working as farm or factory laborers, their jobs were usually unstable and low-paying; frequently they found themselves objects of racial hatred or exploitation; and their inability to speak English helped isolate them (Maldonado, 1982:172–173).

In this difficult situation, Chicanos tended to find the family a source of strength. One prominent factor encouraging this trend was Spanish culture, which has taught that close personal relationships are at the core of people's existence and that relationships establishing individuals' confidence, sense of security, and identity are those formed within the family. From Spanish tradition Chicanos also adopted the use of *compadres*—individuals who, whether related by blood or not, become ritualized kinship members after serving in ceremonies as godparents at a child's baptism or witnesses at a couple's wedding.

In modern times families play an important role in another way, with Mexican Americans tending to migrate to areas where relatives live. As young adults Chicanos tend to have a wide range of kin in the vicinity—grandparents, parents, aunts, uncles, and cousins. Research has suggested that the higher the socioeconomic status, the more likely Mexican Americans will retain close relations with kinship members. In general, however, Chicanos tend to remain in the same area for many years, thus keeping open the distinct possibility of maintaining close contact with relatives (Keefe and Padilla, 1987:142–143).

Some recently arrived Mexicans face a new problem. In November 1994 in response to the large number of illegal, primarily Mexican immigrants coming into the state, California voters passed Proposition 187, which would cut off schooling and nonemergency health care to all undocumented immigrants. Within a week of the vote, a federal judge temporarily restrained the implementation of the proposition, saying that it might cause undue hardship and also might preempt powers reserved for the Immigration and Naturalization Service. Following the ten-day restraining order, plaintiffs began legal proceedings to have the proposition declared unconstitutional. Both supporters and opponents of Proposition 187 agreed on one point—that the fight over the proposition could last for several years (Ayres, 1994).

Like Mexican Americans, Puerto Ricans use *compadres*. Among Puerto Ricans *compadres* have a deep obligation to provide economic assistance, emotional support and encouragement, and even criticism and suggestions for personal improvement. While the Spanish provided a tradition that helped solidify family life, they also produced a distinctly negative influence on it. Between 1511 and 1873, Spanish rulers practiced slavery in Puerto Rico. Even though treatment of slaves was less brutal than in the United States, owners responded to the same economic pressures as their counterparts in the United States and thus bought and sold slaves with little or no regard for the impact on slave families (Fitzpatrick, 1987:69–73).

Like African Americans, Puerto Ricans have suffered the economic legacy of slavery. Often caught in the vicious cycle of poverty, they have experienced substandard education, high unemployment, poverty, and family fragmentation. In 1991, 37.5 percent of Puerto Rican families were living below the poverty level compared to 30.4 percent for African Americans, and the proportion of single-parent families with children under 18 was almost the same—52.4 percent for Puerto Ricans and 52.9 percent for African Americans. Puerto Rican families have tended to concentrate in poor urban neighborhoods in northeastern and midwestern industrial centers which have suffered declining employment opportunities, especially for people with limited education and job training (Moore and Pinderhughes, 1995; U.S. Bureau of the Census, *Statistical Abstract of the United States: 1993*, No. 53, No. 73, and No. 743).

Other factors can affect families. A significant negative reality is that across the nation community life has declined, forcing families within all racial groups to fend for themselves to a greater extent. In the following excerpt, a group of elderly African American men suggest that in the 1920s and 1930s when they grew up in Chicago's black ghetto, adult neighbors took a much greater responsibility for other people's children than they do now:

> Ted began: "On our block you would get chastised by an old lady. 'Boy, what are you doing over here? Does your mother know you are over here?' She'd get you on your toes by the ear and she'd drag you home. 'I found him over on Lafayette.' You could get chastised by anyone in the neighborhood."
>
> "That's true," Slim said. "Oh, yeah. You had about twelve mothers, seventeen fathers. Everybody knew what you did."
>
> Ted continued. "We would be out on the corner. All the police would say is, 'I want this corner. I'll be back in five minutes.' If you weren't off the corner, they'd throw you up against the wall and go through this ritual. And your neighbor would come by and see this and say, 'Ted, what did you do?' 'Nothing, ma'am.' That would not be believed."
>
> "'Yeah," Slim said, "you got looked out for in that old neighborhood." (Duneier, 1994:61)

We now move into the present, assessing major problems in minority families and the impact of racism on their development and perpetuation.

MINORITY FAMILIES AND RACISM

In this section we examine two issues that relate to racism: The first concerns a celebrated racist analysis of the minority, primarily black family, and the second examines current racist outlooks on and programs for minority families.

The Moynihan Report

In 1965 a report titled *The Negro Family: The Case for National Action* appeared. While no individual was listed as author—the Office of Policy Planning and Research, United States Department of Labor received the designation—the public learned that the chief writer was Harvard professor, later New York senator, Daniel Patrick Moynihan.

The so-called Moynihan Report created a furor, because many readers considered it a simplistic indictment of the African American family and thus African Americans. William Ryan, whose concept of blaming the victim was introduced in Chapter 3, felt that the document served as a notable illustration of that process. Ryan wrote:

> Moynihan was able to take a subject that had previously been confined to the Sociology Department seminar room . . . and bring it into a central position in popular American thought, creating a whole new set of group stereotypes which support the notion that Negro culture produces a weak and disorganized form of family life, which in turn is a major factor in maintaining Negro inequality. (Ryan, 1976:64)

Thus, the report emphasized, when African American families were not economically or educationally successful, the major problem was deficiencies within the

African American culture. The victims—African Americans—were designated the source of their own failure. Once again we see the internal-colonialist perspective's emphasis on both a racial minority's supposed cultural inferiority and the necessity for its members to adopt standards of the dominant culture.

Since the Moynihan Report serves as the foundation for this section of the chapter, it seems reasonable to discuss the document in greater detail. The report contained five major conclusions.

First, it emphasized that while the white family had achieved a high degree of stability and was managing to maintain it, the black family, especially the lower-class black family, was highly unstable, with an increasing percentage of female-headed families and a sharp rise in welfare dependency.

Second, the report indicated that slavery had been a major influence on the development of the black family. Along with their cultural heritage and personal rights, slaves were deprived of the opportunity to produce and maintain a stable family. When slavery ended, blacks received liberty but not equality. In particular, the black man, widely seen as a threat by whites, was systematically deprived of rights, including the right to work. Thus black women became the breadwinners and also assumed the dominant role in family life.

Third, the Moynihan Report claimed that high levels of black unemployment, which have existed since the collection of unemployment data started in 1930, have contributed to the increasing fragmentation of African American families—a growing proportion of illegitimacy and female-headed families.

Fourth, Moynihan indicated that "the tangle of pathology"—the combined impact of poverty, the absence of fathers, and exposure to delinquency and crime—make it impossible for poor black children, especially poor black males, to perform effectively in schools and in the work place.

Fifth, the report concluded that "the case for national action" was clear. The United States needed an effective strategy, and because of the extent of current pathology in the black family, it could focus only one place. Moynihan wrote:

> In a word, a national effort toward the problems of Negro Americans must be directed towards the question of family structure. The object should be to strengthen the Negro family so as to enable it to raise and support its members as do other families. (Office of Planning and Research, United States Department of Labor, 1965:47)

At this point perhaps you are wondering why the Moynihan Report deserves so much attention. After all, you might be thinking, the document is now about three decades old and probably forgotten by everyone except the fellow whose book I am presently reading.

Actually the last conclusion is wrong. Discussion—not mere mention but detailed analysis of the Moynihan Report—continues to appear in a variety of sources (see Besharov, Quin, and Zinsmeister, 1987; Blauner, 1989:41; Brewer, 1988; Cockburn, 1989; Darity and Myers, 1984; Demos, 1990; Stewart, 1994; Taylor, 1994).

But more significant than these references is the reason why writers on racism and the African American family continue to provide such analyses. As the opening of this chapter suggests, the plight of poor black families has not improved in

Table 7.1   AFRICAN AMERICANS VERSUS WHITES: FAMILY FRAGMENTATION
AND POVERTY

Female-Headed Families with Children Under 18 (percent)		
	African American	White
1960	22.4%	8.7%
1970	29.5	7.8
1980	46.9	13.4
1985	51.0	15.6
1992	42.1	14.0
Families Below the Poverty Level		
	African American	White
1959	48.1%	15.2%
1966	35.5	9.3
1970	29.5	8.0
1975	27.1	7.7
1980	28.9	8.0
1985	28.7	9.1
1991	30.4	8.8

Note: In 1960 there were 14 percent more female-headed African American families than female-headed white families. By 1992 the difference had increased to 28 percent. While from 1959 to 1991, the proportion of both African American and white families below the poverty line declined, a significant gap between the two sets of families has remained.

Source: U.S. Bureau of the Census. *Statistical Abstract of the United States: 1961,* No. 34; *Statistical Abstract of the United States: 1989,* No. 71 and No. 739; *Statistical Abstract of the United States: 1990,* No. 43 and No. 748; *Statistical Abstract of the United States: 1993,* No. 73 and No. 743.

the past quarter-century. In fact, as Table 7.1 indicates, over the past three decades, there has been an increase in the proportion of female-headed black families. Furthermore in 1985, 60.1 percent of newborn African American children had unmarried mothers. All other major racial minorities had lower proportions of children born out of wedlock. For Chinese Americans the figure was 3.7 percent, for Japanese Americans 7.9 percent, for whites 14.5 percent, for Mexican Americans 25.7 percent, for Native Americans 40.7 percent, and for Puerto Ricans 51.1 percent (U.S. Bureau of the Census, *Statistical Abstract of the United States: 1990,* No. 89).

Nobody disputes the statistics. At the national level, the practical necessity is to determine why minority family fragmentation has been so extensive and then to figure out what measures can alleviate destructive conditions imposed on black and other poor minority families.

But our agenda is more modest—simply to learn about the relationship between racism and minority families. One way to analyze this topic is to consider four major criticisms of the Moynihan Report. This approach not only provides information about current minority families but also points out the racism frequently found in official, government-sponsored investigations of racial issues.

Four Criticisms of the Moynihan Report and Their Application to Modern Minority Families

The four issues to be discussed are the Report's analysis of fragmentation in black families, the role of welfare in the poor minority family, stereotyped minority, especially black families, and deemphasis or omission of minority families' strengths.

Fragmentation of Poor Minority Families   The Moynihan Report concluded that poverty produced "a tangle of pathology" that made it impossible for poor African American children, especially male African Americans to function effectively in schools and in the work world. This image—a tangle of pathology— creates the same sense of jungle immorality and dire hopelessness that Jewell Handy Gresham associated with the 1986 CBS Special Report on the supposedly vanishing black family.

Besides its negative imagery, the phrase is vague. To understand fragmentation within the poor black family, the analyst needs to move beyond slogan-like phrases and examine concretely how economic conditions adversely affect poor African Americans. Hopefully in the following pages, we can begin to untangle ideas related to the tangle of pathology.

A useful place to start is Elijah Anderson's study entitled "Sex Codes and Family Life among Poor Inner-City Youths." In a poor inner-city black area, Anderson interviewed prospective and present teenage parents as well as their family members in an effort to understand the process producing an increasing number of out-of-wedlock children.

Anderson suggested that for a young, inner-city black man, members of his peer group tend to be the most important people in his life. As in most young men's peer groups, there is a strong emphasis on obtaining high status. For these young men, good job prospects are remote or nonexistent, and so economic achievement and the status that goes with it are unrealistic. The most available means for achieving high status is sexual—the conquest of teenage girls.

So the teenage boy develops his sexual "game," focusing on his clothes, dancing ability, and, above all, his style of conversation or "rap." Whether the young man is a winner or loser in his peers' eyes depends on the number of sexual conquests he obtains.

If the teenage girl is inexperienced, the boy's game might fool her. But even if she is not fooled, she is vulnerable to his advances. She has her own agenda—the American dream of living with a loving husband and children in a nice house in a pleasant neighborhood. This dream has been nurtured by love songs that she has heard ever since her early childhood and by soap operas, which show affluent, comfortable middle-class housewives.

The dream is sufficiently powerful that when approached by the boy, the girl simply tends to fit him into the dream. If successful at playing the romantic game, the boy knows what is on the girl's mind and exploits the knowledge. He might take her for walks, visit her family, even go to church with her family to show that he is an upstanding young man.

At times even the boy might get caught up in the dream, but then he recalls job prospects for young African American men in the inner-city, and he rejects the idea of becoming the young woman's provider in the middle-class tradition. So he returns to the game, focusing on sexual conquest by playing the role of the "dream man," who appears to plan to marry the girl and live with her happily ever after. A 23-year-old respondent, who had become a single mother at 17, explained:

> Yeah, they'll [boys will] take you out. Walk you down to Center City, movies, window shop (laughs). They point in the window, 'Yeah, I'm gonna get this. Wouldn't you like this? Look at that nice livin' room set.' Then they want to take you to his house, watch some TV. Next thing you know your clothes is off and you in bed havin' sex, you know. (Anderson, 1989:63)

Peers tend to accord high status to boys who can demonstrate extensive control or exploitation of their girl friends. To achieve this, the boy is likely to try "to break the girl down" in front of his friends. The girl often accepts this treatment if she feels that it will help promote her dream of marriage and domestic happiness. On the other hand, if she believes that aggression or manipulation better serves her interests, then she follows an appropriate course of action. Each of them has a definite goal in mind and will do what's necessary to achieve it. As one respondent said:

> "They trickin' them good. Either the woman is trickin' the man, or the man is trickin' the woman. Good! They got a trick. She's thinkin' it's [the relationship is] one thing, he playing another game, you know. He thinkin' she all right, and she doing something else." (Anderson, 1989:64)

Ultimately the boy wants to demonstrate that he "has the girl's nose open"—that she is so sick in love with him that he has complete control.

Interestingly at the time when the boy believes that he is achieving this objective, the girl is likely to give up birth control. She accepts what he told her about taking care of her and believes that if she becomes pregnant, he will marry her or at least take care of her. She thinks little about the job market or the boy's job prospects; she also underestimates the impact of his peer group. She is in love and the relentless dream of marriage and domestic happiness seems very close.

When the girl becomes pregnant, the boy faces a decision. Should he accept the peer-group ethic of "hit and run," or should he risk the loss of his friends' support by opposing the ethic? Actually he can usually maintain prestige in peers' eyes if he acknowledges the paternity but provides the amount of financial support that he, not the girl, considers appropriate. With pregnancy the boy's economic situation becomes an even more critical reality. He recognizes that it is difficult simply to support himself. The prospect of maintaining at least two others seems difficult or impossible, especially in light of the peer group's contempt for settling down.

The young man's economic situation also creates ambivalence for the young woman. Upon giving birth she must decide whether or not to depend wholly upon the father. She might decide that she would be better off financially receiving regular checks from the welfare office instead of occasional support from a young man who is irregularly employed.

Frequently the expectant father decides that his best interest involves leaving the pregnant girl even if he knows that the baby is his own. His desire for freedom is very strong and receives peer-group support. In addition, in a modern economy offering few job prospects, the young inner-city black man is unlikely to have sufficient funds to give him leverage to control the domestic situation, permitting him to "play house" in what he considers an enjoyable way.

Mercer L. Sullivan's (1989) research provides consistent evidence. Sullivan studied young men living in three low-income neighborhoods in Brooklyn, New York. One area contained primarily white, Catholic third- or fourth-generation descendants of immigrants from Italy and Poland; the people in this district were among the poorest non-Hispanic whites in New York City, but their average income was considerably higher than that of the other two groups. The second neighborhood had predominantly black residents who were first- or second-generation immigrants from the southern United States. The final district was largely Puerto Rican, with a population whose members were first- or second-generation immigrants from Puerto Rico. In the latter two groups, about half the families were living below the poverty level and obtained Aid to Families with Dependent Children (AFDC), the largest government-subsidized welfare program. For the white group, about 12 percent of families were living below the poverty level, and less than 10 percent received AFDC.

Sullivan found that among young men in the three neighborhoods, economic prospects and culture combined to affect their responses to getting a young woman pregnant. Compared to young black men in the study, young white men who got young women pregnant were more likely to marry them. Better job possibilities seemed to be the major factor that produced the stronger inclination to accept marriage. Through family and neighborhood contacts—this is the issue of social networks influencing hiring discussed in Chapter 5—young white men tended to have fairly stable, decently paying blue-collar jobs that permitted them to set up independent households. In contrast, young black men lacked such contacts and jobs produced by them, and so they were much less inclined than whites to marry young women they made pregnant. In many cases, however, black fathers did provide some support for their children.

In addition, culture played a role. Puerto Rican men in the study were as poor as blacks and had equally unpromising job prospects, but coming from a cultural tradition that strongly emphasizes marriage, most of them married the young women they made pregnant. Because the majority were unlikely to find jobs that paid sufficiently well and were steady enough to maintain their families, it seemed likely that many of these marriages would soon end. Most of these men, in fact, had come from homes where their fathers had employment difficulties and as a result had left the home when the research subjects were still young children. Earlier in this chapter, we saw data on illegitimacy that showed Puerto Ricans' rate running a close second to blacks'. Those data suggest that in opposition to the results of this three-culture study, Puerto Ricans' illegitimacy rate is close to blacks'. Probably over time the economic factor plays a larger role than the cultural one, causing Puerto Ricans' family fragmentation to be statistically similar to blacks'.

In a third investigation, Mark Testa et al. (1989) also learned that the dominant issue affecting family fragmentation was the family's economic condition. Examining data from a survey of 2,490 inner-city residents in Chicago, this team of researchers found that among African American, white, Puerto Rican, and Mexican American respondents the likelihood was almost twice as great that a single man eventually would marry the mother of his first child if he were employed than if he were unemployed. In addition, while researchers did not have income data, they learned that the higher the joint educational attainment of unmarried parents—and thus most likely the greater their combined income—the stronger the likelihood that they would marry. Testa and his colleagues concluded their article by observing that "improvements in the economic status of both low-income men and women promise to enable most parents to marry and thus provide a financially and, it is hoped, socially better environment for themselves and their children" (Testa et al., 1989:91).

A study of rates of murder and robbery in 150 American cities took the above conclusion a step further. Robert J. Sampson (1987) learned that as a result of a three-step process, African American men had greater involvement in these two violent crimes than white men. Because their fathers were more likely than whites' fathers to have been unemployed, there was a higher likelihood that they came from single-parent families. As a result African American males received less support, control, and supervision at home. Therefore they were more likely than white males to be vulnerable to involvement in delinquency and crime. Sampson concluded that to alleviate these problems, social policies need to address structural conditions that have maintained a high rate of joblessness among black men, encouraged the fragmentation of poor black families, and helped contribute to the high rate of violent crime among black men.

The following case study relates to the previous material on the relationship between African American men's employment and family structure and activity.

Unemployed or Employed Father: Social Impact on the African American Family

For most Americans there has been a strong expectation that husbands/fathers will be breadwinners supporting their families. As Frank Casey's experience suggests, a black man whose chances to be an effective breadwinner have been limited by institutional racism in education and work is likely to suffer a diminished self-image that adversely affects not only him but also other family members.

During the 1960s Frank Casey was hired by a federally funded project called New Careers for the Poor, that trained low-income minority residents to fill positions in the schools, police departments, and other community organizations. Casey was a liaison between the primarily black parents and children and the largely white teachers and administrators. Previously he had worked irregularly, sweeping floors and cleaning streets, and sometimes he was on welfare.

Casey loved his new job. He felt a special relationship with the children—both African American and white. There was something of the kid in him still, he told sociologist Bob Blauner. Blauner watched him dealing with the children. Casey was relaxed and easy and yet without blaming he'd get kids to explore the process that had produced problems with their teachers and brought them to his office.

Casey indicated that because the job permitted him to help others and also himself, it provided him dignity. Most important of all perhaps, it gave Casey's children a positive image of their fathers.

A few years before, when he had either been working irregularly or was on welfare, Casey was at home a great deal. The children would see him when they left to go to school and then when they returned in the afternoon. They would look at him, Casey indicated, but "they wouldn't see anything." In the sense of a father providing a role model, he simply didn't exist. Casey explained that

> a father will go out with his lunch bucket and come back all dirty and tired. I wasn't that way, because I didn't have no job. And a whole lot built up within me that made me feel that I wasn't no father no more. I wasn't nothing but an empty shell. . . . And I couldn't even help them with homework—not that I didn't know how, but inside of me I felt that I couldn't. (Blauner, 1989:151)

This was the situation, Casey indicated, that many African American men he knew faced at home. They were trapped in the black urban underclass, but he wasn't. Now he had a good job, and the situation had changed dramatically. He was earning money that contributed to the family, and because of the money and the impact of what he was accomplishing with students at the school, his own children were much closer to him. Sometimes Casey's children warned him to watch what he said and not to insult the school administrators, because if he did, he could once more be out of a job and be back where he'd been—diminished in their eyes and in his own.

Casey was convinced that one of the most important reasons to hold on to his job was to provide a role model for his children. They needed to see their father as a breadwinner, contributing to the family income—proud and not stigmatized—and upon reaching adulthood they should expect to fill the same role.

Welfare's Effect on Poor Minority Families   Besides focusing on the supposed fragmented nature of African American families, the Moynihan Report suggested that welfare plays a destructive impact on poor minority families. One can examine three possible ways welfare might negatively affect minority families.

First, there is the claim that AFDC and other welfare programs promote fragmentation. A review of research on the topic indicated that there is a statistically detectable but modest relationship between levels of welfare benefits that different U.S. states provide and the proportion of female-headed families (Jaynes and Williams, 1989:531).

Second, the possibility exists that women on welfare are likely to have an increased number of illegitimate children. A review of studies on the subject concluded that there is no evidence to support such a claim (Hayes, 1987).

Third, perhaps AFDC lowers or even kills poor parents' work incentive. In research on black, female-headed poor families throughout the United States, Jones (1987) found that higher proportions of these women were on welfare when the states in which they lived provided primarily low-paying clerical, service, and operative jobs to modestly educated black women. On the other hand, in states where jobs available to African American female heads of poor families offered higher wages, the proportion of these women supported by welfare dropped.

Reading the preceding paragraph, you might feel that even if wages are low, people should have the pride to work instead of seeking welfare support. The problem is that welfare recipients lose nearly a dollar in benefits for each dollar earned, and in some states they also lose health coverage. In addition, while working, they often need to pay for a babysitter or a child-care program. These economic realities help to explain why among the poorest female-headed families, AFDC and other welfare subsidies tend to encourage women to stay out of the work force (McLanahan and Garfinkel, 1989).

Policy makers often ignore or gloss over such economic realities, focusing instead on what the Moynihan Report considered the tangle of pathology dominating the poor black family. In 1988 Moynihan and senate colleague William Armstrong sponsored a bill which claimed to represent welfare reform and was passed by the Senate. This legislation required all AFDC mothers with children over three to enter the labor force as cheaply paid workers. The bill simply failed to assess such practical problems as obtaining jobs in largely jobless areas, locating effective child-care personnel, and getting children to and from their caretakers.

Examining this legislation, a pair of writers wondered "how many of the men who sit in the halls of Congress have ever played a parenting role in which they had the opportunity to engage in such tasks for even, let us say, one week" (Wilkerson and Gresham, 1989:128).

Still the temptation to provide some easy, money-saving solution to a complicated problem persists. In October 1993 Charles Murray wrote an article published in *The Wall Street Journal* asserting that the elimination of the welfare system and food stamps would serve as a major incentive for the reduction of illegitimate births. Murray asserted that when poor women were unable to force the government to support them and their babies, they would either give up having children or, at least, would be willing to turn to parents, other relatives, boyfriends, neighbors, and other private parties for support. President Bill Clinton agreed with one of Murray's basic ideas—that welfare cutbacks would produce a decline in illegitimate births.

As we have noted, however, research evidence does not support this claim. Furthermore Murray's expectation that the elimination of public assistance would enlist the support of family networks appears overstated. As we see momentarily, some families possess such networks. For many others, however, they have broken down, particularly in the poverty-stricken areas ravaged by drugs, alcohol, and AIDS. A study using data from the National Survey of Black Americans, a stratified random sample of African Americans aged 18 and over, found that kin networks supplied financial assistance to only a quarter of never-married mothers (Jayakody, Chatters, and Taylor, 1993). Thus for many poor single-parent families, the loss of welfare payments would be devastating. One writer concluded, "If welfare were suddenly eliminated, many single mothers would probably turn to selling drugs— or their bodies—to help make up the difference" (Massing, 1994:48).

Perhaps because they tend to be closer to the harsh realities of dire poverty, "nonwhites" are more inclined than whites to believe that welfare recipients need the aid (36 to 27 percent) and to support an increase in current funding (20 to 9 percent) (McAneny and Moore, 1994:4–5).

Whether minority-group members or whites, families in dire poverty need financial assistance. To fail to provide such assistance would be both inhumane and impractical. The challenge this country must face is the determination of the most effective steps to move welfare recipients off the roles into productive economic activity.

Stereotypes of Minority Families Consider two titles—*The Negro Family: The Case for National Action* and "Vanishing Family: Crisis in Black America." These are the precise titles of the Moynihan Report and the CBS Special Report on black family problems. So what, you might say. The point is that in these two works, which appeared 21 years apart, the reference in the title is to *a family*—singular. The analysts suggest that blacks have a single family structure: A stereotype emerges—in particular, Moynihan's idea of "a tangle of pathology." This stereotype has continued to thrive.

A study of 25 textbooks in the sociology of the family indicated that nine of the books analyzed black families under headings suggesting deviance or inadequate functioning. There were statements that black families are more likely to be female-headed and to experience unemployment, illegitimacy, and break-up than white families. Such statements are factually correct, but without further explanation they are misleading. Useful discussion would indicate how factors besides race, such as poverty and unemployment, have come into play. (Our earlier discussion of fragmentation in the poor minority family used such an approach.) Otherwise readers are likely to receive the impression "that black families are innately problem-ridden or dysfunctional" (Bryant and Coleman, 1988).

A review of the 283 data-based articles about black Americans published in the *Journal of Marriage and the Family* between 1939 and 1987 revealed a declining tendency over time to present a distinctly problematic, pathological image of the black family. However, research-related factors have contributed to a somewhat negative image of black families in this journal's articles. Since the early 1960s, the analysis indicated, articles published about black families in the *Journal of Marriage and the Family* were more likely than in earlier years to have been quantitative studies conducted by researchers at large, primarily white universities and subsidized by government grants. These studies tended to present an abstract sense of black family issues, failing to represent respondents' point of view and often, with little or no explanatory analysis provided, highlighting statistical information indicating blacks to be more deviant or less successful than whites. Tendencies for this research to have been conducted at white universities and to have received government support have been consistent with this quantitative trend. White universities can best afford the mainframe computers necessary for this type of investigation, and government sponsors have been more inclined to fund large quantitative projects than qualitative studies. In short, all three trends have dovetailed in support of published studies that present an abstract, somewhat negative view of the black family (Demos, 1990). It would be instructive to know whether other prominent social-scientific journals with articles on minority families have produced similar results.

Some researchers have directly confronted stereotypes of the African American family. *In A New Look at Black Families,* Charles Willie (1991) suggested that his study of black families indicated that they roughly divide into three categories—affluent or middle-class blacks, working-class blacks, and poor blacks.

Affluent black family members tend to be well educated, with one or both spouses college graduates. Both adults generally work hard, obtaining positions in the public sector, industry, education, and in private business. Work is often a consuming experience; little time remains for recreation and other kinds of activities, with the possible exception of regular church attendance. Because of the income limitations of jobs available to blacks, wife and husband usually both work and as a result produce a total income at or above the national median. A recent study of 41 black professional couples concluded that while the respondents considered work a significant part of their lives, they heavily depended upon their marriages for happiness and psychological well-being (Thomas, 1990).

Middle-class African American families want the home to be a pleasant, often elegant place to live—"their home is their castle," Willie indicated—and so they emphasize modern furnishings and appliances.

Affluent African Americans tend to have two or fewer children and to encourage them to go to college directly after high school. The parents hope that their children will have more opportunities than they did, and they consider a college degree important for success in the work world. In their children middle-class African Americans try to develop the same positive emphases toward work and thrift that dominate their own lives.

Among working-class black families, life is a struggle requiring cooperative activity among all family members. Both spouses tend to be employed, with husbands sometimes maintaining two jobs. The sense of unity in this type of family is often less the result of understanding and tenderness than of the joint effort to avoid major economic hardship. Because their salaries tend to be low, working-class black families find that any reduction in the overall income is likely to push them below the poverty level.

Working-class African Americans consider children their special contribution to society, and they tend to have more of them than do affluent African Americans—sometimes five or even more. While these parents value education, they generally draw the limit at high-school graduation. Job expectations for their children are those requiring no more than a high-school or junior-college education—for instance, employment as a secretary, nurse, or skilled manual worker.

The third category—poor black families—has already been discussed. As we have noted, these families have various problems rooted in poverty. Willie indicated that sometimes poor African American families are rebellious, rejecting the society that has rejected them, trusting few if any outsiders, and appearing uncommitted to anyone or anything. However, mothers remain loyal to their children, and brothers and sisters generally accept the obligation to help each other (Willie, 1991).

To break down stereotypes, analysts should keep in mind that minority-group members' experiences can be diverse, producing a variety of outlooks and behaviors, not a single approach. For instance, a recent study of Mexican Americans' child rearing found not one but *two* distinct patterns produced by different sets of influences. Parents, especially mothers of first- and second-generation adolescents, tended to emphasize early autonomy, productive use of time, and strict adherence to rules while third-generation adolescents were reared with greater emotional support. These variations in outlook emerged because of diverse influences on the two sets of parents. The first- and second-generation parents were immigrants from a highly traditional culture and thus had grown up believing that their children's success in an alien world required a disciplined, dedicated approach. On the other hand, third-generation parents, who had all been born in the United States, had two experiences making them more inclined than earlier generations of parents to tune into their children's emotional needs: First, better educated than their own parents, they had been more extensively exposed in school to the importance of providing emotional support during child rearing; second, unlike their own parents, they had been lifelong victims of discriminatory treatment and wanted to compensate their children for a similar exposure by providing extensive emotional support (Buriel, 1993).

Table 7.2 provides economic data on black, Hispanic, Asian American, and white families. Like the previous discussion, it suggests that all three sets of families are too diversified in income to fit an economic stereotype.

Deemphasis or Omission of Minority Families' Strengths   Stereotypes are negative, failing to consider possible positive qualities in a group. For the black family, Moynihan's "tangle-of-pathology" perspective is invariably negative. In contrast, research has suggested positive qualities about minority families.

A study of 41 black families that were poor, urban, and intact found that the husband played a prominent role. In at least seven out of ten cases, the husband was the main provider and was an active decision maker in such issues as choosing household appliances and selecting the residence (Robinson, Bailey, and Smith, 1985).

Since the days of slavery, African American families sometimes have informally adopted the children of fellow family members or friends when medical, financial, housing, emotional, or other emergencies have arisen (Littlejohn-Blake and Darling, 1993). A large investigation revealed that when African Americans faced a serious emergency, eight out of ten had either a relative or friend available to help: 24 percent of the respondents turned to parents or siblings, 21 percent to friends, 12 percent to their children, and 10 percent to in-laws (Taylor, Chatters, and Mays, 1988). A study of poor African American families indicated that resident grandmothers' parenting activity was substantial, second only to mothers in areas of control, punishment, support, and presence at bedtime (Pearson et al., 1990).

A serious reality is that white, middle-class practitioners often lack the knowledge and experience to function effectively in this intergenerational context. Generalizing from their own social world, these individuals often believe that grandparents must be in their 50s or older. Thus when a mother was held by the police and the 34-year-old grandmother showed up to take temporary possession of her grandchildren, the social worker in charge refused to release them, believing that the woman must be an impostor since she appeared too young to be a grandmother. Eventually the issue was resolved, but the incident "did irreparable damage to the relationship between the family and the agency" (Taylor, Chatters, and Jackson, 1993:338).

Native Americans also can often rely on support from a variety of relatives. In spite of government officials' historical efforts to undermine traditional extended

Table 7.2 BLACK, HISPANIC, ASIAN AMERICAN, AND WHITE FAMILY INCOME LEVELS: 1991

	Black Families	Hispanic Families	Asian American Families	White Families
			Percentage in Each Income Category	
Under $9,999	25.0%	17.3%	9.8%	6.8%
$10,000–$24,999	29.6	33.6	18.8	22.2
$25,000–$49,999	29.9	32.0	30.2	36.5
$50,000 or more	15.4	17.0	41.0	34.5
Median income	$18,807	$22,691	$41,907	$38,229

Note: While black and Hispanic families are less affluent than Asian American and white families, a fairly broad distribution of income exists within all four types.

Source: U.S. Bureau of the Census. *Statistical Abstract of the United States: 1993,* No. 717.

family structures, many modern Indians continue to emphasize these family ties. Sometimes young people leave their parents' home and move in with other relatives. They do not need to pay rent, nor must they suffer inquiries about when they plan to leave. One Native American analyst noted that relatives accept that "the child will decide when it is right for him or her to go home" (Edmo, 1990:3).

Findings on the Puerto Rican family suggest that when influenced by the desire for economic advancement on the mainland, second-generation adults are less familistic than parents who were born on the island and migrated to the United States. Such a comparison can be misleading, however, because even adult children who deemphasize family ties tend to turn to their parents for assistance when emergencies strike (Zayas and Palleja, 1988).

A recent analysis concluded that for most of the minority families examined in this chapter—African American, Native American, Chinese American, Japanese American, Mexican American, and Puerto Rican—the extended family has been both a problem-solving and stress-coping system (Harrison et al., 1990).

Nonetheless it is evident that oppressive conditions encourage victims to become oppressive themselves. Thus for minority-group members to interact effectively in families, they are well advised to understand the destructive factors impacting on their lives and work together to overcome the impact of those influences. Consider the following statement from an analyst of the African American family who wrote:

> The stereotypes imposed by white history and by the lack of knowledge of our own past often convince many younger Black males that their struggle is too overwhelming. Black women have a responsibility to comprehend the forces that destroy the lives of thousands of their brothers, sons, and husbands. But Black men must understand that they, too, must overcome their own deeply ingrained sexism, recognizing that Black women must be equal partners in the battle to uproot injustice at every level. (Marable, 1994:77)

In this section we have examined the complex, primarily economic factors affecting minority families. We have also considered the role of racist, victim-blaming official outlooks on and policies toward minority families. Box 7.1 summarizes significant points about minority families raised in this section. For the next issue, similar themes arise once again.

Box 7.1   MAJOR CONCLUSIONS ABOUT THE ANALYSIS OF MINORITY FAMILIES

1. **Family fragmentation:** that limited educational and occupational opportunities have made a major contribution to this problem
2. **Welfare impact:** that analysts and policy makers often fail to assess effectively the complex relationship between welfare and poor minority families
3. **Stereotypes of minority families:** that many investigations, particularly large studies, tend to present a negative or abstract image of minority families; that analyzed by income level, black families divide into three broad types
4. **Deemphasis or omission of minority families' strengths:** that racial minorities' relatives provide considerable extended-family support

MINORITY CHILDREN AT RISK

Recent statistics are impressive. Compared to white children, African American children are twice as likely to have been born prematurely, to have substandard birth weight, to live in inferior housing, and die in the first year. Compared to white children, black children are three times as inclined to be poor, to live in a female-headed household, to have no employed parent, and to be murdered between the ages of five and nine. Finally compared to white children, African American children are five times more likely to be dependent on welfare and nine times more inclined to live with parents who have never been married (Edelman, 1989:22; Taylor, 1990:5–6). Thus it is no exaggeration to conclude that in various life-threatening or life-diminishing ways, black children are at greater risk than their white counterparts. Poor Puerto Rican and Native American children also experience a highly disproportionate exposure to life-threatening or life-diminishing circumstances.

Besides South Africa, the United States is the only modern industrialized nation that does not provide financial or medical aid when the birth or major illness of a child occurs (Rosewater, 1989:11). Since African Americans, Puerto Ricans, and Native Americans are disproportionately poor, this omission clearly suggests institutional racism in government practice: The policy, or absence of a policy, systematically discriminates against a greater proportion of minority than white children.

The relationship between family income and race also affects child-care programs. Because of poverty, low-income parents, who are disproportionately members of racial minorities, must send their children to governmentally subsidized child-care programs. Middle- and upper-income parents enroll their children in fee-based services. The result is that in many residential areas, child-care programs are racially segregated. Because of the Supreme Court decision in *Brown* v. *Board of Education,* racial segregation of schools has been under attack since 1954. However, a similar concern has not developed for preschool child-care programs (Kagan, 1989:77).

A situation that produces major difficulties for some children is homelessness. Among the hundreds of thousands of homeless American children, there are both whites and members of racial minorities. Because of more widespread poverty, minority youth—African American, Puerto Rican, and Native American children—are disproportionately represented.

In 1980 homeless children were rare, but several factors have altered that situation. During the 1980s chronic unemployment rose, especially for young black men. While explicit employment discrimination certainly played a role, the major cause was the restructuring of the American economy, with a shift toward a postindustrial work force most adversely affecting individuals with limited education and job training; during the 1980s minority-group individuals were highly represented here. In addition, the death and incarceration rates rose for African American males. All of these trends accelerated the growth of female-headed single-parent families, which are the most common type of homeless families. Another factor contributing to increased homeless families during the 1980s was a decline in inexpensive rental housing, with rent increases outpacing the growth of personal income; the disparity was particularly acute for welfare recipients, for whom the purchasing power of their grants was only 64 percent in 1990 what it had been two decades earlier (Rossi, 1994). Policy makers and politicians often fail to assess the impact of these conditions on homelessness. As the following account suggests, they are more inclined to take a victim-blaming approach.

On March 6, 1986, David Bright, a ten-year-old, homeless black boy from New York City, testified before the House Select Committee on Hunger in Washington, D.C. When he grows up, David explained, he wants to become president so that he can make certain that "no little boy like me will have to put his head down on his desk at school because it hurts to be hungry" (Hayes, 1989:58).

David's statement left few dry eyes in the hearing room. From Mayor Edward Koch, however, it aroused an angry reply. Koch indicated that David's testimony "simply doesn't reflect reality. New York does more for the homeless than any other city in America" (Rimer, 1986:42). Koch took further action. Trying to prove that David's mother was directly responsible for her son's hunger, Koch had a spokesperson, whom he later appointed a judge of the New York Family Court, leak to the press confidential information from the Bright family's records about the mother's suspected drug abuse.

David Bright took the developing feud in stride, saying that the root of the problem might be jealousy produced by the fact that "I've got hair, and he doesn't." David's school principal declared that while Koch had an effective public presence "he's no match for this kid" (Rimer, 1986:42).

Although David Bright had his moment in the sun, much of his life has been dreary and painful. At the time of the hearing, he was living with his mother and three siblings in two small rooms in New York City's crowded Hotel Martinique, along with 1,500 homeless children and their families. Sometimes his mother would become so depressed that she would tell the children to leave her alone in one room so that she could cry.

But while adults suffer because of homelessness, children perhaps suffer more. There is no physical stability—no place, even though it might fall short of ideal—that provides a basic sense of continuity, a home, during their early years. As one writer indicated, homelessness destroys "the inner beauty of a child" (Hayes, 1989:66).

The impact of racism and poverty are formidable realities that descend on many minority families. Another factor affecting family dynamics is women's perception of their roles. The final section of this chapter addresses that issue.

WOMEN OF COLOR: THROUGH THE CULTURAL MAZE

During the late 1970s, Barbara Omolade became a part-time instructor at an evening college in New York City. The course she taught was for black women on the topic of black women. Since Omolade was completing a master's degree on black motherhood, she was hired immediately in spite of minimum college-teaching experience. She accepted the job reluctantly because she already had a full-time job and was a single mother of three school-aged children.

The course Omolade developed was entitled "The Histories and Experiences of Black Women," and it gave a historical view of African American women's lives as well as analysis of contemporary challenges they faced. Soon she decided that since the students were about her age and came from working-class backgrounds similar to her own, it was most appropriate to act more like a sister than an instructor. As a sister it seemed inappropriate, arrogant in fact, to teach them. The best strategy, Omolade decided, was to present herself as one sister among many railing in a general way against the inadequacies of the current society. Much of the time, Omolade conceded, she simply lacked the background for such critical examination, but she persevered.

Then one day she stopped in the midst of a lecture and stared at the students. Omolade wrote:

> There was silence. Every eye was on me. I was terrified. The students wanted—hungered, really—to know more. They wanted me to teach them, not just to be sisterly and befriend them or rant politics at them. (Omolade, 1993:32)

Responding to the challenge, Omolade worked hard to improve the course. At that time, however, she found it difficult to obtain effective information because there were few available written works about black women.

Less than two decades later, the situation has changed impressively. Ann duCille, the chair of African American studies at Wesleyan University, indicated that she is "alternately pleased, puzzled, and perturbed—bewitched, bothered, and bewildered" by the extensive written analysis currently devoted to black women (duCille, 1994:591). It is difficult, duCille suggested, to know just why this new interest has developed. Perhaps it is because white mainstream culture needs some spicing up.

For not only the topic of black women but also the larger subject of women of color, there is a growing body of literature providing a variety of information. Still the challenges minority women face have not changed greatly in 20 years. In this section I focus on those special challenges, including the feminist option.

The Search for the Right Fit

How should a modern minority woman live? Certainly there is no simple, all-encompassing answer to that question. Comfortably or well, one might suggest. But what this outcome will entail might differ not only from one racial minority to another but for women with varying experiences and preferences within a given ethnic group. Let us consider some of the general social issues coming into play.

Many women of color come from cultures where they are expected to make the family their priority. First and foremost, traditional Mexican culture has emphasized, women are supposed to be mothers, centering their activities in the home. Not only women's own mothers but the entire kinship network along with the greater ethnic community support this orientation. When Mexican American women oppose this emphasis, they are seeking personal empowerment at the expense of a strongly supported traditional family pattern (Segura and Pierce, 1993). Such women can be considered deviants, even designated outcasts.

In cultures where women's lives are supposed to be centered in family activities, they are highly dependent on their families and thus vulnerable to familial changes, particularly divorce. A study of 50 divorced immigrant Asian American women found that since they had been socialized to believe that marriage is their highest goal and that wife and mother their most important roles, they were often psychologically devastated by divorce, with 60 percent of the sample feeling that life was hardly worthwhile without a partner (Song, 1993:188–189).

While women of color can be victimized by traditional conditions, they frequently find that the modern social world opens up new possibilities and options. Lynda Wright, a single black mother of four, was forced to go on welfare when she was divorced after seventeen years of marriage and could not find a job. It was a long haul. Wright found welfare demeaning, with case workers telling her that she had been stupid and failed to plan her life well. She had to struggle to keep her children out of trouble and to find ways to get them the things they needed for a productive life. She had many fights with welfare personnel—over taking college courses, over preparing to be a teacher instead of settling as a jackhammer operator. It was a difficult life, but through it all Wright extended herself. She explained:

> I have a rainbow coalition of friends. It took a lot of growth on my part, because in the sixties I became hostile to whites. I saw hate on people I didn't even know. They didn't try to know me; they just hated me instantly. I had a lot of anger. I did many sit-ins. As I've grown older, I've mellowed. It's all right if somebody else hates. I don't really have the time. I don't try to avoid hate; I just understand it better. (Terkel, 1992:67)

Other minority women have found different kinds of opportunities opening up. In the Coast Salish communities of western Washington and British Columbia, Indian women have become increasingly active politically, now winning about a third of the seats in tribal councils. Several factors seem to contribute. As some women have obtained more schooling and more jobs outside the home, they feel prepared to engage in political activity. A major contributor is that they often receive encouragement and child-care assistance from family members, allowing them to enter politics at an earlier age than most women with families (Miller, 1992; 1994). Other considerations come into play. Before supporting a woman for council membership, tribal members observe her social skills with her own children and with other people. One council member observed that the voters "have seen me work with kids the better half of my life, so I guess they trust in me, and elected me in" (Miller, 1992:376). Among many Coast Salish tribespeople, the belief is strong that women become more emotionally involved than men and more readily will defend the band's interest to the outside world. As one female council member indicated, women are more inclined than men to "really go in and fight" (Miller, 1992:377).

In the course of seeking their identity, some women of color are attracted to feminism.

The Feminist Option

Feminists' struggle is against **sexism**—the belief contending that actual or alleged differences between women and men establish the superiority of men. Sometimes minority women face barriers to engaging in feminist activity.

One reason is that in many instances they find no feminist role models to observe. Kesaya E. Noda, a Japanese American woman, indicated that it has been much easier to establish her sense of self as a person of Japanese ancestry and as a Japanese American than to know herself as a Japanese American woman. The central problem, she explained, is that when she was growing up, her mother did not provide the kind of model that would have promoted a sense of herself as a competent, modern woman. Noda wrote:

> She was my dark self, a figure in whom I thought I saw all that I feared most in myself. Growing into womanhood and looking for some model of strength, I turned away from her. Of course, I could not find what I sought. I was looking for a black feminist or a white feminist. My mother is neither white nor black. (Noda, 1993:48)

As an adult Noda has come to value what she learned from her mother and to appreciate the ways that they are similar. Growing up, however, she felt confused without a more distinct feminist model.

Sometimes women of color deny the need for feminism, declaring that sexism does not exist in their group. Consider the relevance of a traditional African American stance about racism. Since the days of slavery, some African Americans have argued that while racist oppression has been relentlessly imposed on them, they have been able to battle it effectively: The proof has been the continued presence of many strong black families and communities. The basic defect with this analysis, feminist bell hooks suggested, is that it fails to consider that if black women battle only for racial liberation, then they face the distinct possibility that they help establish a society where they are subjected to a black patriarchal order (hooks, 1994).

Minority women considering the feminist option often face significant challenges. Sometimes they find that the white feminist world is hardly a hospitable place, with historical relationships between minorities and whites playing a role. For several centuries the chief relationship between black and white women was a hierarchical one, with the former in the role of slave or servant and the latter in the position of mistress. Such cultural patterns are not readily forsaken, and thus in spite of claims of equality, it appears that some white feminists still want to dominate black women, who often conclude that a true sisterhood is impossible (hooks, 1994:150).

Nonetheless many black and other minority women are interested in feminism and must figure out how to pursue this issue. One place to start can be a discussion with a few immediate associates—friends or perhaps colleagues at work. In small-group settings, women can talk about their perceptions and experiences, learning that the "personal is political"—that only a critical self-evaluation can provide a starting point for a clear understanding of the nature of one's current existence. As women of different economic and racial backgrounds get together and discuss their experiences, they can begin to appreciate both their differences and their commonalities. Feedback from other group members is critical for the development of that understanding. This process is often difficult, requiring participants to evaluate and perhaps reject set ways of thinking, but it is essential for personal growth. Unless individuals' consciousness changes, they will be incapable of altering their actions or encouraging change from others.

The key, bell hooks suggested, is that women belonging to different racial groups understand the "realities of sex, race, and class, the ways they divide us, make us different, stand us in opposition, and work to reconcile and resolve these issues" (hooks, 1992:447). With such realizations in mind, feminists' ability to overcome differences and cooperate in mutually beneficial ways can rapidly evolve.

However, some minority feminists see a major roadblock to such progress. Emphasizing minority women's frequent exclusion from effective participation in feminist organizations, Helen Zia (1993), a Chinese American feminist, indicated that minority feminists must build their own support networks, especially when they are employed in the diverse political, educational, economic, and health-oriented organizations concerned with women's rights and dominated by white feminists. Zia concluded that women of color in these organizations must require that policies mandating minority representation be written into each group's by-laws. A long-term goal should be the destruction of the "old girls' network"—a primarily white informal friendship and support network within the leadership of the women's movement. For instance, in Washington, D.C., the prestigious President's Council composed of the presidents of major feminist organizations has almost no women of color. As a result minority women in Washington, D.C., have formed their own networking group, which is called the Women of Color Leadership Council.

CONCLUSION

Throughout this chapter we have repeatedly encountered two points. First, minority families are often the victims of institutional racism, disproportionately suffering more limited educational and occupational opportunities and thus encountering greater risk of poverty and its associated problems than white families. Second, in the tradition of the Moynihan Report, a victim-blaming strategy has prevailed. With African American and other minority families, this approach emphasizes, the source of serious problems resides in the family itself. If one focuses on the tangle of pathology or other supposed indicators of what internal colonialism labels racial minorities' cultural inferiority, then one can overlook economic and political roots of minority families' problems. To date this racist strategy has remained alive and well.

REFERENCES

Anderson, Elijah. 1989. "Sex Codes and Family Life among Poor Inner-City Youths." *Annals of the American Academy of Political and Social Science* 501 (January):59–78.

Ayres, B. Drummond, Jr. 1994. "Court Blocks California on Alien Rules." *New York Times* (November 17):A16.

Besharov, Douglas J., Alison Quin, and Karl Zinsmeister. 1987. "A Portrait in Black and White: Out-of-Wedlock Births." *Public Opinion* 10 (May/June):43–45.

Billingsley, Andrew. 1968. *Black Families in White America*. Englewood Cliffs, NJ: Prentice-Hall.

Blauner, Bob. 1989. *Black Lives, White Lives.* Berkeley: University of California Press.

Brewer, Rose M. 1988. "Black Women in Poverty: Some Comments on Female-Headed Families." *Signs* 13 (winter):331–339.

Bryant, Z. Lois, and Marilyn Coleman. 1988. "The Black Family as Portrayed in Introductory Marriage and Family Textbooks." *Family Relations* 37 (July):255–259.

Buriel, Raymond. 1993. "Childrearing Orientation in Mexican-American Families: The Influence of Generation and Sociocultural Factors." *Journal of Marriage and the Family* 55 (November):987–1000.

Cockburn, Alexander. 1989. "Beat the Devil." *Nation* 249 (July 24/31):113–114.

Corry, John. 1986. "TV: 'CBS Reports' Examines Black Families." *New York Times* (January 25):49.

Daniels, Roger. 1988. *Asian America: Chinese and Japanese in the United States since 1850.* Seattle: University of Washington Press.

Darity, William A., Jr., and Samuel L. Myers, Jr. 1984. "Does Welfare Dependency Cause Female Headship? The Case of the Black Family." *Journal of Marriage and the Family* 46 (November):765–779.

Demos, Vasilikie. 1990. "Black Family Studies in the *Journal of Marriage and the Family* and the Issue of Distortion: A Trend Analysis." *Journal of Marriage and the Family* 52 (August):603–612.

DuBois, W. E. B. 1967. *The Philadelphia Negro.* New York: Benjamin Blom. Originally published in 1899.

duCille, Ann. 1994. "The Occult of True Black Womanhood: Critical Demeanor and Black Feminist Studies." *Signs* 19 (spring):591–629.

Duneier, Mitchell. 1994. *Slim's Table: Race, Respectability, and Masculinity.* Chicago: University of Chicago Press.

Dunn, Ashley. 1994. "Southeast Asians Highly Dependent on Welfare in U.S." *New York Times* (May 19):A1+.

Edelman, Marian Wright. 1989. "Children at Risk." *Proceedings of the Academy of Political Science* 37:20–30.

Edmo, Ed. 1990. "Cradleboards and Development." *American Indians for Development Newsletter* 5 (May/June):2–3.

Fitzpatrick, Joseph P. 1987. *Puerto Rican Americans: The Meaning of Migration to the Mainland.* Englewood Cliffs, NJ: Prentice-Hall. Second edition.

Franklin, John Hope, and Alfred A. Moss, Jr. 1988. *From Slavery to Freedom: A History of Negro Americans.* New York: Alfred A. Knopf. Sixth edition.

Frazier, E. Franklin. 1957. *Black Bourgeoisie.* Glencoe, IL: Free Press.

Furstenberg, Frank F., S. Philip Morgan, Kristin A. Moore, and James L. Peterson. 1987. "Race Differences in the Timing of Adolescent Intercourse," *American Sociological Review* 52 (October):511–518.

Genovese, Eugene D. 1994. "The Myth of the Absent Family," pp. 20–25 in Robert Staples (ed.), *The Black Family: Essays and Studies.* Belmont, CA: Wadsworth. Fifth edition.

Gresham, Jewell Handy. 1989. "White Patriarchal Supremacy: The Politics of Family in America." *Nation* 249 (July 24/31):116–122.

Harrison, Algea O., et al. 1990. "Family Ecologies of Ethnic Minority Children." *Child Development* 61 (April):347–362.

Hayes, Cheryl D. 1987. *Risking the Future: Adolescent Sexuality, Pregnancy, and Child-bearing.* Washington, DC: National Academy Press.

hooks, bell. 1992. "Feminism: A Transformational Politic," pp. 441–448 in Paula S. Rothenberg (ed.), *Race, Class, & Gender in the United States: An Integrated Study.* New York: St. Martin's Press. Second edition.

hooks, bell. 1994. "Black Women and Feminism," pp. 148–153 in Richard C. Monk (ed.), *Taking Sides: Clashing Views on Controversial Issues in Race and Ethnicity.* Guilford, CT: Dushkin Publishing Group.

Ima, Kenji. 1982. "Japanese Americans: The Making of 'Good' People," pp. 262–302 in Anthony Gary Dworkin and Rosalind J. Dworkin (eds.), *The Minority Report.* New York: Holt, Rinehart and Winston. Second edition.

Jayakody, Rukmalie, Linda M. Chatters, and Robert Joseph Taylor. 1993. "Family Support to Single and Married African American Mothers: The Provision of Financial, Emotional, and Child Care Assistance." *Journal of Marriage and the Family* 55 (May):261–276.

Jaynes, Gerald David, and Robin M. Williams, Jr. (eds). 1989. *A Common Destiny: Blacks and American Society.* Washington, DC: National Academy Press.

Johnson, Michael P. 1989. "Upward in Slavery." *New York Review of Books* 36 (December 21):51–55.

Jones, John Paul, III. 1987. "Work, Welfare, and Poverty among Black Female-Headed Families." *Economic Geography* 63 (January):20–34.

Kagan, Sharon L. 1989. "The Care and Education of America's Young Children: At the Brink of a Paradigm Shift?" *Proceedings of the Academy of Political Science* 37:70–83.

Keefe, Susan E., and Amado M. Padilla. 1987. *Chicano Ethnicity.* Albuquerque: University of New Mexico Press.

Kitano, Harry H. L., and Roger Daniels. 1988. *Asian Americans: Emerging Americans.* Englewood Cliffs, NJ: Prentice-Hall.

Kivisto, Peter. 1995. *Americans All: Race and Ethnic Relations in Historical, Structural, and Comparative Perspectives.* Belmont, CA: Wadsworth.

Littlejohn-Blake, Sheila M., and Carol Anderson Darling. 1993. "Understanding the Strengths of African American Families." *Journal of Black Studies* 23 (June):460–471.

Li, Wen Lang. 1982. "Chinese Americans: Exclusion from the Melting Pot," pp. 303–328 in Anthony Gary Dworkin and Rosalind J. Dworkin (eds.), *The Minority Report.* New York: Holt, Rinehart and Winston. Second edition.

McAneny, Leslie, and David W. Moore. 1994. "Public Supports New Programs to Get People Off Welfare." *Gallup Poll Monthly* (May):2–5.

McLanahan, Sara, and Irwin Garfinkel. 1989. "Single Mothers, the Underclass, and Social Policy." *American Academy of Political and Social Science* 501 (January):92–104.

Maldonado, Lionel A. 1982. "Mexican-Americans: The Emergence of a Minority," pp. 168–195 in Anthony Gary Dworkin and Rosalind J. Dworkin (eds.), *The Minority Report.* New York: Holt, Rinehart and Winston. Second edition.

Marable, Manning. 1994. "The Black Male: Searching beyond Stereotypes," pp. 69–77 in Richard G. Majors and Jacob U. Gordon (eds.), *The American Black Male: His Present Status and His Future.* Chicago: Nelson-Hall Publishers.

Massing, Michael. 1994. "The Welfare Blues." *New York Review of Books* 41 (March 24):45–48.

Miller, Bruce C. 1992. "Women and Politics: Comparative Evidence from the Northwest Coast." *Ethnology* 31 (October):367–383.

Miller, Bruce C. 1994. "Woman and Tribal Politics: Is There a Gender Gap in Indian Elections.?" *American Indian Quarterly* 18 (winter):25–41.

Moore, Joan, and Raquel Pinderhughes. 1995. "The Latino Population: The Importance of Restructuring," pp. 227–236 in Margaret L. Andersen and Patricia Hill Collins (eds.), *Race, Class, and Gender.* Belmont, CA: Wadsworth. Second edition.

Noda, Kesaya E. 1993. "Growing Up Asian in America," pp. 45–50 in Anne Minas (ed.), *Gender Basics: Feminist Perspectives on Women and Men.* Belmont, CA: Wadsworth.

Office of Policy Planning and Research, United States Department of Labor. 1965. *The Negro Family: The Case for National Action.* Washington, DC: United States Department of Labor.

Omolade, Barbara. 1993. "A Black Feminist Pedagogy." *Women's Studies Quarterly* 21 (fall/winter):31–38.

Parker, Seymour, and Robert J. Kleiner. 1977. "Social and Psychological Dimensions of the Family Role Performance of the Negro Male," in Doris Y. Wilkinson and Ronald L. Taylor (eds.), *The Black Male in America: Perspectives on His Status in Contemporary Society.* Chicago: Nelson-Hall.

Pearson, Jane L., et al. 1990. "Black Grandmothers in Multigenerational Households: Diversity in Family Structure and Parenting Involvement in the Woodlawn Community." *Child Development* 61 (April):434–442.

Price, John A. 1984. "North American Indian Families," pp. 245–268 in Charles H. Mindel and Robert W. Habenstein (eds.), *Ethnic Families in America: Patterns and Variations.* New York: Elsevier. Second edition.

Rimer, Sara. 1986. "'Hotel Kid' Becomes Symbol for the Homeless." *New York Times* (March 6):42.

Robinson, Ira E., Wilfrid C. Bailey, and John M. Smith, Jr. 1985. "Self-Perception of the Husband/Father in the Intact Lower Class Black Family." *Phylon* 46 (June):136–147.

Rosewater, Ann. 1989. "Child and Family Trends: Beyond the Numbers." *Proceedings of the Academy of Political Science* 37:4–19.

Rossi, Peter H. 1994. "Troubling Families: Family Homelessness in America." *American Behavioral Scientist* 37 (January):342–395.

Ryan, William. 1976. *Blaming the Victim.* New York: Vintage Books. Revised edition.

Sampson, Robert J. 1987. "Urban Black Violence: The Effect of Male Joblessness and Family Disruption." *American Journal of Sociology* 93 (September): 348–382.

Segura, Denise A., and Jennifer L. Pierce. 1993. "Chicana/o Family Structure and Gender Personality: Chodorow, Familism, and Psychoanalytic Sociology Revisited." *Signs* 19 (autumn):62–91.

Song, Young I. 1993. "Asian American Women's Experience in the Crossfire of Cultural Conflict," pp. 186–203 in Young I. Song and Eugene C. Kim (eds.), *American Mosaic: Selected Readings on America's Multicultural Heritage.* Englewood Cliffs, NJ: Prentice-Hall.

Staples, Robert. 1984. "The Black Amerian Family," pp. 217–244 in Charles H. Mindel and Robert W. Habenstein (eds.), *Ethnic Families in America: Patterns and Variations.* New York: Elsevier. Second edition.

Staples, Robert. 1994. *The Black Family: Essays and Studies.* Belmont, CA: Wadsworth. Fifth edition.

Stewart, James B. 1994. "Neoconservative Attacks on Black Families and the Black Male: An Analysis and Critique," pp. 39–58 in Richard G. Majors and Jacob U. Gordon (eds.), *The American Black Male: His Present Status and His Future.* Chicago: Nelson-Hall Publishers.

Sullivan, Mercer L. 1989. "Absent Fathers in the Inner City." *Annals of the American Academy of Political and Social Science* 501 (January):48–58.

Taylor, Robert Joseph, Linda M. Chatters, and James S. Jackson. 1993. "A Profile of Familial Relations among Three-Generation Black Families." *Family Relations* 42 (July):332–341.

Taylor, Robert Joseph, Linda M. Chatters, and Vickie M. Mays. 1988. "Parents, Children, Siblings, In-laws, and Non-kin as Sources of Emergency Assistance to Black Americans." *Family Relations* 37 (July):298–304.

Taylor, Ronald L. 1990. "Black Youth: The Endangered Generation." *Youth and Society* 22 (September):4–11.

Taylor, Ronald L. 1994. "Black Males and Social Policy: Breaking the Cycle of Disadvantage," pp. 147–166 in Richard G. Majors and Jacob U. Gordon (eds.), *The American Black Male: His Present Status and His Future.* Chicago: Nelson-Hall Publishers.

Terkel, Studs. 1992. *Race: How Blacks & Whites Think & Feel about the American Obsession.* New York: New Press.

Testa, Mark, et al. 1989. "Employment and Marriage among Inner-City Youths." *Annals of the American Academy of Political and Social Science* 501 (January):79–91.

Thomas, Veronica G. 1990. "Determinants of Global Life Happiness and Marital Happiness in Dual-Career Black Couples." *Family Relations* 39 (April):174–178.

U.S. Bureau of the Census. 1989. *Statistical Abstract of the United States: 1989.* Washington, DC: U.S. Government Printing Office. 109th edition.

U.S. Bureau of the Census. 1990. *Statistical Abstract of the United States: 1990.* Washington, DC: U.S. Government Printing Office. 110th edition.

U.S. Bureau of the Census. 1993. *Statistical Abstract of the United States: 1993.* Washington, DC: U.S. Government Printing Office. 113th edition.

Wilkerson, Margaret, and Jewell Handy Greshman. 1989. "Sexual Politics of Welfare: The Racialization of Poverty." *Nation* 249 (July 24/31):126–130+.

Willie, Charles V. 1991. *A New Look at Black Families.* Dix Hills, NY: General Hall. Fourth edition.

Willie, Charles V. 1993. "Social Theory and Social Policy Derived from the Black Family Experience." *Journal of Black Studies* 23 (June):451–459.

Ying, Yu-Wen. 1994. "Chinese American Adults' Relationship with Their Parents." *International Journal of Social Psychiatry* 40 (spring):35–45.

Zayas, Luis H., and Josephine Palleja. 1988. "Puerto Rican Familism: Considerations for Family Therapy." *Family Relations* 37 (July):260–264.

Zia, Helen. 1993. "Women of Color in Leadership." *Social Policy* 23 (summer):51–55.

Chapter
8

Distorted Image: Racial Minorities in the Mass Media

*C*onvicted of armed robbery, Nathan McCall was sent to the Norfolk jail to await transmission to a prison. Time hung heavy on his hands, and he decided to relieve the boredom by volunteering for one of the jail jobs. Eventually he became the inmate librarian.

Besides reading a few short stories in high school, McCall had done very little recreational reading. Now, however, with books all around him, he started leafing through a number of them. One day he picked up a book with a black man's picture on the cover. It was Richard Wright's *Native Son*, and once he started reading it, McCall couldn't put it down.

The story was about a confused, angry young black man named Bigger Thomas, whose racial fears led him to accidently suffocate a white woman. Knowing that nobody would believe that her death was accidental, he dismembered the body and tried to incinerate it in the furnace. Soon, though, he was apprehended, tried, and sentenced to die.

McCall identified with Bigger. They were both 20 years old and had ended up in prison. They shared the same conflicting feelings: "restless anger, hopelessness, a tough facade among blacks and deep-seated fear of whites—that I'd sensed in myself but was unable to express." Like Bigger, McCall had felt himself "headed down a road toward a destruction that I couldn't ward off, beaten by forces so large and amorphous that I had no idea how to fight back" (McCall, 1994:157). He was surprised to find that someone had written a book that so clearly represented his experiences and feelings.

Not accustomed to books, McCall read slowly—through the days and during the nights by the dim light of the hall lamps. Toward the end of the book, there is a passage where a lawyer talks to Bigger shortly before his execution. The man explained that while Bigger was trying to find a way to feel good about himself, his mind kept getting in the way. All through his life people had told him he was bad and that invariably when a person receives that message over and over, he will have doubts about himself. The challenge, the lawyer continued, is to help people to understand and accept their feelings and to appreciate that they are just as significant and worthy as anybody else's.

After reading that passage, McCall sat up in his bunk, buried his face in his hands, and wept. The tears, however, brought relief. Finally he was releasing feelings that he had held for years—feelings that he was unaccustomed to deal with and that he didn't understand. McCall wrote, "*Native Son* confirmed for me that my fears *weren't* imagined and that there were rational reasons why I'd been hurting inside" (McCall, 1994:158).

In school nearly all of the books were about whites' feelings and experiences. The only time African Americans' lives received any attention was during Black History Week, and then time was only spent on "Booker T. Washington and a few other noteworthy, dead black folks I couldn't relate to" (McCall, 1994:158). Reading *Native Son* was a very different experience, however, and McCall was now stimulated to look for more books that could help him learn more about himself and about a society where so many young black men ended up in prison.

While Nathan McCall's encounter with *Native Son* was dramatic, we see that it was hardly unique. In various ways books and other forms of mass media can affect people's perceptions of race and racism and also how they feel about themselves.

The central subject in this chapter is the **mass media,** which are the instruments of communication that reach a large audience without any personal contact between senders and receivers. Books, records, newspapers, magazines, radio, television, and movies are the most significant mass media.

Prominent in these discussions is a concept we have already used extensively. A **stereotype** is a highly exaggerated, greatly oversimplified image, maintained by prejudiced people, of the characteristics of the group members against whom they are prejudiced.

In this chapter we discuss mass media from the internal-colonialist perspective. Then we consider the impact of mass media on racial minorities.

MASS MEDIA AND INTERNAL COLONIALISM

Three tenets of internal colonialism apply to racial minorities' relationship to the mass media. The colonial-labor principle is relevant: Members of racial minorities tend to be kept out of powerful, desirable jobs, with few minority-group members in leadership positions in the popular mass media. The second principle of internal colonialism is restriction of racial minorities' freedom of movement. In this chapter we see how minorities' stereotyped portrayal in the mass media has helped impose restrictions on them. Finally stereotyped representations of racial minorities in the media have served to represent them as culturally and even genetically inferior.

Racial Minorities' Participation in Mass Media

The number of minorities who have been able to enter white-owned print media has been small but growing. In 1990 the nation's daily newspapers had about 55,700 journalists; about 5,000—9 percent—belonged to minorities, up from 5.6 percent seven years earlier. In addition slightly over half the nation's newspapers—51 percent—contained no minority representation, down from 60 percent seven years earlier (*Crisis,* 1985; Timbs, 1994). While the number of minority reporters has steadily increased, the top of the ladder remains white. In 1993 only 2 percent of the estimated 5,000 newsroom managers in the nation's daily newspapers were minority-group members. Assuming minorities do not suffer significant discrimination in the promotion process, that percentage should gradually increase in the years ahead. In 1993 two newspapers named their first minority managing editors while nine dailies appointed their first minority assistant managing editors (*Editor & Publisher,* 1994).

William Hilliard, editor of the *Portland Oregonian* and past president of the American Society of Newspaper Editors, is an African American; he is fairly optimistic about minority hiring by newspapers. Hilliard indicated that

> our profession took giant strides toward cultural diversity when professors in our schools of communication and journalism stopped telling people of color, especially young blacks, as one professor told me, that big newspapers wouldn't hire them. (Hernandez, 1994a:24)

True diversity in newspaper journalism will have been achieved, Hilliard concluded, "when the differences among us don't make any difference" (Hernandez, 1994a:24).

Statistics also show that blacks are underrepresented in the broadcast industry and cable television. While blacks comprised nearly 12 percent of the population in 1983, they held 8.9 percent of the broadcast jobs and 7.6 percent of the cable-television positions (*Crisis,* 1985).

Throughout all mass media, African Americans and other minority-group members have had low representation in leadership positions—such as editors, managers, and, in particular, owners. At present about 2.7 percent of the nation's television and radio stations are minority-owned, and frequently these are among the weakest in their markets. One distinctive impact of minority ownership is that a greater number of minorities is likely to be hired. Research, however, has not established to what extent minorities' presence on the job affects programming. While some observers believe that an increase of minorities in radio and TV invariably influences news coverage and entertainment choices, others argue that career pressures on the decision makers have the dominant impact (Fabrikant, 1994). Most likely both factors come into play.

People belonging to different minority groups tend to support their own members' involvement in the mass media. When representative samples of African Americans, Hispanic Americans, and Asian Americans across the country were asked whether a news story primarily involving their respective group should receive coverage by a reporter belonging to their ethnic group, 58 percent of African Americans, 54 percent of Hispanic Americans, and 61 percent of Asian Americans indicated that it was very important or somewhat important to provide that same-group coverage (McAneny, 1994:35).

Since the 1940s there has been a number of African American novelists, playwrights, poets, and other writers whose works have been published or produced widely. One specialist on African American literature suggested that white Americans have met more black men through their portraits in novels and autobiographies than they have encountered in person (Andrews, 1994:60). Following World War II, talented and versatile black actors have performed on the stage and on the screen, and since the 1940s black actors have appeared on television, starting to play major characters in situation comedies during the early 1950s. By the late 1980s, Bill Cosby and Oprah Winfrey were the highest-paid entertainers on television.

Perhaps African American artists have been best known in popular music. During the 1950s a number of African American singers and singing groups were commercially successful. In the past three decades, such performers as Ray Charles, Stevie Wonder, Diana Ross, and Michael Jackson have achieved the "crossover" effect, becoming as popular with white as with African American audiences (Abarry, 1990; Franklin and Moss, 1988:374–375; 431–432; Jaynes and Williams, 1989:101–102). But the number of successful African American singers and entertainers is relatively small.

Other racial minorities, for instance Asian Americans, have also had limited prominence in the major mass media. In such low-budget movies as *Dim Sum*, *Chan Is Missing*, and *Hito Hata*, Asian American filmmakers have had some popular and commercial success portraying the Asian American experience. It appears, however, that most white Americans do not want Asian Americans represented in dominant roles in the popular media (Kitano and Daniels, 1988:176).

Even when they are successful, some minority artists face an indifferent, even hostile commercial world. Rudolfo Anaya's novel *Bless Me, Ultima* was first published in 1972, selling over 250,000 copies and still producing 13,000 sales annually. While the book remains popular among Mexican Americans, no major publisher has issued a mass-market edition. John Randall, who runs a bookstore featuring

Chicano and Native American material, feels that censorship is common with writers like Anaya whose works help members of their racial group understand and rebel against political and economic oppression. Referring to Chicano writers breaking into mainstream publishing, Anaya said, "It's just that we see how important it is for the culture that our voices be heard and known to a wider readership. So while we're struggling to maintain our culture, lack of attention to it helps ensure that cultural genocide goes on" (M. Jones, 1990:30).

Population increase, however, bodes well for Hispanic Americans' representation in the media. By the year 2010, Mexican Americans, Puerto Ricans, and other Hispanic groups will represent the largest minority group. In recognition of the growing size of the Hispanic American populace, the number of Spanish-language newspapers has been increasing. In some cases such publishing heavyweights as Capital Cities/ABC, the *Los Angeles Times,* the *New York Times,* and the *Miami Herald* have produced Spanish-language entries. Instead of starting new papers, some companies have developed free weekly tabloids that emphasize culture and entertainment and are distributed independently of their parent papers, or they provide Spanish-language inserts for the Sunday edition or a daily page in Spanish (Garza, 1994).

As the market for Hispanic readers continues to grow, a struggle is likely to develop. Tino Duran, owner of four Hispanic weeklies in Texas, indicated that the giant companies have entered the competition because they want an increasing share of the disposable income from the Hispanic market—projected to rise from $220 billion in 1993 to $477 billion in 2000. Their reach for advertising dollars, Duran contended, could doom Hispanic publications. "Without our share of advertising revenues, we will shrivel and die." Duran added that buying space in Hispanic media is a smart move because their papers "are culturally and community relevant" (Stein, 1994:11–12).

Sometimes modern minority-group members can identify an area where they have been excluded from media participation and then take decisive actions to alter the situation. For example, in 1992, three African American women formed a company called Black Books Galore, which conducts book fairs and festivals providing hundreds of childrens' books about blacks, Native Americans, and other racial minorities. Such books do exist, but they are not well publicized or distributed. Christine Dina, a black woman who had grown up without such books and was experiencing the same deficiency with her 15-year-old daughter, explained:

> I never imagined there were so many books about different ethnic groups. Before we had the book fairs, which have been tremendously successful, I just thought there was not that much good literature about blacks and other minorities. I was wrong. (*New York Times,* 1994a:42)

With mainstream bookstores failing to meet the needs of African Americans and other minorities, a company like Black Books Galore has a continuing opportunity to address and resolve a glaring need.

The relevance of the colonial-labor principle to racial minorities in the mass media concerns not simply their extent of participation in the mass media but also

their portrayal. Consider the following television advertisement that was prominent in 1989 and 1990. The ad, which involved a major airline, showed a black airline attendant suddenly realizing that his last customer, a well-dressed white businessman, had left his briefcase at the check-in counter. Grabbing the briefcase, the
attendant took off at full speed, skirting people, vaulting over chairs and other
obstacles, and showing, the narrator informed the viewers, the moves he displayed
as a first-string halfback. Just as the passenger reached the gate, the attendant
handed him the briefcase. They exchanged smiles—they didn't shake hands, which
would have suggested their equality—the white man thanked the black man, and
the black man, still smiling but breathing heavily, said, "Piece of cake."

Now there is nothing racist about this situation, you might be thinking: It just
represents one person helping another. But the core issue concerns how the people, especially the black man, are portrayed. With a great display of physical energy and grace—the area of physical prowess has often been reserved for blacks
since the days of slavery—the black employee exerted himself on behalf of the
white man who needed to make no special effort, and then the black man downplayed the contribution he made—a modesty that implicitly undercut his own significance. What would have been the public reaction, one might wonder, if the
roles had been reversed?

The colonial-labor principle has another, somewhat different application to
the mass media (defined in this case somewhat more broadly than is usual). Steven
C. Dubin (1987) studied African Americans' representation on objects like salt and
pepper shakers, cookie jars, lawn statues, and ashtrays. These media often portray
African Americans with grossly distorted features and dressed like slaves ready to
perform menial domestic tasks. Dubin described the representations as "symbolic
slavery." Such a designation conveys a sense of the colonial-labor principle: that the
purchasers would be comfortable with a world where blacks and members of other
racial minorities were restricted to menial, slave-like jobs. Such stereotyped
images on objects were most popular from the 1890s to the 1950s and have
become much less prevalent in the past three decades as whites have realized that
they are insulting to blacks.

In contrast, a recent event—the overthrow of South Africa's oppressive
apartheid system—has produced minority-group members' triumphal representation on objects. In the spring of 1994, South Africans could buy a four-foot-high
wall clock with Nelson Mandela, the most prominent black hero, pictured on it,
and Mandela's political party produced a sun visor, with Mandela in the center of
it. In addition, *Oppression,* a Monopoly-style game, replicated the segregationist
rules of *apartheid:* Draw a card and pay a $10 fine for letting your children play at
an all-white playground; or roll doubles and reclassify a rival as a minority-group
member—black, Indian, or Colored (Keller, 1994).

Back in the United States, many of us have observed that over the past several decades, suburbanites with lawn statues of black lackeys have either removed
them or painted the face white, thereby preserving the statue and a sense of the
elitest lifestyle it implies. The latter action seemed to represent such people's sen-

sibility about racism—that all that's needed to remove racism is a symbolic coat of paint.

Media Stereotypes and Restriction of Minorities' Activity

Why have stereotypes been used in the mass media? One answer is that through the centuries their use has proved profitable (Clifton, 1990:19–20). By the middle of the nineteenth century, writers learned that they could become wealthy writing Indian-captivity narratives, which barraged readers with sensationalized accounts of tortures and sexual abuse inflicted on captives, especially female captives (VanDerBeets, 1984).

Early films about Indians grew out of this tradition, recognizing that lurid, blood-thirsty sensationalism would bring patrons streaming into the theatres just as it had sent them running to the bookstores. Once film makers obtained proof that flaming arrows, burning forts and wagons, and screaming, soon-to-be-raped white women would effectively sell tickets, they gave up efforts to produce historically accurate portraits of Native Americans. Sensationalism in Indian films caught on so quickly, in fact, that in 1911 members of four western tribes travelled to Washington, D.C., to protest their treatment in films to Congress and to President William Howard Taft (Stedman, 1982:157–158).

Certainly stereotyped media representations can make fortunes. But we look further and speculate about what conditions in American society encourage support for stereotypes. Once more the internal-colonialist perspective seems relevant: Stereotypes prove useful in controlling racial minorities' activities.

The mass media, especially written accounts, played a role in this endeavor. Mary Rowlandson, a seventeenth-century homemaker, authored the earliest effort. Captured during an Indian raid in 1675, Rowlandson was held by her captives for 12 weeks, then released after a ransom payment. Rowlandson's book described the atrocities she supposedly observed—the torture and killing of numerous white women and children. For decades the book was reprinted, and it became the prototype for Indian-captivity novels. Unlike later fictionalized victims, Mary Rowlandson apparently was not sexually violated by her captors. Nonetheless, Raymond William Stedman indicated, even modern readers have found her account gruesome and terrifying:

> How much more unsettling it must have been when the depicted menaces were still only a night's march away from frontier cabins. It is well to remember that for two centuries and more the Rowlandson capture reflected elements of actual threat to many Americans—and a convenient excuse for land grabbing and Indian damning to others. (Stedman, 1982:75)

Indian attacks ceased about a century ago. Undoubtedly African Americans have been the source of contemporary white Americans' greatest racial fears. Sometimes those fears have been so great that they have even affected whites trained to provide calm, objective analysis. During the 1960s urban riots, many journalists claimed that strategically placed snipers launched carefully planned and coordinated attacks on whites. Professional investigators looked into 25 such reports and found little or no supportive evidence. This research, however, received almost no publicity. The press's accounts of systematic insurrection carried the day and contributed substantially to a stereotype of brutal blacks dedicated to the systematic murder of whites (Hartmann and Husband, 1974:156). Obviously the idea that such people had to be controlled by any means necessary was readily forthcoming. The same implication applies to the following situation.

In late 1989 in Boston, a highly publicized murder occurred. Carol Stuart, a pregnant white woman, was shot and Charles Stuart, her white husband, was wounded. Stuart indicated that the assailant had been black. The police systematically searched an African American neighborhood where Stuart claimed the assailant had forced him to drive before shooting Stuart and his wife. Even though Stuart's story had suspicious overtones, journalists accepted his account, not following standard procedure of seeking verifying sources. One reporter indicated that press coverage was "voluminous and dramatic" (A. Jones, 1990:A21). On its front page, the *Boston Globe* published a picture of Mrs. Stuart's shattered head, and local radio and television kept replaying Mr. Stuart's desperate conversation with the police dispatcher, a conversation in which he referred to an unknown black assailant. Eventually evidence made it clear that Stuart should be the chief suspect, and at this point he committed suicide. African American leaders were enraged that police and press so readily mobilized to seek a black suspect when from the beginning there was ample reason to regard Stuart suspiciously (Butterfield, 1990). The incident suggests that with only flimsy evidence, many journalists are still inclined to represent African Americans as a major source of threat which implicitly must be controlled.

As Table 8.1 indicates, many members of three minority groups believed that when covering crime stories, the local daily newspapers as well as local and national television news treated their group unfairly.

Other evidence has addressed the issue of controlling racial minorities, albeit in a more subtle manner. A study of African Americans' portrayal in popular magazines' advertisements produced between 1950 and 1982 found that whites and African Americans were much more likely to appear together on equal social terms in later ads. However, even recently the chances were substantially greater that the people in the pictures would be interacting with each other if all were white than if they were both black and white (Humphrey and Schuman, 1984). Thus in the course of three decades, advertising specialists have concluded that popular magazines' primarily white audiences have been increasingly willing to support African Americans' entrance into their social world but have continued to want limited interaction with them.

Media Stereotypes of Racial Minorities' Cultural Inferiority

In a history of the relationship between American blacks and television, J. Fred MacDonald wrote, "In terms of utilization of black professional talent, and in the

Table 8.1   RESPONSE TO MEDIA COVERAGE OF CRIME STORIES INVOLVING ONE'S OWN GROUP (PERCENT)

	African Americans	Hispanic Americans	Asian Americans	Whites
Local newspapers				
Fairly	38%	61%	69%	85%
Unfairly	47	30	10	10
No opinion	15	9	21	5
Local TV news				
Fairly	35%	64%	73%	83%
Unfairly	53	31	15	10
No opinion	12	5	12	7
National TV news				
Fairly	34%	60%	75%	77%
Unfairly	55	34	14	17
No opinion	11	6	11	6

Note: Among the four groups represented here, distinct differences existed in the extent to which members felt that media coverage of crime stories involving their group was unfair. African Americans were the most inclined to perceive unfair coverage followed by Hispanic Americans, Asian Americans, and whites.

Source: Leslie McAneny. "Ethnic Minorities View the Media's View of Them." *Gallup Poll Monthly,* August 1994, pp. 31–41.

portrayal of Afro-American characters, TV as a new medium had the capability of ensuring a fair and equitable future" (MacDonald, 1983:21).

So far it has not succeeded in this regard. In the late 1940s, as TV became popular, African Americans appeared in very selected roles as singers, dancers, and clowns. One of the most popular programs was "Amos 'n' Andy," a televised recreation of a radio show that had been very popular in the 1920s and 1930s with both black and white audiences. In spite of NAACP protests, the program premiered on CBS television in June 1951, bringing "the old minstrel stereotype of blacks as slow, footshuffling, fun-loving, slightly dishonest people from the radio to television for all the world to see" (Staples and Jones, 1985:12).

As a child I sometimes watched the show, and the character who most vividly comes to mind is George "Kingfish" Stevens, a clumsily deceitful man who inevitably managed to trick Andy and all the other dumb nice guys portrayed on the program. I can remember thinking that if this slow-talking lightweight could outwit the others, then they must be dense indeed. It didn't consciously come to mind that these characters might be considered representative of all African Americans, but psychically speaking that idea couldn't have been very far away.

During the 1950s African Americans were generally limited to small roles on television. As an exception Ethel Waters and later Louise Beavers starred in "Beulah," which started in 1950 and was the first television program with a black actor in the lead. The show contained many stereotypes. Beulah was a maid for a prosperous white family and in that role she served as an update of the southern domestic slave—the "mammie" who was warm, loving, dedicated, and so accepted in her role that she could scold and lecture the children. In 1956 the "Nat King Cole Show" premiered on NBC. It was the first time that an African American appeared on TV in a dignified, unstereotyped way, and the program never did well, expiring in 1957 when it could no longer obtain sponsors. Apparently the American public simply was not ready to accept an African American entertainer in anything but stereotyped roles.

Bill Cosby was the first person to break that particular barrier on television. In 1965 he starred with Robert Culp in "I Spy," playing a basically nonstereotyped role in a successful, three-year program where race was not the central issue. Racist overtones to the role did exist, however. As a spy, Cosby's cover was trainer for a tennis player, casting him in a subordinate role within one of blacks' traditional realms—sport. Furthermore the show's producers permitted Cosby no explicit romantic involvement, thereby reducing whites' possible anxieties about displaying a black man's sexual activities.

Perhaps the late 1960s was the heyday of African Americans' prominence on television. Diahann Carroll, Teresa Graves, Leslie Uggams, and Flip Wilson obtained their own shows, and a host of other programs had African Americans in supporting roles. While the percentage of black actors never approached their proportion of the population, they had an unprecedented chance to display their abilities relatively unhampered by stereotyped roles.

By the early 1970s, however, the civil-rights movement was in decline, and most Americans appeared to return to the asocial outlook of the 1950s and early 1960s. The situation comedy, with its trivialization of social issues and barrage of one liners, became the rage and has remained prominent to the present day. Following the success of a number of all-white shows, there appeared such all-black or black-dominated shows as "The Jeffersons," "Good Times," "What's Happening," "In Living Color," and "Fresh Prince of Bel Air." Many African American analysts have widely criticized these shows, suggesting that the actors' style, particularly their use of "black humor," presents the same kind of witless and deceitful stereotypes of blacks found 30 or 40 years earlier on "Amos 'n' Andy."

An exception has been "The Cosby Show." No longer in production but still popular in reruns, it features black actors, but it does not display traditionally black-stereotyped situations—no ghetto, no drugs, an intact family. The variety of struggles and encounters involving Dr. and Ms. Huxtable and their children are typically American, not African American. Some critics have pointed out that the show does not address poverty and racism, issues of extreme importance to many blacks, but its significance lies elsewhere: It has presented a middle-class black family in nonstereotyped roles, and it has been a resounding success.

"The Cosby Show" is a clear illustration that African Americans can break long-accepted stereotypes and still be successful. Circumstances surrounding the program, however, are instructive. Selling his show to NBC, Cosby had the distinct advantage of being a popular, successful entertainer who was dealing with a network that at the time was dead-last in the ratings (Staples and Jones, 1985). The circumstances producing the success of "The Cosby Show" are unusual, and thus it is reasonable not to expect a great flood of nonstereotyped black shows. Nonetheless black entertainers will probably be able to find some opportunities to step outside narrow roles. In recent years "The Oprah Winfrey Show" has become very successful, convincing the American public that an intelligent, quick-witted, outgoing black woman can be an effective talk-show host.

Other hopeful signs exist. For the years 1985 and 1986, a pair of researchers examined the three half-hour, prime-time situation comedies that featured an entact African American family. They found a more positive representation of black families than in earlier programs. In particular, it was apparent that the spouses interacted frequently, lovingly, and equally with each other; that the children were treated with respect and taught achievement-oriented values emphasizing the importance of staying in school, keeping out of trouble, and working hard at all one's endeavors; and that family activity was generally nonconflictful (Merritt and Stroman, 1993).

Like African Americans and Indians, Asian Americans have had stereotyped roles in the visual media. One analysis indicated that in films, "The evil Jap of World War II and the Communist gooks in Korea, China, and Vietnam—faceless, fanatic, maniacal, willing to die because life is not valued—are endlessly recycled with changes in nationality as our foreign policy changes" (Kitano and Daniels, 1988:176). Less politically explicit, the karate films, that became commercially successful in the 1970s, provided similar stereotypes. In 1988 ABC television offered a short-lived series titled "Ohara," which starred Pat Morita, a Japanese American in the lead role. Ohara was a small, elderly Japanese American behind whose unassuming bearing lurked an endless series of one-line putdowns reminiscent of the pre–World War II Charlie Chan films, along with, of course, the full martial-arts package. It was hardly the series to challenge prevailing stereotypes of Asian Americans developed in films.

Since the Mexican War in the 1840s, white Americans have maintained stereotypes of Mexican Americans. The contemptuous term "greaser" appeared at that time, probably because some Mexicans worked to grease wagon axles. The image that Mexicans were lazy, immoral, untrustworthy, stupid, and dirty was well established by the time films started. The visual media sustained the stereotype. In movies Mexicans were often portrayed as bandits. In the case of the famed Pancho Villa, who conducted raids into Texas, violence and criminality were emphasized, but the films neglected to show that white settlers' exploitation of Mexicans motivated the raids. On television Mexican or Mexican American men were generally presented as lazy, fat, carefree, and immoral and women as flirtatious and promiscuous. Media advertising has also contributed to the Chicano stereotype. Frito ads represented Mexicans as criminals ("Frito Banditos"), and a deodorant ad showed a grubby-looking Mexican bandit with the caption, "If it works for him, it will work for you" (Feagin and Feagin, 1993:266; Maldonado, 1982:193).

About two-thirds of Puerto Rican characters on television are criminals (Staples and Jones, 1985:15). Undoubtedly the best-known entertainment feature involving Puerto Ricans has been *West Side Story,* first a Broadway musical and later a successful film. While one might concede that it presented a moving Romeo-and-Juliet-type story and appealing music, it only supported prevailing stereotypes of Puerto Rican men as violent, vicious gang members who physically intimidate and dominate their girl friends.

In his book *A Puerto Rican in New York,* Jesus Colon noted that Puerto Ricans are frequently stereotyped by the mass media, which harp on "what is superficial and sentimental, transient and ephemeral, or bizarre and grotesque in Puerto Rican life" (Colon, 1961:9).

So far discussion in this section has focused on fictional representations. Stereotyping, however, also occurs in the news area. A study based on 4,000 articles obtained from seven major, general-interest newspapers and the three major newsmagazines indicated that most issues were presented from a mainstream, white-male cultural orientation. What would this mean concretely? For example, articles pertaining to Barbara Jordan's keynote speech at the 1992 Democratic Convention played up the fact that her call to end white and black racism caused elevated emotions among both blacks and whites, but most accounts provided few or no quotes from Jordan elaborating on her remarks. The study found many articles about the competition for black votes but little detailed discussion about the issues, perceptions, and leaders that are prominent among African Americans. The researchers concluded that while minorities are receiving more press coverage, the coverage often fails to reveal the key issues related to their lives (Bridge, 1994).

A similar deficiency has occurred with reporting about Hispanic Americans and Asian Americans. For instance, while mainstream media readily report stories about illegal Asian immigration, the additives in Chinese food, or other issues enforcing stereotypes, they are much less inclined to give effective coverage to issues that Asian Americans consider significant but that avoid stereotypic representations of them. Because such stereotypes are so common and often go unchallenged, many Americans, including journalists, are simply unaware when they are stumbling into using them. To restrict stereotyping in reporting, news media need to hire diverse minority-group members and permit them a significant role in the planning and development of stories involving ethnic groups. (Hernandez, 1994b; 1994c).

Majority-group members often enjoy stereotypes of racial minorities' cultural inferiority, finding that they make them feel amused and superior. Whether intended or not, the suggestion of cultural inferiority supports a contention discussed in several chapters, especially the family chapter—that racial minorities' personal inadequacies and not economic, political, and social conditions outside of them are responsible for their lack of success. As we have seen, this victim-blaming perspective forces racial minorities to adopt the majority group's cultural standards after rejecting their own. Only then do they have a chance of receiving full acceptance and associated rewards within the society. Box 8.1 summarizes major conclusions from this section.

Sometimes minority-group members have mounted significant campaigns to change the media use of stereotypes. The following illustration is a case in point.

Dropping Indian Nicknames

When in 1991 and 1992 the Atlanta Braves twice reached the World Series, a now controversial issue came to national attention: Should professional and college

Box 8.1   MASS MEDIA AND INTERNAL COLONIALISM

Tenet of Internal Colonialism	Example
1. Colonial-labor principle	Blacks' limited participation in newspapers and television
2. Restriction of minorities' activities	Response to the sense of threat created by Mary Rowlandson's book and Indian-captivity novels
3. Racial minorities' supposed cultural inferiority	Past and present television representation of stereotyped black, Japanese American, Native American, and Mexican American characters

sports teams continue to use nicknames and actions that suggest Indian stereotypes?

Tim Giago (1994), the editor/publisher of the weekly newspaper *Indian Country Today,* suggested that a useful measure is to ask if one would use the nickname if the team were just starting out today. With all the nicknames, Giago concluded, the answer would be negative. Invariably the nicknames and the costumes, implements, and actions associated with them perpetuate internal-colonialist standards, denigrating a people and their cultural tradition: Supporters' claims that there is "no big deal" and that the whole thing is just "good, clean fun" become highly suspect (Churchill, 1994).

Let's examine the situation a bit more closely. If one attends an Atlanta Braves baseball game or a Kansas City Chiefs football game, the tomohawk chop in which many fans engage suggests the idea of brutal killing—a perpetuation of the centuries-old stereotype that Native Americans are savage and warlike (Marger, 1994:170). Furthermore the "smirking faces painted in Dayglo colors" suggest to Indians that a spiritual experience in which their ancestors engaged represented no more than a Halloween-like masquerade. Finally the wearing of feathers or feathered headdresses traditionally signified honoring or blessing the wearer, a significance that the sporting context denigrates.

Hold on there, some readers might say. The call to eliminate Indian nicknames establishes a double standard. After all, white groups are sometimes used for nicknames. Consider, for instance, the Pittsburg Steelers, the Green Bay Packers, and the Dallas Cowboys. The fact is, however, that none of these are ethnic groups, and thus the stereotyping to which racial minorities are subjected does not occur. Well, then what about the Minnesota Vikings, some might contend. It is true that Vikings represent a one-time ethnic group, but Vikings no longer exist while

Indians do. Finally those citing a double standard might point to the Notre Dame Irish. Here, they could triumphantly conclude, the nickname refers to a living ethnic group. Yes, that is true, but one must mention two considerations. First, it was Irish Catholic officials who created the nickname and not hostile or indifferent outsiders. Second, at rallies and sporting events, Notre Dame supporters have maintained a positive, respectable image. For instance, at football games students do not dress up as popes or cardinals, or ridicule Irish characteristics or culture. One can imagine that if students did engage in such an action, then school administrators would take quick steps to repress what would be labelled mischievous or even malicious student behavior.

In the latter case, the key issue would be respect. It is disrespectful to have someone dressed like the pope doing somersaults or backflips, or to have Notre Dame spectators take a swig from a huge mug filled with green beer each time their basketball team scores.

Some observers would say that while this discussion might be interesting, it pales in importance compared with extensive poverty and other significant problems from which many Native Americans suffer. However, it might be well to appreciate that if racial minorities want to mobilize economically and politically, respect and self-respect are important incentives.

In recent years some outsiders have been starting to appreciate the nickname issue. As long ago as 1972, Stanford University changed the athletic team's name from "Indians" to "Cardinal." Recently both St. John's (Redmen) and Marquette (Warriors) have eliminated their traditional nicknames (Giago, 1994; Marger, 1994:170). Those implementing these changes have developed some ability to see the issue of respect through Indians' eyes. Implicitly they appreciate that the linguistic labels that represent a carryover from the internal-colonialist past represent a destructive, demeaning tradition.

Having analyzed mass media's treatment of racial minorities, we can examine some impacts of that treatment.

EFFECTS OF MASS MEDIA ON RACIAL MINORITIES

We discuss two issues—the impact on racial minorities of stereotypes in the mass media and actions taken by minority groups to offset discrimination in the media.

Stereotypes and Other Distortions: Impact of Media Representations on Minority-Group Members

One particularly troubling aspect of black stereotyping in the media involves children's TV programming. African American children watch television extensively. A number of studies have suggested that when family income level is held constant, African American children tend to watch more television than their white age mates. What they see presents blacks neither extensively nor positively. In children's shows blacks are represented well below their proportion of the population, constituting about 7 percent of the characters in weekend programming and about 3 percent in after-school shows. Furthermore African Americans presented are much more likely than whites to be poor, jobless, or in low-status jobs. Such results certainly justify many black parents' and professionals' concern that limited and stereotyped roles for African Americans on television are likely to promote low self-concepts and negative views toward African Americans in general (Stroman, 1984).

In addition, Henry Taylor and Carol Dozier (1983) suggested that commercial television has developed a fairly new stereotyped black character—the black superhero. This person is a policeman or other upright citizen, cut very much in the mold of white counterparts, and he tirelessly and often violently enforces order and keeps society safe for the good, law-abiding people of all races. Such programming both legitimates violence when used by law-enforcement officers and encourages young African Americans to join the police and pursue the same violent agenda.

Television viewing can produce other distorted impressions. A study of 161 adult African Americans concluded that heavy viewers were more inclined than light viewers to have mistaken impressions that racial integration is extensive and that blacks are primarily middle-class members. The author argued that when exposed to a glut of commercial television, African Americans readily obtain the false sense that an effective confrontation of racism now occurs and that political activism demanding social justice and equality no longer remains necessary (Matabane, 1988).

Sometimes the potential impact of blacks' representation on television is complex. As we noted, "The Cosby Show" has avoided the stereotyped African American characters of the past. Dr. Cliff Huxtable and his family are successful, upper-middle-class people. They are much more successful than most blacks, and as a result the socioeconomic world in which they live and challenges and problems they face are as remote to the majority of African Americans as if the program focused on a white, upper-middle-class family. The Huxtables, in fact, are in most regards like successful whites. It appears that one of the reasons that the program has become so popular is that it never addresses tough issues related to race—in particular, political and economic conditions that have promoted limited opportunities for many blacks since the days of slavery. With these issues unaddressed, "The Cosby Show" and the steady flow of other sitcoms featuring middle-class blacks imply that blacks who are not economically successful are personally responsible for their situation (Gates, 1989).

Commercial-television programs featuring black characters seldom provide significant commentary on the issue of racial identity. When one or more characters start to explore this topic, they tend to do it in a highly specific but nonconducive context—in a comedy situation involving black children located in a largely white environment. Seldom does the program examine the issue in depth, and usually the conclusion emerges that either it is not productive to pursue the search for black identity or, if it appears that this is a positive course of action, viewers obtain little sense of how to go about the search (Peterson-Lewis and Adams, 1990).

Not surprisingly, as Table 8.2 indicates, minority-group members are often upset by the way mass media cover their group.

Do Your Own Thing

In early 1985 at the University of California at Santa Barbara, there was a symposium on news-media coverage of black America. One of the participants was James Cleaver, executive editor of the *Los Angeles Sentinel*, an African American newspaper. Not only are African Americans and other racial minorities underrepresented in the mass media, Cleaver pointed out, but a more important issue, regardless of whether reporters are black or white, involves the presentation of topics about blacks. Unless black reporters have lived and worked in black communities, they are unlikely to be sensitive to urban black residents. Cleaver analyzed a recent story in the *Los Angeles Times*, a major white-owned newspaper. It discussed African Americans' criminal activities in white residential areas. The factual material was accurate, Cleaver conceded. However, he noted that "the manner in which this was presented led the reader to believe that every person in the black community was a criminal. It led people to believe that they could not be safe in the black community" (*Center Magazine*, 1983:9). To present African Americans positively, Cleaver concluded, African American mass media must continue to exist.

Table 8.2   MINORITY-GROUP MEMBERS' FREQUENCY OF BEING UPSET BY MASS MEDIA COVERAGE OF THEIR GROUP (PERCENT)

	African Americans	Hispanic Americans	Asian Americans
Local daily newspaper			
Every day	4%	6%	—
At least once a week	39	21	20%
Less than once a week	31	22	32
Never	20	44	38
No opinion	6	7	10
Local TV news			
Every day	8%	6%	1%
At least once a week	37	27	19
Less than once a week	28	29	35
Never	24	35	43
No opinion	3	3	2
National TV news			
Every day	9%	1%	1%
At least once a week	33	27	18
Less than once a week	30	36	42
Never	23	36	36
No opinion	5	—	3

Note: While members of all three minority groups expressed discontent about media coverage of events or issues involving their group, African Americans were more upset than Hispanic Americans, who in turn were more disturbed than Asian Americans.

Source: Leslie McAneny. "Ethnic Minorities View the Media's View of Them." *Gallup Poll Monthly,* August 1994, pp. 31–41.

Certainly there is historical precedent for this position. Often African Americans have not been represented effectively in the mass media, nor have they been permitted to participate extensively in them. Their alternative has been to found their own media. In the middle of the nineteenth century, Frederick Douglass's *North Star* condemned slavery, and late in that century, T. Thomas Fortune's *New York Age* blasted African Americans' treatment as second-class citizens. In the twentieth century, African American newspapers in many cities became vehicles operating on behalf of African Americans. During World War I, they encouraged many readers to move to industrial centers for jobs. While supporting the war, African American newspapers urged the complete integration of African Americans into American life. Many of the newspapers prospered, with several having weekly circulations of over 100,000 by 1920 and more than 200,000 twenty years later. Large black papers published several editions to service different sections of the country, and a few were sufficiently prosperous to form chains in various cities.

During the late nineteenth and early twentieth centuries, no black journalist was more celebrated than Ida B. Wells, who dedicated her life to fighting racism. Just recently her remarkable achievements have started to receive public attention, and it seems fitting to summarize them here.

Wells's first public action involving racism occurred when at the age of 22, she sat in the all-white "ladies car" of a train and refused to move when ordered to do so; she was removed forcibly from the train. Wells's articles about her protest led to her entrance into journalism, and she soon became the editor and co-owner of the *Memphis Free Speech.*

As a journalist Wells condemned the lynching of three black friends whose grocery store had successfully competed against a white-owned store. Lynchings became Wells's chief target, and she believed that the only effective way to convince whites to stop killing blacks was to punish the oppressors economically—to deprive them of black workers. Wells wrote editorials urging blacks to pack up and move to the newly opened Oklahoma Territory, and thousands went. Analyzing sources of white violence toward African Americans, Wells wrote that sometimes there seemed to be an intense attraction between white women and African American men. Whites were infuriated and stormed her newspaper, destroying the presses.

Wells, who was in the North at the time, was forced into exile and threatened with death if she ever returned to the South. First in New York City and then in Chicago, Wells worked as a journalist for African American newspapers in an effort to alleviate violence against African Americans and to promote African Americans' basic rights. Continuing to believe that economic pressure was the most effective means of ending lynching, she travelled to England, which was a major market for southern cotton. She spoke with prominent individuals and lectured to groups, providing detailed information about the torture and killing of southern blacks and seeking to convince the English to boycott southern cotton if lynching continued. As a result of Wells's action, the English applied some pressure on southern business people.

At the age of 60, Wells risked death, returning to the South for the first time in 30 years. Unrecognized by white authorities, she managed to interview 12 black farmers who had been sentenced to death for defending themselves against a white mob. Back in Chicago, Wells wrote a pamphlet describing the case in detail and demanding the men's freedom. Largely because of Wells's effort, the prisoners were released (*Public Broadcasting System,* 1989).

While the largest black newspapers have lost circulation in recent years, there is still a substantial number of black print media. In 1979 there were over 350 black newspapers, magazines, and bulletins published on a regular weekly, monthly, or quarterly basis. The most recent growth has involved monthly or quarterly magazines such as *Ebony* and *Jet; Tuesday,* a Sunday supplement in many white newspapers; and *Monitor,* a supplement in many African American weeklies. At present there are only two African American newspapers published daily (Franklin and Moss, 1988:379; Jaynes and Williams, 1989:171).

Because of their tradition of free expression, those working for black newspapers sometimes find themselves in dangerous situations. In March 1994 following death threats against a reporter who had recently published in the *Cincinnati Herald,* the black weekly was firebombed. In spite of serious damage, the staff produced its next edition four days later. The publisher declared, "Nobody is going to tell me who is going to write in the paper and who is not" (Fitzgerald, 1994:46).

Like African Americans other racial minorities are significantly underrepresented in the mass media. Some Native Americans have followed blacks' lead, realizing that the only way to publicize their interests effectively is to establish their own newspapers. For instance, *Daybreak* is a quarterly publication, and its editorials and articles discuss historical and contemporary Native American cultures and activities, and, in particular, racist oppressions. Next to the paper's masthead is a statement with a distinctly anti-internal-colonialist tone: "*Daybreak* is written by contemporary Indians to reflect ancient tribal values in new ways, to transfer knowledge to the future generations. Join us today and enjoy our insights about Indian realities" (*Daybreak,* 1989:3).

Like African Americans and Native Americans, Puerto Ricans have limited exposure in popular mass media. Newspapers, which have served a prominent role for blacks, have had a less significant impact on Puerto Ricans. In New York City, for example, Spanish-language papers have not been owned by Puerto Ricans and have not focused on their interests and problems. While generally not concentrating on Puerto Ricans, Spanish-language radio and television stations have provided music, news, and entertainment that has helped give Puerto Ricans a sense of being "at home" in a strange land (Fitzpatrick, 1987:59–60).

Sometimes when minority-group individuals control a media event, controversy can develop about its presentation. In the fall of 1994 as part of its continuing effort to present elements of black history that will help people better understand its harsh realities, the African American department at Colonial Willamsburg decided to enact slave auctions. The Virginia branch of the NAACP received numerous calls, most of which expressed outrage about the auction, and eventually the NAACP political director decided to organize a protest against the event (Janofsky, 1994).

As one performance with about 2,000 spectators was just about to begin, six demonstrators pushed through the audience and started singing "We Shall Overcome." Costumed employees of Colonial Williamsburg tried to push them back behind the ropes. During the altercation Jack Gravely, the organizer of the protest, shouted that the actors were turning black history into a sideshow. At that point Christy Coleman, a black actress who was to portray a pregnant house slave, grabbed a microphone and with tears running down her cheeks shouted to the protesters, "I want you to judge with honest hearts and honest minds." Two protesters sat down on nearby steps and challenged officials to call the police. They did not, and the show went on. When the sale occurred, Ms. Coleman cried and hid her face in her apron. Among those moved was Mr. Gravely, who startled people by retracting his objections. "Pain had a face," he said. Indignity had a body. Suffering had tears" (*New York Times*, 1994b:A16).

REFERENCES

Abarry, Abu. 1990. "The African-American Legacy in American Literature." *Journal of Black Studies* 20 (June):379–398.

Andrews, William L. 1994. "The Black Male in American Literature," pp. 59–68 in Richard G. Majors and Jacob U. Gordon (eds.), *The American Black Male: His Present Status and His Future.* Chicago: Nelson-Hall Publishers.

Bridge, Junior. 1994. "Media Mirror: Distorted Relations—Distorted Treatment." *Quill* 82 (April):16–17.

Butterfield, Fox. 1990. "Boston in Uproar over Murder Case." *New York Times* (January 8):A12.

Center Magazine. 1983. "American Blacks as Seen by the Media: Getting the Story Straight." 16 (January/February):8–15.

Churchill, Ward. 1994. "Crimes against Humanity," pp. 73–77 in John A. Kromkowski (ed.), *Race and Ethnic Relations 94/95.* Guilford, CT: Dushkin Publishing Group. Fourth edition.

Clifton, James A. 1990. "Cultural Fictions." *Society* 27 (May/June):19–28.

Colon, Jesus. 1961. *A Puerto Rican in New York.* New York: Mainstream Publishers.

Crisis. 1985. "Blacks & Mass Media: Where Do We Stand?" 92 (June/July):27–31+.

Daybreak. 1989. "Masthead Statement." 3 (spring):3.

Dubin, Steven C. 1987. "Symbolic Slavery: Black Representations in Popular Culture." *Social Problems* 34 (April):122–140.

Editor & Publisher. 1994. "Minorities Still Underrepresented on Top of the Corporate Ladder." 127 (February 19):10.

Fabrikant, Geraldine. 1994. "Slow Gains by Minority Broadcasters." *New York Times* (May 31):D1+.

Feagin, Joe R., and Clairece Booher Feagin. 1993. *Racial & Ethnic Relations.* Englewood Cliffs, NJ: Prentice-Hall. Fourth edition.

Fitzgerald, Mark. 1994. "Black Weekly Firebombed." *Editor & Publisher* 127 (April 23):46.

Fitzpatrick, Joseph P. 1987. *Puerto Rican Americans: The Meaning of Migration to the Mainland.* Englewood Cliffs, NJ: Prentice-Hall. Second edition.

Franklin, John Hope, and Alfred A. Moss, Jr. 1988. *From Slavery to Freedom: A History of Negro Americans.* New York: Alfred A. Knopf. Sixth edition.

Garza, Melita Marie. 1994. "Growth Market: Mainstream Media Vie for Latino Readers." *Quill* 82 (April):18–21.

Gates, Henry Louis, Jr. 1989. "TV's Black World Turns—But Stays Unreal." *New York Times* (November 12):Sect. 2, p. 1+.

Giago, Tim. 1994. "Drop the Chop! Indian Nicknames Just Aren't Right." *New York Times* (March 13):Sect. 8, p. 9.

Hartmann, Paul, and Charles Husband. 1974. *Racism and the Mass Media.* Totowa, NJ: Rowman & Littlefield.

Hernandez, Debra Gersh. 1994a. "A Call for Diversity." *Editor & Publisher* 127 (April 30):24.

Hernandez, Debra Gersh. 1994b. "The Race Quotient: Unity Panelists See Race Playing a Hand in the News." *Editor & Publisher* 127 (August 20):12–13.

Hernandez, Debra Gersh. 1994c. "Stereotypes Refuse to Die." *Editor & Publisher* 127 (August 27):21.

Humphrey, Ronald, and Howard Schuman. 1984. "The Portrayal of Blacks in Magazine Advertisements: 1950–1982." *Public Opinion Quarterly* 48 (fall):551–563.

Janofsky, Michael. 1994. "Mock Auction of Slaves Outrages Some Blacks." *New York Times* (October 8):7.

Jaynes, Gerald David, and Robin M. Williams, Jr. (eds.). 1989. *A Common Destiny: Blacks and American Society.* Washington, DC: National Academy Press.

Jones, Alex S. 1990. "Bias and Recklessness Are Charged in Boston Reporting of Stuart Slaying." *New York Times* (January 14):A21.

Jones, Margaret. 1990. "Salt of the Earth Books." *Publisher's Weekly* 237 (October 12):29–30+.

Keller, Bill. 1994. "Nelson Mandela on a Mug? It's the Rage in South Africa." *New York Times* (April 13):A1+.

Kitano, Harry H. L., and Roger Daniels. 1988. *Asian Americans: Emerging Minorities.* Englewood Cliffs, NJ: Prentice-Hall.

MacDonald, J. Fred. 1983. *Blacks and White TV: Afro-Americans in Television since 1948.* Chicago: Nelson-Hall.

Maldonado, Lionel A. 1982. "Mexican Americans: The Emergence of a Minority," pp. 168–195 in Anthony Gary Dworkin and Rosalind J. Dworkin (eds.), *The Minority Report.* New York: Holt, Rinehart and Winston. Second edition.

Marger, Martin N. 1994. *Race and Ethnic Relations: American and Global Perspectives.* Belmont, CA: Wadsworth. Third edition.

Matabane, Paula W. 1988. "Television and the Black Audience: Cultivating Moderate Perspectives on Racial Integration." *Journal of Communication* 38 (autumn):21–31.

McAneny, Leslie. 1994. "Ethnic Minorities View the Media View of Them." *Gallup Poll Monthly* (August):31–41.

McCall, Nathan. 1994. *Makes Me Wanna Holler: A Young Black Man in America.* New York: Random House.

Merritt, Bishetta, and Carolyn A. Stroman. 1993. "Black Family Imagery and Interactions on Television." *Journal of Black Studies* 23 (June):492–499.

New York Times. 1994a. "Minority Book Fairs Fill Retailing's Cultural Gap." (March 13):42.

New York Times. 1994b. "Tears and Protest at Mock Slave Trial." (October 11):A16.

Peterson-Lewis, Sonja, and Afesa Adams. 1990. "Television's Model of the Quest for African Consciousness: A Comparison with Cross' Empirical Model of Psychological Nigrescence." *Journal of Black Psychology* 16 (spring):55–72.

Public Broadcasting System. 1989. "Ida B. Wells: A Passion for Justice." (December 19).

Staples, Robert, and Terry Jones. 1985. "Culture, Ideology and Black Television Images." *Black Scholar* 16 (May/June):10–20.

Stedman, Raymond William. 1982. *Shadows of the Indian: Stereotypes in American Culture.* Norman: University of Oklahoma Press.

Stein, M. L. 1994. "Hispanic Publishers Take Aim at Mainstream Press." *Editor and Publisher* 127 (February 12):11–12.

Stroman, Carolyn A. 1984. "The Socialization Influence of Television on Black Children." *Journal of Black Studies* 15 (September):79–100.

Taylor, Henry, and Carol Dozier. 1983. "Television Violence, African-Americans, and Social Control, 1950–1976." *Journal of Black Studies* 14 (December):107–136.

Timbs, Larry. 1994. "Future of Minority Workshop in Doubt." *Editor & Publisher* 127 (May 14):18–19+.

VanDerBeets, Richard. 1984. *The Indian Captivity Narrative.* Lanham, MD: University Press of America.

Chapter

9

South Africa and Brazil: Comparative Contexts of Racism

On May 10, 1994, Nelson Rolihlahla Mandela stood before a crowd of world leaders who had shunned South Africa during its years of racial separatism and in a husky, resolute voice swore the oath to become the tenth leader of South Africa since its union in 1910. Mandela was the first black president, and the first president elected with the participation of blacks.

In his acceptance speech, Mandela spoke about the shared patriotism of all South Africans, their common pain for their country's humiliation before the world, and the national relief at being readmitted to the company of civilized nations. Mandela promised, "Never, never, and never again shall it be that this beautiful land will again experience the oppression of one by another and suffer the indignity of being the skunk of the world" (Keller, 1994c:A1).

A few minutes later before a crowd of 50,000 ordinary citizens, Mandela held aloft the hand of F. W. de Klerk, the former president and Mandela's chief rival in the recent election. Mandela hailed his predecessor as "one of the greatest reformers, one of the greatest sons of our soil" (Keller, 1994c:A1). This tribute was consistent with a conciliatory pattern black and white leaders had maintained through the election process. At the end of a hard-hitting presidential debate a month earlier, Mandela had leaned across the table, grasped de Klerk's hand, and said, "My criticism of Mr. de Klerk should not obscure one fact. We are a shining example of people drawn from different race groups who have a common loyalty, a common love for their common country" (Gevisser, 1994:626).

The final returns in the election showed that Mandela's African National Congress (ANC) had received over three-fifths of the popular vote—12.3 million votes representing 62.7 percent of the total and along with the presidency accorded the majority party 252 seats in the new parliament. The National Party, the former white ruling unit, obtained nearly 4 million votes, representing 20.4 percent of the total and 82 seats in the parliament. The other organization receiving substantial support was the Inkatha Freedom Party, which obtained 10.5 percent of the vote and 43 parliamentary seats (Keller, 1994b:8).

For this chapter South Africa provides one comparative case study and Brazil the other. Stepping outside our own cultural boundaries, we can get different perspectives on how racism affects human relations. On the surface, certainly, South Africa, in spite of the recent remarkable developments, provides even more devastating racism than the United States and Brazil a considerably milder picture. At the end of the discussion, will we have new insights about whether, as we noted in Chapter 1, race is a "persistent category of advantage and privilege"? Let's wait and see.

THE SOUTH AFRICAN CASE

We begin with a look at the country's history, then discuss current racial policies, and finally consider its future.

Development of *Apartheid*

At the end of the eighteenth century, four large blacks groups dominated what would eventually become the Republic of South Africa. Conflict among these groups was frequent, including a series of bloody wars in the 1820s known as the *difaqane*. One significant impact of these wars was that many black tribal settlements were disrupted, making it much easier for recently arrived white immigrants to occupy unchallenged large sections of land.

In the 1650s white settlement started with Dutch immigrants brought over by the Dutch East India Company. During the 1820s over 3,000 British citizens arrived in the Cape Colony, and for the rest of the century, thousands of European immigrants settled in that area. Beginning in the late 1830s, about 15,000 primarily Dutch-speaking whites who were dissatisfied with British rule and seeking more land left the Cape Colony and spread into the interior in what became known as "the Great Trek." When white settlers encountered blacks, they either expelled or conquered them. Conflicts between British and Dutch-speaking settlers (Afrikaners) frequently occurred over land or other natural resources, and eventually the Anglo-Boer War of 1899 produced the British conquest of what had been two independent Boer states. Afrikaners were defeated but not subdued. They produced an Afrikaner version of South African history, widely celebrating its central events, heroes, and martyrs. Much like nineteenth-century white Americans professing "manifest destiny," Afrikaners stressed that theirs was a divine destiny— to lead the way to wealth and prominence in a white-supremicist nation (Oberholster, 1988; Thompson, 1990).

British rule was brief. Afrikaners outnumbered the British, and in 1948 their political party—the National Party—won control of the government and maintained it until 1994. Shortly after the 1948 election, the policy of *apartheid* began. **Apartheid,** which means separate development, is a government policy involving racial segregation of major facilities—residential areas, hotels, restaurants, buses, work locations, and even staircases, benches, and toilets. *Apartheid* represents the implementation of internal colonialism on a scale never attempted in this country since the days of slavery. To many modern Americans, *apartheid* has become a term suggesting hatred and bigotry, the epitome of racism, but precisely what the policy involves is not well known. Let's examine it.

In the 1950s the winds of change were sweeping across Africa, and a host of new nations emerged from what had been former European colonies. Hendrik Verwoerd, the prime minister of South Africa, recognized that in this social climate Great Britain would be unwilling to agree to a long-time South African request that three British territories bordering on South Africa be incorporated by it. Acknowledging Britain's outlook, Verwoerd declared that he would set aside his country's previous position and encourage Great Britain to permit these territories to become independent.

On the surface Verwoerd's decision might have seemed progressive, even humane. Actually because of the poverty dominating these areas, the proposed course of action, which Britain quickly accepted, simply assured South Africa's legal separation from land and people that represented an economic liability. These black nation states and other African homelands were largely overcrowded with no mining, very little manufacturing, and hardly any arable land. Under *apartheid* there were ten of these territories. Four became independent, and the other six, though maintaining some degree of autonomy, remain part of the Republic of South Africa. With the end of *apartheid,* all homelands were reincorporated into South Africa. These areas remain poor.

To survive, many blacks left independent states and impoverished rural homelands within South Africa itself and migrated into South African cities. Often men went alone, living in barracks and leaving their families behind. In addition, blacks frequently settled in the sprawling black communities on the outskirts of cities. In either case because of *apartheid*'s requirement that races remain residentially separated, they seldom could avoid long commutes to work.

With a surplus of cheap labor available, whites often made it more difficult for blacks to move into the cities. The dominant group used two major techniques. First, since the middle 1960s, the central government deliberately slowed and in some cases even stopped the construction of African housing in cities. Second, there was the outright destruction of black communities; in several instances bulldozers flattened shelters and huts housing 10,000 to 15,000 people (Badsha, 1986:10–14). It was apparent, in short, that under *apartheid* white leadership harshly applied the internal-colonialist principle of restricting racial minorities' activity, including residential location.

Brutal realities dominated racial minorities' lives, and yet during the 1980s the leadership learned to temper its restrictions, allowing some actions that might strike the outside observer as surprising. For instance, authorities relaxed extensive censorship. In the record section of the O.K. Bazaar, a big department store in Cape Town, an American woman heard Stevie Wonder's "Master Blaster," a song celebrating the independence of neighboring Zimbabwe. Among the white elite, there were a host of encounter groups in which the participants, including a few minority-group members, discussed and even debated the country's future.

But historically most apparent softenings of *apartheid* had an underside. At the very moment "Master Blaster" was heard in the O.K. Bazaar, South African undercover units were taking steps to overthrow the black government in Zimbabwe. And while a few members of racial minorities took part in elites' encounter groups, these participants were carefully chosen "responsible" individuals who were considerably less militant than thousands of other possible spokespeople for racial minorities (Lelyveld, 1985:29–31). Thus in the 1980s, the South African government permitted some activities that contrasted with the harshness of *apartheid*, but the policy itself remained a daily reality.

THE EVE OF *APARTHEID*'S FALL

We look briefly at prominent South African institutions and then, to make the reality of what's being discussed more vivid, examine *apartheid* in everyday life. First, though, as a background for this discussion, we briefly examine the size of different racial groups in the last years of *apartheid*.

South Africa's Racial Composition

In 1985 the population of the Republic of South Africa was 23,385,645. Of the total, 4,568,739 people (19.5 percent of the population) were white, with nearly twice as many Afrikaners as whites of British descent. The Coloreds, who are of mixed white, black, and sometimes Malay ancestry were 2,832,705 in number (12.1 percent). Indians, who arrived in nineteenth-century South Africa to work on sugar cane plantations, comprised 821,361 individuals (3.5 percent). Finally blacks were the largest group, with 15,162,840 people (64.8 percent) (South African Foundation, 1988:5).

A feature of South Africa which has made it unique among African territories located south of the Sahara Desert is that for over a century and a half, it has contained a relatively large white group which has made the country its homeland and committed itself to maintaining its position of dominance and privilege. Most sub-Saharan African territories were former European colonies, which contained a small resident white contingent, often less than 1 percent of the country's total population. Zimbabwe, formerly Southern Rhodesia and located directly north of South Africa, was once controlled by its white settler class, but eventually the whites stepped down when a black ticket headed by Robert Mugabe won at the polls. Through the 1980s both extensive verbal and guerrilla attacks against the South African ruling class originated from Zimbabwe.

As we look at institutional structures in South Africa, we begin to obtain a more detailed sense of how the ruling whites imposed their control on racial minorities.

Racism in South Africa's Major Institutions

In western democracies people grow to adulthood believing that with the inalienable right to vote in free and open elections, they participate in the process of choosing their rulers. In spite of possessing this right, they realize that tyranny can occur; without it, however, tyranny is inevitable.

In 1984 the South African government adopted a new constitution after a two-thirds majority of the white electorate had approved it the previous year. This document made some concession to the existing policy excluding all minority-group members from national elections. Now, along with whites, Coloreds and Indians could choose their own representatives. Each racial group would elect members to its own parliamentary house, which was proportional to its size in the population—thus 4:2:1 for whites, Coloreds, and Indians respectively (South African Foundation, 1988:16–17).

Opponents to this "reform" pointed out that with exclusion of blacks, whites' supremacy was assured. But the supporters of the new plan were quick to emphasize that blacks were permitted political participation: They could elect representatives within their own townships. Most blacks did not buy this idea, boycotting all-black elections which in their eyes could do nothing or almost nothing to alleviate the crushing oppression produced by *apartheid*. Furthermore both Coloreds and Indians turned out for elections in small numbers, realizing that with continued white control they inevitably remained second-class citizens.

Above all, this constitutional reform did not change the economic picture for racial minorities. In 1985 the average monthly earnings for the four racial groups were R418 (418 Rands) for blacks, R561 for Coloreds, R770 for Indians, and R1,561 for whites (South African Foundation, 1988:18–19). In South Africa an average African wage earner receives about 26.7 percent—barely a quarter—what an average white person makes.

This is a pretty grim picture, but it becomes even grimmer when one considers that it does not include the vast number of unemployed South Africans, who are primarily Africans. One can be working and still remain poor, but one is infinitely poorer without any economic resources. South Africa has no accurate figures on unemployment, but it is certain that large numbers of blacks forced out of farms, towns, and villages all over the country and onto the overcrowded reserves have been without employment and also without any prospect of finding any. One indication of the terrible poverty many Africans face is the estimate that in a given year about 50,000 black children die of malnutrition and other related diseases (Badsha, 1986:7).

A relationship among political power, income, and education exists in all countries. Not surprisingly whites, who have the lion's share of power and income in South Africa, also have the best educational opportunities. In 1987 for whites, the average per-capita governmental expenditure for education was R2,160; for Indians it was R1,450; for Coloreds R818; for blacks it was R368, or about 17 percent the per-capita government expenditure for whites. Inevitably the overall quality of children's educational experience corresponded with the expenditure. For instance, the teacher-pupil ratio for white students was one teacher to every 19 students and for blacks it was one teacher for every 41 students (South African Foundation, 1988:56–62). Such a situation represents a perpetuation of internal colonialism's colonial-labor principle, with racial minorities' limited educational opportunities keeping them restricted to low-paying jobs that primarily benefit the white controllers.

Those with power and wealth are best situated to obtain quality education, and, in turn, superior education helps them maintain their dominance. In South Africa, of course, whites have been decisively helped in this regard by the *apartheid* system, which, as we see in the following pages, promoted their dominance with a variety of concrete, drastic measures.

Maintenance of *Apartheid* in the Recent Past

For white South Africans, the country has long been a democracy, but for Indians, Coloreds, and most decisively blacks, one could persuasively argue that until 1994 it remained a totalitarian government, even with recent constitutional "reforms." Consider the follow situations, which show the impact of *apartheid* on racial minorities.

Since Afrikaners took control of the South African government in 1948, there was an effort to limit the migration of blacks to cities and their environs—a clear illustration of internal colonialism's principle of restricting racial minorities' activity. In Cape Town this policy was sufficiently successful that by 1970 black men in the area of that major South African city outnumbered black women by three to one, and in the African township of Langa, where thousands of workers were kept in barracks, the ratio was eleven to one.

Many men driven to the cities because it was the only place to find work felt that living without their families was wrong. One worker, who had brought in his family illegally, complained bitterly, saying that the construction firm which employed him and was about to build a first-class hostel for single men was failing to acknowledge the importance of the family in a country's development. He said, "That is why I am critical of its approach. Because it neglects the very core of nation building" (Badsha, 1986:42).

This man lived in Crossroads, a squatter settlement outside of Cape Town. Blacks resided illegally in this area for a number of reasons. Some, like the man quoted above, refused to live in single housing provided by their companies, risking the wrath of the law to be with their families. Others had been forced out of the city as the economy expanded and the legal areas for black residence became hopelessly overcrowded. Still others streamed into the area from outlying black areas looking both for jobs and a place to live. During the 1970s thousands of shacks and modest houses were built.

Authorities reacted harshly. The infamous pass law, which required blacks to have passes to enter so-called white areas, was reinstated, employers were threatened with huge fines if they hired "illegal" blacks, and, finally the flimsy cottages and shacks of about 25,000 people living nearby were destroyed. The word was out that Crossroads would be bulldozed shortly afterwards.

But Crossroads had become a community. Despite the absence of all modern conveniences and effective housing, life was better there than any place else in the vicinity blacks were permitted to reside. Crime rates were low, work was fairly plentiful, and the nutritional status of children was considerably better than that of children living in the countryside.

Eventually in 1979 the people of Crossroads won a stay of execution from the government, but the situation remained uncertain as officials refused to make a long-term commitment. Then in 1985 there was a battle between stone-throwing youngsters and police that left 22 people dead. In 1985 the government finally declared that Crossroads would remain and be upgraded (Badsha, 1986:110). The residents of the community had won a substantial victory.

Difficult as it was, life in urban areas tended to be much better than in the homelands and independent territories restricted to blacks under *apartheid*. In the Qwa Qwa reserve, for instance, a government commission reported that by 1920 the area was already overcrowded with 5,000 inhabitants; by 1970 the number had risen to 24,000.

The level of impoverishment is apparent in the following family history. The Serote family arrived in Qwa Qwa from a nearby white-owned farm in 1974. Since then Mr. Serote worked at a variety of jobs, but in 1982 tuberculosis made him too ill to continue. In that same year, Mr. Serote's eldest son obtained a job some distance away in the gold-mining town of Welcom. He too became ill but clung to the job because it was the family's only source of income. The second son was removed from school halfway through that year; he would have gone to work but he was too young to apply for a job as a migrant worker and could find nothing within the territory.

By the middle of the year, the family faced a severe crisis. Mrs. Serote and her youngest daughter were both diagnosed as suffering from pellagra, an extreme form of malnutrition, and a younger child was sent home from school because he was fainting from hunger in class. Drought and exhaustion meant that even the small vegetable garden near the house no longer received care. Begging or borrowing from neighbors was no longer possible, and because of the impersonal system of blacks' relocation, neither Mr. nor Mrs. Serote had relatives in the vicinity. When interviewed both parents spoke of their anxiety for and guilt about their children, confessing that they had failed as parents. "I cannot sleep at night any longer," said Mrs. Serote, "because my son was so ill when he last came home, but I sent him back to work [in Welcom] because his is the only income we have. I am forced to kill one child in order to feed the others" (Badsha, 1986:15) Neighbors were "appalled and ashamed" by the horrible sight of a family literally starving to death before their eyes while, besieged by their own poverty, they could do little to help.

Blacks are the poorest, most vicitimized racial group in South Africa, but other racial minorities are also poor and exploited by racism. In Durban, for instance, blacks, Indians, Coloreds, and whites once shared neighborhoods, but *apartheid* laws have forced all but whites out of the choice areas, compelling minority-group members to move elsewhere. Indians were ordered to leave prime locations close to the Indian Ocean, and in the vacated areas, real-estate speculators cashed in on high-rise apartments and shopping centers restricted to whites. In the middle 1980s, an irate Indian leader explained, "They don't need their laws anymore! They've done it! Whoever comes into power will not be able to change *this*" (Lelyveld, 1985:26–27). In this view racial minorities' displacement has been accomplished: *Apartheid* has triumphed.

A recent study of racial minorities' residential location in South African cities supported this conclusion, indicating that racial segregation has expanded through the twentieth century, with a marked increase since the 1960s when urban segregation laws were most strongly enforced. The highest level of racial segregation has been among blacks, followed by Asians, and then Coloreds. By the early 1990s, racial segregation in housing prevailed. As a result even with official elimination of *apartheid,* prospects for urban integration are remote (Christopher, 1990).

In South Africa, blacks customarily lived in a police state. The significance of that statement is apparent in the following section.

Being Black in South Africa: Living in a Police State

While racism continues to exist in the United States, its victims often have the opportunity to confront it—with an appeal to the appropriate agency, some type of legal action, or public protest.

In South Africa few blacks have had such opportunities. Under *apartheid* they knew that they were considered racially inferior and that the best they could expect was the opportunity to make a modest living and away from work to be left alone by whites. Often, however, black South Africans have been subjected to the stringent controls internal-colonialist theory analyzes.

In his autobiography Mark Mathabane, a black South African who was born in 1960, described the experience of growing up in Alexandra, a black ghetto near Johannesburg. Both then and now, violence has been an intimate part of residents' daily lives.

As internal-colonialist theory emphasizes, the white power structure controlled blacks' physical activity—in this case through police action. Once a year in Alexandra they designated "Operation Clean-up Month," during which black policemen led by white officers would comb the ghetto searching for gangsters, prostitutes, people whose passbooks (which indicated that they were permitted to live and work in the city) were not in order, or families living illegally in the area.

One winter in the middle of the night, the police raided the shack rented by the Mathabane family. Twice they banged at the kitchen door, yelling that if it weren't opened immediately, they would break it down. Five-year-old Mark was sleeping on a piece of cardboard close to the door, and he was so frightened that he urinated, soaking himself and the blanket in which he was wrapped. From the bedroom his mother whispered not to open the door until she and Mark's father had a chance to hide themselves. When Mark opened the door, two tall black policemen in starched brown uniforms rushed into the room and shined a flashlight in his eyes. One kicked the young boy in the side, sending him crashing into a crate in the corner. Mark tried to stand up, but another kick flattened him. "What took you so long to open the bloody door?" the policeman shouted. He was about to kick the boy again when his partner stopped him.

They began searching for Mark's parents. The bedroom door was locked from the inside, and when no one responded to the policemen's demand to open it, they knocked it down.

Looking under the bed, they spotted Mr. Mathabane, who was naked, and ordered him out. "I'm coming, *nkosi* [lord]," Mark's father whimpered. They asked him where his wife was, and he said she was sleeping at the residence where she was employed as a kitchen girl. Apparently the policemen believed him.

One interrogator demanded to see Mr. Mathabane's passbook, quickly noting that several taxes were unpaid and that one entry indicated that Mrs. Mathabane was expected to sleep at home. How could he account for his wife's absence, the policeman asked, and playfully began prodding Mr. Mathabane's penis with his nightstick. Mark's father offered an excuse for his wife.

Why, the policeman continued, did an old man want to remain in the city. Mr. Mathabane, who was only in his 30s but was prematurely aged by an impoverished life, replied that there were no jobs in the reserves.

The policeman said that the statement was wrong—that until recently he had been living in the reserves and that people like his own father continued to lead comfortable, productive lives there. In Alexandra and other black ghetto areas, residents knew that the white leadership preferred black policemen with a rural background. Such recruits resented the more affluent, sophisticated urban blacks and enjoyed acting as cruel instruments of the white power structure.

The policeman summarized the offenses displayed in Mr. Mathabane's passbook and asked whether he could figure out a solution. Looking up for a moment from the floor, Mr. Mathabane forced a smile—not a spontaneous smile but "a begging smile, a passive acceptance of the policeman's authority. After smiling my father again dropped his eyes to the floor" (Mathabane, 1986:22). The policeman whispered in Mr. Mathabane's ear, giving him the chance to buy his way out of the predicament with a bribe. But Mark's father had no money, and so he was forced to serve two months of hard labor on a white man's potato farm.

In 1966 the raids increased, and frequently they occurred in daytime. Children became adept at observing and analyzing police actions and would rush home to warn their parents. But Mark was unable to do so. He wrote:

> That brutal encounter with the police had left indelible scars. The mere sight of police vans now had the power of blanking my mind, making me forget all I had learned, making me rely on my instincts, which invariably told me to flee, to cower, lest I end up face-to-face with a policeman and get flogged. I became a useless sentry. (Mathabane, 1986:28)

Many black South Africans have grown to maturity with similar experiences. They found that living in *apartheid,* where the brutalities of oppressed status was a constant reality, was a continuous nightmare. Such experiences remain a significant part of South Africa's legacy, but change has been occurring.

RECENT DEVELOPMENTS

Seldom does significant social change occur so quickly. Consider events in South Africa occurring at the time of this book's first edition. Well past the normal deadline for manuscript correction, Alan McClare, the sociology editor, permitted me to slip in a paragraph about a momentous event that had just occurred—the March 1992 referendum of white voters calling for a formal end to *apartheid.* This was an extraordinary event, but what would follow from it? Three years later we can begin to answer the question.

To eliminate *apartheid* South Africa's leaders needed to open up the political process to all racial groups. This course of action was fraught with danger. White separatists committed to their long-established control of power and privilege might have engaged in sustained violence to sabotage the election. In addition, African groups vying for political dominance might have taken violent measures or simply boycotted the event, undermining its universal legitimacy. In spite of threats from both camps, general cooperation prevailed: In a country where violence has been widespread, the months leading up to the election produced surprisingly limited violence (Keller, 1994a).

The election process involved major governmental efforts to prepare black voters, many of whom were illiterate, to do something they had been prevented from doing all their lives—to vote. Because of *apartheid,* blacks, representing three-quarters of the potential voters, were often located in the most inaccessible parts of the country. To acquaint these individuals with the voting process, organizers in vans toured both rural and urban areas. On television and radio, different public-service messages anticipated specific dangers: that in traditional tribal areas, husbands would try to dictate their wives' choice or that tribal chiefs would require subjects to make a payment for the privilege of voting; that white overseers would confiscate their black workers' identity cards to hinder their voting (Clines, 1994a).

Frequently election organizers ran a mock presidential ballotting to acquaint new voters with the process. A week before the election, Mike Tukai was conducting a mock election with mine workers at a company barracks in Cape Province. The men were concerned that their white overseers might punish them, but still they were determined to participate. As the activity began, the "men were instantly wide-eyed as they saw, then took in their hands sample ballots that they treated like holy writ" (Clines, 1994b:A10). Lucas Mlungana, a 50-year-old quarry worker, suggested why they showed this respect. "Whether my life changes depends on who gets elected," Mlungana explained (Clines, 1994b:A10). He yearned for fast improvement in a life where he had to sleep in a rickety, gloomy barracks 11 months of the year and then journey a long distance to spend a precious month with his wife and children.

With nearly two-thirds of the popular vote, the African National Congress had to face the huge challenge of leading the country during the momentous conversion from white rule to racial democracy. At the top of the ANC ticket was Nelson Mandela—in the eyes of both South Africans and outside observers a remarkable leader. But Mandela is vulnerable both to age—he was 75 when elected president in 1994—and the possibility of assassination. So were Mandela to die or be incapacitated, who would succeed him?

Immediately below Mandela in the ANC hierarchy are two men—Cyril Ramaphosa and Thabo Mbeki. Ramaphosa, aged 41 in 1994, fought *apartheid* inside South Africa, forming the black National Union of Mineworkers in 1982 and leading it until 1991. Ramaphosa rose rapidly within the ANC, becoming its secretary general, and played a significant role in the negotiations leading up to the election, but he supposedly lacked Mandela's confidence. So after the election, he remained secretary general with an eye to building up the party. Mbeki, son of one of the men imprisoned with Mandela in 1962, had spent 28 of his 51 years in exile, where he frequently negotiated with diplomats to promote the end of *apartheid*. Moderate and aristocratic, Mbeki struck many people as similar to Mandela, whose confidence in him was apparent when Mbeki was made first executive vice president and the leading candidate to succeed the president.

To fill its seats in parliament, the ANC presented a diversified set of candidates. A third were women, and there was a distinct range of ethnic groups—including Zulus, who dominated the rival Inkatha Freedom party, Indians, and diverse whites, with even a few Afrikaners. Perhaps the party's greatest challenge has been that beneath the surface of its polished leadership, this large organization, with its 400 branch offices, lacks skilled administrators.

Another problem the party faces has been the maintenance of constituent support. Many of its backers are poor, often unemployed, and radical. In the 1980s the ANC built extensive support among dispossessed blacks by making black residential areas ungovernable: Tactics included strikes, school boycotts, mass refusals to pay rent, mortgages, and utility payments, and killing of such agents of the white rulers as black police officers and councilmen (*Economist*, 1994a; Keller, 1994b:5). But, to put it mildly, times have changed, and the ANC is now in power and the old white enemies are now considerably less formidable. The party's new challenge has been to maintain its support while promoting significant change that will improve the lives of *apartheid*'s victims.

Before examining some of those challenges, we consider the reasons why in recent years South Africa has undergone such a significant transformation. It is an involved issue requiring analysts to consider a complex set of factors. First, as South Africa has become increasingly urbanized and industrialized, the maintenance of *apartheid* has become more cumbersome and difficult. With modern mass media providing so much information about whites' luxurious lives, economic inequalities became blatantly and painfully visible. In addition, forced to live in completely segregated areas, black organizers found ample opportunity to mobilize social movements based on members' shared oppressions. Furthermore in an era when an increasing number of countries around the globe were democratizing, South Africa stood seriously out of step with all other modern industrial countries.

While these factors undoubtedly have had a significant impact over time, one must consider why the end of *apartheid* occurred just when it did—in the early 1990s. Certainly the barrage of protests both inside and outside the nation played a significant role. These activities encouraged, even forced foreign governments and companies to restrict or eliminate economic relations with South Africa. The boycotts, in turn, set the groundwork for negotiations between such exiled ANC leaders as Thabo Mbeki and major South African business leaders, who were losing out financially because of economic bans imposed on their country. While details of their discussions are sketchy, it does appear that the ANC leaders made it clear that they were willing to compromise their radical positions on such issues as the redistribution of wealth if the white businesspeople would pressure F. W. de Klerk and other top politicians to support the end of *apartheid*. The impact of these business leaders appears to have been heightened by the fact that theirs has been a fairly small group of highly organized individuals—in sharp contrast to the less cohesive, much larger combination of white farmers and small businesspeople who represented the core supporters of *apartheid*.

Finally one should consider a factor that generally makes sociologists somewhat uncomfortable—the contribution of individuals, in this instance two individuals. Could the fairly bloodless transition to the end of *apartheid* have been accomplished without two, quite remarkable individuals—Nelson Mandela and F. W. de Klerk? Appropriately de Klerk has received much less credit than Mandela; yet as the most prominent white leader, he played a significant role in orchestrating a peaceful transition to the post-*apartheid* state. Since released from prison in 1990, Mandela has been able to move the process of ending *apartheid* calmly but persistently ahead. Commenting on Mandela, sociologist S. M. Miller declared, "I am not a devotee of the great man in history approach but Mandela's role does not seem foreordained nor that a stand-in could have performed it" (Miller, 1994:12).

With the formal end of *apartheid* completed, South Africa still faces many significant race-related problems.

THE CHALLENGES IN THE YEARS AHEAD

The national election of spring 1994 produced two significant results. First, *apartheid* was abolished, at least in a formal, legal sense. Second, for the first time in its history, all the major groups within the country engaged in "one bonding action of civil responsibilities." At least for a while, people felt a sense of shared nationhood (Breytenbach, 1994:6).

After the election South Africa has been forced to confront the effects of the most developed system of internal colonialism in the entire industrial world. A journalist summed up the situation in the following way:

> Mr. Mandela's government will find that 46 years of *apartheid* have bequeathed it a fearsome legacy. A huge economic and social divide separates black from white. A "lost generation" of black children has gone unschooled. Families have been divided through imprisonment and exile. Perhaps the most devastating and intractable problem of all will be that of dealing with the muddled ethnic identities and feuds that *apartheid* has bred: a process that has not only turned black against white but also black against black. (*Economist,* 1994b:21)

Considering some of the major issues, we might start with the fiercest manifestation of the ethnic-identity issue: violence. Between 1990 and mid-1994, 13,000 South Africans were killed in politically motivated violence, with the rivalry between the ANC and the Zulu-dominated Inkatha Freedom party providing the context for most of those deaths. Beyond explicitly political violence, South Africa has become a country where unpleasant encounters can quickly turn violent and then lethal. Robberies and car hijackings often escalate quickly into savage killings. A factor contributing to deadly violence is that cheap weapons have been readily available from neighboring wars: In 1994 a semiautomatic rifle from Mozambique could be bought for less than $20 (*Economist,* 1994b:21;Keller, 1994a:1).

Long-run efforts to curtail violence in South Africa require policy makers to address the sources of the anger and frustration that promote it: in particular, the poverty and limited opportunity facing the country's huge poor population. In the short term, however, a critical factor must be effective policing.

In May 1994 officials of the new Mandela-headed government announced a reorganization of the South African police beginning with a name change—the South African Police Service instead of the South African Police Force. While some observers might be skeptical about the significance of a name change, it well might be important in a country where the police have traditionally been a force dedicated exclusively to affluent whites' interests and goals. Thus while until the early 1990s, a police sweep through the mixed-race township of Manenberg in Cape Town would have focused on a search for political dissidents or an harassment of local people, in June 1994 it signified an effort to root out the violent gangs that have plagued all the racial groups in this township. Instead of terrorizing local blacks, police were protecting them.

The buzzwords "community policing" are as prevalent in South Africa as in Los Angeles, New York, Houston, Miami, Chicago, and a host of other American cities. Details on police reorganization have been limited, but some guidelines are apparent. The country's interim constitution declares that within a given locale, reforms will be the result of consultations between police and local leaders, and the new South African Bill of Human Rights protects all citizens from many oppressive acts the police routinely used in the past—such as searches without warrants and detention without trial (Holmes, 1994a).

Another reorganized system of authority in post-*apartheid* South Africa is local government. With a racial democracy in effect, black officials are now elected to positions previously held only by whites. However, as we saw in the discussion of minority politicians in Chapter 4, election is only the beginning of the battle. Consider the case of Port Elizabeth. This industrial city on the Indian Ocean has the country's first black mayor, Nceba Faku, who spent 13 years in prison for recruiting anti-*apartheid* guerrillas. As mayor Faku has been widely admired for his emphasis on racial conciliation and energetic plans for political reform, but there has literally been a heavy price to pay: Change is going to be expensive, with whites paying higher property taxes and costlier utilities while waiting longer for their potholes to get filled and their leaky sewers repaired. The great cost and need involves the other three racial groups: By the year 2000, the formerly disenfranchised minority groups are going to have fresh water, electricity, sewers, garbage removal, decent roads, clinics, fire departments, access to libraries, and recreation services—goods and services they were often denied under *apartheid*. A journalist summarizing the policies established by the Faku administration in Port Elizabeth concluded, "It is the first [local government] to confront a blunt reality Mr. Mandela has tended to play down: that whites have a large bill to pay for the past" (Keller, 1994e:3). In most cities the election of local governments will occur in 1995. Among whites concern runs deep about the sacrifices they will be required to pay—especially with the case of Port Elizabeth already starting to set precedents.

Another political challenge involves the nation's bloated bureaucracy. The pre-*apartheid* government had 18 education departments, which are certain to be trimmed, but such trimming, though fund-saving overall, will meet resistance from incumbents who lose their jobs. Each of the ten black homelands created for blacks in the name of *apartheid*'s separate development had its own bureaucracy of thousands of civil servants who find themselves without function now that with the official end of *apartheid* the homelands have been reintegrated into the nation. As part of governmental streamlining, the civil servants are supposed to be retrained and relocated, but just what that means so shortly after the election is not yet apparent (*Economist,* 1994a; Keller, 1994d).

Besides the political challenges, the new government faces myriad complicated economic issues. The current reality is that foreign investment in South Africa, which had been significantly curtailed by widespread economic boycott during *apartheid,* can now resume. Early returns, however, have not been promising. Ten months after Nelson Mandela formally invited business to return and three months after the election, South Africa had not seen the surging investment needed to produce new jobs and economic growth. Major impediments are that the labor force is costly, largely unskilled, and militant. Furthermore American investors tend to be unsophisticated about Africa, often identifying South Africa with Rwanda, the tiny, impoverished country 1,500 miles to the north where ethnic hatreds have produced political chaos and a massive number of deaths. The fact that South Africa is part of the industrial world and that Rwanda is not does not prevent South Africa from losing out through the comparison. Japanese companies looking for investment opportunities tend to head toward Southeast Asia because labor costs are lower, skills are greater, and sometimes loyalty to an employer is stronger. Still, hope persists that investors will turn to South Africa. The most promising investment areas appear to be tourism; processing of natural resources to produce such products as aluminum, stainless steel, and paper; and specialty manufacturing, like a BMW subsidiary that makes leather auto seats (Keller, 1994f).

Another optimistic economic sign was that in October 1994, Moody's Investor's Service, a major credit-rating agency, provided South Africa an investment-grade rating that would permit the country to borrow money to build roads, provide electricity, and create jobs for millions of poor black citizens. Balancing this positive development was the fact that Standard and Poor's, the other major rating agency, gave South Africa a rating just below investment grade, in part because the firm wanted more time to evaluate the economic and political changes occurring in the country (Ramirez, 1994).

Not only do poor blacks desperately need the financial benefits of an improving economy, but they are understandably impatient for a better life. Consider the legacy of the *apartheid* laws depriving most blacks of land ownership. Not waiting for the new government to supply public housing, landless blacks have initiated a wave of "land invasion" on a variety of public and private spaces in and around various cities. This development has provoked the wrath of multiracial homeowners fearing a decline in housing values. In addition, such action disrupts government plans for a systematic public-housing registration where landless people would place their names on waiting lists.

In spite of such problems, these settlements appear quite promising. For instance, in Canana, a recent settlement about 40 miles from Johannesburg, a committee composed of some of the original settlers runs the community. Committee members have laid out wide swaths for streets and have marked off lots. Newcomers are assigned numbers that are painted on the outside of their corrugated iron shacks so that one day the postal service will be able to deliver mail. Pit latrines are dug near the street to make it easier for authorities when they install sewer lines. Plots of land are set aside for a clinic, stores, churches, and a nursery. A member of the ruling committee indicated that there had been no conflict or violence since the community was established. Another committee member said, "If the government wants to remove us from here, they must build houses where there are services where poor people are satisfied" (Holmes, 1994c:A4).

In the former black homelands, grinding poverty prevails. A portion of Gazankuku, one of the former homelands, contains about 500,000 people crammed into 140 square miles where local blacks have been restricted to wrenching a meagre living from agriculturally marginal land. Separated only by a wire fence is the Sabi Sand Game Reserve, where wealthy, generally white tourists sip drinks on shaded verandas and roam about the bush in Land Rovers photographing cheetahs, lions, rhinos, elephants, and other game.

Until the recent election, the wealthy white land owners in the reserve saw little reason to pay much attention to their poor neighbors. Now, however, they have become responsive to blacks' recent efforts to develop laundries, auto-repair shops, film-developing enterprises, and other businesses that can contribute to the local tourist industry. Such cooperation represents a form of insurance. Otherwise, land owners realize, they face the distinct threat that local blacks will petition the government to force whites to give up their land (Holmes, 1994b).

Prosperous blacks face their own challenges. Moving into previously all-white neighborhoods in a country where until recently segregated housing for blacks was the law, they often encounter coldness, isolation, hostility, suspicion, and even white flight. Although blacks moving into white areas obtain better housing, paved streets, and nights without gunfire, they feel deprived of the camaraderie their poor communities offered. "You miss your people," said Gladness Ncobo, a real-estate agent. "Here you are like in jail, like on Robben Island. Here you don't know if your neighbor is alive or dead. Then you see the car drive up, and you know that he's alive. That's not life" (Wilkerson, 1994:A3).

With modern South Africa, one sees a country in the midst of momentous social change. In the past several years, formal *apartheid* has been eliminated. Now the structural effects of that virulent internal-colonialist policy remain. How effectively current government efforts can erradicate those effects and whether or not violence will develop remains to be seen.

Race relations in Brazil offer a contrasting picture.

THE BRAZILIAN CASE

Since the emancipation of slaves a century ago, Brazil has had the international reputation of being a racial paradise, or at least close to it. In recent years, however, that image has begun to tarnish. In 1978 and 1979, for instance, Brazil's leading television network, *Rede Globo,* presented a series for children adapted from stories written by Monteiro Loboto, a well-known Brazilian author, and the series was widely acclaimed. In 1979 the African country of Angola, which is also Portuguese speaking, decided to show the series. After seven installments, however, Angolan television abruptly cancelled the series, charging that it was racist, depicting blacks only in inferior positions. Most offensive to Angolan viewers was the role of Tia [Aunt] Nastácia, an elderly, black cook whom the Angolans considered a racial caricature. Brazilians were surprised and asked many questions. Were the Angolans justified? How should blacks be represented in the media? (Skidmore, 1985:15). If this had been an isolated incident, then concern about racism probably would have soon passed. But it was only one illustration of widespread criticism.

In the following pages, we briefly examine the racial history of Brazil, then analyze current racial inequalities, and consider future race relations.

History of Brazilian Race Relations

Predominantly three groups have produced the current racial composition of Brazil—European, initially Portuguese whites, Indians, and African blacks.

In the sixteenth century, Portuguese colonists, primarily men, began immigrating to Brazil, and in many cases these men fathered numerous children whose descendants are currently found both among whites and racial minorities. Some of these early immigrants became sugar plantation farmers while others, former Jews known as "new Christians," settled in small ports along the sea coast and engaged in skilled trade, skilled labor, and the professions and became moneylenders to the sugar planters, who were often heavily in their debt. In the nineteenth century, immigrants from other European countries began to come to Brazil. At first Germans and Swiss arrived, followed by Italians, Poles, and Spaniards.

To supply laborers for the first sugar plantations, early Portuguese colonists hunted down and enslaved Indians—substantial numbers of them because each large sugar plantation required about 200 workers. Early settlers had a few black slaves and found them more manageable than Indians since they had been subdued by the slavery system. However, because of wars with Holland during the colony's first two centuries, whites were unable to add appreciably to the number of black slaves. When the wars with Holland finally ended, African slaves replaced Indians in agricultural work; Indians were often used to care for livestock (Smith, 1972:52–55).

For about a century, the slave trade occurred in Brazil. While the number of slaves brought to Brazil is unknown, it certainly was a significant number. In 1819 the population of the country was about 3.6 million people, with about 80 percent—2.9 million—blacks or mulattoes (people of mixed blood). In contrast, in the United States, the ratio was reversed, with whites forming about 80 percent of the population, and racial minorities—blacks and Indians—comprising the remaining 20 percent. Even in the American South, where blacks most heavily concentrated, they never represented more than 38 percent of the population.

The different proportions are significant, because, unlike the United States, nineteenth-century Brazil simply did not have enough whites to fill key positions in a commercially expanding country, and so blacks and mulattoes could become skilled tradesmen, cowboys, small food growers, and boatmen (Drimmer, 1979:102). Out of economic necessity, in short, the colonial-labor principle applied less drastically to Brazil than to the United States.

Nonetheless most slaves remained unskilled agricultural workers. When blacks were freed in 1888, they found few jobs available. At that point they had to compete for agricultural jobs with Indian laborers now willing to work for wages and with a steady stream of European workers better prepared to function in the postslavery economic system. Many blacks could not find jobs and quickly slipped into terrible poverty (Fernandes, 1969:1–3). For many Brazilian blacks, that poverty has carried into the present era.

Thus historically racial minorities in Brazil have had diversified economic opportunities. Socially modern Brazilian society gives the impression of being racially liberated. Currently racial intermarriage is common, and explicit racial segregation is both unusual and illegal (Webster and Dwyer, 1988). Historically racial practice in Brazil has been fairly progressive, generally more progressive than in either South Africa or the United States.

But many Brazilians have not been content with such modest claims. Since about 1950 governmental officials and other leading citizens have vocally asserted that Brazil is a racial democracy. They have emphasized two themes—that under no circumstances should people admit that racism occurs in Brazil and that any claim about the existence of racism should be attacked as "un-Brazilian" (Smith, 1972:59).

In the 1970s such attacks were extensive. For instance, when a major newspaper ran a feature story describing the "black is beautiful" movement in Rio de Janeiro, powerful whites sharply criticized the paper, claiming that publicizing such "un-Brazilian" groups was itself "un-Brazilian." The white elite, in fact, went much further to protect the country's racially democratic image: In particular, prominent faculty members at the University of São Paulo were forced to retire. While ideologically varied, these men all were involved in race-relations research, where they raised questions members of the white elite found troubling. In addition, the federal government confiscated a modern journal of opinion, *Argumento*, which featured a hard-headed analysis of Brazil's racial situation. But an even more significant action occurred. Government officials decided to omit the topic of race from the census of 1970, thereby preventing researchers' access to a potentially revealing data source. Without this information or any other large studies on race in Brazil, meaningful analysis and discussion of the issue was impossible. Thus supporters of the doctrine of racial democracy temporarily defeated a potential major threat (Skidmore, 1985:15–17).

By the late 1970s, however, the tone of the times had changed, and as we see, a major study of race in Brazil produced some important, interesting findings.

Racism in Modern Brazil

A 12-year-old black boy reached through a car window and snatched a woman's necklace. As he fled, four white men grabbed him and started beating his face and ribs. A black woman intervened, and she too was beaten. Eventually the police arrived and carried off the badly bruised boy. In such situations angry crowds often lynch young thieves on the spot.

Currently there are about 36 million Brazilians under 18, with about 60 percent of them needy and about 7 million of them maintaining few or no links with their families (Riding, 1985). The most desperate poor in Brazil—abandoned children, youths who live from muggings, robberies, and other crimes, and families who must remove children from school to perform menial jobs contributing to the family's survival—are overwhelmingly black (Sundiata, 1987:68).

About 44 percent of Brazil's population is black or mulatto (Christmas, 1988), and many Brazilian minority-group members suffer life-threatening poverty. Two factors contribute significantly to making poor racial minorities' situation in Brazil worse than in the United States. One major difference is that since Franklin Roosevelt's New Deal in the 1930s, the American government has been willing to supply a welfare "safety net," albeit an increasingly flimsy one, for the nation's poor, and Brazil offers the poor no similar support.

The second major advantage in the United States has been the strength of the black professional class, whose members, unlike blacks and mulattoes in Brazil, have historically been denied full participatory rights in society. As a result American black professionals have developed a race consciousness that has extended concern to all members of their race, even the poorest (Sundiata, 1987:68). The irony is that in Brazil the relatively open racial situation has tended to discourage a sense of black consciousness, including a systematic concern by affluent blacks for poor members of their race.

The historical insignificance of a black-consciousness movement in Brazil does not imply that blacks have been spared diverse effects of racism. Using data from the large 1976 National Household Sample Research, investigators revealed clear indications that racism in Brazil has occurred and continues to occur.

As in the United States, in Brazil educational attainment links to occupational success. Among whites about 27 percent reported no schooling or less than a year while the comparable figure for racial minorities was 46 percent. As the amount of education increased, the gap between whites and racial minorities expanded. Thus while 19 percent of whites and 12 percent of minority-group members completed five to eight years of school, 11 percent of whites and only 3 percent of racial minorities obtained nine or more years of education. For the five- to eight-year bracket, whites had a 1.55 greater chance of completion, but at the nine-year-and-more level, their chance was 3.15 times greater.

Income differences were equally distinct. Among racial minorities 54 percent received the minimum wage or less while a considerably smaller percentage of whites—23 percent—fell into this category. At the affluent end of the income distribution, 24 percent of whites and 15 percent of minority-group members had an income two to five times the minimum wage, and 16 percent of whites and 4 percent of minority-group individuals received over five times the minimum wage. Overall whites' income was about twice minority-group members'.

For both education and income, the gap between Brazilian racial minorities and whites increases when one evaluates higher status categories. Data on these topics indicated racial inequality, but what needs more analysis is whether racial minorities' inferior job attainments occurred simply because they started from disadvantaged positions, or, in addition, because they encountered racism. Research on social mobility provides clues.

Social mobility is the movement of a person from one social class or status level to another, either upward or downward with accompanying gains or losses in wealth, power, and prestige. The following analysis of social mobility involves people in three broad occupational levels—manual, nonmanual, and upper; the manual and nonmanual categories are also subdivided.

Among people born into families where the father was employed at the lower-manual level (workers in domestic services, traditional industries, and local trade), only 21 percent of minority-group individuals compared to 38 percent of whites rose to nonmanual positions. Among those coming from the high-manual level (workers in modern industries and unskilled workers in services), 29 percent of minority-group members and 41 percent of whites obtained nonmanual occupations. Among those born into the nonmanual category, 64 percent of whites and 53 percent of minority-group people in the lower-nonmanual level (lower-clerical workers and small owners in commerce and services) achieved positions equal to or higher than their fathers', and in the higher-nonmanual category (high-level clerical workers and small farmers), the proportions were 44 percent for whites and 26 percent for racial minorities. At the upper level (professionals, managers, and big-business owners), 47 percent of whites and 24 percent of minority-group individuals stayed in this highest occupational category; or, reversing the focus, one sees that 76 percent of minority-group people compared to 53 percent of whites at the upper level were downwardly mobile from their fathers' upper-level occupations.

These data involve situations where racial minorities and whites originated from families with about equal socioeconomic status, and yet whites' upward social mobility or sustained high status was consistently greater than minority-group members'. Since no other factors influencing these outcomes are readily apparent, it is hard to avoid concluding that racism plays a significant role.

More recent research produced a notable refinement of this conclusion. Data obtained from 74 metropolitan areas with populations of 100,000 people or more found that the more industrialized a district, the greater racial equality across occupations. However, at the higher occupational levels of managerial/professional and white-collar jobs, whites were favored, even with the educational level controlled. Most industrial jobs in modern Brazil are blue-collar, and thus many minority-group members benefit significantly from industrialization. However, those who attempt to move toward the top of the occupational ladder are disproportionately unsuccessful compared to whites. It appears that in Brazil poor whites have less negative racial attitudes than middle-class whites; in addition, whites in general seem to accept blacks and browns in even highly skilled blue-collar positions while they are uncomfortable with their presence in white-collar jobs.

Racial inequality persists in Brazil's occupational structure. There are two major processes. First, racial minorities obtain less education, and as a result they enter the labor market with fewer qualifications. Second, racial discrimination affects workers' hiring and promotion. Because of these processes, racial minorities suffer "a cycle of cumulative disadvantage" in their quest for status attainment (Hasenbalg, 1985; Silva, 1985; Telles, 1994).

These are harsh, important facts that might strike some readers as somewhat abstract. If that be the case, the following illustration should help clarify how racial discrimination can occur in Brazil. José (a pseudonym), a well-known black lawyer and legal scholar, tried in 1970 to pass a set of examinations to receive an appointment to the Law Faculty of the University of Bahia. In a competition organized within the University, José received the highest score on the written examination but failed on the oral examination, which could be attended only by candidates and their examiners. In the following four years, José continued to fail the oral examination, and while he was reluctant to conclude that racism was involved, he saw no alternative explanation. Then in 1974 the oral examinations were opened to the public. José invited friends and legal colleagues to attend, and this time he not only received the highest score on the written examination but also passed the oral (Turner, 1985:76). He had triumphed but not without extensive exposure to racist treatment.

On basic survival issues, racial differences also exist. Recent research indicated that whites outlived minorities (classified as "nonwhites") by 6.7 years in 1980—no more than a modest reduction from the 7.5-year margin in 1950 (Wood and Lovell, 1992).

Besides blacks and mulattoes, Indians also suffer racial oppression in Brazil. In the state of Roraima, the government has failed to take active steps to prevent illegal gold mining and drug smuggling on Indian reserves. In Roraima and the nearby state of Acre, forest Indians' traditional way of life is rapidly disappearing as poor people from the rest of Brazil move in and clear the forests (*Economist*, 1987).

In the fall of 1993, there occurred a celebrated, savage incident in which Indians were victimized in a situation fitting the frustration-aggression theory described in Chapter 2. Since 1990 gold miners have been trying to enter the Yanomamö homeland located near the Venezuela border. To discourage this illegal activity, Brazilian police raided a mining camp in August 1993, destroying the miners' water pumps, generators, and air strip. Infuriated, the miners struck not at the most logical object of their wrath—the police—but at a more vulnerable group—local Yanomamö. Attacking a nearby village, the miners massacred 20 Yanomamö: They shot the men and then used machetes to slit women's and children's throats. Ten children were killed, with some of them decapitated. Two months later 23 Brazilian miners were charged with the murders and scheduled to stand trial (Brooke, 1993; Chagnon, 1993).

The following situation illustrates some complexities of blacks' discrimination in modern Brazil.

The African Connection: An Uncomfortable Policy

During a major holiday in Rio de Janeiro, ambassadors from Ghana and Nigeria appeared in a street celebration, singing in the Yoruba language and dancing with a well-known Brazilian dance troop. Many onlookers were confused about their identity, and in his column a journalist asked, "Who are these two personalities with complicated names?" (Dzidzienyo, 1985:135). We can consider why African ambassadors' public appearance was a distinctly incongruous event in Brazilian society.

Throughout the book we have noted that racial oppression involves restrictive norms imposed on a racial minority, particularly limited access to the prized economic, political, and social rewards within the society.

Suppose, however, the nation's dominant group—in this case Brazil's white power structure—wants to establish close, mutually beneficial economic and political relations with groups racially and culturally linked to their own oppressed racial group—in this instance African nations. Let's consider how Brazil's African connection has developed in the past three decades.

Since the early 1960s, Brazilian leaders have encouraged increased relations between their country and independent African countries. Such connections interest many Brazilian groups, including political leaders seeking to increase the nation's stature through broader political alliances, white business people wanting to develop new markets for their products, and black Brazilian groups trying to establish a variety of political, economic, and cultural ties to citizens in African countries.

During the 1960s the all-white Brazilian leadership acted efficiently to advance the African connection— condemning *apartheid* while maintaining political and economic ties to South Africa; encouraging an increasing number of African leaders to make official visits to Brazil; and giving repeated affirmations of historical and cultural linkages between Africa and Brazil.

But from the African viewpoint, something critical was usually missing—visible involvement of black Brazilians in the official relations between Brazil and African nations. For instance, many black Africans consider the city of Bahia the place where black culture thrives in Brazil. However, when the *Asantehene,* the monarch of the Ashantis of Ghana, visited Bahia, he was not officially introduced to any black Bahians during his two-day stay. In contrast, in São Paulo his party met a large number of black Brazilians, including federal and state politicians, professionals, journalists, and students. The reason for the difference was that in São Paulo, Adalberto Camargo, a black elected official, played a major role in planning the *Asantehene's* schedule.

Sometimes the African connection produces controversy among black Brazilians. For instance, Abdias do Nascimento, a well-known writer, painter, and activist, has criticized black organizations in Bahia for failure to promote black Brazilians' involvement in relations with African officials. Nascimento's critics, in turn, have accused him of being argumentative and antiwhite.

At present black Brazilians are minimally involved in their nation's official relations with African countries. While the white political and economic leadership in Brazil would like the involvement to remain modest, many black Brazilians and African officials take an opposing view. How this situation unfolds will affect not only the African connection but also many black Brazilians' political, economic, and social status in their own society.

Future of Brazilian Race Relations

Recently an upsurge of black consciousness has occurred in Brazil. Groups involved have differed in style and goals but have shared the strongly held belief that the myth of racial democracy has been harmful for blacks and mulattoes and must be destroyed (Turner, 1985). Yet it is doubtful that such a movement can significantly change racial minorities' plight in Brazil.

Certainly racism thrives in that society. While internal-colonialist policies are toned down in Brazil, whites hold minority groups in check. A larger if related problem in that in this society dire poverty exists for an enormous number of people, primarily members of racial minorities, whose plight results principally from historical racial oppression, not explicit racist practice today. Elimination of current racist practices would do little to benefit most of them. To significantly change their lives, the government would need to enact drastic economic reforms, beginning with a "safety net" welfare program.

But such a policy is not likely to develop soon as the following event illustrates. In 1990 Fernando Collor de Mello was elected president, campaigning as a champion of the "shirtless and shoeless" and an enemy of the "corrupt elite." Once in office, however, his policies reversed these priorities: Brazil's poor racial minorities faced new rounds of layoffs and income cuts while the Collor government protected elites' economic interests (Silverstein, 1990).

CONCLUSION

The material in this chapter offers distinct contrast to the American racial picture, and at the end we find ourselves with three quite different situations. In recent years certainly the greatest change has occurred in South Africa; in the near future, that country probably remains the least predictable of the three, with the possibilities ranging from the development of a successful multiracial democracy to a significant political deterioration where violence and chaos dominate. Even though *apartheid* has been officially dismantled, its negative impact in politics, work, housing, education, and the family will persist indefinitely.

In the United States, the mainstream ideology involving race has been changing, showing signs of lessened racism. Survey data suggest that most white Americans don't like to think of themselves as racist, don't wish to assert a sense of racial superiority. Nonetheless ample evidence of racism exists. One might conclude that the U.S. racial picture is somewhat like Brazil's. In both cases current ideology differs from the present reality of sustained racism.

Furthermore another parallel between the two societies might be growing. Earlier we noted that because of more pronounced historical racism in the United States than in Brazil, the black professional class has maintained closer ties to poor blacks than their affluent counterparts in Brazil. That connection, however, is starting to change. Perhaps 10 to 15 percent of young U.S. blacks are completely removed from any contact with poor people (Clark, 1979), and thus like successful Brazilian blacks, they are developing an insensitivity to the combined impact of poverty and racism.

What is unique about Brazil is that for decades there has been an ideology of racial democracy, which the elite has strongly supported and even defended. If a Brazilian makes the claim that racism occurs in their country, they are unpatriotic—un-Brazilian.

In all three countries, notable parallels occur: In each of these societies, minority-group members tend to be considerably poorer and more deprived educationally, economically, and politically than whites; in addition, all three societies offer explicit illustrations of recent racial discrimination. Unfortunately we have found cross-cultural evidence from three very different societies indicating that race continues to be a remarkably "persistent category of advantage and privilege."

REFERENCES

Badsha, Omar, (ed.). 1986. *South Africa: The Cordoned Heart.* Cape Town, South Africa: Gallery Press.

Breytenbach, Breyten. 1994. "Dog's Bone." *New York Review of Books* 41 (May 26):3–6.

Brooke, James. 1993. "Miners Kill 20 Indians in the Amazon." *New York Times* (August 20): A10.

Chagnon, Napoleon A. 1993. "Covering Up the Yanomamö Massacre." *New York Times* (October 23):21.

Christmas, Rachel Jackson. 1988. "In Harmony with Brazil's African Pulse." *New York Times* (November 20):43.

Christopher, A. J. 1990. "*Apartheid* and Urban Segregation Levels in South Africa." *Urban Studies* 27 (June):421–440.

Clark, Alisha. 1979. "African-American College Students' Attitudes." *Journal of Black Studies* 10 (July):243–248.

Clines, Francis X. 1994a. "South Africa Tries to Prepare Those It Long Denied Ballot." *New York Times* (April 12):A1+.

Clines, Francis X. 1994b. "Enrollment Teams Hunt the Forgotten Corners." *New York Times* (April 21):A10.

Drimmer, Melvin. 1979. "Neither Black Nor White: Carl Degler's Study of Slavery in Two Societies." *Phylon* 40 (March):94–105.

Dzidzienyo, Anani. 1985. "The African Connection and the Afro-Brazilian Condition," pp. 135–153 in Pierre-Michel Fontaine (ed.), *Race, Class, and Power in Brazil.* Los Angeles: Center for Afro-American Studies, University of California, Los Angeles.

Economist. 1987. "An Amazonian Tragedy." 305 (October 17):52.

Economist. 1994a. "The ANC on the Road to Power." (February 19):46+.

Economist. 1994b. "South Africa's Election: The Second Struggle." (April 23):21–22+.

Fernandes, Florestan. 1969. *The Negro in Brazilian Society.* New York: Columbia University Press.

Gevisser, Mark. 1994. "Race against Hope: Fear Campaign in South Africa." *Nation* 258 (May 9):624–626.

Hasenbalg, Carlos A. 1985. "Race and Socioeconomic Inequalities in Brazil," pp. 25–41 in Pierre-Michel Fontaine (ed.), *Race, Class, and Power in Brazil.* Los Angeles: Center for Afro-American Studies, University of California, Los Angeles.

Holmes, Steven A. 1994a. "South Africa Tries to Take the Force Out of Police." *New York Times* (June 18):3.

Holmes, Steven A. 1994b. "Trying to Bridge South Africa's Rich-Poor Chasm." *New York Times* (June 29):A4.

Holmes, Steven A. 1994c. "Mandela Is Facing Squatter Challenge." *New York Times* (July 6):A4.

Keller, Bill. 1994a. "Can South Africa Do It?" *New York Times* (April 24):Sec. 4, 1+.

Keller, Bill. 1994b. "Mandela Picks Old Comrades to Fill His New Government." *New York Times* (May 7):1+.

Keller, Bill. 1994c. "Four Years after Release from Jail, Mandela Assumes Control." *New York Times* (May 11):A1+.

Keller, Bill. 1994d. "Mandela's Inheritance: Bloated Bureaucracy." *New York Times* (May 15):14.

Keller, Bill. 1994e. "Now the Hard Part in South Africa: Local Taxes." *New York Times* (July 9):3.

Keller, Bill. 1994f. "In Mandela's South Africa, Foreign Investors Are Few." *New York Times* (August 3):A1+.

Lelyveld, Joseph. 1985. *Move Your Shadow: South Africa, Black and White.* New York: Times Books.

Mathabane, Mark. 1986. *Kaffir Boy.* New York: Macmillan.

Miller, S. M. 1994. "Theorizing South Africa." *Footnotes* 22 (summer):12.

Oberholster, A. G. 1988. "Evolution of South African Society," pp. 39–58 in H. C. Marais (ed.), *South Africa: Perspective on the Future.* Pinetown, South Africa: Owen Burgess Publishers.

Ramirez, Anthony. 1994. "Upgrading for South Africa Debt." *New York Times* (October 4):D1+.

Riding, Alan. 1985. "Brazil's Time Bomb: Poor Children by the Millions." *New York Times* (October 23):2.

Silva, Nelson do Valle. 1985. "Updating the Cost of Not Being White in Brazil," pp. 42–55 in Pierre-Michel Fontaine (ed.), *Race, Class, and Power in Brazil.* Los Angeles: Center for Afro-American Studies, University of California, Los Angeles.

Silverstein, Ken. 1990. "Collor's 'New Brazil': Shock Treatment for the Poor." *Nation* 251 (November 12):554–557.

Skidmore, Thomas E. 1985. "Race and Class in Brazil: Historical Perspectives," pp. 11–24 in Pierre-Michel Fontaine (ed.), *Race, Class, and Power in Brazil.* Los Angeles: Center for Afro-American Studies, University of California, Los Angeles.

Smith, T. Lynn. 1972. *Brazilian Society.* Albuquerque: University of New Mexico Press.

South African Foundation. 1988. *1988 Information Digest.* Johannesburg, South Africa: South African Foundation.

Sundiata, I. K. 1987. "Late Twentieth Century Patterns of Race Relations in Brazil and the United States." *Phylon* 48 (March):62–76.

Telles, Edward E. 1994. "Industrialization and Racial Inequality in Employment: The Brazilian Example." *American Sociological Review* 59 (February):46–63.

Thompson, Leonard. 1990. "South Africa: The Fire This Time?" *New York Review of Books* 37 (June 14):12+.

Turner, J. Michael. 1985. "Brown into Black: Changing Racial Attitudes of Afro-Brazilian University Students," pp. 73–94 in Pierre-Michel Fontaine (ed.), *Race, Class, and*

Power in Brazil. Los Angeles: Center for Afro-American Studies, University of California, Los Angeles.

Webster, Peggy Lovell, and Jeffrey W. Dwyer. 1988. "The Cost of Being Nonwhite in Brazil." *Sociology and Social Research* 72 (January):136–138.

Wilkerson, Isabel. 1994. "The Suburbs of South Africa Stay Cold to Blacks." *New York Times* (November 3):A3.

Wood, Charles H., and Peggy A. Lovell. 1992. "Racial Inequality and Child Mortality in Brazil." *Social Forces* 70 (March):703–724.

Chapter
10

Racism in the Land of Dreams

"*L*et me tell you what it was like when we were children," the old woman told me defiantly. "We weren't spoiled! As soon as we could walk, our parents set us to work. It was that way in the old country, and there was no reason to change it once we got over here."

Others nodded, and another participant said, "You know, professor, soap and water aren't expensive. The problem with those people today," and she rolled her eyes, "is that they expect the world on a silver platter. Nobody, and that includes God, gives you something for nothing. You've got to work for it!"

"There's no doubt," I replied, "that when you and your families came to the United States you worked hard. I'd never dispute that, but something else needs to be put on the table. For modern African Americans poverty is different." I paused, wondering just what to say. I felt the need to be as expressive as the members of this senior group; yet the easiest course of action would be to summarize relevant research.

While I hesitated, the priest who had asked me to lead the discussion spoke up. "A colleague and I were driving downtown a few days ago," he began. "Several blocks from here we saw a young black man heading our way. We offered him a ride, and as we drove, he started speaking about what it's like to be black and poor in America. 'If I had anywhere else to go, I'd leave,' he told us. 'This is a terrible country—a terrible country in its heartless treatment of so many people.' Then he told us how he'd lost his job, his family, and his place to live—how he'd felt pushed out of life in his own country." The priest paused for a reply but none came. Then he added, "That man's experience and conclusion are shared by millions of people of color. Difficult as your lives were, you were spared that acute sense of being so systematically deprived."

There was silence as people absorbed the message, and afterwards the debate continued but in a subdued form. I found the moment instructive. In a straightforward, effective way, the priest had presented a form of the idea that runs throughout this book—Troy Duster's claim that throughout the nation's history race has been "the most persistent category of advantage." As the discussion demonstrated, it is a reality that is widely examined and disputed in our society. Yet it can be difficult to present the idea effectively.

In this text I have used the theory of internal colonialism to explore the persistent impact of racism. Internal colonialism emphasizes that since whites' earliest occupation of this land, they have systematically controlled racial minorities in governance, physical activity, and work, and criticized and condemned their traditional cultures. These points in the internal-colonialist theory help us to see that while racism has toned down in modern times, it remains healthy.

We have seen that racism persists in all the substantive areas we have examined. At times, perhaps, some of you might have been surprised at how widespread racism is. Professional sports has long been considered an area where a person of ability can find success, regardless of race. Yet research has shown clearly that racial discrimination exists in professional football, basketball, and baseball. It might seem clear that if a family can afford a certain house, then they can buy it. But if the family is African American or Puerto Rican, then residential discrimination has been prevalent.

Through these chapters three phases in race relations have been implied—an early time period when whites' superiority was the dominant trend; a second embodying a growing recognition of the injustices of racial inequality; and a painfully emerging third focusing on the necessity to implement structural changes eliminating the historical injustices. In this chapter we focus on the third phase.

COMBATTING RACISM

Public-service announcements, sermons, and classroom lectures often stress that racism is wrong. But in spite of many notable efforts to condemn racism, the impact is limited. The problem is that such efforts do not alter structures supporting racism.

Public officials often either fail to appreciate or simply deny that reality. When a major racial incident occurs in a city or at a college or university, authorities are likely to call meetings, create task forces which issue reports but make few meaningful changes.

Nor can one hold the mayor of a city or the president of a college or university mainly responsible for failing to eliminate racism. As we have seen throughout this book, racism permeates American society: The steps to restrict it significantly go well beyond the capacities of political or university officials. What needs to be done?

To begin, we must keep the internal-colonialist perspective firmly in mind. What is the significance of that focus in this context? It seems to be twofold. First, internal colonialism suggests that racism has been relentless and widespread throughout the history of American society. Second, the implication of this conclusion is that measures to eliminate or even restrict racism require major efforts. Inexpensive, painless solutions to racism won't work. In several chapters we have considered some specific courses of action. Now the approach becomes more general, moving beyond specific topic areas.

Stephen Steinberg (1989) contended that an effective policy to eradicate the historical impact of racism must address fundamental problems. The following discussion includes several of Steinberg's issues, along with an additional point:

1. There must be a national commitment to eliminating ghettoes. Poverty inherited from the days of slavery and discrimination in housing have produced and maintained ghettoes, and ghetto residence restricts a person's educational and occupational opportunities. Yet on television news and in textbooks, ghettoes are discussed with the same neutrality shown suburbs. That shouldn't be: Ghettoes are among the most stark representations of internal colonialism's emphasis on the restriction of racial minorities' physical movement.

   Steinberg pointed out that to implement effectively such a multibillion-dollar program, organizers would need to keep a vigilant watch on its activities, making certain that it did not become simply another scandal-ridden opportunity for construction, real-estate, and political interests. In addition, it would be essential to enlist the participation of local individuals and groups whose perspective on ghetto dwellers' needs and interests emerge out of daily experience, not from some removed, possibly misguided, or even racist viewpoint.

   On this topic we should consider one cautionary idea. A clear distinction exists between eliminating negative aspects of ghetto life and destroying vital if poor inner-city communities. Herbert Gans (1962) and Jane Jacobs (1961) produced classic studies stressing that most city planners tend to view poor, urban neighborhoods negatively, simply assuming that they are destructive for their residents and the city at large. As a result their orders are to bulldoze indiscriminately, with the frequent tragic result that vital communities developed over long periods of time are destroyed. Eliminating ghettoes, in short, should not mean destroying vital communities. Before determining appropriate alterations, each area must be carefully examined to assess its strengths and weaknesses.

2. Affirmative action needs continued support and growth; it represents a direct attack on the colonial-labor principle. Historically racial minorities were restricted in education and work, limited to training and jobs that would directly benefit white controllers. Affirmative-action programs attempt to address historical wrongs.

   Consider some impressive successes. American Telephone and Telegraph Company, one of the largest private employers in the United States, established an agreement in 1973 with the Equal Employment Opportunities Commission to redress past discriminatory hiring practices. By 1982 the percentage of minority craft workers had increased from 8.4 percent to 14 percent of the work force, and among management the proportion of minority-group members had risen from 4.6 percent to 13.1 percent. Between 1962 and 1968, the number of black employees at IBM rose nearly tenfold—from 750 to 7,251—and then in 1980 more than doubled to 16,546. Under threat of court orders, government agencies have aggressively pursued affirmative-action policies, and the results have been decisive. One result has been that since the late 1960s, the number of black police officers has increased by 20,000 (Steinberg, 1989).

In general, research found that between 1966 and 1973, companies forced to establish affirmative-action programs because they were doing business with the federal government increased their percentage of black workers more than companies not required to meet affirmative-action standards. Between 1974 and 1980, the number of African Americans receiving jobs because of affirmative action increased even more than in the previous seven-year period. In fact, between 1968 and 1991, the number of blacks in the work force grew by 50 percent—a solid advance even considering the expanding black population (Gleckman et al., 1993; Jaynes and Williams, 1989:316–317; Leonard, 1985). Reviewing investigations on the topic, a team of researchers concluded that "affirmative action seems to have effected educational and occupational gains for women and for racial minorities" (Crosby and Clayton, 1990:65).

A criticism frequently directed against affirmative action is that it has promoted racial minorities' opportunities for white-collar positions and ignored their involvement in blue-collar positions. But this has not been the case. The focus of many affirmative-action initiatives has been law enforcement, construction work, and craft and production jobs in large companies.

Another criticism is that giving minority-group members a hand up undermines their morale and self-confidence. Each affirmative-action program needs to be examined and reexamined for its impact on participants, and if clear indications of destructive impact appear, then alterations are necessary. In particular, minority-group individuals given preference must have all significant job skills and experiences.

Most opponents of affirmative action praise the value of individualism while conveniently forgetting structural factors underlying racism and poverty. A significantly greater concern seems to be that the vicious cycle of poverty enveloping so many minority-group members continues to expand. To help alleviate that, affirmative action must proceed with all deliberate speed.

With the groundwork for affirmative action now established, it appears just and reasonable to extend its programs into all educational and work areas. Inevitably resistance will continue, but if this society truly is dedicated to elimination of racism, this policy must persist.

3. Another difficult issue, which is also related to jobs, involves immigration policy. In the past quarter century, this nation has lost 3 million industrial

jobs and also absorbed over 11 million legal immigrants, along with count-less millions of illegal arrivals. Frequently immigrants have taken jobs for which Americans, particularly minority Americans, could be trained.

Consider the area of nursing. To meet a critical shortage of nurses, the United States has been importing tens of thousands of foreign nurses. At the same time, nursing schools throughout the country have been closed. A program oriented to needs and interests of American minorities would emphasize that the nursing shortage could be met with a radically different approach—expand nursing schools, publicize and promote the opportuni-ties for nursing throughout the public-school system, especially in areas where there are large numbers of minority students, and, ultimately, stop importing large numbers of foreign nurses (Steinberg, 1989:51–54).

4. So far we have covered two major issues addressed by internal colonialism: The first point relates to the restriction of physical activity and the last two address problems associated with the colonial-labor principle. The final issue relates to the tenet declaring minority cultures inferior and the dom-inant culture superior.

Even specialists on racial issues find themselves contributing to racism. Stephen Steinberg raised this point with his analysis of the term "under-class," which became popular in the early 1980s. The term focuses on indi-viduals' and groups' failures to attain conventional rewards, thus keeping them "under" the established class system. It is a vague term, lumping together diverse ethnic and racial groups and failing to single out specific conditions, especially racism for racial minorities, that have played a crucial role in limiting their opportunities (Steinberg, 1989:43–44). This term has racist, blaming-the-victim overtones, implying minorities' cultural inferior-ity; and it is used widely, with even experts on race relations sometimes fail-ing to see that their analysis of racial situations is simplistic.

The above point might seem inconsistent with the book's emphasis on the overriding importance of institutional structures producing racism. Why empha-size the importance of individuals' attitudes? While altering institutional structures producing racism must be the priority, perhaps an individual or group's starting point should be recognition that successful steps must be modest but concrete, located in immediate realities.

As this book draws to a close, however, we need to return to the structural con-ditions maintaining racism and consider one promising approach to altering these conditions.

Regionalism: To Salvage Cities

We have noted a number of prominent suggestions for confronting specific racist outcomes. While all of them are somewhat promising and have already produced some positive results, a new, quite different approach is currently gaining momen-tum.

Regionalism is a strategy where urban and suburban groups which recognize the mutual interdependence of their residential areas collectively confront local political, economic, and social problems, with the aim of negotiating mutually beneficial outcomes. The starting point needs to be visualization: Historically whites have often contributed time and energy to what seemed to be solutions to minorities' problems. Seldom, however, did it appear that such people considered that minorities' plight was a shared condition. With the recognition that the massive poverty and hardship inflicted on large numbers of minorities is adversely affecting a broad area of cities and towns, regionalism takes a very different view. From the internal-colonialist perspective, the emerging idea is that the dominant group's legacy of exploitation has come home to roost, adversely affecting not only the traditionally exploited groups but whites too. The challenge has become the discovery of means to confront this unfortunate, difficult situation.

In *Cities without Suburbs,* David Rusk, a leading proponent of regionalism, indicated that when cities have a sustained population loss, a large proportion of poor, minority-group inhabitants, and a sustained income difference between city dwellers and nearby suburban residents, they are in serious trouble (Rusk, 1993). Within such cities financial resources tend to be shrinking, and thus the city has less and less funding to maintain itself. Local roads, bridges, public transportation, public buildings, and public services like the police, fire, and sanitation departments suffer. Local businesses that can afford to do so often leave. As a result the city's capacities continue to shrink. The local population, especially poor minorities who suffer more in difficult times, receive the brunt of the problems. Their schools, health care, recreational facilities, and employment opportunities are adversely affected. Alcoholism, drug use, crime, and violence increase, and the city declines.

Traditionally suburban residents have considered themselves immune to urban problems. Yes, they realize that they need to be careful about travelling to the local city at night or even entering certain areas, but basically the city's problems are just that—its problems. A regional perspective attempts to demonstrate that this view is shortsighted, failing to recognize that the city's difficulties are moving beyond its own borders into the suburbs. Rising crime, declining property values, deteriorating schools, loss of urban jobs for commuting suburbanites, and other tangible effects appear. No longer can the primarily white suburbanites comfort themselves that the inner cities, with their high proportion of minorities, are a world apart: With a vengeance the two worlds have started coming together.

Consider recent developments in New Haven, Connecticut, and its suburban environs—a region containing a poor, crime-ridden city that is surrounded by fairly affluent towns. The two worlds are interconnected. Forty-six percent of the people working in New Haven live in the encircling 14 towns; two-thirds of Yale-New Haven Hospital's patients reside outside the city; at New Haven's major threatre, the Long Wharf Theatre, 50 percent of the season subscribers come from New Haven suburbs and only 10 percent from the city itself. While a national study of 28 metropolitan areas revealed that suburbs around a declining city can continue to prosper for some time, the interdependence of a city and its suburbs sets a time limit—about five years (Bass, 1994a).

To many analysts examining New Haven, the interrelation of the city and suburbs seems painfully obvious. The challenge is to spread that perception—to get segments of the local public, particularly in the suburbs, to see that reality.

Outrage is not a bad mechanism for helping to spread the word. In suburban Guilford, Mary Summers, a long-time civil-rights activist, became angered and frustrated over the Rodney King beating and the subsequent Los Angeles riot. Summers concluded that greater New Haven was no different from Los Angeles—that similar problems existed in her locale. Summers and a number of other predominantly white suburbanites started developing a relationship between their church group and the members of a black New Haven church.

At first they simply attended each others' services and afterwards talked with each other. But then what became the Interfaith Urban/Suburban Task Force began bringing in experts to address such topics as how to improve public schools through desegregation and how to make the entire region work more effectively by engaging in more equitable taxation. In the course of the interaction, Summers and her associates learned that the traditional approach to suburban-urban relations needed to change—that racially tinged stereotypes seemed to dominate on both sides. She explained that many suburban people consider the urban poor, particularly the minority poor, the source of the city's problems. Inner-city residents, in turn, label suburban dwellers as selfish, racist, and uncaring. Such stereotyped thinking, Summers concluded, makes people defensive and hopeless. But, Summers indicated, communication has started to change the situation:

> "When we start to talk, we start to realize how much most of us have in common, how much we want the same things: good schools, safe streets, and a future for our children. We all need the benefits of city institutions: hospitals, universities, museums, theaters, libraries, parks, and neighborhoods. We all want to enjoy the landscapes and festivals of the countryside. We all want to feel safe, welcome, and comfortable wherever we are." (Bass, 1994b:13)

In greater New Haven, other groups have begun examining regionalism. During the winter of 1994, in several local towns, sometimes reluctant parents and educators opened discussions on the prospect of regionalizing education. Jack Hasegawa, the state official in charge of organizing the process, had participated in civil-rights activity as a student in the early 1960s. While he personally has seen his new task as in keeping with his civil-rights past, Hasegawa perceived a different orientation: The moral language and motivation that dominated the civil-rights movement was less common now. Hasegawa said, "What I hear more often is: 'My kids won't be prepared to go to work if they don't understand diversity'" (Bass, 1994b:13).

The Greater New Haven Chamber of Commerce's support has been equally practical. In 1987 officials at the Chamber started taking a number of initiatives—inviting suburban and urban-government and business leaders to meetings to discuss common interests; becoming the state's first business group to push for a state income tax; developing a local coalition to start a shoreline commuter train; convincing business and citizens groups to lobby the state to modernize the small local airport (a factor that experts felt retarded the region's commercial growth); and hammering away at the regionalism theme in dozens of Rotary Club and church-group meetings (Bass, 1994b). In addition, Chamber personnel played a major role in forming a group of local citizens in greater New Haven interested in developing strategies and goals involving regionalism and then committed to carrying them out.

We should recognize the historically derived significance of regionalism. In the late 1960s, some African American leaders began to advocate a new phase in the civil-rights movement. It was time, they said, for whites promoting blacks' rights to stop working with blacks and return to their own communities where there was plenty of work to be done. At the time the message had limited impact, but now, with regionalism, its meaning assumes a new, powerful importance. For whites concerned about racial minorities' rights and needs, the chief battle seems to have moved to their own back yards, where they need to convince their friends and neighbors that everyone will benefit from the promotion of regionalism.

CONCLUSION

In the years ahead, Americans will be forced to make tough decisions about race. What programs will most effectively curtail or eliminate the legacy of racism? Throughout this book we have examined the inhumanity of racism. Certainly it is fitting to do everything to be humane—to give all citizens an opportunity to participate fully in the bounty of our great nation.

But as the discussion of regionalism emphasized, the issue goes beyond altruism. It has become painfully apparent that a great shadow has spread across our society—fear of the ever-expanding violence of people who have been denied access to valued opportunities and rewards. It is now painfully apparent that no token measures are going to buy them off. If the United States doesn't make a frontal attack on the combined forces of racism and poverty, then those formidable foes are going to grow in strength and in the terror they produce. Analyzing race relations in the 1990s, sociologist Lewis Killian concluded that new taxes and a more equitable distribution of wealth are necessary. He warned that without such measures "the new enemy will be our own underclass" (Killian, 1990:13).

At the moment American culture is a racist culture. This condition is undeniable, regrettable, but potentially changeable. Collectively Americans should do what those addicted to alcohol or hard drugs are required to do: Look hard and long at themselves and face their problem head on, saying, "We are racist. How can we change this hateful condition?" A heartfelt realization can be a first step toward effective action.

REFERENCES

Bass, Paul. 1994a. "Cities without Suburbs: A State without Borders." *New Haven Advocate* (February 3):15+.

Bass, Paul. 1994b. "It Can Work." *New Haven Advocate* (February 10):13+.

Crosby, Faye, and Susan Clayton. 1990. "Affirmative Action and the Issue of Expectancies." *Journal of Social Issues* 46:61–79.

Gans, Herbert J. 1962. *The Urban Villagers*. New York: Free Press.

Gleckman, Howard, et al. 1993. "Race in the Workplace: Is Affirmative Action Working?" pp. 152–159 in John A. Kromkowski (ed.), *Race and Ethnic Relations 93/94.* Guilford, CT: Dushkin Publishing Group. Third edition.

Jacobs, Jane. 1961. *The Death and Life of Great American Cities.* New York: Vintage Books.

Jaynes, Gerald David, and Robin M. Williams, Jr. (eds.). 1989. *A Common Destiny: Blacks and American Society.* Washington, DC: National Academy Press.

Killian, Lewis M. 1990. "Race Relations and the Nineties: Where Are the Dreams of the Sixties?" *Social Forces* 69 (September):1–13.

Leonard, Jonathan. 1985. "The Effectiveness of Equal Employment and Affirmative Action Regulation." Report to the Subcommittee on Civil and Constitutional Rights of the Judiciary Committee, U.S. Congress. Berkeley, CA: School of Business Administration, University of California, Berkeley.

Rusk, David. 1993. *Cities without Suburbs.* Washington, DC: Woodrow Wilson Center Press.

Steinberg, Stephen. 1989. "The Underclass: A Case of Color Blindness." *New Politics* 2 (summer):42–60.

Glossary

Apartheid South African government policy involving racial segration of major facilities—residential areas, hotels, restaurants, buses, work locations, and even staircases and toilets.

Authority Power that people generally recognize as rightfully maintained by those who use it.

Caste system A socially legitimated arrangement of groups in which the ranking of the different groups is clearly designated, members' expected behavior is specified, and movement of individuals from one group to another is prohibited.

Conflict theory A perspective contending that the struggle for power and wealth in society should be the central concern for society.

Discrimination The behavior by which one group prevents or restricts a minority group's access to scarce resources.

Ethnocentrism The automatic tendency to evaluate other cultures by outsiders' cultural standards.

Frustration-aggression theory A perspective emphasizing that people blocked from achieving a goal are sometimes unable or unwilling to focus their frustration on the true source, and so they direct the aggression produced by frustration toward an accessible individual or group.

Index of dissimilarity A calculation indicating the proportion of a particular racial group that would need to change residential location in order to achieve racial evenness—a condition in which that racial group's representation throughout a city's census districts would be dispersed proportionate to its overall representation in the city.

Individual racism An action performed by one person or group that produces racial abuse.

Institutional racism Discriminatory racial practices built into such prominent structures as the political, economic, and education systems.

Internal colonialism A theory emphasizing that the control imposed on indigenous racial minorities passes from whites in the home country to whites living within a newly independent nation.

Looking-glass self Individuals' understanding of what sort of person they are is based on how they think they appear to others.

247

Lynching One group's use of mob action to kill a member of an oppressed group, thereby warning members of that oppressed group either to accept an even more lowly status or to forsake any developing plans to rise above their subordinated position.

Macro level The large-scale structures and activities that exist within societies and between one society and another.

Majority group A category of people within a society who possess distinct physical or cultural characteristics and maintain superior power and resources.

Mass media The instruments of communication that reach a large audience without any personal contact between senders and receivers.

Mentoring A process by which people of higher rank and achievement instruct and guide the intellectual or career development of less experienced individuals outside of classrooms.

Micro level The structure and activities of small groups.

Minority group Any category of people with recognizable racial or ethnic traits that place it in a position of restricted power and inferior status so that its members suffer limited opportunities and reward.

Norm Standard of desirable behavior.

Normification Behavior that gives the impression that an individual widely considered inferior is trying to deny being different.

Pluralism A theory emphasizing that a dispersion of power exists in government or other structures within American society.

Political incorporation Inclusion of racial minority-group members as significant players in political coalitions which contain some whites and successfully challenge established white conservative groups for control over a city's political activity.

Political institution The system of norms and roles that concerns the use and distribution of authority within a given society.

Power The ability of an individual or group to implement wishes or policies, with or without the cooperation of others.

Prejudice A highly negative judgment toward a minority group, focusing on one or more characteristics that are supposedly uniformly shared by all group members.

Race A classification of people into categories falsely claimed to be derived from a distinct set of biological traits.

Racism The belief contending that actual or alleged differences between different racial groups assert the superiority of one racial group.

Regionalism A strategy where urban and suburban groups which recognize the mutual interdependence of their residential areas collectively confront local political, economic, and social problems, with the aim of negotiating mutually beneficial outcomes.

Self-fulfilling prophecy An incorrect definition of a situation that comes to pass because people accept the incorrect definition and act on it to make it become true.

Sexism The belief contending that actual or alleged differences between women and men establish the superiority of men.

Social distance The feeling of separation between individuals and groups.

Social mobility The movement of a person from one social class or status level to another, either upward or downward with accompanying gains or losses in wealth, power, and prestige.

Stereotype Exaggerated, oversimplified image, maintained by prejudiced people, of the characteristics of the group members against whom they are prejudiced.

Structural-functional theory A perspective suggesting that interacting groups tend to influence and adjust to each other in a fairly stable, conflict-free pattern.

Vicious cycle of poverty A pattern in which parents' minimal income significantly limits children's educational and occupational pursuits, thereby keeping them locked into the same low economic status.

Index